Cultural Competence
A Primer for Educators

SECOND EDITION

Jean Moule
Oregon State University

WADSWORTH
CENGAGE Learning™

Australia • Brazil • Japan • Korea • Mexico • Singapore • Spain • United Kingdom • United States

WADSWORTH
CENGAGE Learning™

**Cultural Competence:
A Primer for Educators,
Second Edition**
Jean Moule

Publisher: Linda
Schreiber-Ganster

Executive Editor:
Mark David Kerr

Assistant Editor:
Rebecca Dashiell

Editorial Assistant:
Genevieve Allen

Marketing Manager:
Kara Kindstrom

Marketing Coordinator:
Dimitri Hagnere

Senior Marketing
Communications Manager:
Tami Strang

Content Project
Management:
PreMediaGlobal

Senior Art Director:
Jennifer Wahi

Print Buyer: Mary Beth
Hennebury

Production House/
Compositor:
PreMediaGlobal

Rights Acquisition
Specialist: Don Schlotman

Cover Image: Jeff Bane,
CMB Design Partners,
illustrator; Back Cover Photo
by Daniel Markoya

For product information and technology assistance, contact us at
Cengage Learning Customer & Sales Support, 1-800-354-9706
For permission to use material from this text or product,
submit all requests online at **www.cengage.com/permissions**.
Further permissions questions can be emailed to
permissionrequest@cengage.com.

Library of Congress Control Number: 2010936253

ISBN-13: 978-0-495-91529-4

ISBN-10: 0-495-91529-7

Wadsworth
10 Davis Drive
Belmont, CA 94002
USA

Cengage Learning is a leading provider of customized learning
solutions with office locations around the globe, including Singapore,
the United Kingdom, Australia, Mexico, Brazil and Japan. Locate your
local office at **international.cengage.com/region**

Cengage Learning products are represented in Canada by
Nelson Education, Ltd.

For your course and learning solutions, visit **www.cengage.com**.

Purchase any of our products at your local college store or at our
preferred online store **www.cengagebrain.com**.

Printed in the United States of America
1 2 3 4 5 6 7 14 13 12 11 10

CONTENTS

PART II
Becoming Culturally Competent in the Classroom and Community 113

PREFACE

Cultural Competence: A Primer for Educators is a basic textbook for people in education. It opens pathways for effective and competent cross-cultural teaching. It presents a clear understanding of how a complex variety of social and psychological factors come together to shape a teacher's ability to work with K-12 students who are culturally different. I have called this work a primer. According to Webster, a "primer" is a book of elementary or basic principles. The objective of this text is to initiate a process of learning that will ultimately lead you toward greater cultural competence as a teacher. Included are chapters on cultural competence; racism; culture, ethnocentricity, and privilege; ethnic children, parenting, and families; multicultural issues in education; bias in curriculum delivery; and the practical dynamics of getting started. In addition, there are chapters focusing specifically on working with African Americans, Latinos/as, Asian Pacific Americans, Muslims, and American Indian/Alaskan Natives written by expert educators from those communities as well as a final chapter on European Americans.

The first edition was well-received by both students and faculty. Its accessibility through anecdotal and classroom examples as well as the interviews with experts in specific cultures made it a popular introductory text for multicultural education classes, student teachers, and teachers in the field. The book can be used as a primary text for multicultural issues and cultural diversity courses in education as well as for student services programs in community colleges, four-year colleges, and beginning graduate programs. It can also be used as a supplementary text in basic education and field experiences courses where the intent is to sensitize students to the cultural dimensions of teaching and learning. Finally, it can be a valuable asset in the continuing education of teachers interested in broadening their theoretical and practical knowledge of what has become the fastest-growing content area in the field of education.

New to This Edition

Since the first edition of this cultural competence primer appeared in print, the racial and ethnic population of the United States has grown tremendously. This growth has sometimes caused a pushback on immigration and acceptance of the growing diversity. Feelings about 9/11 and our growing conflicts in many parts of the world have caused many to hold biases against our Muslim communities, and the need to know more about this group caused the addition of a chapter by a scholar who understands the nuances and wide variety of this culture. As teachers and educators, our need for increased understanding of culturally diverse populations has grown to become a requirement: Even in the most homogenous communities, school districts are experiencing a slow rise in the number of culturally and linguistically diverse student populations.

Besides the addition of a chapter on Muslim students, the chapters on racism have been expanded. I have updated the citations in each of the chapters and included more stories and voices from my students. The ends of Chapters 1–9 now include reflective and practical applications for personal and classroom use to help bridge the gap from theory to practice. All graphics are new, and all chapters have a new focused bibliography to be found in the companion website for those who wish to make a deeper connection to the chapter topic.

Chapter 1, formerly the introduction chapter, now includes material from Chapter 2 on becoming culturally competent and a table detailing changing demographics. Former Chapter 3 is now Chapter 2 and includes a new section on racism in children.

Chapter 3 is completely new, with material on understanding our unconscious and unintentional racism as well as microaggressions, the last explored through a flow chart. Other specific changes in the first section of the book include a table on racial attitudes and how to be an ally in Chapter 4 and new ways to connect culture and multiple intelligences as well as an iceberg graphic on culture in Chapter 5.

In the second part of the book, the introduction highlights changes in teachers' attitudes and related instruction by way of a comprehensive table. Chapter 6 includes additional classroom scenes and a graph on how President Obama is racially perceived. Stereotype threat is closely considered in Chapter 7 through a new flow chart and suggestions for overcoming the threat. Textbook biases and ways to reform curriculum are greatly expanded and a new section on teacher expectations appear in Chapter 8. In Chapter 9, multiple types of immersion programs and their effects have been added and the section on bilingualism has been replaced.

Each chapter (10–13) on a Community of Color has updated demographic statistics and a new relevant graphic. Chapter 11 has a new interviewee, while the interviewee in Chapter 12 updated his interview. Chapter 14 is the new chapter on working with Muslim students and includes a new interview. Chapter 15 on working with European American students is entirely new. I end the book with new encouragement from my own prior words and current thoughts on making a difference.

In addition to the suggested revisions from faculty reviewers and other users of the book, I asked students to suggest revisions for their favorite chapters. One surprise was that each chapter was chosen as a favorite by about the same number of people. I trust you will find chapters that speak especially well to you.

Unique Features

The book is unique in its breadth of coverage as well as its organization and style. It integrates theory with hands-on practical knowledge and does so from the perspective of asking what kinds of information a student needs to grasp the essentials of culturally competent teaching. Its treatment of topics is comprehensive. For example, racism—a vital issue summarily addressed in most multicultural texts—is explored from a variety of perspectives. What is it? How does it operate in the individual and in society's institutions to oppress people? Why do many mainstream individuals find it so hard to acknowledge racism and their own privilege? How do teachers' prejudices compromise the learning process? How does one become aware of and alter unconscious biases, unintentional racism and negative racial attitudes? What are the psychological consequences of racism and oppression on People of Color, especially the developing child? And how does racism operate within schools and the teaching professions? To assist the reader in personalizing these questions, a self-assessment tool is included at the end of Chapter 1, and self-awareness exercises are provided for every other chapter. Chapters end with discussion questions, and practical applications, including classroom activities that allow the reader to engage further with the chapter material. In the companion website you will find for each chapter a summary of key points and a focused bibliography.

A second unique feature of the book is its accessibility. Although it is rich in theoretical and practical material, it is not overly academic. For example, rather than exhaustively reviewing multiple studies within a given subject area, it succinctly surveys critical questions and issues and supports them with detailed descriptions of exemplary research. In addition, anecdotes, personal practical experiences, and real-world examples are generously included. It is easy to read and written for and to the student educator, anticipating questions, concerns, and anxieties that the topic has regularly elicited from course participants during my many years of teaching experiences. For most students, cultural diversity is a loaded topic, and the more roadblocks that can be removed—making it more accessible—the more likely significant learning will occur on this journey. For example, it is important to acknowledge White students' concerns over being called racists and to normalize their anxieties over cultural differences as well as to acknowledge the enormous frustration

People of Color feel at the denial of racism by Whites. Part of the motivation for writing this text comes from experiences of seldom having found a textbook on cultural diversity that truly engaged students while educating them. Many books on the topic are overly academic and hard for the average student to wade through. However, such engagement is imperative if students are to not only grasp a body of knowledge but to also become sensitized to their own biases and discomfort with difference. Most efforts to define cultural competence begin with acknowledging the importance of self-awareness in the teacher. This book thoroughly understands and clarifies the psychological components of that self-awareness.

A third unique feature of the book is its treatment of Students of Color and Whites and the presentation of specific cultural knowledge. Five educators—each with extensive practical experience working with students from their respective groups—were interviewed and asked to discuss the following topics: professional and ethnic autobiographical material, demographics and shared characteristics of their community, group names, history in a nutshell, learning styles, family and community characteristics, cultural style, values and worldview, common school-based problems, socioeconomic issues, subpopulations at risk, tips for developing rapport, effective teaching strategies, and a short classroom example. Christine Sleeter, a leader in the field of multicultural education, concludes the book with an analysis of her own European American heritage and what such an understanding means to educators. The result is six highly informative and engaging chapters, each filled with rich cultural material and practical hands-on suggestions and cautions, relayed with passion by six educators strongly committed to working with students from their communities. While I am aware of the dangers of assuming major similarities within groups, these interviews allow us to go more deeply below the surface and become aware of subtle differences that can help teachers widen their perspectives and improve their pedagogical skills when working with specific groups. The interviews are only lightly edited to retain their personal and cultural flavor.

Focusing on Race and Ethnicity

There are many forms of human diversity: race and ethnicity, gender, socioeconomic class, age, sexual preference, religion, ability and disability, and more. Each affects the individual differently and operates by its own unique set of rules and subtleties. Rare is the text that can adequately and comprehensively cover all forms of diversity. Some writers even argue that coverage of too many forms of diversity in a single treatment tends to be superficial and minimizes the importance of each. For this reason, I have chosen to focus on teaching students from different racial and ethnic groups. The decision to highlight only race and ethnicity is pragmatic, builds on my own research and strengths and in no way minimizes the importance of gender, class, age, sexual preference, and so on. Furthermore, as a foundation for teaching competently in the many areas of diversity, confronting the process and harm of potential oppression in one area leads one to learn many of the skills needed to address and make a difference in other areas where oppression may occur.

This textbook also focuses extensively on the diversity within racial and ethnic groups. Differences in class, gender, age, geography, and social and political leanings—among others factors—can lead to such diverse life experiences that members of the same ethnic or racial group may feel they have little in common. For example, a lower-class White teacher who grew up in a major city may experience difficulties when working with middle-class White students from a rural mountain setting. On the other hand, teachers and students from different cultural backgrounds who share similar demographics of class, gender, geography, and so forth, may feel that they have much in common on which to build a teaching/learning relationship.

Prologue: Beginning the Journey

I wish to address the reader in a more direct way regarding the pursuit of cultural competence and this book. The old adage is still true: You get as much out of reading and the related activities as you put in. There is much useful information in the following pages that cannot help but contribute to your growth as a culturally competent educator. But it can also be the beginning of a journey that may change you in deep and unpredictable ways. Engaging in the serious pursuit of cultural competence can be transformational—not so much in a religious sense but rather in a perceptual one. You may in time think very differently than you do now. I can also guarantee that at times, if you take this latter course, you will be disturbed or disoriented or find yourself feeling very lost and alone. The material on racial identity development in Chapters 4 and 7 will help you negotiate this journey. I continue to experience these insights, and I continue to grow as I delve into cultural material. Gaining cultural competence can provide you with enormous personal growth in the form of increased self-awareness, cultural sensitivity, nonjudgmental thinking, and broadened consciousness.

A theme that will reverberate throughout this book is the critical nature of self-awareness. Again, it is not just a question of whether one holds racist attitudes and stereotypes or if one is involved with practices of institutional or cultural racism. We all do and are at some level. Rather, the issue is discovering the ways a teacher's thinking is slanted racially, how this will affect his or her role as an educator, and what can be done to change it. The questions and reflections at the end of each chapter are meant to stimulate increased self-awareness. They are necessary in counteracting natural tendencies toward denial, avoidance, and rationalization in matters of race and ethnicity. They are useful to the extent that the reader takes them seriously, allows sufficient time to adequately process and complete them, and approaches them with candor.

Two things will make a difference in how you relate to this book and ultimately in your pursuit of cultural competence. The first is self-honesty and humility. There is an aspect of ethnocentrism that is deceiving. It seeks to hide the fact that human experience can be relative—that there might be another show in town. As shall become evident in Chapter 3, there is also a strong tendency to deny and hide from consciousness many of the negative feelings about race, ethnicity, and cultural differences that one has learned over the years. Together, these factors conspire to keep one in the dark. Only by pushing oneself to critically engage the concepts and material of this book and discovering precisely how they play themselves out in the confines of individual lives can one truly begin to understand.

Second is a sustained commitment to gaining cultural competence. The learning in this book is long-term. It is as much process as content, tends to be cumulative in nature, and is highly developmental, meaning that the learner goes through various predictable stages of growth, emotion, and change. This book is only a beginning. What happens next—what additional cultural learning experiences you seek and the extent to which you seriously engage in providing culturally competent teaching—is up to you.

The needs of children, especially the needs of culturally diverse children, are not limited by the confines of the classroom. Children are privy to and defined by cultural and social forces that have deep emotional impacts on their psyches and shape the very essence of what and how they learn. As teachers of culturally diverse students, you will be called on to interact with and enter the lives of not only your students but also their parents, siblings, families, and communities. At times, you may find yourself acting as babysitter, confidant, culture broker, social worker, or counselor as well as teacher. The broader your knowledge and insights, the better you will be able to perform and meet the needs of these children. May the journey begin.

Supplements: Provisions and Itinerary for the Journey

End of Chapter Materials

At the end of each chapter, you will find new sections to give you sustenance and guidance as you take and continue on the cultural competency journey.

You will find discussion questions labeled "Connections and Reflections: Emerging Views." Many of my students find that they discuss the readings and coursework with those outside of the classroom and often outside of their field. The journey involves your life as well as your classrooms, and some of the questions may be helpful to you beyond your role as a teacher. These emerging views help you more personally consider the material and gain additional perspectives on the topics in each chapter. "Classroom: Adventures in Learning" sections are for your current or future students, and most may be adapted for different grade levels. You will find in the companion website two additional resources for each chapter: "Key Points: Landmarks for Your Journey," a point-by-point summary, and a "Focused Bibliography: Sites and Insights for the Journey" section. The focused bibliography, mostly websites, will open new pathways for your learning.

Companion Website

The book companion website at www.cengage.com/education/moule offers students a variety of study tools and useful resources, such as exercises related to cultural competence, downloadable surveys and forms, cultural competence videos, links to related websites, and more.

About the Author: Jean's Journey So Far

I bring to this text and my work my passion as a human being that wants to make a difference in her world. I have discovered that becoming culturally competent is a complex and lifelong process that needs constant care and reflection. It is my goal to provide a *margin of safety* for those who undertake this difficult journey to prepare themselves to teach culturally diverse students. To meet this goal, I work to more closely connect theory to practice in the area of cultural competency.

I am a wife, the mother of three biracial children, and grandmother to six. My journey in these roles included and continues to include work with schools. My teaching experiences have ranged from pre-kindergarten to doctorate level and from talented and gifted students to people in prisons. I balance my professional life with work on ski patrol and traveling over the world to understand other cultures and broaden my own horizons.

I have worked in intergroup relations for over twenty years: teaching courses on multicultural issues in education, consulting with various districts and private organizations, working within my own institution. As an isolated Person of Color on the faculty of Oregon State University, I have a unique perspective and unique challenges. My research is among preservice teachers of primarily European descent, who themselves will be teaching primarily

European American students and, increasingly, Students of Color. Many of the preservice teachers in my courses react to their simultaneous introduction to multicultural issues and their first African American professor. I am a link between the institution as it is and the institution as it wishes to become—more welcoming and diverse in its faculty and students, with greater multicultural awareness. Teacher education is changing. In order to meet the increasing need for culturally competent teachers beginning in 1998, we have worked to place our OSU students full time in culturally and linguistically diverse classrooms in Portland and Salem, Oregon. This book has presented me with an opportunity to disseminate much that I have learned in this preservice teacher work. Writing also has allowed me to delve deeper and further understand my role within teacher education as I help diversify the teacher workforce and prepare teachers for diversity.

Yet, for all my experiences and understanding of cultural competence issues, I feel humbled by the prospect of speaking about those who are culturally different from me. Keeping my own journey and limitations in mind, I have revised the chapters dealing with the broader conceptual issues, drawing on research as well as examples from my own experience, and have invited experts from five Communities of Color and a White educator to speak about working with students from their respective groups.

The first edition of *Cultural Competence* was co-written with Jerry V. Diller, who brought a male, Jewish heritage as well as a strong psychological perspective to the work. This second edition continues to reflect his and my richness of diversity—of race, gender, ethnicity, and scholarly discipline. We had both lived these realities as well as studied them. As I continue to revise and update this text, my appreciation goes out to Jerry, who outlined a fine way of addressing a difficult topic and saw the importance of the interviews with experts in the field. I continue to use much of his work and the questions he originally wrote for the interviews.

Of special value in our writing together was the fact that one of us is a teacher and teacher educator and the other a psychologist and professional counselor. Bringing these two perspectives together in a book on culturally different students and what happens to them in the classroom offers unique insights into the psychology of multicultural education. The task of becoming culturally competent is usually viewed from one perspective or the other—as an educational challenge or as a psychological one. However, neither is sufficient by itself to provide the richness of analysis necessary to truly appreciate the educational and psychological factors that define the experience of culturally different students and the classrooms and worlds they face. By bringing together knowledge and insights from both disciplines, I feel we created a unique text that, especially in its revision, is best-suited to teaching teachers about becoming culturally competent.

Acknowledgments: Companions Along the Way

On the home front, I would like to thank my husband Rob, who fed me encouragement and many meals. My three children, six grandchildren, and parents gave me life experiences and stories that I have shared. My friend Bonnie Morihara gives my written work serious attention, close editing, useful insights, and support beyond measure. Also on my personal side, I thank my ski patrol and geocaching buddies as well as those unnamed ones who have supported me in many ways during the revision of this text.

Among colleagues in the field, I am especially grateful to people who completed a section in the book, agreed to an interview, or gave me extensive feedback: Cornel Pewewardy, Christine Sleeter, Karim Hamdy, Valerie Ooka Pang, William Cross, Aurora Cedillo, Jim Loewen, Kathryn Ciechanowski, Rick Orozco, Franklin Fisher, and Angela Freeman. Other colleagues at Oregon State University who have been supportive in this and closely related work: Karen Higgins, Ken Winograd, Chris Ward, Kay Stephens, Allan Brazier, Gene Newburgh, Terryl Ross, Juan Trujillo, and Catherine Porter. On the subject of immersion programs, I especially thank Lynn Penland, Diane Triplett, Davies Bellamy, Ruth Ann Angell, Linda Wallace, Joy Williams, Chris Cartwright and Nancy Meltzoff. My colleagues in and through my work with NAME, the National Association for Multicultural Education, have either contributed to the text or helped shape my perspectives and expanded my networks: Bette Beaver, Gennie Harris, Arun Toké, Arbrella Luvert, John Lockhart, Keylah Frazier, and Bill Bigelow. This list is not complete, for there are numerous students and fellow educators—some quoted in this work—who have been companions on the way as we work toward a more culturally competent world for all our students.

I would like to thank the following individuals at Cengage for their contributions to the development and production of this text: Linda Schreiber-Ganster, senior publisher; Mark Kerr, executive editor; Rebecca Dashiell, assistant editor; Kara Kindstrom Parsons, marketing manager; and Dimitri Hagnéré, marketing coordinator; Pradhiba Kannaiyan, project editor; and Christopher Stolle, copy editor. Finally, special thanks to the following people who served as readers and reviewers in preparation for the second edition of the text: Dionne Clabaugh, Gavilan College; Sandra Hackley, Midlands Technical College; Geraldine Jenny, Slippery Rock University; Misty Rodeheaver, West Virginia University; and Andrea Zarate, Hartnell College.

PART I

Foundations for Becoming Culturally Competent

"There is so much good in the worst of us, and so much bad in the best of us, that it hardly behooves any of us to talk about the rest of us."

—Edward Wallis Hoch

An example of cross-cultural misunderstanding in the classroom:

> Mrs. Gussman is one of the best English teachers in the school. She spends every weekend reading her immigrant students' compositions and making careful comments in red ink. To soften her criticisms, she says something positive before writing suggestions for improvement, using the students' names to make the comments more personable. "Jae Lee, these are fine ideas." These red-inked notes send shock waves through the families of her Korean students, but Mrs. Gussman is unaware of this until the principal calls her into the office. She is told that— Koreans, particularly those who are Buddhists, only write a person's name in red at the time of death or at the anniversary of a death. Therefore, to see the names of their children in red terrified the Korean parents. (Dresser, 1996, pp. 38–39)

Contained in this simple scenario is the crux of a serious problem currently facing teachers and educators. How can we hope to teach cross-culturally when we lack basic knowledge about the students we hope to educate?

One of my web course students anticipated her journey toward cultural competency with the following reflections that reveal her personal history, her encounter with new material, and an understanding of the long journey ahead:

> I grew up in what felt like a very mono-cultural place, but my parents made great pains to give us wider cultural experiences. Most of my Oregon experience

has been an even "whiter" experience than Utah was, which is one reason why living in the culturally diverse family student housing appealed to me.

Like many naive students of my generation who grew up as a majority in a not-very-diverse culture, I used to think the big "isms" were a thing for history books. Institutionalized segregation was fixed through laws, and things are better. I believe the first time I experienced outright obvious sexism was a wake-up call. I knew racism still existed, but thought it was confined to KKK rednecks in the south. I'd like to think I know better now.

I am concerned that the current culture of discussion about race, between races, simply breeds ignorance for those benefiting from it and anger in those suffering from it. I don't believe we will make the necessary progress until open dialogue is standard practice.

This student is clear on some of the problems and solutions in becoming culturally competent. She had already grown from seeing racism only in a stereotypical group in one area of the country to recognizing it in some form in herself. Her story, like many you will read, may draw one of your own stories out of yourself.

Another one of my students explains with great understanding: "When we learn our own story and share it, we begin to understand how our past has brought us to where we are today and how we can learn from it.... Becoming familiar with one's own life story is a powerful process." I begin most of my writing with a story, and stories, past and present, permeate my work. I believe that stories are the key to learning, and this is supported by our knowledge of how the brain functions. Schank (1990) explained: "Human memory is story-based.... Not every experience makes a good story, but if it does, the experience will be easier to remember" (p. 12). One part of human memory breaks down experience into "facts." From a day's happenings, the mind retains e-mail addresses, directions, and the next day's errands. But another part of memory, which Schank labeled "episodic memory," assembles experience into stories. And because stories contain lived experiences, lessons, and wisdom, they are remembered long after facts fade (Watson, 1997).

You will find this section—indeed, the whole book—laced with real-life stories. Ours is a world of stories. Schank said, "We know them, find them, reconsider them, manipulate them, use them to understand the world and to operate in the world, adapt them to new purposes, tell them in new ways" (p. 241).

Introduction to Chapters 1, 2, 3, 4, and 5

The first five chapters of this book establish foundational understandings for the reflections and personal growth that underlie culturally competent teaching. Chapter 1 defines cultural competence and many of the terms we use in discussing and understanding cross-cultural teaching.

Next, we move on to discuss the difficulty of this journey. As one of my students said: "I think it might be natural for people in the majority to get defensive. I don't want to be guilty of doing or saying insensitive things toward anyone so naturally I would feel very embarrassed and want to defend myself. Hopefully, now that I know this is an issue I will try to actually hear and listen to what people are telling me, even when it may feel critical."

Chapters 2 and 3 examine racism and prejudice, both conscious and unconscious. Unintentional actions and words that may cause distance between individuals are also detailed as we come to understand microaggressions. Chapters 4 and 5 examine two sides of one coin: whiteness and culture and how they are deeply and closely related. In the next section, I have introduced each chapter through the voices of students who are also on this journey.

Student Voices: Fellow Travelers on This Journey

Chapter 1, "What It Means to Be Culturally Competent," discusses the need for cultural competence, the skill areas cultural competences comprise, and the benefits gained by educators who choose to pursue it. It ends with a self-assessment of current competency. One graduate student commented on the assessment: "For the question of where I want to be, I answered for each question that I want to be somewhere in the application [AP] and facilitation [F] range. If I wasn't an educator then I think that striving for the application level would be sufficient, yet in working with students I realize that I have the chance to make a difference on how they look at the world not just in math but in all aspects, and thus being able to facilitate their learning of these matters will be extremely powerful."

Chapter 2, "Understanding Racism and Prejudice," describes the dynamics of racism and prejudice as they operate at individual, institutional, and cultural levels and how they may restrict learning in the classroom. Another student's reflection: "Ya know Jean, not until I signed up to get the ESOL endorsement, which triggered me to take this class, did I realize that I have MANY questions regarding racial everything. All these thoughts on this matter have been stored up in some box in my brain since my childhood when I often wondered to myself 'why does grandma call the people across the street colored?'"

Chapter 3, "Recognizing Unconscious Bias and Unintentional Racism and Microaggressions," examines studies and examples that help us pay attention to our unconscious biases, stereotypes, and unintentional racism, including micro-aggressions and how they may affect us in our teaching and lives. One student's comment: "Stereotypes consist of thoughts that help us make sense of our world and the people around us. The problem is that our emotions [around these stereotypes] transmit into our actions, which ultimately may lead to hostility between two people who are different."

Chapter 4, "Understanding Privilege and Racial Consciousness among Whites," highlights the ways racial attitudes are structured among Whites and how Whites unconsciously protect the privilege their racial identity affords them in our society. One student said: "My question after reading this chapter is what makes it so difficult for many white people to see that they are indeed privileged? Is it because everyone struggles to some degree just to get through life? Or maybe it hurts to realize that while life may be challenging for me, it's actually easier because there are so many things I don't face because of my race?" Another said: "I ... hadn't put myself in the 'White privilege' category, because I've certainly never thought of myself as privileged because I'm White—you hear about it all the time, and how we have to fight racism, so I'm not saying it doesn't exist—I know it does—I'm just saying I never consciously thought I was part of it.... I'm surprised that now that I know about this, that it will take a lifetime to fight it, but I can see that it's like anything else—a lifelong habit, especially one you haven't been aware of, will certainly take a very long time to break."

Chapter 5, "Understanding Culture and Cultural Differences," focuses on the elusive concept of culture and its various dimensions, how to make sense of and deal with cultural differences, and the meaning of multiculturalism. This chapter helps teachers begin to be aware of their cultural values that may be at odds with the culture of their students. A teacher in one of my classes said: "I faced this once when I first started teaching. I was trying to talk with a student about hitting his friends and he kept looking at the ground. I asked him to look at me while I was talking so I knew it was listening. He refused. I figured out that his culture believed that looking someone in the eyes was a sign of disrespect. I was amazed. That taught me to pay attention to the beliefs and traditions of other cultures." And: "Before this course, I thought that being culturally aware meant understanding and respecting people of different cultures and races. Period. I now feel that although understanding and respect are a good start (and true understanding never ends), they only represent the beginning of a long, introspective and complex journey."

CHAPTER 1

What It Means to Be Culturally Competent

"They just understand some things outside, but they cannot understand some things in our hearts."

–Hoang Vinh

Hoang's parents immigrated to the United States with hopes of better life and education opportunities for their children. Noella, a Latina classmate, also has parents who came to America to offer her a chance at a better education than they had—aided by her teachers, who encouraged her and helped her reach her potential. Were their teachers well-prepared? Could you have been their teacher? How deep and wide are the new demographics in our country, and what does it mean to become culturally competent to meet the needs of Hoang and Noella?

Defining Cultural Competence

What is *cultural competence*? Put most simply, it is the ability to successfully teach students who come from cultures other than your own. It entails developing certain personal and interpersonal awarenesses and sensitivities, learning specific bodies of cultural knowledge, and mastering a set of skills that, taken together, underlie effective cross-cultural teaching. Individuals begin this journey with specific lived experiences and biases, and working to accept multiple worldviews is a difficult choice and task.

Most teachers regularly, although unknowingly, discriminate against culturally different students by lacking the sensitivity, knowledge, and skills necessary to teach them properly. Research consistently shows that schools are not welcoming places for culturally different students. On average, these students drop out earlier and achieve at lower educational levels than their mainstream counterparts (Garcia, 2001; Taylor & Whittaker, 2003). Several reasons explain this disparity. As in the red ink scenario, schools may inadvertently make students feel uncomfortable or unwelcome. Students and parents may not trust the motives or abilities of educators because of past experiences with the system. They may believe they will not be understood culturally or have their needs met. Students from culturally different backgrounds and home environments may require more support in order to succeed in mainstream school settings.

This book's purpose is to sensitize preservice teachers and those already in classrooms to the complex issues involved in cross-cultural education. Only when culturally competent teaching is routinely available will culturally different students have a chance to reach their full potentials. As Oregon state superintendent Susan Castillo said about teachers, "If we are going to hold them accountable for achievement levels of all populations of students, then we better also train them and give them the skills they need to achieve that" (McLain, 2005, p. C3).

As professionals, educators are expected to demonstrate expertise in transmitting curriculum and structuring the classroom for optimal learning. Cross-cultural teaching also requires mastery. Only by gaining the requisite awarenesses, knowledge, and skills necessary to become culturally competent can teachers hope to actualize their professional commitment to ensure academic success for all students.

Discrimination in education involves more than merely ignoring the contributions of ethnically and racially different people in the curriculum. It also includes being unaware of one's own prejudices and how one may inadvertently communicate them to students; being unaware of differences in cultural style, interactive patterns, and values and how these can lead to miscommunication; being unaware that many of the theories taught in many teacher education programs are culture-bound; being unaware of differences in cultural definitions of success as well as the existence of traditional cultural learning styles; and being unaware of the necessity of matching learning modalities to the cultural styles of students or of adapting teaching to the specific cultural needs of culturally diverse students.

Developing empathy and gaining an appreciation for the life experiences of those who are culturally different are equally important for effective cross-cultural teaching. Why do so many culturally different students and parents harbor fears about and mistrust those who represent the system? Why are so many angry and frustrated? Why do many culturally different people tend to feel tenuous and conflicted about schools? Why is parenting these students such a challenge? What is the source of the stress felt by many culturally different students and their parents? Why do they so often feel that majority group members have little awareness of or concern for the often harsh realities of their daily lives? Without keen insight into the complex answers to these questions, educators cannot hope to teach their students sensitively and successfully.

At a deeper and foundational level cultural competency, the need to teach all students successfully, "is connected to our ability to give each student, regardless of differentiated circumstances, 'permanent value' also known as 'unconditional positive regard' (some would simply use the words 'unconditional love'). How do we help teachers 'learn' that?" (Moule, 2008, p. 468). It begins with a respect for other ways of knowing and interacting, and a humility about our own assumptions.

The life experiences and college learning of educators have made them familiar with the inner workings of the educational system. Therefore, teachers need to take special care to recognize their own strong assumptions about schooling. As a result of interacting with teachers and the system, culturally different students may be unintentionally socialized into the dominant culture's ways. For example, Latino/a students may inadvertently be pressured to be competitive or self-assertive or students with Asian backgrounds to be informal in relations with authority—characteristics that are devalued in their home cultures. A second danger is overdependence on teachers. Culturally different students are especially susceptible because their knowledge of mainstream culture may be limited. Teachers may inadvertently perpetuate dependence rather than help students learn to function independently. For example, it is often easier and more expedient to expose students to dominant paradigms than to teach them to negotiate a parallel course that works better for them culturally. However, teaching is most useful when it facilitates students' interaction with the system on their own terms and in light of their own cultural values and needs. In the literature, this is called *empowerment*. It involves supporting and encouraging students to become self-directed lifelong learners.

Teachers and students from culturally different backgrounds do not come together in a vacuum. Rather, each brings preconceived ideas about the ethnicity of the other. For example, a student may initially feel mistrust, anger, fear, suspicion, or deference in the presence of teachers. In turn, a teacher may respond with feelings of superiority, condescension, discomfort, fear, or inadequacy. Each may also perceive the other in terms of cultural stereotypes. Such reactions may appear subtle or covered up, but they exist and—for at least a while—will prevent the forming of a successful learning interaction and environment.

The least helpful thing a teacher can do is to take these reactions personally and respond defensively. A much better strategy is to acknowledge the different perspectives and raise them as topics of discussion. Although students may initially feel more comfortable with teachers from their own culture, the truly successful learning environment builds on the sensitivity, caring, and commitment of the teacher, regardless of race or ethnicity. Because of the serious shortage of non-White teachers, Students of Color will likely find themselves working with dominant group teachers. This is where cultural competence comes in. Basic trust can develop cross-culturally. But it is not easy. It requires the right skills, a sincere desire to help, a willingness to openly acknowledge and discuss racial and ethnic differences, and a healthy tolerance for being tested. Distance and discomfort will fade with time as the student and the teacher come to know each other as individuals instead of stereotypes.

Demographics

U.S. population demographics are changing dramatically, and central to these changes is a significant increase in non-White populations. This "diversification" of America began in the 1980s. Between 1980 and 1992, the relative percentages of population increase for ethnic groups were as follows: Asians and Pacific Islanders, 123.5 percent; Latino/as, 65.3 percent; Native Americans/Eskimos/Aleuts, 30.7 percent; African Americans, 16.4 percent; and non-Hispanic Whites, 5.5 percent. These percentages represent not only a sizable increase in the numbers of People of Color in the United States but also a significant decline in the relative percentage of Whites from almost 80 percent to less than 75 percent. It will not take many years before non-Hispanic whites are a numeric minority of the U.S. population.

Based on U.S. census data estimations, in 2008, the population percentages for ethnic groups were as follows: non-Hispanic White, 65 percent; African American, 12 percent; Latino/a, 16 percent; and Asian, 5 percent. By 2020, it is estimated that the percentages will be non-Hispanic White, 64 percent; Latino/a, 17 percent; African American, 13 percent; and Asian, 6 percent. And by the year 2050, population estimates will be non-Hispanic White, 47 percent; Latino/a, 29 percent; African American, 13 percent; and Asian, 9 percent. While Native Americans are projected to remain below 1 percent of the population, actual numbers will triple during this period. As shown in Figure 1.1, by 2050, it is estimated that non-Hispanic Whites will represent less than 50 percent of the population.

Such changes are even more dramatic for certain subpopulations and regions of the United States. By 2008, for example, 43 percent of all U.S. elementary school children were Children of Color. By 2020, half will be. In California (a clear pacesetter for diversity), such parity was reached in 1990, when one school-aged child out of every four came from a home where English was not the primary language, and one out of every six was born outside the United States. By 2020, four states—New Mexico, Hawaii, California, and Texas—and Washington, D.C., will have minority majority populations. Even in states with a small population of racially diverse students, a slow and steady percentage increase continues.

These population changes are largely due to two factors: immigration and birthrates. The United States has a larger foreign-born population than any other country—approximately 12 percent of the total U.S. population in 2005.

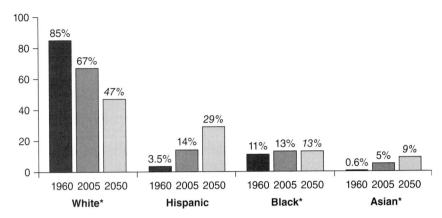

FIGURE 1.1   Population by Race and Ethnicity, Actual and Projected: 1960, 2005, and 2050 (% of total). Note: All races modified and not Hispanic (*); American Indian/Alaska Native not shown. Projections for 2050 indicated by light gray bars

Source: Pew Research Center, *U.S. Population Projections: 2005–2050,* Copyright © 2008 Pew Research Center.

For comparison, historical highs of foreign-born immigration was 15 percent in 1890 and 1910. The last forty years have seen an unprecedented wave of immigration to the United States, with yearly numbers rising to one million. The new arrivals are primarily non-European; approximately a third come from Asia and a third from South and Central America. In 1998, for example, while 9 percent of all U.S. citizens were foreign-born, 63 percent of Asian Americans and 35 percent of Latinos/as were foreign-born. By 2050, one in five Americans will be immigrants (Pew, 2008).

Differential birthrates of ethnic groups in the United States are equally skewed. Birthrates of Latino/a populations tend to be approximately 1.7 times those of Whites, and Asian Americans' birthrates are between three and seven times greater, depending on the specific subpopulation.

In the 2000 census, for the first time, there was an attempt to identify multiracial individuals, and 6.8 million people—or 2.4 percent of the population—reported multiracial backgrounds. Of these, 93 percent reported being biracial. Thirty-two percent of this group reported being White and some other group; 16 percent White and American Indian or Alaska Native; 13 percent White and Asian; and 11 percent White and Black or African American.

Reactions to the Changing Demographics

What has been the reaction to this growing diversification? First, many White Americans have clearly felt threatened by the changes. The sheer increase in numbers has stimulated a widespread political backlash. Most prominent has been a rise in anti-immigrant sentiment and legislation and a strong push to repeal affirmative action practices, which were instituted over the last several decades to level the economic and social playing fields for oppressed peoples. As economic times have worsened for working-class and middle-class Whites, frustration has increasingly been directed at non-White newcomers, who have been blamed for "taking our jobs" and told to "go back to where you came from if you're not willing to speak English." In a similar vein, White supremacist, militia, and antigovernment groups—playing on racial hatred and a return to "traditional values" and "law and order"—have attracted growing numbers. The result has been even greater polarization along Color lines. People of Color, in turn, have sensed in their growing numbers an essential appeal to White America: "Soon, you won't even be the numerical majority. How can you possibly continue to justify the enormous injustice and disparity?"

For those in the teaching professions, a major implication of these new demographics is a radically different student base. More and more, educators will be called on to teach students from diverse cultures. Job announcements will increasingly state "experience with diverse student populations required" and "fluency in a second language preferred." At the same time, a growing awareness exists that it is not sufficient to merely channel new students into the same old structures and programs or to hire a few token Teachers of Color. Rather, what is needed is a radical reconceptualization of effective teaching of those who are culturally different. At the center of such a renewed vision is the notion of cultural competence.

Basics for Understanding Cultural Competence

In its broadest context, cultural competence is the ability to effectively teach cross-culturally. It is a "set of congruent behaviors, attitudes, and policies that come together in a system, agency, or among professionals and enable that system, agency, or those professionals to work effectively in cross-cultural situations" (Cross, 1988, p. 13).

It is not a new idea. It has been called "ethnic sensitive practice" (Devore & Schlesinger, 1981), "crosscultural awareness practice" and "ethnic competence" (Green, 1981), and "ethnic minority practice" (Lum, 1986) by human service providers. It has been referred to as "intercultural communication" (Hoopes, 1972) by those working in international relations and as "cross-cultural counseling" (Petersen, Draguns, Lonner, & Trimble, 1989) and "multicultural counseling" (Ponterotto, Casas, Suzuki, & Alexander, 1995) in the field of counseling psychology. In education, early efforts at preparing for cultural competence were labeled "ethnic studies" and then "multiethnic education" (Banks & Banks, 2004). Other early terms included "education of the culturally different" and "education for cultural pluralism" (Gibson, 1976). Today, "cultural diversity" (Marshall, 2002), "culturally responsive" (Gay, 2010), "cultural proficiency" (Lindsay, Nuri-Robins, & Terrell, 2009) and "multicultural education" are most frequently used (Banks & Banks, 2004) as umbrella terms for approaches and strategies under girding culturally competent teaching.

What is new is the projected demand for such teaching and the urgent need for a comprehensive model of effective educational strategies for culturally competent teaching.

Basic Terms

Many different terms are used to refer to culturally different students. Anyone familiar with this field is aware of the power of such terms. First of all, they possess subtle connotations and, at times, implicit value judgments. They have often been used to oppress and demean devalued groups. They may be powerful sources of empowerment and pride. It is not surprising that ethnic group members pay serious attention to the ways in which they label themselves and are labeled by others. Finding out which term is preferable is a matter of respect, and teachers who are in doubt should ask students and parents which name they prefer. I have seldom seen anyone offended by that question. I have, however, repeatedly watched educators and others unintentionally alienate students, parents, and members of the community through their use of outdated and demeaning terms like "colored" and "Orientals" or insensitive general references to "you people."

The following terms are used in this text:

- *Culture* is viewed as a lens through which life is perceived. Through its differences (in language, values, personality and family patterns, worldview, sense of time and space, and rules of interaction), each culture generates a different experience of reality. The same situation (such as the first day of school in a kindergarten classroom) may be experienced and interpreted very differently, depending on the cultural backgrounds of individual students and teachers.
- *Cultural competence* is the ability to successfully teach students who come from cultures other than your own. It entails mastering complex awarenesses and sensitivities, various bodies of knowledge, and a set of skills that, taken together, underlie effective cross-cultural teaching.
- *Cultural diversity* refers to the array of differences that exist among groups of people with definable and unique cultural backgrounds.
- *Culturally different* is used synonymously with *cross-cultural* or *ethnic* and implies that the student comes from a different culture than the teacher.

It includes no value judgment about the superiority of one culture over the other—only that the people have been socialized in very different ways and may find communication problematic.

- An *ethnic group* is any distinguishable group of people who share a common culture and see themselves as separate and different from the majority culture. Their observable differences—whether physical, racial, cultural, or geographic—frequently serve as a basis for discrimination and unequal treatment within the larger society.

- A *racial group* or *race* is perceived as a biologically isolated, inbreeding population with a distinctive genetic heritage. Socially, the concept of race has created many difficulties. The distinction between race as a social and biological category is made in Chapter 2.

- *People of Color* and *Students of Color* are terms used to refer to non-White students and their families.

- *Communities of Color* are collectives of ethnic groups that share certain physical (racial), cultural, language, or geographic origins features. In naming specific Communities of Color, I try to use the term or referent that is most current and acceptable to members of that group (although there is always some debate within communities about what names are most acceptable). In relation to students, parents, and Communities of Color, the following terms are generally used: *African American, Latino/a, Native American/Alaska Native* or *Native People,* and *Asian American* or *Asian.* In quotations and in references to research, terms are used as they appear in the original texts.

- *Whites* or *European Americans* are members of the dominant or majority group of European origin.

This book assumes that all ethnic and culturally different students share certain psychological characteristics and experiences. First is the experience of belonging to a group that is socially stigmatized and the object of regular discrimination and oppression. Second is the stress and harm this causes to the psyche and the resulting adaptations—some healthy and empowering and others unhealthy and dysfunctional—that ethnic individuals and families make in order to survive. Third is the stress and harm that result from problems regularly associated with prejudice and racism (poverty, insufficient health care, crime, drug abuse). Fourth are problems in ethnic identification and racial consciousness that are often evident in ethnic students. *Ethnic identification* refers to the attachment that individuals feel to their cultural group of origin. *Racial or ethnic consciousness* refers to people's awareness of the impact of race or ethnicity on their lives. In one form or another, most ethnic students exhibit some modicum of these four factors and share in their impact.

Basic Assumptions

Whether in a school system or an individual, cultural competence is an ideal toward which to strive. It does not occur as the result of a single day of training, a few consultations with experts, reading a book, or even taking a course. Rather, it is a developmental process that depends on the continual acquisition of knowledge, the development of new and more advanced skills, and ongoing reflective self-evaluation of progress.

An effective and culturally competent education system must begin with a set of unifying values—or what might be called assumptions—about how to best educate diverse communities. These values share the notions that being culturally different is positive, that education must be responsive to specific cultural needs, and that teaching should be offered in a manner that empowers students. One model states that a culturally competent system:

- Respects the unique, culturally defined needs of various student populations.
- Acknowledges culture as a predominant force in shaping behaviors, values, and institutions and that culture has an impact on education.
- Views natural systems (family, community, church, healers) as primary mechanisms of support for culturally diverse populations.
- Recognizes that the concepts of family, community, and the like are different for various cultures and even for subgroups within cultures.
- Understands that culturally diverse students are usually best served by persons who are part of or in tune with their cultures.
- Educates students in the context of their minority status, which creates unique educational issues for them, including issues related to self-esteem, identity formation, isolation, and assumptions about the role of schooling.
- Recognizes that the thought patterns of non-Western peoples, although different, are equally valid and influence how students view problems and solutions.
- Respects cultural preferences that value process rather than product and harmony or balance within one's life rather than achievement.
- Recognizes that taking the best of both worlds enhances the capacity of all (my personal favorite).
- Recognizes that culturally diverse people have to be at least bicultural, which in turn creates educational and psychological issues such as identity conflicts resulting from assimilation.
- Understands when values of diverse groups are in conflict with dominant society values. (Adapted from Cross, Bazron, Dennis, & Isaacs, 1989, pp. 22–24).

Taken together, these assumptions provide the psychological underpinnings for a truly cross-cultural model of education. First, they are based on the experiences of People of Color and those who have worked intimately with them.

Second, they take seriously notions that are not typically included in dominant-culture educational models. These include the impact of cultural differences on education, the family and community as a beginning point for teaching, school accountability to the constituent community, and biculturalism as an ongoing life experience for People of Color. Third, they provide a yardstick against which existing educational institutions can measure their own philosophies and assumptions.

Individual Cultural Competence Skill Areas

Related to these basic assumptions about cultural competence are individual skill areas associated with the development of cultural competence in individual teachers. Five basic skill areas necessary for effective cross-cultural teaching: (1) awareness and acceptance of differences, (2) self-awareness, (3) dynamics of difference, (4) knowledge of the student's culture, and (5) adaptation of skills (Cross et al., 1989). Each can be assessed on its own continuum, although growth in one tends to support positive movement in the others. It is believed that these skills must infuse not only a teacher's work but also the general climate of the school and the educational system as a whole. These skill areas should be taught, supported, and, even more basically, introduced as underlying dimensions of everyday functioning within schools. For example, one skill area involves being aware of and accepting differences. For teachers, this means respecting differences in students. At a school level, however, a similar commitment to accepting and valuing diversity should also be evident in the educational practices that are adopted, in the philosophy that is shared, and in the relationship between colleagues and with parents.

Awareness and Acceptance of Differences

A first step toward cultural competence involves developing an awareness of the ways in which cultures differ and realizing that these differences may affect the learning process. While all people strive to meet the same basic educational needs, they differ greatly in how they have learned to do so. Cultural differences exist in values, styles of communication, the perception of time, the meaning of success, community, and so on. In aligning one's educational efforts to work with students from other cultures, acknowledging and looking at differences are as important as highlighting similarities. The discovery of exactly what dimensions of living vary with culture is an ever-changing exploration. Each individual begins life with a singular experience of culture, which is taken as reality. Only with exposure to additional and differing cultural realities does one begin to develop an appreciation for the diversity that is possible in human behavior.

Equally critical to becoming aware of differences is accepting them. Perhaps differences in beliefs and cultural views—rather than a reaction to race itself—are at the heart of prejudice and racial conflicts (Rokeach, 1960). Accepting cultural ways and values that are at odds with our own is difficult. For example, a success-oriented, hyperpunctual individual of European ancestry might find it difficult to accept the perpetual "lateness" of those whose cultures view time as flexible and fluid.

What eventually emerges in educators who are moving toward cultural competence, however, is a broadening of perspective that acknowledges the simultaneous existence of differing realities and requires neither comparison nor judgment. All exist in their own right and are different. Farther along the continuum, differences are not merely accepted or tolerated but are truly valued for the richness, perspective, and complexity they offer. A culturally competent educator actively and creatively uses these differences in the service of teaching and learning.

Self-Awareness

It is impossible to appreciate the impact of culture on the lives of others, particularly students, if one is out of touch with his or her own cultural background. Culture is a glue that gives shape to life experience, promotes certain values and experiences as optimal, and defines what is possible. As a skill area, self-awareness involves understanding the myriad ways culture impacts human behavior. "Many people never acknowledge how their day-to-day behaviors have been shaped by cultural norms and values and reinforced by families, peers, and social institutions. How one defines family, identifies desirable life goals, views problems, and even says hello are all influenced by the culture in which one functions" (Cross, 1988, p. 2).

In addition, the skill of self-awareness requires sufficient self-knowledge to anticipate when one's own cultural limits are likely to be pushed, foreseeing potential areas of tension and conflict with specific student groups and then accommodating them. A White European American culture exists and is sensed as embedded background. Specific cultural self-awareness is an especially difficult task for many White teachers who grew up in households where intact European cultural pasts have been lost. What remains are bits and pieces of cultural identity and personal history that were long ago cut loose from extended family, traditions, and community and as a result lack deep meaning (see Chapters 4, 5, and 15 for more on this topic). Without such a felt sense of the role of culture in the lives of People of Color, certain areas of student experience become difficult to empathize with and understand.

Dynamics of Difference

Related to self-awareness is the *dynamics of difference*. When students and teachers come from different cultures, there is a strong likelihood that sooner or later, they will miscommunicate by misinterpreting or misjudging the behavior of others (Fox, 1993). An awareness of the dynamics of difference involves knowing what can go wrong in cross-cultural communication and knowing how to set it right. Cultural miscommunication has two general sources. The first relates to past experiences of students, their parents, and teachers with members of the other's group or to the nature of current political relations between groups. For example, Mexican immigrants—due to border crossing and immigration policy enforcements that may be Draconian—may tend to be hypervigilant in relation to anyone who is perceived as White and authoritarian. Dynamics of difference also involve differences in cultural style. If a teacher from a culture that interprets direct eye contact as a sign of respect works with a student who has been taught to avert eyes as a sign of deference, there is a good chance that the teacher will come away from the interaction with erroneous impressions of the student. If educators are prepared for the possibility of such cross-cultural miscommunication, they are better able to respond to a potential problem with openness and respect.

Knowledge of the Student's Culture

It is also critical for teachers to familiarize themselves with a student's culture so that behavior may be understood within its own cultural context. Many serious mistakes can be avoided if the teacher begins each attempt at motivating students and encouraging academic success by considering what it might mean within the context of the student's cultural group. Similarly, other kinds of cultural information can be educationally useful. Interpreting the learning behavior of someone who is culturally different without considering cultural context or ethnocentricity (that is, from one's own cultural perspective) is fraught with danger, as the following anecdote amply demonstrates.

Several years ago, during a period of particularly heavy immigration from Southeast Asia, Children's Protective Services received a rash of abuse reports on Vietnamese parents whose children had come to school with red marks all over their bodies. A bit of cultural detective work quickly turned up the fact that the children had been given an ancient remedy for colds called *cupping*, which involves placing heated glass cups on the skin, leaving harmless red marks for about a day. The result was a group of upset Vietnamese parents, always attentive to the needs of their children, who were deeply insulted by accusations of bad parenting, and several teachers who felt foolish about their cultural ignorance.

Given the variety of populations that must be taught and the diversity that exists within each, it is not reasonable to expect a single teacher to be conversant in the ways of all cultures and subcultures. However, it is possible to learn to identify the kinds of information that is required to understand what is going on in the teaching/learning situation and to have cultural experts and resources to consult. Additionally, an open, listening attitude will allow a teacher to gain information directly from the parents and students that will help bridge the gap between theory and practice.

Adaptation of Skills

The fifth skill area involves adapting and adjusting teaching practices (that in reality, as we shall see, have their roots in the dominant cultural paradigm) to accommodate cultural differences. Such adaptations can take a variety of forms. Educational goals can be altered to better fit cultural values. For example, a Korean family may not feel comfortable about being involved in conflict resolution in the classroom (see the scenario in Chapter 6).

A teacher's style of interaction in which he or she carries out the learning process can be adjusted to become more familiar to the student. For example, in many cultures, teaching practices are highly *authoritative,* with advice freely given by experts. Asian students may tend to respond to teachers by showing deference. For their part, African American students may not even believe a teacher cares unless he or she is highly authoritative (Delpit, 2006).

The definition of who is a family member—and accordingly should be included in parent/teacher conferences—can also vary greatly from culture to culture. For example, meeting with families of African American or Latino/a students may involve the inclusion of multiple generations as well as nonbiological family members, such as good friends, neighbors, or godparents. The time and place of meetings can be modified to fit the needs of those who could not ordinarily be available during traditional hours, perhaps due to inflexible or double work schedules, or who would find it difficult or threatening to come to school.

Defining Professional Standards

James Banks and his colleagues (2001) offer a somewhat different approach to defining cultural competence in an educational system. According to the authors, the goal of multicultural education is two-fold: to prepare all students for the responsibility of citizenship and to do so by valuing and considering the cultural background of all students in the learning process. In the authors' words, "to forge a common destiny, educators must respect and build upon the cultural strengths and characteristics that students from diverse groups bring to school" (p. 5). To emphasis the mutual benefits of such work, they have titled their model *Diversity Within Unity: Essential Principles for Teaching and Learning in a Multicultural Society.*

Based on research related to diversity, Banks et al. (2001) begin by asking what we currently know about culture and education and then proceed to define a comprehensive set of principles of culturally competent teaching and educational delivery. They group these principles into five categories: teachers, students, cross-cultural relations, school structure and equity, and evaluation.

Consider a school system with which you are familiar. Are teachers knowledgeable about the cultural dynamics that might occur within the classroom? Are all students afforded access to all aspects of the curriculum and school resources? Do school personnel actively promote positive interaction between students of different cultural backgrounds? These are the kinds of questions that their work directs you to ask. Their joined research and theorizing provide a comprehensive model for current thinking as to what a culturally competent school looks like.

Why Become Culturally Competent?

In the past, gaining what is now called cultural competence was an ethical decision by educators with a particularly strong moral sense of what was right and fair. Usually, such individuals sought cultural knowledge with the express purpose of working with specific cultural groups and thus gravitated toward urban schools. Mainstream teachers with a predominantly White student base had little reason to pursue cultural competence. But today, the picture is quite different. For example, preservice teachers in Oregon are surprised by the steady increase in recent years of Students of Color from perhaps 1 percent to 4 percent of the student bodies in the "all-White" rural communities from which they come. All schools, especially those in urban settings, are seeing more culturally diverse students walking through their doors, and it may not be long before cultural competence becomes a professional imperative. In time, cultural competence may be a routine requirement for all jobs, not just those in the teaching professions. If projections are correct, most Whites will find themselves in close working relationships with colleagues who are culturally different. Whether it is a matter of working under a superior who is a Person of Color, supervising others from different backgrounds, or just retaining good relations with colleagues who are culturally different, being skilled in cross-cultural communication will increasingly be an asset.

Given the dramatic diversification that is currently underway in the United States, cultural competence may someday reach a status comparable to computer literacy. Twenty-five years ago, computer skills were an isolated novelty. Today, it is difficult to successfully compete in any job market without them. The same may eventually be true of cultural competence.

The Fear and Pain Associated with Moving toward Cultural Competence

It is my experience that most people are rather apprehensive about learning about race and ethnicity and that they approach the topic with reluctance and even dread. The same may be true for readers of this book. When I start a new class, the tension in the room is palpable. Students do not know what to expect. Race is a dangerous subject for everyone. People can come unglued when discussing it. White students wonder if they will be attacked, called racists, and made to feel guilty (Jensen, 2010). Students of Color wonder if the class is "going to be for real" or just another "exercise in political correctness." All students wonder whether they will really have the chance to speak their minds, whether things might get out of control, and whether we will, collectively, be able to handle what happens. Their concerns are understandable. Few Whites have had the experience of talking openly about race and ethnicity, especially cross-racially. Society has evolved strong taboos against it. Specific viewpoints and fear are embedded into children at young ages (Copenhaver-Johnson, 2006).

Rather than talking openly, what is more familiar are accusations and attacks, name-calling, and long, endless denunciations. Consider people's views about racial profiling, affirmative action, anti-immigrant legislation, and what constitutes terrorism. What one does not hear about or talk about and what must become a focus of attention if there is ever going to be positive change are the pain and suffering caused by racism and the ways in which everyone is touched by it. It is impossible not to think of past students and their stories: the young White woman who was traumatized as a young child when her mother found her innocently touching the face of their Black maid; the Latina girl who was never the same after being accused of stealing the new bike that her parents had scrimped and saved to buy her; the man who discovered at the age of twenty-five that his parents had been hiding from him the fact that they were Jews; the Asian woman, adopted at birth by White parents, who could not talk to them about how difficult she found living in an all-White world; and the European American woman consumed by guilt because of what she felt to be an irrational fear of African American and Latino men. There is clearly as much fear and nervousness about expressing such feelings as there is about working with students from other cultures.

It is possible to alleviate some of the anxiety by reviewing the ground rules and assumptions that define how we will interact in our college classrooms:

1. There will be no labeling or blaming each other and, of course, no name-calling. There are few heroes or villains in this drama; few fully good people or bad. We all harbor our own negative reactions toward those who are different. It is nearly impossible to grow up in a society and not take on its prejudices. Consequently, it is not a matter of whether one is biased. We all are. Rather, it is a question of what negative racial attitudes one has learned so far and what, from this moment on, one is willing to do about them.

2. Everything that is said and divulged in this classroom is handled with sensitivity. Students often censure, measure their words, and are less than honest in what they say out of fear of looking bad or of having their personal disclosures treated insensitively or as gossip.

3. As much as possible, students will personalize their discussion and talk about their own experiences. There is much denial around racism that serves as a mechanism for avoiding responsibility. By personalizing the subject and speaking in the first person—rather than the third person—this can be avoided.

4. Students can say whatever they believe. This may, in turn, lead to conflict with others. That is okay. But they should be willing to look at what they say, take responsibility for their words, and learn from what ensues. Anything that happens during class is a learning opportunity. It can and may be analyzed as part of the process. The class is a microcosm of the outer racial world, with all of its problems, and honest interaction in class can shed valuable light on the dynamics of intergroup relationships and conflict.

5. The intention of this class is to create a safety zone where students can talk about race in ways that they cannot talk about race in most parts of the real world.

As an educator, I also try to lessen anxiety in the classroom by modeling transparency and openness. I try to talk openly and honestly about myself and my personal experiences with race and ethnicity and to react and relate to students in the same open and honest manner. I hope that students will mirror such modeling in their own conversations and writings. This process is particularly encouraged by certain classroom activities and practices I have developed. For example, I ask students to self-evaluate their reactions and progress throughout the course.

In some courses, they are asked to keep journals of their reactions and experiences related to the course and the topic of race and ethnicity. For comfort, students are allowed to choose or propose their own reading lists (beyond certain basic requirements) and also selectively participate in a choice of various venues. For example, they can choose to avoid class presentations and do more introspective activities, such as interactive journal writing with the instructor, or they can choose small discussion groups or participate in online discussion forums. I try to respond to all remarks and sharing in an affirming manner or I help students resolve for themselves any dissonance between conflicting facts and other voices in the classroom. I may also use nonverbal affirmations or gentle challenges, usually posed as a question, that do not raise defenses.

Most students have serious questions about race and ethnicity that need to be answered or experiences that have to be processed and better understood. Significant learning and unlearning about race and ethnicity cannot proceed without this happening. Opportunities to do so are rare in most people's lives, yet it is through such occasions that growth and healing begin. Once some safety has been established, the floodgates may open, and students become emboldened by others' frank comments to share what is really on their minds. The following are the kinds of concerns that emerge:

- "Why do so many immigrants refuse to learn English? If they want to live here and reap the benefits, the least they should be willing to do is learn our language. My parents came over from Italy. They were dirt poor, but they made successful lives for themselves. They didn't have all this help. I really don't understand why it should be any different for People of Color."

- "This is all really new to me. I grew up in a small town in rural Oregon. There was one Black family, but they stayed to themselves mostly. It's confusing and, to be perfectly honest, it is also pretty scary. If I had a Friend of Color, I'm not sure I would know what to say or do."

- "My biggest issues are with Black men. I try to be supportive of them and understand the difficulties they face. But when I see them with White women, overlooking me and my sisters and all we have to offer, I get really frustrated."

- "To be perfectly honest, I hate being White. I feel extremely guilty about what we have done to People of Color and don't know how to make up for it. I don't feel I have any culture of my own. We used to joke about being Heinz 57 variety Americans. And I envy People of Color for all of their culture and togetherness. We tried practicing some Native American ways, but that didn't seem exactly right, and besides, we were never made to feel very welcome."

- "I've come to realize how much racial hatred there was in my family while I was growing up, and this disturbs me greatly. I find it very hard to see my parents in this negative light and don't know what to do with all of this."

- "It's gotten pretty hard being a White male these days. You've always got to watch what you say, and as far as getting a job, forget it. There's a whole line of women and minorities and disabled in front of you. I guess I sort of understand the idea of affirmative action, but just because I'm White doesn't mean I have it made. I find it very difficult just getting by financially. I don't see where all of this privilege is."

- "I just can't buy all this cultural stuff. People are just people, and I treat everyone the same. I grew up in an integrated neighborhood. I always had a lot of Black and Latino friends and never saw them as different. Frankly, I think all of this focus on differences is creating the problem."

- "I'm Jewish but am finding it hard to discover where I fit in all of this. I don't feel White, but everyone treats me and classifies Jews as White. My parents were very involved in the civil rights movement a number of years ago—even worked down in the South for a summer registering voters. But that seems so far away, and now Blacks hate Jews. What did we do?"

- "I'm in this class because I have to be. I don't need to take a class on racism. I've lived it all my life. White people don't get it. They just don't want to see, and no class is going to open their eyes. What I'm not willing to do is be a token Person of Color in here."

I keep these perspectives in mind, even when they may not be openly shared. I also keep in mind and appreciate the alternative viewpoints expressed by my students who understand the road ahead yet embrace it for the doors it will open not only in their classroom but also in their lives. In the very first week, one student shared this:

> While learning about how to discuss race, racism, and identity formation is a professional pursuit, for me, it is also a pursuit I take on personally as a parent trying to raise confident, social justice–minded kids in a multicultural world full of race, class, and gender inequities. Through this reading, I hope to gain a better understanding of racial identity formation (and identity development in general) and specific steps to interrupt racism and other forms of oppression, especially in our schools.

Moving toward cultural competence is hard emotional work. Personal issues such as those just described have to be given voice and worked through. Students need good answers to their questions and support in finding solutions to personal conflicts. Each of the five skill areas described earlier in the chapter represents a new set of developmental challenges. It is as if a whole new dimension of reality—that of culture—has been introduced into a student's phenomenological world. Old beliefs about oneself, others, and what one does and does not have in common need to be examined and adjusted where necessary. In addition, there are vast amounts of information to learn and new cultural worlds to explore. Perhaps most exciting, however, are the ways in which one's mind has to stretch and grow to incorporate all this new material. Students who have progressed in their learning about cultural matters often speak of a transformation that occurs in the ways they think about themselves and the world.

Regarding these cognitive changes, of particular interest is the qualitative shift that occurs in a person's frame of reference: movement from *ethnocentrism* to *ethnorelativism* (Bennett, 1993). In typical ethnocentric thinking, culturally different behavior is assessed in relation to one's own cultural standards; it is good or bad in terms of its similarity to how things are done in one's own culture. In ethnorelative thinking, "cultures can only be understood relative to one another and ... particular behavior can only be understood within a cultural context.... Cultural difference is neither good nor bad, it is just different" (Bennett, 1993, p. 26). People who make this shift increase their empathic ability and experience greater ease in adopting a process orientation toward living. When the actions of others are not assessed or judged but are just allowed to exist, it is far easier to enter into their felt experience and thereby empathize with them. Similarly, realizing that behavior, values, and identity itself are not absolute—but are rather constructed by culture—frees one to more fully appreciate the ongoing process of living life instead of focusing entirely on its content or where one is going or has been. These skills not only transform how people think but also prepare them for working more effectively with culturally different students.

In our increasingly global and diverse world, the ability to work with people whose backgrounds and lived experiences are different from our own has become a necessary skill. Perhaps you have worked in a diverse school setting or placement. You may have learned valuable lessons about how to work with African American students or how to teach children with dual languages. Cross-cultural knowledge is a natural by-product of such placements. Equally important are other kinds of cultural learning: how to listen, how to value different experiences, how to call into question the norms with which you were raised. Such skills transcend the specific knowledge gained in individual placements and are highly transferable. This process has been called "post holing" and reflects the fact that going deeply into a single aspect of curriculum content permits one to expand knowledge laterally. For example, a person grows in relation to cultural competence along racial and ethnic lines and discovers that he or she has also developed insights and sensitivities to gender and class diversity and so on. The result is growing competence in being more sensitive and just when working with an increasing array of diverse populations and issues.

Connections and Reflections: Emerging Views

How personally ready are you to engage in the needed introspection to become culturally competent? What obstacles or consequences do you foresee as you undertake this task?

I developed this survey for your personal reflection and growth. Each day in the classroom, you will be challenged by ideas, interactions, and experiences. What will you make of them? How will they affect your growth as a teacher? Teaching others provides a continuing set of experiences and opportunities to reflect on the educational process and these reflections on educational practice and perspectives improves them. This survey gives you an opportunity to reflect on your current and future self in ten important areas of cultural competence. You may revisit it after reading this text and as your journey continues.

The present survey focuses on race and ethnicity. However, it is most useful to think of it as an index of your growth in learning about differences that reflects an ever-widening perspective. An example of the item on the use and power of words to reinforce stereotypes comes from an analysis of reporting in the aftermath of Hurricane Katrina. In shelters, relief agencies routinely separated residents by race (Knight-Richardson, 2005) and the media followed this division. There was a widely disseminated juxtaposition of an Associated Press photo that showed a black man wading through chest-high water "after looting a grocery store" (read the caption) with an AFP/Getty photo of a white woman doing the same thing. However, the caption with the second photo described her as "finding" food "from a local grocery store" (Charles, 2010). This illustrates how the choice of words affects our perspectives.

Many educators believe that active and ongoing growth of the kind assessed in this survey is the hallmark of a well-educated teacher. The survey is developmental. In relation to each dimension of cultural competence, it asks you to assess your cross-cultural knowledge as it currently exists and then the ultimate goal you set for yourself, no matter how challenging or distant.

Self-Assessment for Cultural Competence

Use the following key to assess your level of competence for each of the statements.

U	Unfamiliar	The information is totally new to me.
AW	Awareness	I have heard about it, but I do not know its full scope, such as its principal components, applications, and modifications.
K	Knowledge	I know enough about this to write or talk about it. I know what it is, but I am not ready to use it. I need practice and feedback.
AP	Application	I am ready to apply or have applied this information in my own work and/or life.
F	Facilitation	I am ready to work with other people to help them learn this. I feel confident enough to demonstrate and/or teach this to others, yet I know that my learning is a lifelong process.

Where I Am Now	Where I Want to Be	Competencies
U AW K AP F	U AW K AP F	I am aware of the problem of language, images, and situations that suggest that most members of a racial or ethnic group are the same (e.g., "All Asians are good at math").
U AW K AP F	U AW K AP F	I substitute factual and meaningful information for ethnic clichés. For example, I avoid using terms and adjectives that reinforce racial and ethnic stereotypes.
U AW K AP F	U AW K AP F	I try to address stereotypical statements when I hear them used by others.
U AW K AP F	U AW K AP F	I avoid patronizing and tokenism of any racial or ethnic group (e.g., "One of my best friends is Black").

U AW K AP F	U AW K AP F	I understand the histories of oppressed groups (Native American, African American, Latino/Chicano, Asian/Pacific American) in the United States.
U AW K AP F	U AW K AP F	I thoughtfully view books and films to see if all groups are fairly represented.
U AW K AP F	U AW K AP F	I am aware of how my membership in different groups influences the power that I possess, and I am aware of how to constructively use that power.
U AW K AP F	U AW K AP F	I understand racial identity development. I know how to evaluate personal attitudes, emotions, and actions around my own racism and prejudices.
U AW K AP F	U AW K AP F	For White individuals: I am conscious of my White racial identity and its relationship to racial oppression in the United States. I think critically about what it means to be White in this country.
U AW K AP F	U AW K AP F	For Individuals of Color: I am conscious of my racial identity development and its relationship to racial oppression in the United States. I think critically about what it means to be of Color in this country.
U AW K AP F	U AW K AP F	I understand the concept of levels of curriculum reform (contributions/additive, transformation, social action; see Chapter 8).

(This survey may be copied and freely used).

Classroom: Adventures in Learning

As you move through this book, you may experience the will and desire to directly discuss race and culture in your classrooms. For a beginning of work in your own classrooms, consider including books with Protagonists of Color or stories that help your students move toward the competencies in the survey you just took. Such reading will help both you and your students get "factual and meaningful information" and "understand the histories of oppressed groups."

- Lower grades: Consider such books as *White Socks Only* by Coleman or the *Story of Ruby Bridges* by Coles. Even first graders will understand these books. "In fact, children were noticing subtleties in the themes that I hadn't even noticed. We too often underestimate what children can handle" (Copenhaver-Johnson, 2006, p. 18).
- For both upper and lower grades: Begin to post pictures, charts, and posters that engage and educate regarding different peoples and culture. For upper grades, I especially recommend the poster that comes with Jim Loewen's book *Lies My Teacher Told Me about Christopher Columbus* because it juxtaposes what we have come to know as "the truth" and actual facts. Once students begin to see two sides of a story, they become more aware in other areas and become critical thinkers. Additionally, such controversy usually stimulates students and increases learning.

CHAPTER 2

Understanding Racism and Prejudice

"Not everything that is faced can be changed, but nothing can be changed until it is faced."

–James Baldwin

Ron Takaki begins his book *A Different Mirror* by recounting a simple but powerful incident:

> In a taxi from the airport to a hotel in a large Eastern city on his way to a conference on multiculturalism, Takaki and the cab driver engaged in casual conversation. After the usual discussion of weather and tourism, the driver asked, "How long have you been in this country?" Takaki winced and then answered, "All my life ... I was born in the United States. ... My grandfather came here from Japan in the 1880s. My family has been here, in America, for over a hundred years." The cab driver, obviously feeling uncomfortable, explained, "I was wondering because your English is excellent!" (1993, p. 1)

Encapsulated in this incident are the basic feelings that increase racial tensions in the United States. The cab driver was giving voice to a belief shared by the majority of White Americans that this country is European in ancestry and White in identity and that only those who share these characteristics truly belong. All others—no matter how long they have resided here—are often viewed and treated with suspicion and considered outsiders. Takaki's wince tells the other side of the story. People of Color who call the United States home are deeply disturbed by their second-class citizenry. Being reminded of their unequal and unwanted status is a daily occurrence. They make a case that this country has grown rich on the labor of successive generations of immigrants—both voluntary and involuntary—and that their reward should be the same as Whites: full citizenship and equal access to resources as guaranteed in the Constitution.

The situation is further exacerbated by White America's seeming indifference to the enormous injustice in the system.

Culturally competent teaching is most usefully viewed against this backdrop. After all, the educational system is a microcosm of broader society and is susceptible to the same racial tensions and dynamics. In fact, as we will investigate later, there is some evidence that schools are the breeding grounds for racism (Lewis, 2003).

The discussion in Chapter 1 suggested that cultural competence depends on self-awareness, which includes, above all, awareness of the attitudes and prejudices that teachers bring to their work. Neither teacher nor student exists in a vacuum. Both carry into the classroom prejudices and stereotypes about the ethnicity of the other, and if unaddressed, these cannot help but interfere with learning. This chapter explores the dynamics of racism: its structure and meaning, the functions it serves for the individual and for society, how it operates psychologically, and why it is so resistant to change.

Defining and Contextualizing Race

First, what is *race*? The concept of race as used by the Census Bureau "reflects self-identification by people according to the race or races with which they most closely identify. These categories are socio-political constructs and should not be interpreted as being scientific or anthropological in nature" (2010). How real is race? Race is not a "scientific valid biological category, and yet … there are certainly observable physical differences among people—skin color, nose and eye shape, body type, hair color and texture" (Mukhopadhyay & Henze, 2003, p. 669).

Physical anthropologists have shown quite conclusively that what were assumed to be clear and distinct differences between the races are not clear or distinct. In fact, there is as much variability in physical characteristics within racial groups as there is between them. For example, it is not uncommon to see a wide array of skin colors and physical features among individuals who are all considered members of the same racial group. There has been so much racial mixing throughout history that many groups that may have once been genetically distinct are no longer distinguishable. Besides, defining race biologically and genetically opens the door to pseudo-scientific arguments about intellectual and other types of inferiority among People of Color.

U.S. census classifications of race and color have changed over time to reflect changing racial attitudes. In 1890, they included "White, Black, Mulatto, Quadroon, Octoroon, Chinese, Japanese, and Indian." In 1998, they included "White, Black, Indian, Eskimo, Aleut, Asian or Pacific Islander, Chinese, Filipino, Hawaiian, Korean, Vietnamese, Japanese, Asian Indian, Samoan, Guamanian,

Other." What is particularly interesting about the redefinition of racial groups every ten years is that the list closely parallels increased immigration restrictions. An increased desire for entry into the United States from groups that are perceived as threats by the White establishment results in reduced immigration quotas. Have racial categories been used throughout U.S. history to simultaneously oppress People of Color and justify White privilege?

Defining and Contextualizing Racism

My students love to say, "There is one race—the human race." And that would be fine, except that race matters. Does anything really change if we pretend that race does not matter? If we try to be colorblind, does that mean that African Americans are less likely to be followed around in stores? Are people going to stop thinking of Asians as good in math or as the "model" minority? Are teachers going to confront their own unconscious biases that produce low expectations of some students?

Racism is "the systematic subordination of members of targeted racial groups who have relatively little social power ... by members of the agent racial group who have relatively more social power" (Wijeyesinghe, Griffin, & Love, 1997, p. 88). Racism is supported simultaneously by individuals, the institutional practices of society, and dominant cultural values and norms.

Racism is a universal phenomenon, exists across cultures, and tends to emerge wherever ethnic diversity and differences in perceived group characteristics become part of a struggle for social power. In the United States, African Americans, Asian Americans, Latinos/as, and Native Americans—groups we have been referring to as People of Color—have been systematically subordinated by the White majority.

There are three important initial points to be made about racism. The first is the distinction between prejudice and racism. Allport (1954) defines *prejudice* as an *antipathy*—that is, a negative feeling, either expressed or not expressed, "based upon a faulty and inflexible generalization which places [a group of people] at some disadvantage not merited by their actions" (p. 10). Prejudice is a negative, inaccurate, rigid, and unfair way of thinking about members of another group. All human beings hold prejudices. This is true for People of Color as well as for majority-group members. But there is a crucial difference between the prejudices held by Whites and those held by People of Color. Whites have more power to enact their prejudices and therefore negatively impact the lives of People of Color than vice versa. It is not that members of one group can garner more animosity than the other. Rather, it is the fact that one group (in this case, Americans of European descent)—because of its position of power—can more fully translate negative feelings into educational, social, political, economic, and psychological consequences for the targeted group. Because of this difference, the term *racism* is used in relation to the racial attitudes and behavior of majority-group members. Similar attitudes and behaviors on the part of People of Color are referred to as *prejudice* and *discrimination* (a term commonly used to mean actions taken on the basis of prejudice). Another way of describing this relationship is that "prejudice plus power equals racism." The literature on racism suggests that "while old-fashioned racism has declined significantly, it has manufactured a new face: it is more covert, has become implicit, and is not under conscious control," as we will examine in the next chapter (Sue, 2010, p. 143).

Second, racism in all its forms is a broad and all-pervasive social phenomenon that is mutually reinforced at all levels of society. It is like the air we breathe. "Because racism is so ingrained in the fabric of American institutions, it is easily self-perpetuating. All that is required to maintain it is business as usual. I sometimes visualize the ongoing cycle of racism as a moving walkway at the airport" (Tatum, 2003, p. 11).

There are three levels of racism: individual, institutional, and cultural. *Individual racism* refers to "the beliefs, attitudes and actions of individuals that support or perpetuate racism" (Wijeyesinghe, Griffin, & Love, 1997, p. 89). *Institutional racism* involves the manipulation of societal institutions to give preferences and advantages to Whites and restrict the choices, rights, mobility, and access of People of Color. While individual racism resides within the person, the institutional variety is wired into the very fabric of social institutions: into their rules, practices, and procedures. Some forms of institutional racism are subtle and hidden; others are overt and obvious. However, all serve to deny and limit access to those who are culturally different. *Cultural racism* is the belief that the cultural ways of one group are superior to those of another. In the United States, it takes the form of practices that "attribute value and normality to White People and Whiteness, and devalue, stereotype, and label People of Color as 'other,' different, less than, or render them invisible" (Wijeyesinghe, Griffin, & Love, 1997, p. 93). Cultural racism can be found in both individuals and institutions. In the former, it is often referred to as *ethnocentrism.* Each level of racism supports and reinforces the others, and together, they contribute to its general resistance to change. Later sections of this chapter explore the workings of each in depth as well as inquire into the relevance for teachers working with culturally different students.

The third point is that people tend to deny, rationalize, and avoid discussing their feelings and beliefs about race and ethnicity. Often, these feelings remain unconscious and are brought to awareness only with great difficulty. It is hard to look at and talk about race because there is so much pain and hurt involved. Children's natural curiosity about human differences is quickly tainted and turned into negative judgments and discomfort. Often imperceptibly, they pick up parental prejudices with little awareness (at least at first) that the racial slurs and remarks that come so easily cut to the very core of their victim's self-esteem.

In a society so riddled with racial tensions, everyone is eventually hurt by racism. Accompanying the pain is often anger—and whether held inside or directed toward someone else, anger is hard to deal with. When such emotions become overwhelming, people defensively turn off or distance themselves from the source of the feelings. Such defenses become habitual, and by adulthood, they are usually firmly in place, effectively blocking emotion around the topic of race.

There is an interesting dynamic that exists around empathizing with those who have been the target of racism. When young children hear the stories of People of Color, they tend to deeply and sincerely share the feelings of the storyteller, for they are able to connect with the lived experiences of others. "We are really sorry that you had to go through that" is the most common reaction of children. By the time they reach adulthood, however, the empathy is often gone. Reactions instead tend to involve minimizing, justifying, rationalizing, or otherwise blocking the emotions. Teachers are no less susceptible to such defensive behavior. Preservice teachers increasingly have more open attitudes toward diversity and social justice and may even reside in diverse communities. Yet, "residing in a diverse neighborhood or attending a diverse high school does not always equate to increased contact with culturally diverse others," (Castro, 2010, p. 206). We need to go beyond open attitudes and minimal racial interactions due to the deeply embedded racism in our society. We must force ourselves to look inward if we are sincere in our commitment to effectively teach cross-culturally.

An Example

Consider the following experience of a teacher-in-the-making—a student in my class—as she struggles to understand her racial awareness. She is discovering the prejudices that reside within herself and the young child she cares for.

> Since the beginning of this class a situation that I encountered recently has continually been popping in to my mind. I figure that this situation has been surfacing for a reason, so I decided that this class presents a good opportunity for me to discuss it. Throughout the past two years I have babysat for a young girl on a regular basis. Throughout this time we have shared a lot of quality time together, and I feel I have played a fairly significant role in her first three years of life.
>
> About six months ago I was watching her on a beautiful sunny day and I asked her if she would like to go outside and play. She looked at me very seriously and replied "no." I thought this was unusual so I asked her why she did not want to play outside. She responded by saying, "I don't want to play out there when it's sunny because I'm afraid my skin will turn dark like yours." She continued on and explained to me that she wants to keep her light white skin and she is afraid that if she goes outside on sunny days she will become dark. She said that she does not think that dark skin is pretty like her white skin. I have to say that I was pretty taken back by the fact that this child was only three years old and she was expressing this concern to me. I know her parents very well and they both value diversity and show

respect for individual differences. I was struggling to decipher just what this child's words meant and how I should respond to her. I could not believe that at such a young age this child had somehow developed the notion that a dark skin tone was not as pretty as a light skin tone.

I bring this situation up mainly because I want to talk about how I felt when she talked this way. I have a very olive tone complexion, and in the summer my skin gets fairly dark. I noticed that I began to become very defensive when she talked this way. In a sense I became offended. She continued to state her concern about going outside in the summer because she did not want to be dark like myself. I decided that I should talk to her about how everyone has different skin tones and that no one color is better than the next. I explained to her that even her skin tone was slightly different than her mother's and brothers'. I told her that I thought my skin color as well as hers was beautiful in many ways.

I would like to hear your response to this particular situation. Specifically, I want to know if you feel that this young child was actually forming some biases that a parent should be concerned about, or if you think this was just common curiosity. I also would like to know how you would respond to a young child's comments such as these. Also, I would like to start to discover why I felt hurt and defensive when she was talking about my skin color in the manner she did. What do you think about all of this?

The child's reactions provided an opening for the preservice teacher to examine both her charge's and her own biases about skin color with increasing sensitivity and clarity. I responded in this manner:

First, studies have shown that children in the USA develop this sense of the value of skin color by about age 3 or 4 regardless of parental efforts (or color). Our cultural racism is just that deep and "unconscious" (isn't that incredibly sad?). Second, I think you gave an admirable answer: you might want to carefully select a few children's books with protagonists of color to give to her.

As to your own defensiveness … Ah … I think of how my father must have felt when I, at about 5, wished I had blond hair and blue eyes. I hope our session on racial identity development will help you make meaning of your feelings.

The material on racial identity development in Chapters 4 and 7 will also help the reader to negotiate such reactions and feelings. Such encounters as shared by the student in my class open the door for deeper understanding of prejudice and racism. Let us look at racism at three different levels: individual, institutional, and cultural.

Individual Racism and Prejudice

The burning question that arises when one tries to understand the dynamics of individual racism is, "Why is it so easy for individuals to develop and then retain racial prejudices?" The answer lies in the fact that racial prejudice has its roots in the "normal and natural tendencies" of how human beings think, feel, and process information (Allport, 1954). For example, people tend to feel more comfortable with those who are like them and to be apprehensive of those who are different. They tend to think categorically, to generalize, and to oversimplify their views of others. They tend to develop beliefs that support their values and basic feelings and avoid those that contradict or challenge them. And they tend to blame the people who are most vulnerable and subsequently rationalize their own behavior. In short, racism grows out of these simple human traits and tendencies.

Traits and Tendencies Supporting Racism and Prejudice

The idea of in-group and out-group behavior is a good place to begin. There seems to be a natural tendency for human beings to stick to their own kind and separate themselves from those who are different. One need not attribute this to any despicable motives; it is just easier and more comfortable to do so. Ironically, inherent in this tendency to love and be most comfortable with one's own are the very seeds of racial hatred. As Allport suggests, "We prize our mode of existence and correspondingly under value or actively attack what seems to us to threaten it" (1954, p. 26). Consequently, what is different can always be and often is perceived as a threat. The tendency to separate oneself from those who are different intensifies the threat because separation limits communication and therefore heightens the possibility of misunderstanding. With separation, knowledge of the other becomes more limited, and this limited knowledge seems to invite distortion, the creation of myths about members of other groups, and the attribution of negative characteristics and intent to them.

Prejudice is also stimulated by the human proclivity for categorical thinking. Organizing perceptions into cognitive categories and experiencing life through these categories is a basic and necessary part of the way people think. As one grows and matures, certain categories become detailed and complex; others remain simple. Some become charged with emotions; others remain factual. Individuals and groups are also sorted into categories. These categories can become charged with emotion and vary greatly in complexity and accuracy. On the basis of the content of these categories, human beings make decisions about how they will act toward others. For example, a colleague reported the following experience:

> I have the category "Mexican." As a child, I remember seeing brown-skinned people in an old car at a stoplight and being curious about who and what they were. As we drove by, my father mumbled, "Dirty, lazy Mexicans," and my mother rolled up the window and locked her door. This and a variety of subsequent experiences, both direct and indirect (such as comments of others, the media,

what I read), are filed away as part of my Mexican category and shape the way I think about, feel, and act toward those I place in the category Mexicans.

It is even more complicated than this, however, for categorical thinking by its very nature leads to oversimplification and prejudging. Once a person has been identified as a member of an ethnic group, he or she is experienced as possessing all the traits and emotions internally associated with that group. For example, one may believe that Asian Americans are very good at mathematics and dislike them because of it. A person who meets and identifies individuals as Asian American will assume that they are good at mathematics and therefore hold a prejudged, negative feeling toward them. Consider the African American female student, one prejudged as not good in math, whose classmates were stunned by her "unexpected" top-of-the-class test score. The "usual" expected top performers were all Asian American and male.

Related to prejudice is the concept of stereotype. A *stereotype* is "an undifferentiated, simplistic attribution that involves a judgment of habits, traits, abilities, or expectations ... assigned as a characteristic of all members of a group" (Weinstein & Mellen, 1997, p. 175). For example, Jews are short, smart, and money-hungry; Native Americans are stoic, violent, and abuse alcohol. What is implied in these stereotypes is that all Jews are the same and all Native Americans are the same (in other words, they share the same characteristics). Ethnic stereotypes are learned as part of normal socialization and are amazingly consistent in their content. As a classroom exercise, I asked students to list the traits they associate with a given ethnic group. Consistently, the lists contain the same characteristics down to minute details and are overwhelmingly negative.

One cannot help but marvel at society's ability to transmit the subtlety and detail of these distorted ethnic caricatures. Not only does stereotyping lead to oversimplification in thinking about ethnic group members, but it also provides justification for the exploitation and ill treatment of those who are racially and culturally different. Because of their negative traits, "they deserve what they get." Because they are seen as less than human, it is easy to rationalize ill treatment of "them." Categorical thinking and stereotyping also tend to be inflexible, self-perpetuating, and highly resistant to change.

Theories of Prejudice

Psychologists suggest that in-group and out-group behavior, categorical thinking and stereotyping, avoidance, and selective perception together set the stage for the emergence of either active (overt) or passive (covert) racism. In *overt* racism, an individual actively engages in or advocates violence and oppression against People of Color, in contrast to *covert* or passive racism that is either hidden or unconscious. Various theories have been offered about the psychological motivation behind prejudice and racism. In reality, there does not seem to be a single theory that can adequately explain the impetus toward racism in all individuals. More likely, there is some truth in all the theories, and in the case of a given individual, one or more may be actively at work.

Probably the most widely held theory of prejudice is known as the frustration-aggression-displacement hypothesis. This theory holds that as people move through life, they do not always get what they want or need and, as a result, experience varying amounts of frustration. Frustration, in turn, creates aggression and hostility, which can be alternately directed at the original cause of frustration, directed inward, or displaced onto a more accessible target. Comically, if my boss reprimands me, I go home and take it out on my spouse, who in turn yells at the kids, who then kick the dog. According to this theory, such displacement is the source of racism.

How does one choose an appropriate target for displacement? There are a number of competing theories. Williams (1947) believes that the target must be "visible and vulnerable." Dollard (1938) sees any group with which one is in competition as a potential target. Still others believe that the target often symbolizes certain attributes that the individual detests. Another theory holds that societal norms dictate the acceptable targets for displacement. Finally, there is the belief that the choice of targets depends on the "analytic" mechanism of projection. Individuals displace their hostility on groups who possess "bad" attributes, which are in reality similar to attributes they unconsciously detest in themselves. The irrationality of displacement requires the person to find justification for the hatred. This is often done by creating myths about why the group being discriminated against really deserves such treatment or by drawing on existing stereotypes, negative traits, and theories of inferiority. During the period of American slavery, for example, many slave owners asserted that African Americans were subhuman and incapable of caring for themselves, and because of this, slavery was actually a benign and kindly institution.

Other theories suggest that racial prejudice is manipulated within a society to promote certain economic and political objectives; that it is a means of buoying up self-esteem by viewing members of other groups as inferior; that it is socially sanctioned in certain geographical areas against specific ethnic groups and that many people who discriminate are adjusting to a social norm; and that it is based not on racial differences as much as on perceived dissimilarities in belief systems (that is, people tend to dislike those who think differently than they do).

What all these theories share is the idea that racist beliefs and actions help individuals meet important psychological, emotional, and socioeconomic needs. To the extent that this process is successful, their hostility remains energized and reinforced. Within such a model, the reduction of prejudice and racism can occur only when alternative ways of meeting emotional and other needs are found.

Implications for Teachers

What does this information about individual racism have to do with teachers? Put most directly, it is the source of—or at least a contributing factor to—many of the problems that culturally different students face in schools. Some students experience academic difficulties related to dealing with racism. They live with it on a daily basis. Dealing with racism in a healthy and non-self-destructive manner is, therefore, a major life challenge for many students. To be the continual object of a person's antagonism as well as the animosity of an entire social system is a source of enormous stress, and such stress often produces educational problems. For example, it is no accident that disproportionate numbers of African American males are often referred to special education programs. Or that African Americans suffer an unusually high degree of stress-related health problems.

The most important factor, though, for teachers is the deeply embedded "lower expectations" that may unconsciously surface when working with Brown or Black students (Holbrook, 2006; Landsman, 2004; Milner, 2009). In some ways, low expectations are the worst form of racism because they are insidious, constant, and long-lasting. Think about your own favorite or not-so-liked teacher. Think of the moments you still remember from your own schooling. From my own schooling, I still vividly remember the teacher who praised my artwork (perhaps eventually leading me to an undergraduate art major?), and I also remember the teacher who accused me of plagiarism (perhaps leading me to a hatred of the subject?). Unless we counter stereotypes in our own or others' minds, we will act on them. Worst, at some points, vulnerable students in your classroom may take on your expectations. I recall a student saying, "_____ is the first place I have been that has low expectations for Black students—and the students buy into it."

Yet, even after years of experiencing "lower expectations," a student's life maybe turned around by *one* teacher: "[The teacher] seemed to understand that my negative behaviors coupled with my propensity for daydreaming masked a fertile, imaginative mind" (Holbrook, 2006, p. 117). In this case, the student lived a chaotic life for many years, but eventually, the memory of this *one* eighth grade teacher's encouragement stayed with her and helped her pursue a career in literary arts. Holbrook adds, "There is no mistaking the lasting power that teachers have in shaping children's lives, for good or for ill" (2006, p. 117).

For younger children, especially, teacher awareness of racism and its impact is crucial. "One of the dire consequences of adult denial is that young children of color tend to bear the burdens of racism without acknowledgement and support from their caregivers" (Copenhaver-Johnson, 2006, p. 14).

Other educational problems are more indirect consequences of racism. Many Students of Color are poor and have limited resources and skills for competing in a White-dominated school system. Yet, more-affluent Students of Color are no less susceptible to the far-reaching consequences of racism. Life goals and aspirations are often blocked or at least made more difficult because of the color of their skin. There is a saying among People of Color that one has to be twice as good as a White to succeed. This is also a source of inner tension, as are the doubts a Person of Color may have about whether he or she earned a grade, either higher or lower, because of ability or skin color.

It is important for teachers to become aware of the prejudices they hold as individuals. "It is vitally important that teachers, no matter their racial or ethnic background, be honest with themselves about how they feel about certain young people" (Holbrook, 2006, p. 120). If the exercises at the end of this chapter and throughout the book are undertaken with honesty and seriousness, they can provide valuable insight into your feelings and beliefs about other racial and ethnic groups. Without such awareness, it is all too easy for teachers to confound their teaching with their own prejudicial reactions. For example, if I think stereotypically about Students of Color, it is very likely that I will narrowly define their potential, miss important aspects of their individuality, and even unwittingly guide them in the direction of taking on the stereotyped characteristics I hold about them. My own narrowness of thought will limit my success in teaching culturally different students. It is critical to remember that prejudice often works at an unconscious level, as we will explore in the next chapter, and that educators are susceptible to its dynamics. It is also important to be aware that after a lifetime of experience in a racist world, Students of Color are highly sensitized to the nuances of prejudice and racism and can identify such attitudes very quickly.

Prejudice and racism are considered value conflicts. It is important to re-emphasize that schools are places where one should carefully consider action and attitudes based on personal values and beliefs in order to embrace a position of wholesome neutrality in areas of difference.

At this point, you may be thinking: "we are all God's children," "we are all the same under the skin," and "we are all human beings or Americans" (Sue, 2010, p. 247). Expressing such color blindness not only has advantages for White people, but those who focus on race from a Christian perspective often have a more difficult time recognizing racism (Harris, 2008). Color blindness— whatever its basis—is often an indicator of bias on the part of those claiming it. The following are perceived advantages:

- It allows one to not acknowledge race and racial differences in the classroom.
- It allows one to maintain the illusion that one is unbiased and does not discriminate.
- If race is unimportant, then everyone has equal access and opportunity (Sue, 2010).

As a character in the film *Skin Deep: College Students Confront Racism* concluded, "God created us equal, but man made it so we ain't" (Reid, 1995).

Institutional Racism

Consider the following statistics from Hacker (2003) about African Americans in the United States.

- The infant mortality rate for African American babies is twice that of White babies.
- Of African American children, 45 percent live below the poverty level.
- In Illinois, 85 percent of African American children attend segregated schools.
- The income of African American families is 58 percent that of White families.
- Unemployment among African Americans is 2.8 times that of Whites.
- African Americans are overrepresented in low-paying service occupations (for example, they make up 30 percent of nursing aides and orderlies) and underrepresented among professionals.
- Whites are nearly twice as likely to have attended college for four or more years than are African Americans.
- African Americans comprise 45 percent of the prisoners behind bars in the United States.
- Life expectancy of African Americans is 93 percent that of Whites.

These are examples of the consequences of institutional racism: the manipulation of societal institutions to give preferences and advantages to Whites and to restrict the choices, rights, mobility, and access of People of Color. In each instance, African Americans are at a decided disadvantage or at greater risk compared to Whites. The term *institutions* refers to "established societal networks that covertly or overtly control the allocation of resources to individuals and social groups" (Wijeyesinghe, Griffin, & Love, 1997, p. 93). Included are the media, police, courts, jails, banks, schools, organizations that deal with employment and education, health system, and religious, family, civil, and governmental organizations.

Something within the fabric of these institutions causes discrepancies such as those listed to occur on a regular and systematic basis. In many ways, institutional racism is far more insidious than individual racism because it exists beyond the attitudes and behaviors of the individual in the bylaws, rules, practices, procedures, and culture of organizations. Consequently, it appears to have a life of its own, and those involved in the daily running of such institutions can more easily disavow responsibility for it.

Determining Institutional Racism

How does one go about determining the existence of institutional racism? The most obvious manner is through the reports of victims—those who regularly feel its effects, encounter differential treatment, and are given only limited access to resources. But such firsthand reports are often considered suspect, and people who may not—for a variety of reasons—want to look too closely at the workings of institutional racism can try to explain them away as "sour grapes" or claim "they just need to pull themselves up by their own bootstraps."

A more objective strategy is to compare the frequency or incidence of a phenomenon within a group to the frequency within the general population. For example, one would expect that a group that comprises 10 percent of this country's population would provide 10 percent of its doctors or be responsible for 10 percent of its crimes. When there is a sizable disparity between these two numbers (when the expected percentages do not line up, especially when they are very discrepant), it is likely that some broader social force, such as institutional racism, is intervening.

One might alternatively argue that something about members of the group rather than institutional racism is responsible for the statistical discrepancy. However, such explanations—with the one exception of cultural differences (to be described)—must be assessed very carefully, for they are frequently based on prejudicial and stereotypical thinking. For example, members of Group X consistently score lower on intelligence tests than do dominant-group members. One explanation may be that members of Group X are intellectually inferior. But there is a long history of debate over the scientific merit of taking such a position. An alternative and more scientifically compelling explanation is that intelligence tests are culturally and social class biased and, in addition, favor individuals whose first language is English.

There are indeed aspects of a group's collective experience that do predispose members to behave or exhibit characteristics in a manner different from what would be expected statistically. For example, because of ritualistic practices, Jews tend to experience relatively low rates of alcoholism. Therefore, it is not surprising to find that the percentage of Jews suffering from alcohol abuse is disproportionately lower than their representation in the general population. While reactions to alcohol use are sometimes genetic, such differences tend to be cultural rather than biological.

Consciousness, Intent, and Denial

Institutional racist practices can be conscious or unconscious and intended or unintended. "Conscious or unconscious" refers to the fact that those working within a system may or may not be aware of the practices' existence and impact. "Intended or unintended" means that the practices may or may not have been purposely created, but they nevertheless exist and substantially affect the lives of People of Color. A similar distinction was made early in the civil rights movement between *de jure* and *de facto* segregation. The former refers to segregation that was legally sanctioned and the existence of actual laws dictating racial separation. De jure segregation was both conscious and intended. De facto segregation, on the other hand, implies separation that exists in actuality or after the fact but may not have been consciously created for racial purposes. This type of school segregation has been increasing in recent years, with Black and Latino/a children more separate from White children than any time since the civil rights era (Brown & Wiessler, 2009).

It is important to distinguish among consciousness, intent, and accountability. A person may have been unaware that telling an ethnic joke could be hurtful and may not have intended such harm. But the person is still responsible for the consequences of the action. Similarly, a school may unintentionally track Students of Color into low-level classes. It was never the school's intention to concentrate Students of Color into these classes and thereby resegregate the school, yet the policies had this effect. Intention does not justify consequences, and teachers in that school should be aware of the racist effects of its policies. Lack of intent or awareness should never be regarded as justification for the existence of institutional or individual racism.

Although denial is an essential part of all forms of racism, it seems especially difficult for individuals to take personal responsibility for institutional racism. Acknowledging one's own prejudicial thoughts or stereotypes is far easier than feeling that one has played an active role in the creation of a racist institution, organization, or school.

First, institutional practices tend to have a history of their own that may precede the individual's own participation in the system. To challenge or question such practices may seem presumptuous and beyond the person's power or status. Or the individual might feel that he or she is merely following the prescribed practices expected of an employee or the dictates of an administrator or school district and, therefore, cannot be held responsible for them. Similar logic is offered in discussions of slavery and White responsibility: "I never owned slaves; neither did my ancestors. That happened hundreds of years ago. Why should I be expected to make sacrifices in my life for injustices that happened long ago and were not of my making?"

Second, people tend to feel powerless in relation to schools and school districts. Sentiments such as "You can't fight central administration" and "What can one person do?" seem to prevail. The distribution of power and the perception that decisions about curriculum and school functioning are made "above" contribute further to feelings of powerlessness.

Third, schools are by nature conservative and oriented toward maintaining the status quo. Change requires energy and is generally considered only during times of serious crisis and challenge. Specific procedures for effecting change are seldom spelled out, and important practices tend to be subtly yet powerfully protected.

Fourth, systems are strong forces and determinators in the academic outcome for all students. "Our schools and curriculum are monocultural in nature and come primarily from a White Western European perspective that omits, distorts, or demonizes the history of non-White Groups in America" (Sue, 2010, p. 119). The policies and practices of a school district that support institutional racism (that cause underachievement for many students) are multiple, complicated, mutually reinforcing, and therefore all the more insidious. Even if one were to undertake such efforts sincerely, it is often difficult to know exactly where to begin.

Implications for Teachers

What, then, are the implications of institutional racism for teachers? First and foremost, the vast majority of teachers work in schools and school districts that may suffer in varying degrees from institutional racism. To the extent that the general structure, practices, and climate of a school make it impossible for Students of Color to receive culturally competent teaching, the efforts of individual teachers, no matter how skilled, are drastically compromised.

What happens between a teacher and students is strongly connected to the larger context of the school. Culturally different students may have their achievement incentive affected if they sense racist or biased practices. (Such information travels very quickly within a community.) Even though they must attend school, their willingness to engage in the learning process with the teacher to whom they are assigned may be seriously compromised. Again, their work with an individual staff member is affected by how they perceive and experience the school as a whole. In their eyes, the teacher is always part of the school and responsible for what happens within it.

Finally, the ability to do what is necessary to meet the needs of culturally different students may be limited by the rules and atmosphere of the school. Does the school provide support, resources, and knowledgeable supervision for working with culturally different students? Is the teacher afforded enough flexibility so as to be able to adapt teaching to the cultural demands of students from various cultural groups? If the answer to either of these questions is no, then the teacher must be willing to try to initiate changes in how the classroom (and even the school) functions—in its structure, practices, and climate—so that it can be more supportive of efforts to provide more culturally competent education.

Cultural Racism

Closely intertwined with institutional racism is cultural racism: the belief that the cultural ways of one group are superior to those of another. Whenever I think of cultural racism, I remember a Latino student once telling a class about painful early experiences in predominantly White schools:

> One day a teacher was giving us a lesson on nutrition. She asked us to tell the class what we had eaten for dinner the night before. When it was my turn, I proudly listed beans, rice, tortillas. Her response was that my dinner had not included all of the four major food groups and, therefore, was not sufficiently nutritious. The students giggled. How could she say that? Those foods were nutritious to me.

Schools, like ethnic groups, have their own cultures: languages, ways of doing things, values, attitudes toward time, standards of appropriate behavior, and so on. As participants in schools, students are expected to adopt, share, and exhibit these cultural patterns. If they do not or cannot, they are likely to be censured and made to feel uncomfortable in a variety of ways. In the United States, White European culture has been adopted by and dominates most social institutions. The established norms on how things are done are dictated by the various dimensions of this dominant culture. Behavior outside its parameters is judged as bad, inappropriate, different, or abnormal. The Latino family's eating habits—to the extent that they differed from what White culture considers nutritious—were judged to be unhealthy, and the student was made to feel ashamed and inadequate.

Herein lies the real insidiousness of cultural racism: those who are culturally different must either give up their own ways and therefore a part of themselves and take on the ways of majority culture or remain perpetual outsiders. (Some people believe it is possible to be bicultural—that is, learn the ways of and function comfortably in two very different cultures. This idea is discussed in Chapters 6 and 7.) In many ways, institutional and cultural racism are two sides of the same coin. Institutional racism keeps People of Color on the outside of society's institutions by structurally limiting their access. Cultural racism makes them uncomfortable if they do manage to gain entry. White society's ways are not their ways, and they know that their own cultural traits are judged harshly.

Here are some examples of cultural racism:

- Personal traits: Characteristics such as independence, assertiveness, and modesty are valued differently in different cultures.
- Language: "Standard English" usage is expected in most institutions in the United States. Other languages are sometimes expressly prohibited or tacitly disapproved of.

- Standards of dress: If a student or faculty member dresses in clothing or hairstyles unique to their culture, they are described as "being ethnic," whereas the clothing or hairstyles of Europeans are viewed as "normal."
- Standards of beauty: Eye color, hair color, hair texture, body size, and shape ideals exclude most People of Color. For example, Black women who have won the Miss America beauty pageant have closely approximated White European looks.
- Cultural icons: Jesus, Mary, and Santa Claus, for example, are portrayed as White. The devil and Judas Iscariot, however, are often portrayed as Black. (Wijeyesinghe, Griffin, & Love, 1997, p. 94)

Racism in the Media

Cultural racism is supported by the media and by advertisements. Take Los Angeles, a multiethnic city since its beginning on Olvera Street as a northern outpost of Mexico. "While Los Angeles County's population is nearly 45 percent Hispanic, Hispanics accounted for only 14 percent of the characters seen on the eight 2004 prime-time series set in Los Angeles" and there were *no* regular Asian American characters, although the group makes up 12 percent of the county's population (Chartock, 2010, p. 81).

An example from advertisement: A few years ago, I picked up a sales brochure from Target. The cover said that the two named children's parents no longer had their disciplining tool: The two children, Zoe and Nik, so enjoyed their Target-supplied bedrooms that they did not mind being sent to them. I remember looking at the photo spreads on the inside and seeing that the girl child had many books and sat dreamily on her bed. The boy child was active in a room with balls, sports equipment, games and no books. Not a good visual, I thought, in regard to gender stereotyping. I was about to put down the flyer when I happened to look at the back cover: There, unnamed, was a brown child, a Latina. She is also in a lovely room. What is she doing? She is serving tea to her teddy bear! Here is subtle racism:

#1. The brown child is not named.

#2. She is on the back cover.

#3. She is serving.

I would call this indirect and ingenious racism. At the time, however, I honestly did not want to believe that the designers of the flyer were even conscious of the subliminal message they were sending in their choices. Yet, here was a confirmation of the "baby maid" (in the next section).

Hoping to find other, more wholesomely neutral material, I returned to the display of brochures at the store. I picked up a flyer that had many people of diverse skin color and occupations. Ah ah, I thought, this is better. Yet, as

I looked, I discovered that all the people in one flyer were looking directly at the photographer ... except for the lone Black male. While this could just be a random coincidence, we do know that eye contact or lack of it has cultural significance as well as perceived threat (Sue, 2010). Perhaps the designer just felt more comfortable with the image of the Black guy not looking at him.

Racism in Children

Cultural racism is probably more responsible for racism in children than specific modeling from their parents. We are able to see this most clearly when we look at Children of Color whose parents would have validated them personally. Babies as young as six months can distinguish race (*Newsweek*, 2009) and children in homogenous settings begin to see their own group as "better" very early.

Yet, the influence of television and ads embed the dominant standards of beauty and desirability in their minds. An excellent illustration of this phenomenon is a recent experiment that repeated Clark's classic 1954 doll study. In a video, completed by a 17-year-old film student and disseminated through the media, a young black child clearly reflects society's prejudice: The child describes the black doll as looking "bad" and the white doll as "nice" (Edney, 2006). Children internalize our society's biases and prejudices, as have all of us; they are just a little less able to hide it. I am reminded of the story of a 4-year-old in an affluent suburb who remarked to her mother upon seeing a young Latina while in line at the grocery store: "Mommy, look! A baby maid" (Romero, 1992, p. 92).

School observations of young children of six years of age showed their preferences based on race. The children sat in heterogeneous groups at their assigned tables during class time, yet during recess and at lunchtime, the girls segregated themselves by race. While this behavior was not seen as clearly in boys and segregation itself is not a problem, the researcher noted that already, the Black children recognized that the White children were making the decisions to sit or not sit by them and that it had a negative racial undertone (Copenhaver-Johnson, 2006). The White children had already learned to not name race or admit that that was a basis of choice of playmates. "White children's reluctance to discuss race or racism can be considered symptomatic of their socialization into color-blindness, at least in adults' presence" (Copenhaver-Johnson, 2006, p. 14). A telling example is noted in White children's dismissal of a Black Santa. The White first graders do not say that the reasons they reject the Santa is because the Santa is Black. It is because Santa is not fat, the beard length wrong, or the style of buttons on the suit is wrong. Black children may also reject the Black Santa; however, they will more likely name race, saying that the Black Santa does not look like "Santa." By the way, these children who reinforce racial ideology on the playground are carefully taught about civil rights in their classrooms and may "speak reverently" about Rosa Parks and Dr. Martin Luther King Jr. (Copenhaver-Johnson, 2006). This insidious silence on race leads to the racism of color-blindness (Copenhaver-Johnson, 2006; Lewis-Charp, 2003; Polite & Saenger, 2003).

Implications for Teachers

Cultural racism has relevance for teachers in several ways. First, teachers need to be aware of the cultural values they bring to the classroom and acknowledge that these values may be different from and even at odds with those of their students. This is especially true for White teachers working with Students of Color. It is not unusual for Students of Color to react to White teachers as symbols of the dominant culture and to initially act out their frustrations with a society that so systematically negates their cultural ways. Remember that the supremacy of White culture has become thoroughly embedded into the lives of those in schools, especially White teachers, usually without consciousness or consent! And these same embedded factors are institutionalized in the schools.

Teaching across cultures must involve some degree of negotiation around the values that define the learning environment. Most importantly, educational goals and the general style of interaction must make sense to the student. Yet, at the same time, they must fall within the broad parameters of what the teacher conceives as sound education. Most likely, the teacher will have to make significant adaptations to standard methods of teaching to fit the needs of the culturally different student. Traditional preparation for teaching and the models that inform preservice education are themselves culture-bound and have their roots in dominant European culture. What exactly are the values and cultural imperatives that teachers bring to the classroom? What relevance do these have for students whose cultural worldviews might be very different?

Cultures differ greatly in how they view success and how they conceive of the role of teacher. The notion of sacrificing peer approval for the sake of academic achievement in a seemingly racist system makes little sense to many students. Similarly, what success is and how one measures it vary greatly across cultures. Given all this cultural variation and the ethnocentricity of traditional teaching and learning methods, teachers must answer a number of very knotty questions. For example, is it possible to expand present culture-bound teaching methods so they can become universally applicable (appropriately applied multiculturally)? If so, what would such teaching look like? Or is there, perhaps, some truth to the contention of many minority educators that something in the European dominant paradigm is inherently destructive to traditional culture and that radically different approaches to teaching must be forged for ethnic populations? These questions are addressed in Chapters 5 and 8.

Connections and Reflections: Emerging Views

These questions are intended to help you identify dynamics and aspects of institutional and cultural racism in schools. Choose a particular school or organization with which you are familiar. It may be one in which you are currently teaching or volunteering or one from your past. Some of the questions may require you to do research or seek additional information.

How many People of Color or other ethnic group members work and teach in this school, and what positions do they hold? How are people hired or brought into the school? Is there anything about this process or the job requirements that could differentially affect People of Color or other ethnic-group members?

Does the school take any position on promoting cultural diversity within its ranks? Do any mission statements, plans, or projections in this direction exist? Can you discern any unwritten feelings or attitudes that prevail around race and ethnicity within the school? Has the school done anything specific to promote greater diversity?

How would you describe the school culture? Do you feel that members of various Communities of Color would be comfortable entering and being a part of it? Specify your answers by group and explain in detail. How do you feel various segments of the school would react to the entry of a Person of Color? How does the school function? Who has the power? Who makes decisions? Is there anything about the school's structure that makes it accessible or inaccessible to People of Color?

What does it feel like to teach or volunteer in this organization? Are there any rules, policies, and styles of working that are unique or unusual? Would you say that the school's culture is predominately Euro-American? Explain.

If it is a school, who are its students? Are any efforts being made (or have there ever been any efforts) to broaden or narrow the racial and ethnic composition of the student body?

You may find it particularly informative to have other teachers or volunteers answer these same questions and then compare answers or use the questions as stimuli for discussing the cultural competence of the school.

Clocks

It is far easier to begin to discuss difficult and challenging material with just one other person. This first activity is simply a fun way to form pairs that may be used when needed. The second activity allows participants to relive and begin to grapple with issues of oppression of whatever kind they choose.

I suggest that you use some form of organization to come up with dyads for discussions and classroom activities. I use a clock. On the first day of class (or when you decide to begin this), each student receives a clock face with a line near each number on the clock. Students go around the room making twelve appointments with others: Each person exchanges clocks with another individual, and they put their names on the same time. I usually use one time slot immediately for an activity. Later, on other days, when it comes time to meet with an appointment, if for some reason the other person is not there, the student comes to the front of the room and I match them with another student in the same situation. If the numbers are uneven, we form one group of three.

I use these appointments for a short 10–12 minute discussion of the book chapters to begin our time together, especially when we are working with challenging material. Sometimes, I save time slots 1–10 for the corresponding week of the quarter for my own convenience. I may also assign a chapter for that week; for example, on week 3, three o'clock appointments will meet to discuss Chapter 3. Occasionally, I instruct students to make plans to meet elsewhere for this content discussion at a time and place convenient for their clock appointment. I use the last pairings for other activities.

Theatre of the Oppressed

This exercise is called "Theatre of the Oppressed" (Boal, 1979). It has also been called the "Game of Dialogue." While it may be elaborately produced with larger audiences and has it roots in the 1960s, I have simplified it for my college classrooms:

- Students sit in groups of four (I put together two sets formed by clock appointments).
- Each student has one minute to tell an *ism* (racism, ageism, sexism, lookism, etc.) that she or he has experienced or witnessed (I time this and tell them when to change).
- The group decides on the most compelling story and makes it into a skit (I allow about five minutes for skit planning).
- I ask for volunteer groups and have the skit acted out for the class.
- As the skit finishes and the group prepares to sit down, I ask them to stay in their positions and ask if anyone in the group would like to change history by re-enacting the skit with different actions and words for any individual in the skit.
- Additional members of the group and then members of the audience are invited to take the place of any character in the skit until there are no more volunteers.

I have seldom had time to do more than three or four skits in a class of fifty. There are benefits at several levels: Regardless of whether a skit is acted out, each member of the class has had an opportunity to define and share an *ism* in a small, safe group. Dialogue has been started, collaborative problem solving has been introduced, and, occasionally, lives are changed. Sometimes, the acted skits with a changed outcome have brought tears and healing to members of the class. Finally, everyone has learned unique stories, seen the reality of oppression, and begun to reflect on such stories and explore ways to disrupt them.

Classroom: Adventures in Learning

- For upper grades, a simplified version of the "Theatre of the Oppressed" may be considered. The activity could be done with a selected group(s) for the audience of the whole class. In order to ensure felt safety for all the students, the need for positive changes could be encouraged or the teacher could be the first to suggest a way to change the past.
- For children in lower grades, one simple way to change the perception of race in the classroom is to insert White before the characters in a book when they are first introduced (not so necessary with picture books, although you might call attention to it). Here is the reasoning:

  Most authors fail to specify race when a character is white, assuming that to be white is to be "us," to be "normal." It is the default setting of much of children's literature. A teacher who merely inserts the adjective "white" or explains that the characters in the story are white doesn't change the story. But that teacher has put "white" on the same footing as "black" and thereby changed everything. This kind of awareness can be powerful for children and for teachers. "We" can be of any race. "They" can be of any race. (Polite & Saenger, 2003, pp. 277–278).

Reading books in this way may deepen the sense of community and eventually build trust for open conversations about race.

CHAPTER 3

Recognizing Unconscious Bias, Unintentional Racism, and Microaggressions

"As long as microaggressions remain hidden, invisible, unspoken, and excused as innocent slights with minimal harm, we will continue to insult, demean, alienate, and oppress marginalized groups."

–Derald Wing Sue

In the blink of an eye, unconscious bias was visible to me, an African American. A man saw my face as I walked into the store and unconsciously checked his wallet. On the street, a woman catches my eye a half a block away and moves her purse from the handle of her baby's stroller to her side as she arranges the baby's blanket. In the airport, a man signals to his wife to move her purse so it is not over the back of her chair, adjacent to the one I am moving toward. On my way to exercise, a man leaving the pool looks up, sees me, and spits to the side. What is happening in these instances? Were these actions general safety precautions? If so, why did the sight only of my brown face, not the others who moved among these White individuals, elicit these actions? And why do these experiences affect my emotions and consciousness?

I believe these are examples of "blink of the eye" racism. Such unconscious biases—such microaggressions—lead to unintentional racism, which is usually invisible even and especially to those who perpetrate it. Most people do not want to be considered racist or capable of racist acts because the spoken and unspoken norm is that "good people do not discriminate or in any way participate in racism" (Dovidio & Gaertner, 2005, p. 2).

Such unconscious biases and microaggressions affect all our relationships, whether they are fleeting relationships in airports or long-term relationships between teachers and students, teachers and parents, or teachers and other educators. Recognizing our own biases is the first step toward improving the interactions that we have with all people and is essential if we hope to build deep community within our schools. Evidence shows that these biases cross racial lines (both Blacks and Whites may have biases against Blacks) and are almost impossible to change.

Unconscious Bias

Biases are rooted in racism, prejudices, and stereotypes, as we discussed in Chapter 2. A *stereotype* is a simplistic image or distorted truth about a person or group based on a prejudgment of habits, traits, abilities, or expectations (Weinstein & Mellen, 1997). These stereotypes—both conscious and unconscious—cause most of us to make links that we do not even believe in: "The problem arises when we form associations that contradict our intentions, beliefs and values. That is, many people unwittingly associate 'female' with 'weak,' 'Arab' with 'terrorist,' or 'black' with 'criminal,' even though such stereotypes undermine values such as fairness and equality that many of us hold dear" (Carpenter, 2008, p. 2).

Uncovering Biases

Because people are more likely to act out of unconscious or hidden bias, knowing that you have a bias for or against a group may cause you to compensate and more carefully consider your possible responses or actions. Acknowledging biases often opens doors for learning and allows people to consciously work for harmony in classrooms and communities (Polite & Saenger, 2003).

How do we find a key to unlock this door to the mind? Several websites have been developed to help people examine their racial and cultural attitudes. They offer a quick, hands-on opportunity to assess the attitudes and beliefs you will bring into the classroom. The Implicit Association Test (IAT) has helped millions of people—those who accept the often startling results—reveal their unconscious biases to themselves. Psychologists from Yale University and the University of Washington for the Southern Poverty Law Center developed this website: http://www.tolerance.org/activity/test-yourself-hidden-bias. It includes a number of implicit association tests, each taking only five minutes, that together provide a broad picture of an individual's racial and cultural biases. The following introduction appears on the website.

> What is an implicit association? Sometimes called "unconscious" or "automatic," an implicit association is a mental response that is so well learned as to operate without awareness, or without intention, or without control…. Equality is a birthright in the United States, protected by the Constitution…. Yet, not a day passes without reports of unequal treatment of individuals. This discrimination is based

on negative stereotypes and prejudice that, according to social psychologists, linger in most of us. Even if we believe in our hearts that we see and treat people as equals, hidden biases may nevertheless influence our actions. A new suite of psychological tests measures unconscious bias. We invite you to take these tests online and reveal to yourself what may be hidden in your psyche.

I encourage you to take the full range of tests and read the various interpretations of your scores. Together, they should provide useful information about your own built-in biases:

Anthony Greenwald and Mahzarin Banaji developed the test in the mid-1990s because "it is well known that people don't always 'speak their minds,' and it is suspected that people don't always 'know their minds'" (Greenwald, McGhee & Schwartz, 1998). The IAT "presents a method that convincingly demonstrates the divergences of our conscious thoughts and our unconscious biases," according to the Harvard website for Project Implicit.

Strangely enough, the first evidence of this unconscious bias came from insects and flowers. Greenwald made a list of 25 insect names and 25 flower names and found that it was far easier to place the flowers in groups with pleasant words and insects in groups with unpleasant words than the reverse. It was just difficult to "hold a mental association of insects with words such as 'dream,' 'candy,' and 'heaven,' and flowers with words such as 'evil,' 'poison' and 'devil'" (Vedantam, 2005, p. 3).

Greenwald then took the next step and used stereotypically white-sounding names, such as Adam and Emily, and black-sounding names, such as Jamal and Lakisha, and grouped them with pleasant and unpleasant words. According to Vedantam, Greenwald himself was surprised: "I had as much trouble pairing African American names with pleasant words as I did insect names with pleasant words" (Vedantam, 2005, p. 3). His collaborator, Banaji, was even more self-reflective, "'I was deeply embarrassed,' she recalls. 'I was humbled in a way that few experiences in my life have humbled me'" (p. 3).

This unconscious pairing has direct real-world consequences. Unconscious bias allows people who consciously said they wanted qualified minority employees to then unconsciously rate résumés with black-sounding names as less qualified. With other factors held constant, white-sounding names at the top of résumés triggered 50 percent more callbacks than African American names. Human resources managers were stunned by the results. Explicit bias can occur not only without the intent to discriminate but despite explicit desires to recruit minorities (Bertrand & Mullainathan, 2004).

In *See No Bias*, Vedantam (2005) shares the disappointment and surprise that two recent test takers experienced when they found that their results on the Implicit Association Test did not mesh with their perceived views of themselves. To the dismay of these individuals, the test results were also in conflict with their life and career goals. Vedantam describes in detail a woman, an activist, taking a recent version of the test:

> The woman brought up a test on her computer from a Harvard University web site. It was really very simple: All it asked her to do was distinguish between a series of black and white faces. When she saw a black face, she was to hit a key on the left; when she saw a white face, she was to hit a key on the right. Next, she was asked to distinguish between a series of positive and negative words. Words such as "glorious" and "wonderful" required a left key, words such as "nasty" and "awful" required a right key. The test remained simple when two categories were combined: The activist hit the left key if she saw either a white face or a positive word, and hit the right key if she saw either a black face or a negative word.
>
> Then the groupings were reversed. The woman's index fingers hovered over her keyboard. The test now required her to group black faces with positive words, and white faces with negative words. She leaned forward intently. She made no mistakes, but it took her longer to correctly sort the words and images.
>
> Her result appeared on the screen, and the activist became very silent. The test found she had a bias for whites over blacks.
>
> "It surprises me I have any preferences at all," she said. "By the work I do, by my education, my background. I'm progressive, and I think I have no bias. Being a minority myself, I don't feel I should or would have biases."
>
> "I'm surprised," the woman said. She bit her lip. "And disappointed." (p. 2)

Such reactions should not really be a surprise according to the writings of many white anti-racist activists, including Tim Wise, who acknowledge residual racism still inside themselves. Wise notes how unconscious bias relegates the role of whiteness or race "to a nonfactor in the minds of whites" (2005, p. 18). When the role of whiteness or race becomes clear to a person, such as the activist described above, surprise and disappointment are likely results.

Professional Consequences

In his book *Blink*, Malcolm Gladwell describes the type of circumstances where Blacks and Whites will both engage and disengage around climate and personal relation issues:

> If you have a strongly pro-white pattern of associations ... there is evidence that that will affect the way you behave in the presence of a black person.... In all likelihood, you won't be aware that you are behaving any differently than you would around a white person. But chances are you'll lean forward a little less, turn away slightly from him or her, close your body a bit, be a bit less expressive, maintain less eye contact, stand a little farther away, smile a lot less, hesitate and stumble over your words a bit more, laugh at jokes a bit less. Does that matter? Of course it does. (2005, pp. 85–86)

TABLE 3.1   Biased and Unbiased White Individuals' Time to Complete
Paired Task

White Member of Pair	Time to Complete Task When Paired with a Black Person
Unbiased in word and behavior	Four minutes
Biased in word and behavior	Five minutes
Unbiased by self-report, behavior shows bias	Six minutes

Consider the possible repercussions of these unconscious biases at a job
interview. The same factors will affect behaviors in parent-teacher conferences
or affect student outcomes in classrooms.

Another study describes matching Whites with Blacks for the completion
of a task Table 3.1; (Dovidio & Gaertner, 2005). Whites were first divided into
two groups: those who expressed egalitarian views and those who expressed
their biases openly. These individuals were then observed to see if their
actions, such as those described by Gladwell, showed unconscious biases. Each
White person then engaged in a problem-solving task with a Black person. The
time it took to complete the joint task was recorded.

Two important points bear emphasis here. First, the African American individuals, either consciously or unconsciously, were aware of the behavior that
showed bias. In this study, "blacks' impressions of whites were related mainly to
whites' unconscious attitudes ... the uncomfortable and discriminatory behavior associated with covert racism is very obvious to blacks, even while whites
either don't recognize it or consider it hidden" (Dovidio & Gaertner, 2005,
pp. 3–4). I know that as an African American, when I enter a room of European American people, I pick up subtle clues, either consciously or unconsciously, as to who is a good, open contact for me versus someone who may
have difficulty engaging with me easily based on my race.

Second, White individuals who said they were unbiased yet showed nonverbal biased behavior reported their impressions of their behavior related to
their publicly expressed attitudes and were likely to maintain their stated level
of biases when questioned. Therefore, they are likely to blame the victim, the
Black individual, for their slowness in completing the task (and, incidentally,
possibly reinforce their stereotypes). "We cling to filters that screen out what
people of color try to tell us because we fear losing material and psychological
advantages that we enjoy" (Sleeter, 1994, p. 6).

Changing Consciousness

Do we have the ability to change our attitudes and behaviors? Gladwell
explains the two levels of consciousness in a manner that gives us hope. He

says that in many situations, we are able to direct our behavior using our conscious attitudes—what we choose to believe or our stated values—rather than our "racial attitude on an unconscious level—the immediate, automatic associations that tumble out before we've even had time to think" (2005, p. 84). He continues: "We don't deliberately choose our unconscious attitudes.... We may not even be aware of them" (p. 85). Because our unconscious attitudes may be completely incompatible with our stated values, we must know just what those unconscious attitudes are, for they are, as Gladwell states, a powerful predictor of how we may act in some spontaneous situations.

While I started this chapter with evidence of people who responded to their gut reactions to my brown skin in surprising nonverbal ways, many of the same people would be quite gracious if given another second or two. Recent research shows that while most people have an instant activity in the "fight or flight" amygdala part of their brains upon encountering an unexpected person or situation (Fair et al., 2009), that first reaction is often consciously overridden in a nanosecond by many people in order to overcome built-in biases and respond as their better, undiscriminating selves. This ability to overcome embedded biases is particularly important when we consider that "although many white Americans consider themselves unbiased, when unconscious stereotypes are measured, some 90% implicitly link blacks with negative traits (evil, failure)" (Begley, 2004, p. 1).

Unintentional Racism

It is important to note that the well-intentioned are still racist:

> Because aversive racists may not be aware of their unconscious negative attitudes and only discriminate against blacks when they can justify their behavior on the basis of some factor other than race, they will commonly deny any intentional wrongdoing when confronted with evidence of their biases. Indeed, they do not discriminate intentionally. (Dovidio & Gaertner, 2005, p. 5)

For example, if White individuals who are self-deceived about their own biases were sitting in a position to influence a promotion decision, they might not support the advancement of a "difficult" Black individual and would select another factor as a reason for their action rather than see or acknowledge their own conflicted perceptions.

The study on task completion strongly suggests that we are far better off to acknowledge our possible biases and to try to work together openly with that knowledge. If we mask our true attitudes, sometimes invisible to our own selves, we will continue to work slowly or unproductively. Consider the White individuals whose conflict over their true or hidden selves and their outward statements made a simple task both time-consuming and psychologically diffi-cult for both the Black individuals and themselves (Dovidio & Gaertner, 2005).

Unintentional racism is not always determined by whether an individual possesses prejudiced beliefs or attitudes, and it can take many different forms. These forms include the unconscious gestures mentioned before or "the dom-inant norms and standards." Because many people believe these norms and standards are culturally neutral and universally right, true, and good, they do not understand how these norms and standards oppress others. They are not even aware of this possibility—and, in this sense, such racism is unintentional (Applebaum, 1997, p. 409).

Human beings go to great lengths to avoid new evidence that is contrary to existing beliefs and prejudices. First, they avoid situations in which old beliefs may be challenged or contrary information found. In a similar manner, people holding like views are sought out to reinforce existing beliefs. That is why seg-regated housing and neighborhoods are such an effective means of perpetuat-ing the racial status quo: People of Color are purposefully fenced out.

Often, when contrary information is encountered, it is unconsciously ma-nipulated so as to leave ethnic categories unaffected. For example, consider an office worker who believe that African Americans are lazy. One day, a new employee, an African American, is hired, and no one works harder or more diligently than this person. So, how does the person make sense of this fact, given his or her beliefs about African American laziness? What the person does is to treat the African American worker as an exception—that is, he is not like other African Americans.

The human brain uses a mechanism called *re-fencing* when confronted with evidence contrary to the stereotype. Allport coined the term: "When a fact can-not fit into a mental field, the exception is acknowledged, but the field is hast-ily fenced in again and not allowed to remain dangerously open" (1954, p. 23). This is illustrated by such statements as "some of my best friends are Black." That statement, while used to deny bias, has within it the seeds of a defense of negative feelings toward Blacks. The context of the statement usually means that "my best friend" is an exception to stereotypes and, therefore, that other Blacks would not be my friends.

Thompson (2003) refers to this as *absolution* through a connected relation-ship (i.e., I am absolved from racism because my best friend is Black). Dovidio and Gaertner describe this inability to connect stated beliefs and unconscious bias as *aversive racism*: "The inherent contradiction that exists when the denial of personal prejudice co-exists with underlying unconscious negative feelings and beliefs" (2005, p. 2).

Contrary information is briefly acknowledged. But by excluding this ex-ception to a general stereotype ("He is really not like other African Ameri-cans"), one may retain beliefs about African Americans in light of seemingly contradictory evidence. Recently, many have used this psychological side step in response to the election of Barack Obama as our first African American president. He is seen by many as an "exception" to their perspectives of African American males. They have "re-fenced" their stereotypes with Obama outside of the fence. During the campaign, when Joe Biden (White) and Barack Obama (Black) announced their plans to run for president, Biden was asked by a reporter about the enthusiasm for Obama. Biden responded, "I mean, you got the first mainstream African American who is articulate and bright and clean and a nice-looking guy." Senator Biden could not understand why many in the Black community did not see this as the praise he intended and were angry. There are multiple meanings in his comments, and the hidden message was: "Obama is an exception. Most Blacks are unintelligent, inarticulate, dirty and unattractive" (Sue, 2010, p. 11). Such a statement (a microaggression, as we will discuss later) "allows the perpetrator to acknowledge and praise a person of color but also allows him or her to express group stereotypes" (Sue, 2010, p. 11).

A similar phenomenon involves the actual distortion of perceptions. Social psychologists have demonstrated that individuals perceive and remember material that is consonant with their attitudes and beliefs. They have even shown that perceptions can be distorted to avoid the introduction of contrary information. A classic example is the recall of ambiguous pictures. Pictures are shown to subjects at such high speeds that they can barely perceive the content. The more ambiguous the exposure, the easier it is for the subject to distort perception to support existing prejudices. When shown a drawing of a Black man being followed by a White man who is carrying a stick-like object in one hand, an individual with extremely negative attitudes about African Americans may report seeing an Black man with a knife or club chasing a White man. Here, individuals have reconstructed a situation in order to conform to their stereotypes. The race of the perpetrator of the violence has been reversed in order to make the scene conform to the prejudice.

Another example comes from my class. In reviewing a film, *The Lunch Date*, containing fleeting images of people of different races, I listened as some preservice teachers not only turned the action around but then castigated the filmmaker for perpetrating a stereotype that existed only in the students' mind.

Such unconscious biases have a role in determining the length of jail sentences (Vedantam, 2005) and the fact that, regardless of explicit racial prejudices, police officers are more likely to shoot an unarmed Black target than an unarmed White target (Correll, Park, Judd & Wittenbrink, 2002).

As we understand from our discussion of *re-fencing, absolution,* and *aversive racism,* when we receive evidence that confronts our deeply held and usually unrecognized biases, the human brain usually finds ways to return to stereotypes. Good examples of the ways in which individuals sidestep their biases—conscious or unconscious—come from what I have come to call my "airport story." While I do not usually keep a journal, I did write this one down shortly after it happened. Consider how it made me—an older, nonthreatening grandmother of six—feel to be perceived as a threat to someone's property based on the color of my skin?

Today, September 26, I had about 45 minutes before a flight. I decided to have a bite to eat while waiting. I entered the sports bar and took a seat next to a White couple. As I sit down he signals her, and she moves her purse from the back of her chair, next to me, to the seat between them.

This action intrudes on my consciousness and bothers me. I think of whom to call to process this response to my presence. I call Ken, a White male colleague, and tell him about it, knowing the couple can hear me (I feel a little, just a little bit, both empowered and leery).

I say, "Ken, I just had an encounter that troubled me. I sat about two feet away from a couple at another table. They can hear me. I am troubled that just the color of my skin caused them to move a purse further away from me. I think they may say they just wanted to move the purse and it had nothing to do with me. However, it happened and I am troubled and it disturbs my meal. Being black 24/7, this just happens ... all because of people's reactions."

Ken listens and responds, even returning to the subject when I change to another topic. Among many supportive things he says, trying to be helpful, "We'll never know why they moved it." While there is some truth in his suggestion, at some point there are just too many coincidences.

As I suspected, the couple could not handle having the ball in their court. As I left, they stood to leave as well. She turned towards me, actually blocking my path to the concourse. With venom in her voice, and affront and defense in her stance she began to confront me. Her manner and tone clearly conveyed her biases while her words were her self-report (self-deception?) of non-bias. After each statement I will list what I have come to know as classic responses.

"I'm not racist." (Denial)

"I was just moving my bag from the front to the back." (Aversive racism)

"I live in an integrated neighborhood with Chinese and Blacks." (Absolution)

"It's people like you that cause racism." (Blame the victim)

"And spread it by telling others." (White guilt)

I am laughing just a bit now as I write this. But her anger, her microaggression, hurt and shocked me. I was so shaken that as I went to my gate I sat down for a minute before realizing that everyone else had loaded onto the plane! As I take my seat on the plane, I have the luxury of a full row to myself, I need the space to process what just happened to me.

I had a choice: To accept, as usual, a common situation knowing there was little I could do about it ... or to speak up by calling someone else, as I did. I believe my action was more helpful for all, including the White couple, than if I had remained silent. For no matter how long this man and woman deny and displace their actions and words, they will never again move a purse without thinking about this encounter. Perhaps both they and I made a step towards painful recognition of our paths to better understanding.

When Ken said, "We'll never know," I reflected that the couple did not know, did not consciously consider themselves racist. However, their strong denial and evident discomfort make me believe I uncovered their unconscious bias. It has to be there. I do not believe that it is possible to be raised in America without it ... for Black, White or Brown folk of any age. Such embedded racism is in the air we breathe (not to mention the radio and TV waves). If I do such an *intervention* in a public place again, I think I will give an "Unconscious Bias 101" while on the phone and maybe a "not your fault, raised in America, might as well admit racism" subtext, so that the listeners will not become so defensive (adapted from Moule journal, 2007).

Microaggressions

As we begin to understand and recognize unconscious biases and unintentional racism, we can see that they are so subtle that neither victim nor perpetrator may either see or understand what is transpiring. Yet, "each small race-related slight, hurt, invalidation, insult and indignity rubs salt into the wounds of marginalized groups in our society" (Sue, 2010, p. 95). Recent research by Derald Wing Sue and others have expanded and undergirded the understanding of microaggressions:

> It is the constant and continuing everyday reality of ... indignities visited upon marginalized groups by well-intentioned, moral, and decent family members, friends, neighbors, coworkers, students, teachers, clerks, waiters and waitresses, employers, health care professionals, and educators. The power of microaggressions lies in their invisibility to the perpetrator, who is unaware that he or she has engaged in a behavior that threatens and demeans the recipient of such a communication. (Sue, 2010, p. xv)

Sue describes such events as perceived by some as "harmless and innocent" yet recalls one that left him, feeling as I did, "sitting on the plane, deeply disturbed and bothered, ruminating on my actions, about what I should or should not have done and feeling my blood pressure rise. Yes, the incident alone might appear to be a 'small thing,' harmless and trivial, but it had a major psychological impact on me" (Sue, 2010, p. 51).

Simply stated, microaggressions are brief, everyday exchanges that send denigrating messages to certain individuals because of their group membership. While there are three types of racial microaggressions, two types are more closely connected to unintentional racism. This flowchart (Figure 3.1) from Sue's work gives an overview of microaggressions as well as the major themes that have emerged from his studies.

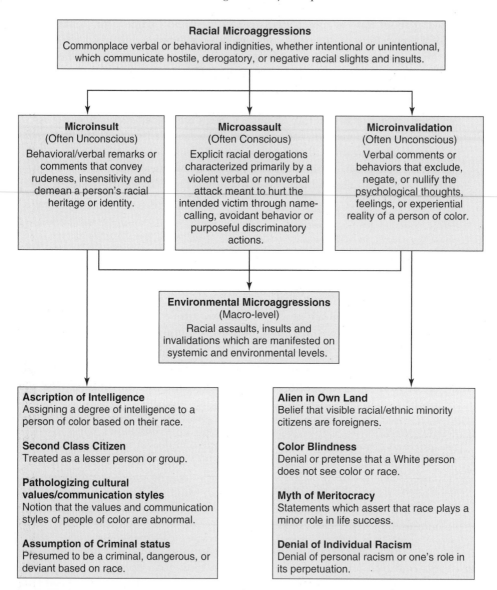

FIGURE 3.1 Categories and Relationships of Racial Microaggressions

Source: Excerpted from *Racial Microaggressions in Everyday Life* by Dr. Derald Wing Sue. Used by permission.

Micro is a good first part for the word, for the incidences are often so small as to be difficult to see. *Aggressions* is a good ending because, like my physical reactions and mental shock in the airport, they are experienced as attacks. Often, neither victim nor perpetrator may understand exactly what is happening, yet the nature of microaggressions has caused many—myself included—to believe that covert racism is more taxing and toxic than overt racism. An Oregon college student put it this way: "What's worse than being a racist is to say you're open minded and then choose not to have a dialogue about race. At least in a place like Mississippi, people will tell you, 'Yeah, I'm a racist.' Here they won't. Everybody will claim to be open-minded, but their actions are to the contrary" (Calhoon, 2006). Other college students agree that overt and obvious racist acts are easier to handle than vague or disguised microaggressions (Solorzano, Ceja & Yosso, 2000).

Microassaults

Explicit, conscious, unambiguous, and intentional actions or slurs, such as racial epithets (calling someone *colored* or *Oriental*), deliberately serving a White person before a person of color in a restaurant or displaying swastikas. These are closer to "old-fashioned," overt racism. Recent examples from my life would be the times I have been seated next to a kitchen in a restaurant when there were many open tables elsewhere. Or the waitress who simply refused to serve my husband and me.

Microinsults

Verbal and nonverbal communications that are rude and insensitive and in some way demean a person's racial identity or heritage. Often, these are unconscious and made by well-intentioned people. A couple of examples come to mind for me; in the first, two other individuals and I were introduced to a fourth person. That person greeted and spoke to the ones on either side of me … and acted as though I were invisible. Another time, an old friend talked to me about "colored" folks. And when my daughter was moving from second grade to third and I heard the only third grade teacher in the school lounge refer to people in her home state as "N—s," we managed to have my daughter skip to fourth grade. I think the hardest microaggression, though, would be the microinvalidation when people would say that these experiences of mine are trivial.

Microinvalidations

Communications that subtly "exclude, negate or nullify the … thoughts, feelings or experiential reality" of a person of color (Sue, 2010, p. 37). Examples from my life would be when the items I shared above are considered trivial and that I was "too sensitive." I also remember with great clarity when my colleagues would say things like, "Race has nothing to do with it," when it clearly does. Or "You play the race card" when I would suggest that race is a reason why we might change our recruiting strategies.

Failure to help instead of a conscious desire to hurt is one facet of microinvalidation. "Most White Americans no longer harbor intense hatred and hostility toward people of color, but instead may express a more 'benign' form of racism that involves feelings of discomfort, uneasiness, and anxiety that result in avoidance or inaction" (Sue, 2010, p. 144). An interesting parallel related to heightism happened to me a few years ago when we had a dwarf, a little person on staff in our office. I felt the discomfort of confronting and working with someone quite different from myself and of a demographic I had never before encountered personally.

Knowing what I know about the need to address such gaps and feelings, I realized that my discomfort around my coworker might be interpreted as rejection and invalidation. I overcame my fear of saying something offensive and simply began to talk—first with superficial conversational and then, quite soon, about his relationships to the university and others on issues related to his height. He came to several of my classes to answer questions my students had about working with little people. I know from my students' reflections months later as well as my conversations with him that these contacts were extremely important for all involved. What if I had let my fears keep me away?

Environmental Microaggressions

In addition to the three types of microaggressions we are considering, *environmental microaggressions* are even more embedded and subtle as we explored under cultural racism in Chapter 2. They may include the simple overwhelming presence of whiteness in leadership, to the stereotypical use of Indian mascots, to the subtle advertising such as the one examined in the last chapter. Sue defines this fully: Environmental microaggressions "can be transmitted through the numerical imbalance of one's own group … mascots or symbols, and inaccurate media portrayals of marginalized groups in films, television, radio, print media, and educational curriculum (books, course content, films, etc.) The sheer exclusion of decorations, literature, and ethnic aesthetic-cultural forms like music, art, language, and food …" (Sue, 2010, p. 27).

The Effects of Microaggressions

Because of their less obvious nature, microinsults and microinvalidations put People of Color in a psychological bind; a person may feel insulted and is not exactly sure why, and the perpetrator is often unaware that an offense has been made. Sue says that the Person of Color is caught in a catch-22: If he or she confronts the perpetrator, the perpetrator will deny it. That denial, as in my airport story, leaves the Person of Color to question what actually happened. The result is confusion, frustration, distraction, and sometimes anger. Most of all, it is a "sapping of energy." Some studies indicate that for African Americans, racial micro-aggressions are more "impactful, harmful, and distressing … than ordinary stressful life events" (Sue, 2010, p. 96). Yet, the nature of the event itself leads to doing nothing for the following reasons:

- Attritional ambiguity—inability to determine whether a microaggression has occurred
- Response indecision—not knowing the best way or how to respond
- Time-limited responding—the incident is over before a response can be made
- Denying experiential reality—engaging in self-deception by believing it did not happen
- Impotency of actions—"It won't do any good anyway"
- Fearing the consequences—interpersonal power differentials determine the degree of threat. (Sue, 2010, pp. 55–57)

"How a person of color … perceives a racial microaggression, the adaptive resources he or she possesses, his or her racial identity development, the presence of familial/social support, what he or she decides to do, and so forth, may moderate or mediate the meaning and impact of the incident" (Sue, 2010, p. 94).

Overcoming Microaggressions

Recently, when a man saw my face and spit to the side, I decided to take action: As our paths crossed, I greeted him and his wife in a friendly manner and said I hoped that they had enjoyed their time in the pool. The fact that the woman responded to me and the man looked away at least confirmed that his initial action was not completely unconscious. It became clearer that he did have an issue with a Black woman in his town and was not simply seeing me as another friendly resident of the area. In some ways, I found his more blatant disregard of my greeting and presence easier to comprehend than the "Was that just the time he happened to spit?" thought that first went through my mind. With his racism a bit more overt, I could just dismiss him for his actions rather than question my own possible misinterpretation. I did feel the support of my husband walking next to me as I made my greeting. At the same time, I felt the impact of the microaggression: As I went into the facility to sign in, I made a simple mistake. Probably due to my shifting emotions and uncomfortable feelings from the act of insult against me, I was distracted from my regular task. How often does that happen to students in our care?

Most of my own reactions to microaggressions have not been so direct. Yet, with the support of two Black colleagues on campus, we came up with following list (Table 3.2) of the burdens of such microaggressions and how we manage them.

While our "lightening the load" choices certainly have helped us survive in the Academy, it is better to have both the terms and processes of microaggressions to mull over and share with others. Sue is correct in his statement: "One of the major contributions of microaggression research has been giving

TABLE 3.2

#	Burden	Lightening the Load
1	People on campus are surprised to see me, based on my color.	Park close to building, limit walks on campus (make office an oasis), go with a colleague for distraction, go to the same place where I am already known, self-talk before walking on campus.
2	Occasionally there is an overtly racist act in my presence that surprises and disturbs me. (Did I really see/hear that? Yes, I did!)	Ignore as possible, but process. Sometimes confront.
3	Reacting to verbal and non-verbal responses to my presence on campus is a level of mental and emotional work that most of my colleagues do not share.	Reduce level of mental and emotional work by limiting exposure to one and two, e.g., less time on campus.
4	People are more likely to exhibit prejudice from unconscious rather than conscious bias, and may not recognize when this is happening. However, the fact that this bias exists IS often in my consciousness and therefore a level of mental and emotional work that most of my colleagues and I do not share.	Act as if it is not there, assume the best. In some situations, it is possible to make unconscious biases conscious.
5	Oregon has a particularly racist past. My race and my reading of Oregon history have made me more consciously aware of this than my colleagues and students. I am more likely to see and be reminded of the current consequences of past racism. For example, while reading a student's statement, "there was little diversity in my community," I am very aware that the person who made the statement is probably totally ignorant of why this phenomenon occurs in Oregon, e.g., exclusion laws, early and wide-spread KKK, numerous sundown towns (Loewen, 2006). Every time I read such statements, I am reminded of the history that produced this student's monocultural upbringing.	Recognize that students' and others' perspectives may simply be a factor of their upbringing. Forgive ignorance.
6	Some of my students question my competency based on their overt or covert racism. This raises the standard I must hold in my teaching.	Continue to do my best.
7	Having faced dead ends because of race or gender in the past, I am more likely to fear such in the future, so I tend to rely on my own resources when possible.	Try to trust and collaborate.
8	I am asked to teach or speak in some areas and am assumed to have specialized knowledge based solely on my race.	Consider each request and respond appropriately if I actually possess the knowledge and perspective needed.
9	My adaptations to these differences and multiple realities include my understanding of these differences and realities and the fact that others may not understand. This causes me to be divided in my perspective taking as I recognize both viewpoints. This may result in my participating in my own oppression through acknowledging and inadvertently accepting the other perspective.	Try to maintain own perspective and not add to my oppression.
10	I am surrounded by people who do not share my racial burden (the items in this list).	Network at conferences. Become involved with integrated school staffs in distant locations so that I am in contact with people who *do* share my racial perspective, and/or work in diverse settings.
11	I have to decide whether to reveal the race-based nature of some of my actions and decisions (such as constructing this list). That may add to the burden of race and may cause increased distance.	Do it when expedient and necessary. Pick and chose battles so that I might live to "fight" another day.
12	My colleagues reading this list may be tempted to say "move on," or come up with an oppression they experience occasionally and say it is the same.	Forgive, understand.

Note: This was adapted from the original publication in *Our Stories*, which was edited by Smith and Taylor-Archer, 2006.

oppressed groups the language and concepts to speak about their experiences, to be able to name the offenses, to be liberated, and to feel empowered by the understanding of their experiences" (Sue, 2010, p. 106).

I expressed it this way: Making this list helped me to see myself better. As attributed to Maya Angelou, "Society's view of the black woman is such a threat to her well-being that she will die daily unless she determines how she sees herself." I understand that the struggle I feel "living this way … with the daily indignities … with a broken heart" (Nile & Straton, 2003, p. 5) is not particularly emotionally or physically healthy.

The openness to dialogue on race is key. "When the oppressed are not allowed to express their thoughts and outrage, when their concerns are minimized, and when they are punished for expressing ideas at odds with the dominant group, their voices are effectively silenced. This allows perpetrators to hold on to a belief that they are good, moral, and decent human beings," (Sue, 2010, p. 112).

A number of times in my classes I have had a White student say that he or she had a Classmate of Color that was a good friend. They would continue on to say that his or her friend had never expressed any feelings of being treated differently based on skin color. In several instances, my students were in a situation where they could meet with or talk with their friend. I would suggest that they return to their friend and just ask them about race-based treatment. Some of my students returned to class or wrote journals about what they considered astounding discoveries: Once the door was open, their friends had *lots* to say about racism in their communities and schools. Their friends—as I have discovered with my colleagues—are precious and appreciated; therefore, the relationship is sometimes worth the silence. However, it is not the high road for making a difference. If we are to work together in a community, we need to overcome this reluctance to just talk.

Hard Work of Honesty

Unpacking our levels of consciousness and intent requires hard work. First, there needs to be unswerving, unnerving, scrupulous honesty. Individuals need to become less focused on feeling very tolerant and good about themselves and more focused on examining their own biases. One must realize and accept that the foundation and continuation of a bias may have, at its root, personal and group gain.

I recall sharing with my graduate and undergraduate students that true equity will be reached when 40 percent of all service people—meaning hotel housekeepers, groundskeepers, etc.—are White men. Can we all embrace such a future? Delpit maintains, "Liberal educators believe themselves to be operating with good intentions, but these good intentions are only conscious delusions about their unconscious true motives" (1988, p. 285). I am not quite that cynical. I believe in change, slow as it may be.

Teaching Tolerance, a group dedicated to reducing prejudice, improving intergroup relations, and supporting equitable school experiences for our nation's children, says, "We would like to believe that when a person has a conscious commitment to change, the very act of discovering one's hidden biases can propel one to act to correct for it. It may not be possible to avoid the automatic stereotype or prejudice, but it is certainly possible to consciously rectify it" (2001, p. 4). In addition, people who report a strong personal motivation to be nonprejudiced tend to harbor less implicit bias (Carpenter, 2008).

While this road should lead to increased racial interaction and understanding, like any journey, there are uphill struggles. For one thing, increased interracial interactions often mean "greater opportunities for microaggressions to occur between students of color and their white classmates, between professors and their students and in exposure to biased curricular topics and orientations" (Sue, 2010, p. 242). These microaggressions may occur through a comment, tone of voice, nonverbals, or insinuations. And, worst, such interactions "often polarize students and teachers rather than contribute to mutual respect and understanding about race and race relations" (Sue, 2010, p. 242).

While the road is more difficult at first, honest acknowledgment accomplishes much in the classroom:

- It frees the teacher from the constant guardedness and vigilance exercised in denying their own racism, sexism, and other biases.
- The teacher can use it to model truthfulness, openness, and honesty to students on conversations about race and racism.
- It can communicate courage in making teachers vulnerable by taking a risk to share with students their own biases, limitations, and attempts to deal with racism.
- It may encourage other students to approach the topic with honesty because their own teacher is equally "flawed" (Sue, 2010, p. 251).

Overcoming Fears

Both implicit biases and microaggressions are complex and deeply embedded. The fears are so great and the feeling of helplessness to make a difference so powerful, many retreat from the dialogue and necessary work. We will look at the fears (adapted from Sue, 2010) and then we will look at some ways to confront the fears and move toward the change most of us want to see.

- Fear of Appearing Racist: Clearly, race is among the easiest and most automatic way to categorize people, yet conscious avoidance is accomplished by invoking color blindness or considering race as a taboo topic. Some people believe that anything they may say will appear racist, yet the avoidance and nonverbals will surface anyway. When self-identity as a nondiscriminatory individual is threatened by any hint of appearing racist, anger and defensiveness arise. The positive side of this fear is that we can see that people *want* to be and appear nonracist.

- Fear of Acknowledging One's Racism: Below the fear of appearing racist is the fear of acknowledging it. Here, the same defenses and anxiety arise. Like the levels of racial identity development detailed in Chapter 4, there is movement from external to internal pressure and recognition. Both produce fear.
- Fear of Acknowledging White Privilege: We will consider details of this privilege in Chapter 4. For now, it is encapsulated in "the possibility that they have benefited from racism and the present racist arrangements and practices of society that oppress one group, but advantage another" (Sue, 2010, p. 125).
- Fear of Taking Personal Responsibility to End Racism: This fear is based on this thought: "How do they deal with their own racism and the benefits and advantages that they have enjoyed individually and collectively? ... [Will] it motivate change and action? Or do Whites deny responsibility for it? ... The magnitude of the change is so overpowering that helplessness and hopelessness may ensue" (Sue, 2010, pp. 126–127). Sue goes on to detail the psychological costs of oppression to the perpetrators: cognitive, affective (including fear, anxiety, apprehension, guilt, and low empathy), behavioral, spiritual, and moral.

Reprogramming Responses

The evidence behind unconscious bias, unintentional racism, and microaggressions may surprise us and cause us pain. Facing the fears and the costs, there are thoughts and actions we can take. As we discussed earlier, many people instantly overcome their initial "flight or fight" responses to those who are different than themselves. With conscious control many are able to overcome built-in biases and respond more openly and fully. This ability to overcome embedded biases is particularly important for classroom teachers who need to develop clear and functional relationships with all students. Carpenter (2008) suggests ways to reprogram our first thoughts and reactions. He says we can reshape our implicit attitudes and beliefs—or at least curb their effects on our behavior. First, environment and context are more important than we realize. Female engineering students who had a male professor held negative implicit attitudes toward math because that caused them to view math as masculine compared to female students who felt differently—more positive toward math—with a female engineering professor. In "college classrooms, students taking a course on prejudice reduction who had a black professor showed greater reductions in both implicit and explicit prejudice at the end of the semester than did those who had a white professor" (Carpenter, 2008, p. 2).

Second, seeing marginalized people in more favorable environments and social contexts can help thwart biases. For example, "seeing a black face with a church as a background, instead of a dilapidated street corner," or "reading about Arab-Muslims' positive contributions to society all weaken people's implicit racial and ethnic biases" (Carpenter, 2008, p. 3). As reported by Carpenter, a study by Payne and Stewart revealed a wonderfully simple means of combating bias: "Those who simply resolved to think of the word 'safe' whenever they saw a black face showed dramatic reductions in implicit racial bias. 'You don't necessarily have to beat people over the head with it,' Payne observes. 'You can just have this little plan in your pocket ("think safe") that you can pull out when you need it. Once you've gone to the work of making that specific plan, it becomes automatic'" (Carpenter, 2008, p. 3).

The following processes and behaviors will also work to change our consciousness and understanding:

- When a person of color brings up race as an issue, listen deeply.
- If the person indicates that he or she is offended, do not be defensive.
- Do not begin talking quickly.
- Do not explain why he or she is misinterpreting the situation.
- Do not begin crying. (These are some of the most infuriating responses People of Color encounter when they challenge a situation that feels wrong.)
- If you hear about something third-hand, do not get angry. Remember that it is almost never completely safe for a Person of Color to challenge a dominant perception. (Dovidio & Gaertner, 2005, p. 5)

Connections and Reflections: Emerging Views

What are some of the feelings you had as you read this chapter? How are you processing them? Are you able to step back and give yourself reflection and growth time?

Teachers in multicultural settings are eventually faced with stereotyping within their classrooms. Such an occurrence represents not only a very teachable moment but also a rich opportunity for attitude change and increased dialogue about race and ethnicity. Knowing how to address the stereotypical statements of others, including students and colleagues, is an extremely valuable skill.

Addressing Stereotypical Statements

Fennimore (1994) offered a four-step method of addressing prejudiced statements. She indicated that teachers and educators must support the goal of accepting the dignity and equality of children, both within and outside the classroom. She quoted Nieto (1992) in further suggesting that educational institutions must continue to confront federal, state, local, and internal practices that reflect negative perceptions of racially, ethnically, or socioeconomically diverse children. These practices include labeling, deficit terminology, and tracking and ability groups, which tend to segregate both more and less advantaged students. She acknowledged that most training in prejudice reduction and multiculturalism seldom offers practical advice about meaningful application. Her four-step method was offered as an antidote to this trend.

According to Fennimore, teachers do not feel comfortable about confronting prejudiced statements for several reasons. They fear that they will become too angry or aggressive or that they will alienate the speaker and invite retaliation or they feel hopeless about what one individual can accomplish. They also lack practice in confronting such statements. Letting such statements go unchallenged not only misses an opportunity to confront what is usually unintended racism, but one can also interpret silence as agreement. Fennimore believed that her method allows educators to gently correct a prejudiced statement in a productive manner without creating a climate of rejection or negativity.

A Four-Step Method

Fennimore indicated that personal responses to prejudiced statements should entail four characteristics:

1. Pull the prejudice out of the comment and restate it in a calm and objective way.
2. State personal beliefs in a clear and assertive manner.
3. Make a positive statement about the specific subjects of the prejudice.
4. Gently turn the subject to a new direction.

   She offered the following two examples.

Example 1

Prejudiced Statement: Why would a talented and well-educated teacher like you choose to work in a neighborhood like that? Aren't most of your students African American (Asian American, Hispanic American, or any group experiencing discrimination)?

Responses

- Many people seem to think that African American (Asian American, Hispanic American, Native American) children, particularly if they live in disadvantaged communities, are less capable. (Characteristic 1)

- I have always acted on my own belief that every child is filled with potential and deserves the finest possible education. (Characteristic 2)
- If you visited my classroom, you might be surprised to see how intelligent and successful my children really are. (Characteristic 3)
- In fact, you might even want to visit sometime. Do you still travel into the city frequently for your work? (Characteristic 4)

Example 2

Prejudiced Statement: I just cannot understand why a wonderful, healthy boy like you would confine yourself to dating that woman in a wheelchair.

Response

- I know that many who haven't had the chance to get to know people in wheelchairs think they are less capable or not as much fun to be with (Characteristic 1), but I have always thought that people's personal strengths and qualities are much more important to a relationship than possible disabilities. (Characteristic 2)
- My friend and I have enjoyed so many social experiences together, and she and her many successful disabled friends have certainly changed my former stereotyped ideas about people in wheelchairs. (Characteristic 3)
- Maybe the three of us could go to a movie sometime. Are you still fond of spy stories? (Characteristic 4)

Fennimore pointed out that training in such a method requires behavior application. Students need assistance in developing self-confidence and assertiveness in regard to such interventions as well as concrete opportunities to practice making assertive responses to prejudiced statements in risk-free classroom environments. They also benefit from observing role models responding to such situations.

Classroom: Adventures in Learning

- For lower grades, move beyond books that have Characters of Color to books that "tell a story" about racism and those who overcome it. While biographies of those who participated in the civil rights movement are a good beginning, remember that children may well grasp the history and the importance of such attitudes yet still exhibit racism in their everyday interactions with those unlike themselves (see more on racism in children in Chapters 6 and 8). As Copenhaver-Johnson, an antiracist educator herself, said about her own child: "I wondered about my child's reluctance to challenge the status quo. Was even she unwilling to bring up race? In her eyes, school is not an 'okay' place to bring up such issues' (2006, p. 12). Be brave, be specific, and address racism directly, especially when a teachable moment comes along.

- For upper grades, consider an active discussion about posters or materials that you have made available. Again, while the environment may make a difference, people need practice learning how to discuss what has become a taboo topic. "Talking to children about race is also helpful because *we* need to learn how to do it, and our children need to observe us actively trying to learn" (Copenhaver-Johnson, 2006, p. 21). For additional challenges, consider teaching about microaggressions at their level (they will probably come up with examples once you open the door). Ask them to share any that they find in the next 24 hours. If you used the "Theatre of the Oppressed" already, do it again—but this time, ask students to use only microinsults and microinvalidations. Also consider showing *The Lunch Date* (available on YouTube). After showing the film, give students one minute to write an anonymous reflection. Wait until you have had an opportunity to read them and prepare some comments on their reflections before you discuss the film. I recommend showing the film as as an end-of-the-day activity.

CHAPTER 4

Understanding Privilege and Racial Consciousness among Whites

"They won't learn the language. They're not assimilating. They don't look like us. I say—put them back on the Mayflower.*"*

–Mike Keefe (cartoonist)

As discussed in Chapters 2 and 3, racism exists on three levels: within the individual, within institutions (such as our schools), and within the culture of the United States. Each aspect reinforces the others, making them all the more difficult to change. Most schools and the teaching styles that define them are Eurocentric and, as such, put Students of Color at an educational disadvantage. These students often feel unwelcome and unwanted; they feel that they do not belong, do not understand the rules of classroom interaction, are not valued, and must give up their cultural identities to succeed. The realities are disproportionate failure and dropout rates, depressed achievement scores, negative attitudes toward education and schooling, and differential funding and educational spending related to the ethnicity of the students being taught. The following analysis of racial disparity and institutional racism within our schools helps to understand the depth of our problem:

> Most students in the United States are still attending segregated schools. Within schools, students are segregated by race and tracked by class.... Segregation and tracking destine most students from a very early age for a particular socioeconomic role in their adult life. There is a vast disparity in what is spent per student. White suburban schools have approximately twice the funds per student as compared with urban schools where students of color are congregated.... When this is multiplied by the number of students in a classroom or school, the disparity is enormous. That money buys fewer students per teacher, classroom necessities like books, pencils and paper, not to mention computers, art and music classes, recreational equipment, teacher's aides, special events and field

trips, and in the long run, the best teachers. Students are given a direct measure of their social worth and future chances by the amount of money they see being spent on their education. When we look at the disparities in educational expenditures we have to acknowledge that most white students have tremendous educational advantages over students of color.... Education is more than money. It includes teachers, curricula, school buildings, safety to learn and many other factors. Racism affects the quality and quantity of each of these resources. Teachers in the United States are disproportionately white, far beyond their representation in the general population, and this disparity is increasing. Few students of color have role models of their own ethnicity, and few white students have contact with people of color in positions of authority. In addition, challenges to white culture-based curriculum are harder to organize because there aren't sufficient numbers of teachers of color to counter traditional curricula. (Kivel, 1996, pp. 186–187)

In order to better understand how such dynamics of inequality are rooted in our schools, we must first understand how majority group members—that is, White Americans—perceive and understand race and ethnicity. To this end, we begin this chapter by looking at the concept of White privilege—the ways in which European Americans are afforded certain benefits and rights based solely on the color of their skin. As will become obvious, Whites have great difficulty acknowledging the existence of such privilege.

Next, we will explore racial consciousness in European Americans—how Whites think about race and racial difference and how White racial identity develops and can progress and mature over time. This material is especially important to White teachers as they move toward cultural competence and a self-understanding of how they perceive, understand, and react to the ethnicity of their students.

On a more personal note, this is a difficult chapter to share. As an African American, I want to come to the aid of my White brothers and sisters even as they confront difficult, challenging material. I know from teaching multicultural issues in education courses how preservice teachers respond. Here are a few of their reactions:

- Chapter 4 made me feel guilty for being White. (White female)
- The most beneficial chapter to me was Chapter 4. I think it is absolutely imperative for an educator of white heritage to face the issue of "white privilege." I don't believe a white educator can truly attain cultural competence unless they come to grips with it. (White male)
- When questions of equality arise, many turn a deaf ear. Being labeled as "privileged" can result in hostility or denial. Until this term in school I had not read much about denial regarding race. I think it is natural for an individual to become defensive when his or her actions are questioned in regard to ethics. I would like to think that few people desire to act or speak in an offensive manner, resulting in a protective backlash. I feel that many are ignorant to white privilege because life is hard no matter who

you are. To think that others have a large disadvantage, in addition to humankind's seemingly endless struggles and hardships, makes me feel weak and embarrassed. (White female)

It is important to note that all these responses came at the end of the course. We worked through the valleys and new viewpoints; we had some difficult moments. You may too.

Becoming White

The social reality of race in the United States does not conform to five distinct groups. Rather, only two bear any real social meaning: White and of Color. For example, the notion of the great melting pot was in actuality only about melting White ethnics. The myth was never intended to apply to People of Color. For White ethnics, upward mobility involved discovering and asserting their group's whiteness to set themselves apart from and above the Groups of Color that perpetually resided at the bottom of America's social hierarchy. When they first arrived in America, various White ethnic groups were met with prejudice and scorn and were merely tolerated because they represented a source of much needed cheap labor. In time, however, as they acculturated into the system, they discovered that they could progress most quickly by identifying themselves as White and by taking on prejudices against People of Color that were an intrinsic part of White culture. A classic example of changing ethnicity may be found in the book *How the Irish Became White*, 1995, by Noel Ignatiev.

An additional consideration is that *White* and *American* have become synonymous in many people's minds. An instructor friend, also a school administrator, told this story:

I have worked in elementary and middle schools for 10 years now and I have heard adults and students describe White people as "American" as if it were a physical characteristic. Here are two recent examples:

Q: "Johnny, what did the girl look like that pushed you?"

A: "She was American."

A psychologist in one building described his granddaughter to me as having the "bluest American eyes."

What does this say about how our society has portrayed what it is to be *American?* (A. Freeman, personal communication, April, 2010)

The question of who is "White" is closely tied to the concept of "White Privilege" and who has it. Looking more carefully at "White Privilege" may help in understanding the stark concept that unless a White person is consciously anti-racist, he or she is participating in and supporting racism, usually both unconsciously and unintentionally.

White Privilege

In a very heated classroom discussion of diversity, several White male students complained bitterly, "It has gotten to a point where there's no place we can just be ourselves and not have to watch what we say or do all the time." The rest of the class—women and ethnic minorities—responded in unison: "Hey, welcome to the world. The rest of us have been doing that kind of self-monitoring all of our lives." What these men were feeling was a threat to their privilege as men and as Whites, and they did not like it one bit. Put simply, White privilege is the benefits that are automatically accrued to European Americans just on the basis of the color of their skin. What is most insidious is that to most Whites, like unconscious biases and microaggressions, White privilege is all but invisible. It is so basic a part of their daily experience and existence and so available to everyone in their "world" that it is seldom acknowledged or given a second thought. Or, at least, so it seems.

If one digs a little deeper, however, there is a strong element of defensiveness and denial. Whites tend to see themselves as individuals, just "regular people," part of the human race, but not as members of a racial group. They are, in fact, shocked when others relate to them racially (that is, as *White*). In a society that speaks so seriously about equality and equal access to resources ("With enough hard work, anyone can succeed in America"; "Any child can nurture the dream of someday being president"), it is difficult to acknowledge one's "unearned power," to borrow McIntosh's (1989) description.

It is also easier to deny one's White racial heritage and see oneself as colorless than to experience the full brunt of what has been done to People of Color in this country in the name of White supremacy. One of my students put it this way: "The husband … is … racist because, by definition, he is white. If you are of the majority, you are racist because you use, consciously or unconsciously, the privileges of the majority. So, based on opinions stated in the books I've read, if you're white … you're racist." Another of my former students, who is now a colleague, closely identified her struggles and changes as she embraced her whiteness. She carefully studied her progression through guilt, shame, and acceptance stages (Burke, 2007).

Such an awareness demands some kind of personal responsibility. If one is White and truly understands what White privilege means socially, economically, and politically, one cannot help but bear some of the guilt for what has happened historically and what continues to occur. If one were to truly "get it," then one would have no choice but to give up one's complacency, to try to do something about it, and ultimately to find oneself with the same kind of discomfort and feelings as the men mentioned in the next paragraph. No one easily gives up power and privilege.

It is easy for Whites to perceive themselves as relatively powerless in relation to people who garner power because of gender, class, age, and so forth, and thereby to deny holding any privilege. One need only look at statistics regarding managers in American industry. White males constitute 40 percent of the workforce yet they hold 80 percent of senior management jobs. The loss from 80 percent of the managerial jobs in this country to 40 percent—their proportion of the population—would be an actual loss in the number of jobs currently allotted to them based on race and gender. That is, they would not have the jobs they may perceive as expected and modeled as their right in the workplace. White women hold 40 percent of middle management positions, compared to Black women and men who hold 5 percent and 4 percent, respectively. Having said this, it is equally important to acknowledge that as invisible as White privilege is to most European Americans, that is how clearly visible it is to People of Color. To those of Color, Whites are clearly racial beings and obviously in possession of privilege in this society. That Whites do not see it is, in fact, mind-boggling to most People of Color because for those of Color, race and racial inequity are ever-present realities. As discussed in cultural racism at a broader level, White privilege is infused into the very fabric of American society and even if individuals wish to deny it, Whites cannot really give it up. There are several reasons why this is so:

- It is "an institutional (rather than personal) set of benefits."
- It belongs to "all of us, who are white, by race."
- It bears no relationship to whether we are "good people."
- It tends to be both "intentional" and "malicious."
- It is "bestowed prenatally."
- It allows us to believe "that we do not have to take the issues of racism seriously."
- It involves the "ability to make decisions that affect everyone without taking others into account."
- It allows us to overlook race in ourselves and to be angry at those who do not.
- It lets me "decide whether I am going to listen or hear others or neither." (Kendall, 1997, pp. 1–5)

Peggy McIntosh, in her classic piece *White Privilege: Unpacking the Invisible Knapsack*, offers a number of examples of the kind of life experiences Whites, as people of privilege, can count on in their daily existence:

- I can if I wish arrange to be in the company of people of my race most of the time.
- I can avoid spending time with people whom I was trained to mistrust and who have learned to mistrust my kind or me.
- If I should need to move, I can be pretty sure of renting or purchasing housing in an area which I can afford and in which I would want to live.

- I can be pretty sure that my neighbors in such a location will be neutral or pleasant to me.
- I can go shopping alone most of the time, pretty well assured that I will not be followed or harassed.
- I can turn on the television or open to the front page of the paper and see people of my race widely represented.
- When I am told about our national heritage or about "civilization," I am shown that people of my color made it what it is.
- I can be sure that my children will be given curricular materials that testify to the existence of their race.
- I can be pretty sure of having my voice heard in a group in which I am the only member of my race.
- I can go into a music shop and count on finding the music of my race represented, into a supermarket and find the staple foods which fit with my cultural traditions, into a hairdresser's shop and find someone who can cut my hair.
- Whether I use checks, credit cards or cash, I can count on my skin color not to work against the appearance of financial reliability.
- I can arrange to protect my children most of the time from people who might not like them.
- I do not have to educate my children to be aware of systemic racism for their own daily physical protection.
- I can be pretty sure that my children's teachers and employers will tolerate them if they fit school and workplace norms; my chief worries about them do not concern others' attitudes toward their race.
- I can swear, or dress in second hand clothes, or not answer letters, without having people attribute these choices to the bad morals, the poverty or the illiteracy of my race.
- I am never asked to speak for all the people of my racial group.
- I can be pretty sure that if I ask to talk to the "person in charge," I will be facing a person of my race.
- If a traffic cop pulls me over or if the IRS audits my tax return, I can be sure I haven't been singled out because of my race.
- I can easily buy posters, post-cards, picture books, greeting cards, dolls, toys and children's magazines featuring people of my race.
- I can go home from most meetings of organizations I belong to feeling somewhat tied in, rather than isolated, out-of-place, outnumbered, unheard, held at a distance or feared.
- I can be pretty sure that an argument with a colleague of another race is more likely to jeopardize her/his chances for advancement than to jeopardize mine.

- I can be pretty sure that if I argue for the promotion of a person of another race, or a program centering on race, this is not likely to cost me heavily within my present setting, even if my colleagues disagree with me.
- If I declare there is a racial issue at hand, or there isn't a racial issue at hand, my race will lend me more credibility for either position than a person of color will have.
- My culture gives me little fear about ignoring the perspectives and powers of people of other races.
- I can worry about racism without being seen as self-interested or self-seeking.
- I can take a job with an affirmative action employer without having my co-workers on the job suspect that I got it because of my race.
- If my day, week or year is going badly, I need not ask of each negative episode or situation whether it had racial overtones.
- I can be pretty sure of finding people who would be willing to talk with me and advise me about my next steps, professionally.
- I can think over many options, social, political, imaginative or professional, without asking whether a person of my race would be accepted or allowed to do what I want to do.
- I can be late to a meeting without having the lateness reflect on my race.
- I can choose public accommodation without fearing that people of my race cannot get in or will be mistreated in the places I have chosen.
- I can be sure that if I need legal or medical help, my race will not work against me.
- I can arrange my activities so that I will never have to experience feelings of rejection owing to my race.
- If I have low credibility as a leader I can be sure that my race is not the problem.
- I can easily find academic courses and institutions which give attention only to people of my race.
- I can expect figurative language and imagery in all of the arts to testify to experiences of my race.
- I can chose blemish cover or bandages in "flesh" color and have them more or less match my skin.
- I can travel alone or with my spouse without expecting embarrassment or hostility in those who deal with us.
- I have no difficulty finding neighborhoods where people approve of our household.
- My children are given texts and classes which implicitly support our kind of family unit and do not turn them against my choice of domestic partnership.
- I will feel welcomed and "normal" in the usual walks of public life, institutional and social. (1989, pp. 10–12)

The opposite of each of these is the experience of People of Color in the United States. Here are two of my experiences. I thought them just rather humorous asides; however, my students remembered them vividly. The first was the day I taught right after receiving a shot for an upcoming trip. We were discussing McIntosh's privileges. I happened to look down and said something about the small, round, flesh-color Band-aid on my upper arm. Even from the back of the room, you could clearly see the light circle on my brown skin. Amazingly, from some of the journals from that day, it was the first time many of my students had ever even thought about the "flesh" color of Band-aids. Later for the class, I found an ad for Band-aids of varying hues. Unfortunately, I could not find any in stores where I usually shop.

The second story is my hair story. Again, I told it on the spur of the moment just to fill a few minutes, yet some students said it made a difference in their perspective. After those responses, I tell it every time I teach face-to-face. Now I wear my hair in locks. At that time, I wore braids. My hair was quite long and it took quite a while to put it into the rows and number of braids I preferred. I knew one person in Oregon's capital city, Salem, about a half hour from my rural setting, who did ethnic hair. Before I left home, I took an hour to unbraid my hair. As time progresses, the waves become more and more filled with moisture and stand up from my head.

When I first came to her shop, the unbraided hairstyle was pleasing; however, I cannot keep it that way, so I looked forward to the wash, parting, and braiding she would do for a wedding I was attending the next day. When I went into the shop, she checked her appointment book and said, "I have you down for *next* Friday." With a three-hour job in front of her for me, she simply could not fit me in. My day's struggle begins:

> I slowly turn around, first asking her if she knows anyone else in the city who would be able to do my hair. She says no. Quite dejected, I slowly walk through the downtown area. My hair is continuing to get, shall we say, more interesting. A number of young people give me a high five or I get stares (more than usual). I try the salon connected to a major department store—no, only older woman with straight silver hair, so I don't even ask. I go by several shops in the malls, including a couple that say "Walk-ins welcome." But I am not. One counter person turns and yells back to all the stylists who are visible from the front door, "Can anyone do her hair?" I am embarrassed as other customers see me turn and walk away.
>
> My steps are getting slower, my gait heavier... and my hair higher. I really don't know what to do. There is no way I can part my hair myself or even comb it out well. I walk past a beauty school. Why not, I think? The receptionist gives me to a young woman to wash my hair. She manages the washing and rinsing fine. When it comes time to comb it, she does not have a comb with teeth big enough to comb it properly. She finds one and, with my help, we are able to comb it out.

Then, she begins to part it. No skill whatsoever. Eventually, the head instructor comes to her aid, and all the students that day surround me as they receive their first ethnic hair lesson. The instructor parts it for me, and I go home to braid it myself.

I shared this story with my students. One said, "Why don't you move to Portland where people know how to do your hair?"

What can be done about White privilege? Mainly, individuals can become aware of its existence and the role it plays in their lives. It cannot be given away. Denying its reality or refusing to identify as White merely leaves White individuals "all the more blind to our silencing of people of color" (Kendall, 1997, p. 6). Perhaps "the ultimate White privilege may be the ability to acknowledge one's privileged position in life and do nothing about it! One would hope that awareness of racial injustice at this level would be powerful motivation to take action against these unfair personal and structural advantages for Whites and disadvantages for people of color" (Sue, 2010, p. 126). By remaining self-aware and challenging its insidiousness within oneself, in others, and in societal institutions, it is possible to begin to address the denial and invisibility that are its most powerful foundation. Like becoming culturally competent, fighting racism and White privilege, both internally and externally, is a lifelong developmental task—a journey necessary if one wishes to make a difference in the lives of Children of Color.

Models of White Racial Attitudes and Identities

Many authors have developed frameworks for understanding how European Americans think about race, racial differences, and racial identity.

A Model of Racial Attitudes

Rowe, Behrens, and Leach enumerate seven different attitudes that Whites can adopt in regards to race and People of Color. They first distinguish between achieved and unachieved racial consciousness. What this refers to is the extent to which racial attitude is "securely integrated" into the person's general belief structure—in other words, how firmly it is held and how easily it can change. Their model is summarized in Table 4.1.

Unachieved racial consciousness can have one or both of two sources. It can reflect the fact that individuals have not thought about or explored matters related to race and ethnicity or that they have no real commitment to a position or set of attitudes.

Avoidant types tend to ignore, minimize, or deny the importance of the issue both in relation to their own ethnicity and that of non-Whites. Example: "Minority issues just aren't all that important to me. We just don't get involved

TABLE 4.1 Racial Attitude Types

Status	Type	Description
Unachieved	Avoidant	Ignore, minimize, or deny race
	Dependent	Unreflective, superficial
	Dissonant	Uncertain
Achieved	Dominative	Entrenched in White supremacy
	Conflictive	Fairness and status quo compete
	Integrative	Favor interracial harmony
	Reactive	Strong anti-racist stance

Adapted from Rowe, W., Behrens, J.T., and Leach, M.M. (1995). "Racial/ethnic identity and social consciousness: Looking back and looking forward." In J.P. Ponterotto, J.M. Casas, L.A. Suzuki, and C.M. Alexander (Eds.), *Handbook of Multicultural Counseling* (pp. 218–235). Thousand Oaks, CA: Sage.

in that sort of thing. I really am not interested in thinking about those things" (p. 228).

Dependent types have adopted their perspective from significant others (often as far back as during childhood). Example: "My thinking about minorities is mainly influenced by my (friends, family, husband or wife), so you could say I mainly learned about minorities from (them, him or her). That's why my opinion about minorities is pretty much the same as (theirs, his or hers)" (p. 228).

The final unachieved type of attitude is dissonant. Such individuals are clearly uncertain about what they believe. Example: "I used to feel I knew what I thought about minorities. But now my feelings are really mixed. I'm having to change my thinking. I'm not sure, so I'm trying to find some answers to questions I have about minorities" (p. 229).

The achieved statuses are ones that are sufficiently explored, committed to, and integrated into the individual's general belief system.

Those with dominative attitudes believe that majority group members should be allowed to dominate. They are ethnocentric, use European-American culture as a standard for judging the rightness of others' behavior and devalue and are uncomfortable with non-Whites, especially in close personal relationships. Example: "The truth about minorities is that they are kind of dumb, their customs are crude, and they are pretty backward compared to what Whites have accomplished. Besides that, they are sort of lazy. I guess they just aren't up to what Whites are. I wouldn't want a family member, or even a friend of mine, to have a close relationship with a minority. You may have to work near them, but you don't have to live close to one" (p. 229).

Although they would not support outright racism or discrimination, conflictive attitude individuals oppose efforts to ameliorate the effects of discrimination, such as affirmative action. Example: "There should be equal chances to better yourself for everyone, but minorities are way too demanding. The media are always finding something they say is unfair and making a big deal out of it. And the government is always coming up with some kind of program that lets them get more than they deserve. We shouldn't discriminate against minorities, but tilting things in their favor just isn't fair. White ethnic groups didn't get a lot of government help, and the minorities of today shouldn't expect it either" (pp. 229–230).

Individuals who possess integrative attitudes tend to be pragmatic in their approach to race relations. They have a sense of their own identity as Whites and favor interracial contact and harmony. Example: "Integration is a desirable goal for our society, and it could significantly improve problems relating to prejudice and discrimination if people would keep an open mind and allow it to work. Race and culture is not a factor when I choose my personal friends. I'm comfortable around minority people and don't mind being one of a few Whites in a group. In fact, I wouldn't mind living next to minority people if their social class were similar to mine. I think we will need racial harmony for democracy to be able to function" (p. 230).

Reactive individuals—the final type—tend to identify with People of Color, may feel guilty about being White, and may romanticize the racial drama. In addition, they are very sensitive to situations involving discrimination and react strongly to the inequities that exist in society. Example: "Our society is quite racist. It is really difficult for minority people to get a fair deal. There may be some tokenism, but businesses won't put minorities in the top positions. Actually, qualified minority people should be given preference at all levels of education and employment to make up for the effects of past discrimination. But they don't have enough power to influence the government, even though it's the government's responsibility to help minority people. It's enough sometimes to make you feel guilty about being White" (p. 230).

According to the originators of these types, these are the most frequently observed White attitudes toward race and race relations. The unachieved types are most changeable, not having been truly integrated into the person's worldview. The four achieved forms are more difficult to change, but under sufficient contrary information or experience, they can be altered.

A Model of Racial Identity Development

Helms (1995) offers a somewhat different model of White racial identity development. Rather than suggesting a series of independent attitudes, she envisions a developmental process defined by a series of stages through which Whites can move to recognize their privilege and, at the autonomy stage, use it to make needed changes in our society. According to Helms's model, each status or stage is supported by a unique pattern of psychological defense and means of processing racial experience.

The first stage—contact—begins with the individual's internalization of the majority culture's view of People of Color as well as the advantages of privilege. Whites at this level of awareness have developed a defense Helms calls "obliviousness" to keep the issues out of conscious consideration. It is a "naive belief that race does not really make a difference" (Bollin & Finkel, 1995, p. 25).

The second stage—disintegration—involves "disorientation and anxiety provoked by unresolved racial moral dilemmas that force one to choose between own-group loyalty and humanism" (Helms, 1995, p. 185). It is supported by the defenses of suppression and ambivalence. At this stage, the person has encountered information or has had experiences that lead to the realization that race does, in fact, make a difference. The result is a growing awareness of and discomfort with privilege.

Reintegration—the third stage—is defined by an idealization of one's racial group and a concurrent rejection and intolerance for other groups. It depends on selective perception and negative distortion. Here, the White individual attempts to deal with the discomfort by emphasizing the superiority of White culture and the imagined deficits in Cultures of Color.

The fourth stage—pseudo-independence—involves an "intellectualized commitment to one's own socioracial group and deceptive tolerance of other groups" (p. 185). It is grounded in the reshaping of reality and selective perception. The individual has developed an intellectual acceptance of racial differences, espouses a liberal ideology of social justice, but has not emotionally integrated either.

A person functioning in the immersion/emersion stage—fifth along the continuum—is searching for a personal understanding of racism as well as insight into how he or she benefits from it. As a part of this process, which has its psychological base in hypervigilance and reshaping, there is an effort to redefine one's whiteness. Entry into this stage may have been precipitated by being rejected by Individuals of Color and often includes isolation within one's own group in order to work through the powerful feelings that have been stimulated.

The final stage—autonomy—involves "informed positive socioracial-group commitment, use of internal standards for self-definition, capacity to relinquish the privileges of racism" (p. 185). It is supported by the psychological processes of flexibility and complexity. Here, the person has come to peace with his or her own whiteness, separating it from a sense of privilege, and is able to approach those who are culturally different without prejudice.

Helms' model of White identity development parallels models of racial identity development for People of Color that are introduced in Chapter 7. All involve consciousness-raising—that is, becoming aware of and working through unconscious feelings and beliefs about one's connection to race and ethnicity. However, the goal of identity development in each group is different. For People of Color, it involves a cumulative process of "surmounting internalized racism in its various manifestations," while for Whites, it has to do with the "abandonment of entitlement" (p. 184). What the two models share is a process wherein the Person of Color or the White person sheds internalized racial attitudes and social conditioning and replaces them with greater openness and appreciation for racial and cultural identity as well as cultural differences. As people move toward the autonomy stage in both models, working together for culturally competence in our schools becomes more possible.

A Practical Interpretation of Racial Identity

In order to make the theories of racial identity development, particularly those of Helms and Cross (delineated in Chapter 7), more immediately understandable by and useful for teachers and students, I proposed and use a four-stage model using colloquial terms that are easy to remember in daily interactions (Moule, 2004). I call this *racial interaction development*.

Stage 1: *I'm OK; you're OK* is the pre-encounter stage. It includes the often-seen "color-blind" perspective.

Stage 2: *Something is not OK* is the basic encounter stage. My hair story is often that for students.

Stage 3: *I'm OK; I'm not so sure about you* includes many substages. In this stage, I summarize many of the dynamics described by the theorists in their stages 3 and 4, including anger, denial, pseudo-independence, immersion, and emersion.

Stage 4: *I'm OK, you're OK, we're OK* is equivalent to the autonomy or independent stage, in which people are ready to work, preferably together, for change in a more fully integrated manner. The superficiality of "I'm OK; you're OK" is replaced by a deeper, more compassionate, and more complex understanding of the issues and the fact that individuals are "all OK" as they continue to progress.

Identity Development in the College Classroom

The racial identity and consciousness development process of White participants in a multicultural learning environment—an educational setting similar to that in which many readers may find themselves—has some specific characteristics. Ponterotto identifies four stages through which most students proceed, and they parallel the earlier work of Helms (1985) for White racial identity and W. E. Cross (1971) for Black racial identity as well as my four stages for racial interaction: (1) pre-exposure, (2) exposure, (3) zealot-defensive, and (4) integration.

In the pre-exposure stage, the student "has given little thought to multicultural issues or to his or her role as a White person in a racist and oppressive society" (Ponterotto, 1988, p. 151). This stage parallels the contact or pre-encounter stage as well as my "I'm OK; you're OK" level.

In the second stage—exposure—students are routinely confronted with minority individuals and issues. They are exposed to the realities of racism and the mistreatment of People of Color, examine their own cultural values and how they pervade society, and discover how interaction is often "ethnocentrically biased and subtly racist" (p. 152). These realizations tend to stimulate both anger and guilt—anger because they had been taught that teaching was "value free and truly fair and objective" and guilt because holding such assumptions probably led them to perpetuate this subtle racism in their own right. This "Something is not OK stage" is often visible to me during my classes. Recognizing that this is a stage—like the stages of grief that will pass—is helpful for continuing the journey.

In the third stage—zealot-defensive—students tend to react in one of two ways: either over-identifying with ethnic minorities and the issues they are studying or distancing themselves from them. The former tend to develop a strong *pro-minority perspective* and use it to manage and resolve some of the guilt feelings. On the other hand, the latter tend to take the criticism very personally and, by way of defense, withdraw from the topic, becoming *passive recipients* of multicultural information. In the real world, such a reaction leads to avoidance of interracial contact and escape into same-race associations. However, in classes—where students are a captive audience—there is greater likelihood that the defensive feelings will be processed either through personal reflection or through thoughtful and safe classroom discussions.

In the last stage—integration—the extreme reactions of the previous stage tend to decrease in intensity. Zealous reactions subside, and students' views become more balanced. Defensiveness is slowly transformed, and students tend to acquire a "renewed interest, respect, and appreciation for cultural differences" (Ponterotto, 1988, p. 153). There is no guarantee that all students will pass through all four stages, and some can remain stuck in an earlier stage.

Implications for White Teachers

White teachers are encouraged to assess their own reactions to the concept of privilege and to locate their current level of development in each of the models. This is a complex process; however, the layers begin to unfold as you are honest with yourself and others. A recent study on teachers that had collectively spent years working with Students of Color uncovered the deeply rooted and rather disheartening findings on their true feelings:

The eight teachers in this study have built a bond of solidarity around their Whiteness and their positions as White teachers in a predominantly Black school. Their likenesses, shared experiences, stories, students, and the school have become the glue that binds them together and is what allows them to reinforce and support each other on a daily basis. As participants shared their stories, perspectives, and feelings, manifestations of their individual and collective racial identity status emerged. Teachers liberally used disclaimers, avoidance techniques, colorblindness, and stereotypes, and spontaneously shared their outsider feelings, as outcomes of their thinking around race throughout the focus group discussions. Findings revealed teachers' attitudes towards students included both caring and deficit thinking. Deficit thinking was found to influence their view of the Black/White achievement gap and the roots of its cause, as well as their classroom management, instruction, and interactions with parents. (Williams, 2008, p. 1)

To what extent is one aware of the existence of White privilege in his or her life? This is an important question because culturally different non-White students view and relate to a White teacher in light of his or her having that privilege. As suggested in earlier chapters, one cannot help but be a magnet for the feelings of culturally different students about White dominant culture and how it has treated them and those they love. A teacher can struggle to fully grasp the meaning and ramifications of White privilege and then communicate that awareness to non-White students.

Trust is more difficult when two people live in perceptually different worlds. A key aspect of unacknowledged White privilege is its invisibility to Whites and its very obvious visibility to People of Color. To the extent that White teachers can acknowledge the centrality of race to a non-White student and at the same time grasp the nature of their own attitudes about racial differences, the cultural distance between them can be dramatically reduced.

A Way Forward

I'm not asking you to apologize or pay for what others have done in the past. I'm only asking you to realize that we wake up in different worlds each day, with different challenges based on the color of our skin alone. As long as you can acknowledge that reality, we're okay.

–overheard by a student, source unknown

Embracing this request means recognizing the differences and becoming an ally. This next list is useful for delineating the difference between a friend and an ally in antiracist work. I found it useful, for I was so aware of my friends' efforts to understand and support me yet could see that they were not fully engaged in the struggle. I need allies. This material helped me to appreciate the friendships and still hope for allies.

A Friend Is Someone Who:

- is a sympathetic listener.
- offers support privately and personally.
- wants to be supportive but is not always sure how.
- is receptive to conversation/discussion of issues.
- takes a reactive stance by responding to inappropriate comments, behaviors, actions, etc., as they arise
- is aware that differences affect people yet is more comfortable focusing on "common humanity."
- offers suggestions or advice for ways to deal with an issue or incident.
- is optimistic/helps cheer up the target group members when incidents occur.

An Ally Is Someone Who:

- addresses issues, not just incidents.
- mobilizes and organizes to respond to issues without being prompted by a target group member.
- is willing to take risks that may affect her own place, position, and authority within his or her (dominant) group.
- is willing to make public mistakes in front of both target groups and his or her own agent group(s).
- is visible, active, vigilant, and public (even when the target person is not in the room).
- is willing to recognize the inherent privilege and power of being a member of the dominant group.
- views membership in the dominant group as an opportunity to bring about change. (Wong, K., 2008)

Connections and Reflections: Emerging Views

What does it mean to be White? (Sue asked this question of random strangers on the streets in one of his studies). How do the answers relate to the different models we have considered?

It can be hard for us to be honest with ourselves about both the existence and the costs of racism in our own lives. These two reflection activities will lead the way.

Becoming Aware of Race

This exercise involves a series of questions about your experiences with ethnicity and cultural differences. Several ask you to identify a time or event in the past. Allow yourself to relax and visualize the time or event you have identified. Try to re-experience it as much as possible. When you are finished, describe the experience in writing. Include how you felt at the time, how you now feel about it, how it has affected you today, and any other associations, images, or strong feelings that may come up. Use as much time and detail as you need.

1. When did you first become aware that people were different racially or ethnically?
2. When did you first become aware of yourself as a member of a racial or ethnic group?
3. When were you first made aware of people being treated differently because of their race or ethnicity?
4. When did you first become aware of being treated differently yourself because of your own race or ethnicity?
5. Are there things about you as a person that make you feel that you are different from other people? Describe them, and describe how having these qualities makes you feel and has affected you over time.
6. When were you proudest being a member of the group to which you belong?
7. When were you least proud of being a member of the group to which you belong?
8. How do you identify yourself racially/ethnically? Culturally? How has your sense of race/ethnicity or culture changed over time?
9. How would you describe the extent of your contact with people who are racially/ethnically different from you? How has this changed over time?

You can increase the intensity and learning value of this exercise by sharing your answers with someone else. After you have shared each answer, use it as a springboard for further soul searching and personal discussion of each topic.

Costs of Racism to White People

The following checklist helps us to evaluate the costs of racism to White people. Check each item that applies to you.

☐ I don't know exactly what my European-American heritage is, what my great-grandparents' names were, or what regions or cities my ancestors are from.

☐ I grew up, lived, or live in a neighborhood or went to a school or a camp, which, as far as I knew, was exclusively White.

☐ I grew up with People of Color who were servants, maids, gardeners, or babysitters in my house.

☐ I did not meet People of Color socially before I was well into my teens.

☐ I grew up in a household where I heard derogatory racial terms or racial jokes.

☐ I grew up in a family where I heard as a child that People of Color were to blame for violence, lack of jobs, or other problems.

☐ I have seen or heard images in magazines, on TV or radio, on cassettes and CDs, or in movies of (check all that apply):

    ☐ Mexicans depicted as drunk, lazy, or illiterate.

    ☐ Asians depicted as exotic, cruel, or mysterious.

    ☐ Asian Indians depicted as excitable or "silly."

    ☐ Arabs depicted as swarthy, ravishing, or "crazed."

    ☐ African Americans depicted as violent or criminal.

    ☐ Pacific Islanders depicted as fun-loving or lazy.

    ☐ American Indians depicted as drunk, savage, or "noble."

    ☐ Any character roles from non-White cultures depicted by White actors.

☐ I was told not to play with children of particular ethnicities when I was a child.

☐ I have sometimes felt that "white" culture was "wonderbread" culture—empty and boring—or that another racial group has more rhythm, more athletic ability, was better at math and technology, or had more musical or artistic creativity than mine.

☐ I have felt that people of another racial group were more spiritual than White people.

☐ I have been nervous and fearful or found myself stiffening when encountering People of Color in a neutral public situation (for example, in an elevator or on the street).

☐ I have been sexually attracted to a person from another racial group because it seemed exotic, exciting, or a challenge.

☐ I was in a close friendship or relationship with a Person of Color, where the relationship was affected, stressed, or endangered by racism between us or from others.

☐ I am not in a close significant relationship with any People of Color in my life right now.

☐ I have been in a close friendship or relationship with another White person where that relationship was damaged or lost because of a disagreement about racism.

☐ I have felt embarrassed by, separate from, superior to, or more tolerant than other White people.

☐ I have worked in a job where People of Color held more menial jobs, were paid less, or were otherwise harassed or discriminated against, and I did nothing about it.

☐ I have participated in an organization, work group, meeting, or event that People of Color protested as racist or which I knew to be racist and did nothing about it.

☐ I have had degrading jokes, comments, or put-downs about People or Color made in my presence and did not protest or challenge them.

☐ I have felt racial tension or noticed racism in a situation and was afraid to say or do anything about it.

☐ I have seen a Person of Color being attacked verbally or physically and did not intervene.

☐ I have had to accept unnecessary limits on my basic civil liberties because of social fears that People of Color are dangerous.

☐ I have felt angry, frustrated, tired, or weary about dealing with racism and hearing about racial affairs.

☐ I live in a community where, for whatever reason, no People of Color are present, so some of these questions do not apply.

(From *Uprooting Racism: How White People Can Work for Racial Justice*, 2002, Paul Kivel, New Society Publishers, Gabriola Island, BC, Canada.)

Classroom: Adventures in Learning

- For lower grades, consider which item(s) from Peggy McIntosh's list might impact or be evident in their worlds. If you can find them, the multi-hued Band-aids will get most children to thinking (although most young ones want a cartoon character on their Band-aid).

- For upper grades, consider the "Step Forward, Step Back" or "Class-Race" Exercise. (There are many lists; here are two: The first is at http://www .rantcollective.net/article.php?id=62, and the second is at http://www .rantcollective.net/article.php?id=37). I have used several lists that I have found, and I combine them and use them as appropriate for the group I am with. Be cautious for which items you choose and also allow the students to not act on an item if they prefer to not share the information with others.

Students line up, usually outside on a warm day, on a line on the grass or playground. They take steps forward and back as you read the items related to race and privilege of different kinds, many in the area of socioeconomics. This activity may be particularly difficult for both those who end up in the rear and the front of the class. I make sure to give a hug or some encouragement to the person in the back, and I expect to see some reflections in the journals from the students who have a hard time processing their ending position in this exercise.

CHAPTER 5

Understanding Culture and Cultural Differences

"Insight, I believe, refers to the depth of understanding that comes by setting experiences, yours and mine, familiar and exotic, new and old, side by side, learning by letting them speak to one another."

–Mary Catherine Bateson

White students often complain that they have no culture; they know nothing and feel nothing about where they came from. What they mean is that they lack the kind of connection to a cultural heritage and community that they often see among People of Color and Whites with strong heritages. When culture is alive and vibrant, it provides a kind of inner programming. It is always there—often beyond awareness. It gives life structure and meaning. However, when it becomes fragmented, a central part of what it is and can offer gets lost. Because White American culture is so embedded and established as a background in our lives, it is often invisible. There are several exercises and links at the end of this chapter that will help illustrate the invisibility of White American culture.

This chapter discusses a number of issues related to culture. What exactly is it, and how does it function in the life of a person? Along what cultural dimensions do groups differ, and in what ways do the cultures of White Americans and People of Color clash? How does all this affect our schools? Are the theories that inform teaching culture-bound, as some educators have suggested? Finally, how do teachers approach cross-culture teaching? Answers to these questions provide a better understanding of the ways culture affects teaching and education in general and what happens in our classrooms when teachers and students from different cultures meet.

An African American parent and school principal gave the following understanding of culture and her position between cultures for herself and her children. This was a response, as an instructional facilitator, to a student in her college web course who questioned cultural connections. This personal perspective on the needs of all children as individuals and as members of specific or dual cultures helps us to understand the porous nature of culture for those in the United States:

> For your question, "Is it possible/okay for a student to decide that they are more American than Mexican American?" I would say that we are getting into that perception of what it means to be "American." I am definitely more culturally American than African. But I am an African American. There are cultural and historical aspects that are specific to being African American that enable me to relate, on some level, to other people of my race/culture. I could not imagine deciding that I am more American than African American for several reasons. One, society will not let me do so, and two, I love who I am.
>
> As I raise my own children as African American, I try to create a home environment that is safe for them to ask questions, get angry and express their feelings in a healthy way. I feel that this gives them a place to gain confidence in themselves as individuals and know what they believe and why they believe it. When they enter the world they can speak with that same confidence and be able to support it.
>
> America is composed of many races and cultures and religions and belief systems. I think we must be careful about the message we send to students when we allow them to ignore/deny their history/culture which are the very things that make them American. (A. Freeman, excerpt from web class, February 2010)

What Is Culture?

Culture is ...

> a unique and ever-changing constellation we recognize through the observation and study of its language, religion, social and economic organization, decorative arts, stories, myths, ritual practices and beliefs, and a host of other adaptive traits and characteristics. The full measure of a culture embraces both the actions of a people and the quality of their aspirations, the nature of the metaphors that propel their lives. And no description of a people can be complete without reference to the character of their homeland, the ecological and geographical matrix in which they have determined to live out their destiny (Davis, 2009, p. 33).

Culture is a difficult concept. It is so basic to human societies and so intertwined with our natures that its workings are seldom acknowledged or thought about. It is so all-encompassing, like water to a fish, that it remains largely pre-conscious and is obvious only when it is gone or has been seriously disturbed. Anthropological definitions point to certain aspects. Culture is composed of traditional ideas and related values; it is learned, shared, and transmitted from one generation to the next; and it organizes and helps interpret life. This iceberg diagram (Figure 5.1) illustrates the difference between surface

The Iceberg Concept of Culture

Like an iceberg, the majority of culture is below the surface.

Surface Culture
Above sea level
Emotional load: relatively low

food ▪ dress ▪ music ▪
visual arts ▪ drama ▪ crafts
dance ▪ literature ▪ language
celebrations ▪ games

Deep Culture

Unspoken Rules
Partially below sea level
Emotional load: very high

Unconscious Rules
Completely below sea level
Emotional load: intense

courtesy ▪ contextual conversational patterns ▪ concept of time

personal space ▪ rules of conduct ▪ facial expressions

nonverbal communication ▪ body language ▪ touching ▪ eye contact

patterns of handling emotions ▪ notions of modesty ▪ concept of beauty

courtship practices ▪ relationships to animals ▪ notions of leadership

tempo of work ▪ concepts of food ▪ ideals of childrearing

theory of disease ▪ social interaction rate ▪ nature of friendships

tone of voice ▪ attitudes toward elders ▪ concept of cleanliness

notions of adolescence ▪ patterns of group decision-making

definition of insanity ▪ preference for competition or cooperation

tolerance of physical pain ▪ concept of "self" ▪ concept of past and future

definition of obscenity ▪ attitudes toward dependents ▪ problem-solving

roles in relation to age, sex, class, occupation, kinship, and so forth

FIGURE 5.1   The Iceberg Concept of Culture (Used by permission of the Indiana Department of Education)

and deep culture. It can "help you go below the surface when considering the relationship between culture and learning. When thinking about the culture students bring to the classroom, often teachers see only the most obvious manifestations of culture and miss its more fundamental expressions... . Like an iceberg, nine-tenths of culture is below the surface" (Grant & Sleeter, 2007, p. 125). As you see on the iceberg, food, dress, music, visual arts, drama, crafts, dance, literature, language, celebrations and games are the surface forms of cultural that are the usual markers of "multicultural education."

Yet, deep culture defines the ways in which a people have learned to respond to life's problems. For example, all human groups must deal with death. But there is great variation from culture to culture in the rituals and practices that have developed around death.

A specific example of how surface and deep culture interact is given by Pang (2005). The surface artifact in the Japanese culture is origami; we will use the paper-folding of a crane, a classroom activity I have witnessed. The customs, practices, and interactional patterns are observable:

1. Child watches another child or adult fold paper.
2. Child folds paper one section at a time, modeling the "teacher."

3. Teacher waits patiently and shows folds several times if needed.
4. Child and teacher treat each other with respect.

Yet, below the surface, there are shared values, beliefs, norms, and expectations:

1. Develops a sense of patience
2. Reinforces a sense of community
3. Teaches respect for the teacher or for someone with skill
4. Cranes represent good luck and long life in Japanese culture
5. Reflects value of simplicity and beauty (p. 58)

How many classroom cultural activities completely miss the mark with an emphasis on surface culture only? What is needed is a better sense of how culture functions in a larger sense, particularly within individuals. To get at this, the concept of paradigm is most useful.

The term *paradigm* describes the totality of the way a science conceives of the phenomena it studies. For example, sciences change over time—not through the slow accumulation of knowledge (as taught in high school physics) but rather through paradigm shifts (Kuhn, 1970). A paradigm is a set of shared assumptions and beliefs about how the world works, and it structures the perceptions and understanding of the scientists in a discipline. For example, when Newton's theory of the way physical matter operated was replaced with Einstein's theory of relativity, this new paradigm was a radical departure from its predecessor and gave physicists a totally different way of thinking about their work. Our beliefs (paradigms) define what we perceive and experience as real.

The notion of paradigm was quickly appropriated by educators to describe the cognitive worldviews through which teachers and students experience their lives. Our paradigms, without our being very aware of them, tell us how the world works and tell us our place in it: what is possible and impossible, what the rules are, how things are done. They shape our experience of reality and the worldview each of us brings into the classroom.

People think through their paradigms, not about them. "I'll see it when I believe it" is a more accurate description of how beliefs can give form to what is experienced as "real." People also grow emotionally attached to their paradigms and give up or change them only with great difficulty and discomfort. A challenge to one's paradigm is experienced as a personal threat, for ego gets invested in the portrayal of how things should be. When the world no longer operates as it "should," people feel cut adrift from familiar moorings, no longer sure where they stand or who they are.

Culture is the stuff that human paradigms are made of. It provides their content: identity, beliefs, values, and behavior. It is learned as part of the natural process of growing up in a family and community and from participating in schools and other societal institutions. These are the sources of culture. In short, one's culture becomes one's paradigm, defining what is real and right for each of us. From this perspective, it is easy to understand why the imposition of one group's cultural paradigm upon members of another cultural group—as occurs in most classrooms, where the European cultural paradigm is the standard against which Students of Color, who view their world through different cultural paradigms, are measured—may be experienced so negatively.

> These cultures do not represent failed attempts at modernity, marginal peoples who somehow missed the technological train of history. On the contrary, these peoples, with their dreams and prayers, their myths and memories, teach us that there are indeed other ways of being, alternative visions of life, birth, death, and creation itself. (Davis, 2009, p. 205)

Before describing the dimensions along which cultures differ, it is useful to remember the difficulties with the concept of race as discussed in Chapter 2. Increasingly, educators and social scientists have found it more useful to distinguish between human groups on the basis of culture rather than race. For example, when they refer to tribal subgroupings within the broader racial category of Native Americans as separate ethnic groups, they are emphasizing cultural differences in defining group identity as opposed to biological or physical ones. In this text, terms such as "ethnic group" and "culturally different students" are used to describe human diversity. *Ethnic group* was defined in Chapter 1 as any distinguishable people whose members share a common culture and see themselves as separate and different from the majority culture. The emphasis is on shared cultural material as a basis for identification. It is not likely that the concept of race and its usual breakdown into distinct human groupings will ever completely disappear. It is too deeply ingrained in the fabric of American society. Rather, its importance as a social as opposed to a biological concept will increasingly be emphasized.

Even though many individuals experience a world more defined by skin color than by culture, we turn to cultural differences as a more useful and less controversial yardstick than race.

The Dimensions of Culture

Cultural paradigms define and dictate how human beings live and experience life. We will look at one set of the dimensions along which cultures can differ. The content and specifics of each dimension vary from culture to culture. Cross-cultural misunderstanding occurs because of differences between cultures and the natural ethnocentric tendency to assume that everyone else views the world the same way we do. Brown and Lundrum-Brown (1995) enumerated the following dimensions of culture: psychobehavioral modalities, axiology (values), ethos (guiding beliefs), epistemology (how one knows), logic (reasoning process), ontology (nature of reality), concept of time, and concept of self.

To support these dimensions, each culture evolves a set of cultural forms—ritual practices, behavioral prescriptions, and symbols. For example, a culture stresses the doing mode on the first dimension. Certain kinds of child-rearing techniques tend to encourage directed activity. Parents differentially reinforce

Psychobehavioral modality: The mode of activity most preferred within a culture. Do individuals actively engage their world (doing), more passively experience it as a process (being), or experience it with the intention of evolving (becoming)?

Axiology: The interpersonal values that a culture teaches. Do they compete or cooperate (competition versus cooperation)? Are emotions freely expressed or held back and controlled (emotional restraint versus emotional expressiveness)? Is verbal expression direct or indirect (direct verbal expression versus indirect verbal expression)? Do group members seek help from others or do they keep problems hidden so as not to shame their families (help seeking versus saving face)?

Ethos: The beliefs that are widely held within a cultural group and guide social interactions. Are people viewed as independent beings or as interdependent (independence versus interdependence)? Is one's first allegiance to oneself or to one's family (individual rights versus honor and protect family)? Are all individual group members equal or is there an acknowledged hierarchy of status or power (egalitarianism versus authoritarianism)? Are harmony, respect, and deference toward others valued over controlling and dominating them (control and dominance versus harmony and deference)?

Epistemology: The preferred ways of gaining knowledge and learning about the world. Do people rely more on their intellectual abilities (cognitive processes), their emotions and intuition (affective processes, "vibes," intuition), or a combination (cognitive and affective)?

Logic: The kind of reasoning process that group members adopt. Are issues seen as being either one way or the other (either/or thinking)? Can multiple possibilities be considered at the same time (both/and thinking)? Or is thinking organized around inner consistency (circular)?

Ontology: How a culture views the nature of reality. Is what's real only what can be seen and touched (objective material)? Is there a level of reality that exists beyond the material senses (subjective spiritual)? Or are both levels of reality experienced (spiritual and material)?

Concept of Time: How time is experienced within a culture. Is it clock-determined and linear (clock-based)? Is it defined in relation to specific events (event-based)? Or is it experienced as repetitive (cyclical)?

Concept of Self: Do group members experience themselves as separate beings (individual self) or as part of a greater collective (extended self)?

activity over passivity and also model such behavior. Cultural myths portray figures high on this trait, and moral teachings stress its importance. The group's language likely favors active over passive voice. What makes a culture unique, then, is the particular profile of where it stands on each dimension combined with the specific cultural forms it has evolved.

The dimensions of culture are not totally independent. Some dimensions tend to cluster with others because they are mutually reinforcing. For example, in relation to ethos, beliefs concerning independence, individual rights, egalitarianism, and control and dominance tend to occur together in the belief system of a culture, as do interdependence, honor and family protection, authoritarianism, and harmony and deference. Likewise, certain cultures share a number of dimensions. For example, the Cultures of Color in the United States have many dimensional similarities and as a group differ considerably from European culture.

Finally, it is important to note that each culture generates a unique experience of living. The quality of life differs in tone, mood, and intensity. So too do educational and learning issues and the emotional strengths members develop. A most dramatic example of this occurred many years ago. A graduate student was running a personal growth group for students at a multicultural weekend retreat. The students who showed up for one group were White, with the exception of one young Latino man, who was there to spend more time with one of the young women in the group. Such groups seldom attracted non-White participants, for most Students of Color believe that they are a "White thing" as well as something that "Whites really need. As for us, we don't have any trouble relating to other people." The group was quite successful, and it did not take long before people were sharing deeply: talking about feelings of disconnection from parents, isolation, and loneliness. At a certain point, the young Latino man could contain himself no longer and blurted out, "I don't understand what you are all talking about. I am part of a big extended family; there is always someone around. I can't imagine feeling alone or isolated." Only from such experiences can one realize that the universal malaise of loneliness and isolation is, in fact, a cultural experience and artifact of the European lifestyle.

Comparing Cultural Paradigms in America

Ho (1987) compared the cultural paradigm of White European Americans to the paradigms of four cultures of People of Color. He used five dimensions: three similar to those identified by Brown and Landrum-Brown's (psychobehavioral modality or work and activity, concept of self or people relations, and concept of time or time orientation) and two of his own (nature and the environment and human nature). It is worth reviewing these in some detail to better appreciate the breadth of difference that can exist. A table with these five dimensions is included in the introduction to Part 3 of this book right before we look at different cultural groups in detail in Chapters 10 through 15. It should be remembered, however, that these comparisons are generalizations and may not necessarily fit or apply to individual group members, especially those who have acculturated. Likewise, individual European American may well have embraced cultural components usually associated with other cultures due to specific family heritage or ancestry or personal choice to become immersed in other ways of knowing and being. Finally, each of the five racial groups described is in actuality composed of numerous subgroups whose cultural content may differ widely. For example, in the United States, there are over 500 federally recognized Native American Indian tribes, each with its own cultural uniqueness.

Nature and the Environment

Ho classified the four Cultures of Color—Asian Americans, Native Americans, African Americans, and Latino/a Americans—as living in "harmony with" nature and the environment, whereas European Americans prefer "mastery over" them. For the former, the relationship involves respecting and co-existing with nature. Human beings are part of a natural order and must live respectfully and nonintrusively with other aspects of nature. To destroy a fellow creature is to destroy a part of oneself. On the other hand, European-American culture views human beings as superior to the physical environment and entitled to manipulate it for their own benefit. The world is a resource to be used and plundered.

The Cultures of Color see the component parts of nature as alive and invested with spirit to be related to respectfully and responsibly. Great value is placed on being attentive to what nature has to offer and teach. Out of such a perspective comes notions such as the Native American idea of Turtle Island, a mythology that views the nonhuman inhabitants of the continent as an interconnected system of animal spirits and archetypal characters. A "mastery" mentality results in environmental practices such as runaway logging, strip mining, and oil drilling as well as the impetus for institutions such as human slavery that exploit "inferior" human beings for material gain.

Time Orientation

There is great diversity among the five cultural groups in regard to how they perceive and experience time. European Americans are dominated by an orientation toward the future. Planning, producing, and controlling what will happen are all artifacts of a future time orientation. What was and what is are always a bit vague and are subordinated to what is anticipated. At the same time, European Americans view time as compartmentalized and incremental, and being on time and being efficient with time are positive values.

Asian and Latino/a cultures are described as past/present–oriented. For both, history is a living entity. Ancestors and past events are felt to be alive and impacting present reality. The past flows imperceptibly into and defines the present. In turn, both Native Americans and African Americans are characterized as present-oriented. The focus is the here and now, with less attention to what led up to this moment or what will become of it.

As a group and as distinct from European-American culture, the Cultures of Color share a view of time as an infinite continuum and, as a result, find it difficult to relate to the White obsession with being on time. Interestingly, each of these groups has evolved a term to describe its looser sense of time: "Colored People's (CP) Time," "Indian time," "Asian time," and "Latin time." Invariably, time becomes an issue when non-Whites enter institutions in which European-American cultural values predominate. Lateness is often mistakenly interpreted as indifference, a provocation, or a lack of basic work skills or interest.

Even seeing time as a continuum fails to give the essence of the difference for those for whom time is simply not important:

> In the Aboriginal universe there is no past, present, or future.... There is no notion of linear progression, no goal of improvement, no idealization of the possibility of change.... The entire purpose of humanity is not to improve anything. It is to engage in the ritual and ceremonial activities deemed to be essential for the maintenance of the world precisely as it was at the moment of creation. (Davis, 2009, p. 158)

For one who lives in a culture where on time rather than early is sometimes considered late, such a universe it difficult to imagine.

People Relations

Ho distinguished European Americans as having an "individual" social focus compared to the "collateral" focus of the four Cultures of Color. *Individual behavior* refers to actions undertaken to actualize the self, while *collateral behavior* involves doing things to contribute to the survival and betterment of family and community. These differences, in turn, become a basis for attributing value to different and opposing styles of interaction. For example, European Americans are taught and encouraged to compete, to seek individual success, and to feel pride in and make public their accomplishments. Native Americans and Latino/a Americans, in particular, place high value on cooperation and strive to suppress individual accomplishment, boasting, and self-aggrandizement.

Having pointed out this shared collateral focus, it is equally important to understand that the four Communities of Color differ significantly in their communication styles and the meaning of related symbols. Native Americans place high value on brevity in speech, while the ability to rap is treated like an art form by African Americans. It is considered impolite in certain Asian-American subgroups to say no or to refuse to comply with a request from a superior. Among Latino/a Americans, differential behavior and the communication of proper respect depends on perceived authority, age, gender, and class.

Work and Activity

On the dimension of work and activity, European Americans, Asian Americans, and African Americans are described as *doing*-oriented, while Native Americans and Latino/a Americans are characterized as *being-in-becoming*. *Doing* is an active mode. It involves initiating activity in pursuit of a goal. It tends to be associated with societies in which rewards and status are based on productivity and accomplishment. But even here, there are differences in motivation. European Americans' work and activity are premised on the idea of meritocracy—hard work and serious effort ultimately bring the person financial and social success. On the other hand, Asian Americans pursue activity in terms of its ability to confer honor on the family and concurrently to avoid shaming the family or losing face. African Americans fall somewhere between these two extremes.

Being-in-becoming is more passive, process-oriented, and focused on the here and now. The world presents opportunities for activity and work rather than individuals seeking them out or creating them. This can easily be misinterpreted as "lazy" or "lacking motivation." On a recent trip to the Sinai in Egypt, a colleague had a traveling companion who was a hardworking lawyer from New York City, clearly high on the doing dimension. After spending several hours visiting a Bedouin village, the lawyer could barely contain his shock at how the men just sat around all day. The guide, himself a Bedouin, suggested that they were not merely sitting but were thinking and planning. "There is a lot to think about: where to find water, missing goats, perhaps a new wife, maybe a little smuggling." This didn't satisfy the lawyer. "I don't understand how they can get anything done without meetings. Give me six months, and I'd have this whole desert covered with condos."

Activity and work, whether of the doing or becoming variety, must occur in the context of other cultural values. For example, in many cultures, work does not begin until there has been sufficient time to greet and properly inquire about the welfare of one's family. To do otherwise is considered rude and insensitive. In White European-American business culture, such activity is seen as lazy, wasteful, and shirking one's responsibilities.

Human Nature

This dimension of culture deals with how groups view the essence of human nature. Are people inherently good, bad, or both? According to Ho, African Americans and European Americans see human nature as being both good and bad and as possessing both potentials. But for each, the meaning is quite different. In African American culture, where behavior involves a focus on co-operation and solidarity, good and bad are defined in relation to the community. Something is laudable if it benefits the neighborhood and bad if it does not. In such a community, human nature is seen as existing in the interaction between the person and the group. On the other hand, European-American culture sees good and bad as residing in the individual. These two sides of human nature—the good and bad—are seen in constant opposition and conflict within the individual.

Ho described Asian Americans, Native Americans, and Latino/a Americans as viewing human nature as good. However, the tendency to attribute positive motives to others has sometimes proven less than helpful in interaction with members of the dominant culture. Early treaty negotiations between Native American tribes and the U.S. government are a case in point. Tribal representatives entered these negotiations under the assumption that they were dealing with honest and honorable men and that agreements would be honored. By the time sufficient experience forced them to re-evaluate their original assumptions, their lands had been stolen. Similarly, in the workplace, when members of such groups exhibit helpfulness, generosity, and caring for fellow workers (behavior that follows from an assumption that others are basically good), they are frequently viewed as naive, gullible, and in need of "getting a clue."

Are Educational Theories Culture-Bound?

In Chapter 2, *cultural racism* was defined as the belief that the cultural ways of one group are superior to those of another. It can exist within the mind of an individual and it can assert itself through the workings of institutions, such as the schools and teacher education institutions in which most teachers work and learn, and through the theories and practices they hold and subscribe to as educators. It is the strong belief of many researchers that the assumptions and practices of mainstream education are based on European cultural values. Sleeter's (2001) meta-analysis of efforts to prepare teachers for culturally diverse schools concludes that the problem is the overwhelming presence of whiteness. Because of this, serious questions exist about whether teachers educated by such theories can adequately serve culturally different students.

Anthropologists draw a distinction between emic and etic approaches to working cross-culturally. *Emic* refers to looking at a culture through concepts and theories that are indigenous to it. For example, making traditional stories available to Native American students is an emic approach to teaching.

Etic means viewing a culture through "glasses" that are external to it. This is the strategy that most educators have adopted. It has been assumed that this approach has relevance for all people, irrespective of their cultural backgrounds, but this is not true. Some argue that because the origins of the teaching profession are European ideas, values, and sensibilities, it is not appropriate for individuals who hold different cultural values and assumptions (LeCompte, 1994). Educational models naively misjudge their own universality and are in reality "emic approaches—that are designed by and for middle-class European Americans" (Atkinson, Morten & Sue, 1993, p. 54).

Conflicting Values in Educational Theory

Many of the assumptions and practices that are central to the teaching professions are in conflict with the cultural worldview or personal paradigms of non-White students. By way of example, we now focus on four such meta-values that are central to mainstream teaching approaches yet are culture-bound—that is, at odds and in conflict with the cultural worldviews of most non-White students and their families. These meta-values include an emphasis on self-disclosure, the value of extensive goal-setting in educational planning, the importance of students' learning to adapt to the world in which they live, and a focus on developing the individual.

Self-Disclosure

A child spends a great deal of time in the classroom. In many ways, teachers and students develop close personal relationships, and this naturally leads to an expectation of personal sharing by the student and possibly by his or her family. Most teachers believe that such self-disclosure is an important part of the educational process and that to the extent that they are in possession of personal information and data about the student, they will be in a position to better understand and adapt the learning environment to their needs.

Individuals from Cultures of Color may not share this value and may not feel comfortable talking about themselves or disclosing personal material to relative strangers. For example, Asian Americans learn emotional restraint at an early age and are expected to exhibit modesty in the face of authority as well as subtlety in dealing with personal problems. To reveal intimate details to strangers is seen as bringing shame on the family and is experienced as losing face. Native Americans and Latino/a Americans may both feel threatened by the demand for such disclosure. For both, intimate sharing is done only with longstanding friends.

Understandably, African Americans tend to be suspicious of requests by WhitesEuropean Americans for intimate life details. The Black community sees not hiding feelings from Whites until their trustworthiness can be assured as dangerous and potentially self-destructive. Educators obviously need to be aware of how culturally different individuals view and experience the teacher's desire for relevant personal information as well as to be careful about drawing conclusions about a student's reluctance to self-disclose. Such behavior is normative in many cultural groups and should not necessarily be interpreted as defensiveness or as reflecting resistance, shyness, or passivity.

In the classroom, culturally different students may hesitate to share details of their lives with volunteers and teachers who are not known to them as long as their motivations and commitment to caring are unknown. Self-disclosure may come much later in the relationship process yet end up being fuller when the barriers to sharing are lifted naturally, according to individual cultural standards. In general, sharing personal information is held suspect in non-mainstream cultures, and this is at odds with the general European penchant for freely exchanging personal information, even with strangers.

Long-Term Goals

Most educational theories place importance on careful planning and setting goals. Teaching is envisioned as an ongoing long-term process in which educator and student interact with the objective of the student's accumulating knowledge, skills, and certain values over time; even the intrapersonal lives of students are seen in developmental terms. However, many People of Color tend to take more action and set short-term goals, and they are less linearly oriented in their approaches to problem solving.

For example, individuals of Color may find directive approaches more helpful than nondirective approaches, and they often express confusion or frustration about setting abstract, long-term goals. The differences may result from differing time orientations, a belief that the individual's purpose is to serve the collective (rather than an all-consuming focus on the self) or the fact that "sitting around and talking" is a luxury most people cannot afford or do not see as potentially helpful (Sue & Sue, 1990). In a school setting, for example, while teachers may be looking forward to end-of-year tests and covering the textbook, culturally different students may want to focus on immediate peer-oriented relationships and an educational process that seems more communally and culturally relevant. A good example of such a value difference is discussed in greater detail in Chapter 8, where we talk about the preference for a more authoritative discipline style by teachers that is found in some Communities of Color, particularly among African American students.

Changing the Individual or Changing the Environment

Educators differ somewhat about the role of schools in bringing about change in the lives of students and exactly where the change process should be located. Is it better to change students to fit their circumstances in the greater society or to educate students to try to change the world around them?

Cultures of Color differ widely on whether to help individuals cope with difficult life situations by accommodating or adapting to them (changing the person) or encouraging or teaching individuals to impose changes on the external environment so that it better fits their needs. For example, Asian-American culture tends to stress passive acceptance of reality and transcendence of conflict by adjusting perceptions so harmony can be achieved with the environment (Ho, 1994). On the other hand, African Americans recognize a racist environment as the cause of many of their distresses and advocate changing it rather than themselves. To this end, in the late 1960s, African American psychologists in California called for and got a moratorium on testing minority children in the public schools (Bay Area Association of Black Psychologists, 1972). They argued that White teachers and administrators—who were not comfortable with students' non-White ways—were using culturally biased psychological assessment to funnel culturally different children into special education classes. For its part, European culture tends to encourage the confrontation of obstacles in the environment that restrict freedom. But this is not necessarily the position taken by most White teachers.

Sue and Sue (1990) offer an interesting perspective on this question. They suggest that most student behavior can be understood as a result of their beliefs about locus of control and locus of responsibility. *Locus of control* refers to whether individuals feel that they are in control of their own fate (internal control) or are being controlled externally (external control) and have little impact on the outside world. *Locus of responsibility* refers to whether individuals believe that they are responsible for their own fate (internal responsibilities) or cannot be held responsible because more powerful forces are at work (external responsibility). Sue and Sue propose four different worldviews based on combining these two dimensions and argue that People of Color may exhibit any of the four.

Generally, European-American teachers believe in internal control and internal responsibility—that individuals are in control of their own fate, their actions affect outcomes, and success or failure in life is related to personal characteristics and abilities. However, this position is at odds with the beliefs of certain Communities of Color. For example, many Latino/a Americans with strong religious beliefs tend to favor external control—that a higher power is in charge of their lives. Similarly, individuals who feel socially and economically powerless also tend to ascribe to a position of external control. The bottom line is that mismatches between a student's and a teacher's perceptions of how the world works are likely to reflect serious differences regarding educational goals and just what constitutes useful learning.

Conflict over the question of changing the child or changing the environment can lead to serious controversy within schools and educational communities. Parents who have chosen to assimilate or accommodate into mainstream

American culture want schools to educate their children to become fully participating members of the school culture—to internalize its values and emulate its personnel. Yet, many culturally different parents are critical of the role of schools in negating the cultures of their family. Although they want students to succeed in school and society, they believe that school culture should be adapted to support the cultural needs of the children.

However, it is possible for both to be in parallel—for a classroom's notion of achievement and the child's culture and values to be mutually supportive of each other. Students are clearly very sensitive to the existence of such discrepancies. Delpit (2006) provided an excellent example of such a dynamic: When Native Alaskan children know they are being watched, they act as if they do "not get it" when their Anglo teacher does or says something that is devaluing of their culture. However, when they believe they are not being observed, they may mock that same teacher, sometimes revealing in their mimicry that they have mastered the material they supposedly had not learned.

Consider the Asian American mother and European-American teacher who experience a basic incongruency in their goals for a child (see the parent/teacher scenario in Chapter 6). The teacher believes that the child should act on the environment and influence other members of the class, while the mother believes that such actions are culturally inappropriate. Their communication is hampered not only by their conflicting goals for the child but also by the cultural reluctance of the mother to question the authority of the teacher and her desire to be in harmony with the school culture. The mother may not say much, but the conflict is still very real and will impact the student. A successful, culturally competent teacher shows respect for the culture of all children and seldom places children in a position where they feel the need to make a choice.

Focus on Developing the Individual

Educators have also tended to adopt European cultural definitions of healthy and normal functioning. Self-reliance, autonomy, self-actualization, self-assertion, insight, and resistance to stress are seen as hallmarks of healthy adjustment and functioning (Saeki & Borow, 1985; Sue & Sue, 1990). These are the characteristics toward which individuals should be encouraged educationally. However, such a focus on developing the strengths of individual character is not shared or seen as of value in all cultures. For example, Asian-American cultures value interdependence, inner enlightenment, negation of self, transcendence of conflict, and passive acceptance of reality (Ho, 1994). This view is highly antithetical to that of mainstream Western thought. What Asian-American cultures share with the other Cultures of Color—and what sets them apart from and in opposition to mainstream White culture—is the diminished importance of individual autonomy and self-assertion. A similar idea is expressed in the ways Native American culture views health and illness. Both mental and physical illnesses are thought to result from disharmony between the individual, the family, and/or the tribe as well as between any of these and the ways of nature and the natural order. Healing can occur only when harmony is restored. Restoring harmony is the goal of traditional healing practices (Duran & Duran, 1995).

Another way to describe this important difference is the distinction between the individual and the extended selves. The individual self is characteristic of European culture. It exists autonomously, is fragmented from its social context, and has the goals of personal survival and betterment. The self develops very differently in cultures where group members conceive of themselves not as individuals but as part of a broader collective. In this extended self, behavior occurs with an awareness of its impact on the larger social group. The subvalues of competition, emotional restraint, direct verbal expression, and help seeking and the sub-beliefs of independence, individual rights, egalitarianism, and control and dominance (all typical of the European cultural paradigm) represent ideas that support the existence of an individual self. Similarly, their opposites, the subvalues of cooperation, emotional expressiveness, indirect verbal expression, and saving face and the sub-beliefs of interdependence, honor and family protection, authoritarianism, and harmony and deference, are more typical of the worldview of Communities of Color and are related to the existence of an extended self (Brown and Lundrum-Brown, 1995). For example, independence allows for greater self-assertion; interdependence allows for greater intergroup harmony. In speaking of the extended self, a graduate Student of Color introduced to a model of identity development that described the final stage of growth as "transcending specific group identities" reacted this way: "This can't be right. How can they see this as optimal growth? The person is no longer a part of the community."

Recent studies on the workings of the brain indicate that this individual vs. extended self conflict is deeply embedded in our brains very early in life. Begley (2010) shares the details in her article "West Brain, East Brain." Her example uses cultures separated by seas: Americans of the United States and Chinese:

> Scientists have been surprised at how deeply culture—the language we speak, the values we absorb—shapes the brain.... To take one recent example, a region behind the forehead called the medial prefrontal cortex supposedly represents the self: it is active when we ("we" being the Americans in the study) think of our own identity and traits. But with Chinese volunteers, the results were strikingly different. The "me" circuit hummed not only when they thought whether a particular adjective described themselves, but also when they considered whether it described their mother. The Westerners showed no such overlap between self and mom. Depending [on] whether one lives in a culture that views the self as autonomous and unique or as connected to and part of a larger whole, this neural circuit takes on quite different functions.

"Cultural neuroscience," as this new field is called, is about discovering such differences. Some of the findings, as with the "me/mom" circuit, buttress long-standing notions of cultural differences. For instance, it is a cultural cliché that Westerners focus on individual objects while East Asians pay attention to context and background (another manifestation of the individualism-collectivism split). Sure enough, when shown complex, busy scenes, Asian-Americans and non-Asian-Americans recruited different brain regions. The Asians showed more activity in areas that process figure-ground relations—holistic context—while the Americans showed more activity in regions that recognize objects. (p. 42)

As in the concept of self and extended self, teachers should be aware of the basic incongruity between their own notions of what is optimally healthy in human development and the kinds of educational goals that should be set for individual students on the one hand and the view of optimal functioning within the culture from which the student comes on the other. Where differences exist, they should be respected, and great care should be taken to not project one's own values onto the educational process or to judge, even unintentionally, a student's behavior as inferior or deficient when it varies from the teacher's internal cultural standards.

Such conflicts can exist at all levels of schooling—from graduate teacher education programs to the ways preschool programs are structured. The daunting task is to allow room not just for moments of cultural congruency as add-ons to the curriculum but for a full-time expression of preferred definitions of successful education and optimal growth for individual students. The basic question turns out to be whether a teacher can allow for choice in everything from the desired lighting level to preferred learning styles to varying forms of peer interaction or instead assumes without reflection that teaching methods and classroom structure must be congruent with his or her own unexamined embedded preferences and cultural assumptions.

Conflicting Strategies about Multicultural Education

In turning to the question of what educators can do about these areas of potential conflict, the easiest and most immediate answer is fairly simple: Alter and adjust education to accommodate cultural differences. Recall from Chapter 1 that one of the central skills associated with cultural competence is being able to adapt mainstream practices to the needs of culturally different individuals. For example, it does not seem unreasonable to expect teachers to alter their expectations—especially when first meeting a student—regarding self-disclosure. Teachers should also be able to adjust the type of interaction that occurs in the classroom and, when helpful, move into a less ambiguous and more directive problem-solving mode. Similarly, it should be possible to adapt the educator's view of where change should take place (changing the individual versus changing the environment) to align with the student's cultural tendencies and to rethink classroom goals and outcomes in light of the student's cultural beliefs.

Two additional strategies will improve teacher credibility. The first is to ensure that students feel that their cultural backgrounds and life experiences are understood by the teacher. This involves both appreciating their worldviews in terms of the intricacies of their cultural backgrounds and being able to communicate that awareness to them. The second is to ensure that students get some immediate benefit or reinforcement from the teaching process. This may involve advocating for them, teaching them a skill or practice that might help them better navigate the system, or even directly intervening in or changing a situation on their behalf. Although such interventions may push the boundaries of what is considered appropriate among mainstream teachers, it should be remembered that educational practices were developed primarily for working with dominant-culture students. Limitations may not make cultural sense when working with Students of Color.

However, some people believe that merely making adjustments to a predominantly European model of education is not sufficient. Their belief is that approaching the problem of cross-cultural teaching in this manner is akin to "rearranging the deck chairs on the *Titanic*." They argue that merely making cosmetic changes in a process whose very nature is destructive to traditional people and their culture does not get to the heart of the problem. For example, European culture and its application through Western educational practices and psychology have been instrumental in fragmenting Native American culture and lifestyle. One need only remember the Indian Boarding Schools and their expressed goal of eradicating Native culture. An inability to tolerate the existence of alternative ways of knowing and experiencing the world is inherent in Western thought:

> The critical factor in cross-cultural psychology is a fundamentally different way of being in the world. In no way does Western thinking address any system of cognition other than its own. Given that Judeo-Christian belief systems include notions of the Creator putting human beings in charge of all creations, it is easy to understand why this group of people assumes that it also possesses the ultimate way of describing psychological phenomena for all of humanity. In reality, the thought that what is right comes from one worldview produces a narcissistic worldview that desecrates and destroys much of what is known as culture and cosmological perspective. (Duran & Duran, 1995, p. 17)

An equally useful concept through which to compare traditional cultures (which include the Cultures of Color in the United States) with the culture of postmodern Europe holds that something is inherently wrong with civilized culture and that something essential has been lost. Through a careful analysis of the dimensions of traditional culture, one can discern that these eight characteristics of "primitive" culture have been lost in the "civilizing" process (Diamond, 1987):

- Good psychological nurturance;
- Many-sided, engaging relationships throughout life;
- Various forms of institutionalized deviance;
- Celebration and fusion of the sacred/natural and individual/society in ritual;
- Direct engagement with nature and natural processes;
- Active participation in culture;
- Equation of goodness, beauty, and the natural environment;
- Socioeconomic support as a natural inheritance.

Not only has the content of primitive cultures been lost but also their traditional methods of socialization and teaching the young. In such cultures, education is a natural function of family structure, where the learning of content and process go hand in hand.

These concerns have led educators to seek alternative and more comprehensive solutions to replace approaches that merely adapt and adjust dominant-group classroom theories and practices for use with culturally different students. One alternative has been to call for the creation of individual ethnic-specific global educational theories, each developed by teachers and researchers from a given ethnic community, aimed at a unique and unbiased understanding of the educational needs of that community (Banks et al., 2001; Foster, 1994; Gay, 2010; Ladson-Billings, 1994). In arguing for such an approach, authors have contended that principles and theories developed to educate European American students do not have sufficient power to engage and take into consideration the behavior that occurs in the African American classroom. Each of the models would dictate a unique and culturally sensitive approach specific to educating members of that community.

Where possible, consider a return to the use of traditional education practices from the student's own culture. Over time, each Community of Color has developed its own conceptions of learning and education in the process of socializing children into the cultural ways of the group. First of all, availing oneself of such approaches helps guarantee that the knowledge being learned has not been compromised by dominant cultural ways. Second, it provides an avenue for strengthening ethnic identity and cultural ties. Finally, introducing such culturally congruent teaching methods is especially useful to students who remain steeped in traditional cultural ways and values, for whom dominant American culture has little relevance and to whom dominant culture feels unsafe.

A logical compromise—at least for the present—is to include traditional learning practices as part of a broad range of educational services within a classroom and a community. Such a strategy above all provides a strong statement about the value of cultural diversity to the teaching profession.

However, most culturally different students have experienced some level of acculturation or, to put it differently, are bicultural in varying degrees. For these individuals, a full return to traditional cultural ways is probably neither possible nor desirable. More relevant to their situation is the use of models of teaching and helping that have been sensitively and extensively adapted to the cultural needs of their group by educators—either indigenous or culturally different—who are truly culturally competent. As the demand for cross-cultural education continues to grow and as increasingly complex and effective strategies for serving culturally diverse students are developed, it is just a matter of time before dominant forms of learning begin to lose their decidedly European perspective and become increasingly infused and informed by the wisdom of a variety of other cultures.

Connections and Reflections: Emerging Views

Which holidays do you celebrate in your family of origin? Are there certain foods that you eat then or when you get together with family? Do the holidays and foods have a cultural connection? Now, think about an extended family meal. Are you able to discern any deeper cultural specifics (return to the iceberg for ideas)?

This exercise is intended to help you become more aware of your own cultural roots and identity as well as prepare you to better understand the material you have read in this chapter. The following is a detailed list of questions to be answered in relation to each ethnic group constituting your culture of origin. In answering them, you are encouraged to seek additional information from your parents or other relatives.

1. What were the migration patterns of the group?
2. If other than Native American, under what conditions did your family (or their ancestors) enter the United States (immigrants, political refugee, slave, etc.)?
3. What were/are the group's experiences with oppression? What were/are the markers of oppression?
4. What issues divide members within the same group?
5. Describe the relationship between the group's identity and your national ancestry. (If the group is defined in terms of nationality, please skip this question.)
6. What significance does race, skin color, and hair play within the group?
7. What is/are the dominant religion(s) of the group? What role does religion and spirituality play in the everyday lives of members of the group?
8. What role does regionality and geography play in the group?

9. How are gender roles defined within the group? How is sexual orientation regarded?
10. What prejudices or stereotypes does this group have about itself? What prejudices or stereotypes do other groups have about this group? What prejudices or stereotypes does this group have about other groups?
11. What role (if any) do names play in the group? Are there rules, mores, or rituals governing the assignment of names?
12. How is social class defined in the group?
13. What occupational roles are valued and devalued by the group?
14. What is the relationship between age and values of the group?
15. How is family defined in the group?
16. How does this group view outsiders in general and educators specifically?
17. How have the organizing principles of this group shaped your family and its members? What effect have they had on you? (Organizing principles are "fundamental constructs which shape the perceptions, beliefs, and behaviors of members of the group." For example, for Jews, an organizing principle is "fear of persecution.")
18. What are the ways in which pride/shame issues of the group are manifested in your family system? (Pride/shame issues are "aspects of a culture that are sanctioned as distinctively negative or positive." For example, for Jews, a pride/shame issue is "educational achievement.")
19. What impact will these pride/shame issues have on your work with students from both similar and dissimilar cultural backgrounds?
20. If more than one group comprises your culture of origin, how are the differences negotiated in your family? What are the intergenerational consequences? How has this impacted you personally and as a teacher? (Hardy & Laszloffy, 1995, p. 232)

As a second part of this exercise and as a way of focusing more specifically on cultural content, carry on an inner dialogue while considering what you have read in this chapter. As different dimensions of culture were introduced and discussed (such as experiencing time), ask yourself where you fit on each dimension and from where in your cultural past this characteristic is likely to have derived.

Classroom: Adventures in Learning

I have developed this activity through my work with students and teachers. It began with a list from George Betts' "Autonomous Learner Model." Then, I adapted it using Howard Gardner's "Eight Intelligences" (Figure 5.2). Finally, I worked to include items that were culturally sensitive, such as "valuing silence," "learns best by watching," and "easily learns language." More importantly, over the years, I have found ways to help in-service and preservice teachers adapt this activity for their grade level.

Self Ranking in the Eight Intelligences

Circle the number that indicates your rating of your ability and/or interest in each item.

	Low				High
Visual/Spatial:					
Learns best by watching	1	2	3	4	5
Reading and using maps	1	2	3	4	5
Drawing	1	2	3	4	5
Building things	1	2	3	4	5
Bodily/Kinesthetic:					
Likes to be moving	1	2	3	4	5
Learns best by touching	1	2	3	4	5
Uses lots of body language	1	2	3	4	5
Making things by hand	1	2	3	4	5
Musical/Rhythmic:					
Listening to music	1	2	3	4	5
Singing or making music	1	2	3	4	5
Recognizing voices	1	2	3	4	5
Dancing/making rhythms	1	2	3	4	5
Verbal/Linguistic:					
Reading books	1	2	3	4	5
Telling stories or speaking	1	2	3	4	5
Writing or writing stories	1	2	3	4	5
Easily learns languages	1	2	3	4	5
Logical/Mathematical:					
Organizing things	1	2	3	4	5
Giving and following directions	1	2	3	4	5
Playing strategy games	1	2	3	4	5
Math and Problem Solving	1	2	3	4	5
Interpersonal:					
Helping others	1	2	3	4	5
Works well in groups	1	2	3	4	5
Making connections	1	2	3	4	5
Spending time with family	1	2	3	4	5
Intrapersonal:					
Valuing silence/quiet times	1	2	3	4	5
Reflecting on experiences	1	2	3	4	5
Journaling	1	2	3	4	5
Knowing own cultural identity	1	2	3	4	5
Naturalist:					
Appreciating nature	1	2	3	4	5
Prefers outdoors to in	1	2	3	4	5
Caring for pets/animals	1	2	3	4	5
Observing plant behavior	1	2	3	4	5

FIGURE 5.2 Multicultural/Multi-Intelligent Chart

Using Multicultural/Multi-Intelligent: Self-Ranking in the Eight Intelligences
First, it may be helpful to use the form, as it is as a conversation or reflection
activity in the college classroom. Numbers one to five are made on a piece of
paper (for multiple uses, laminate on large squares of poster board). Numbers
are placed around the room or on the grass/playground if used outside. Students complete the form and carry it with them.

As the facilitator, I read each item or, depending on the time, choose ones
that I believe are particularly useful to the people participating. As each item is
read, individuals move to the number that corresponds to the one they have
circled after the item. I move to the numbers with the group.

As an educator, I am able to quickly see how the group I am working with
is skewed for different items. No one thinks they can draw? Perhaps that is a
focus if I have time. A couple of students give themselves a five on drawing?
Now I know who to ask for help on bulletin boards.

As the students move from number to number, I am careful to note isolation at either one or five. If I am close to that number myself, I may fudge a
little to join the student. If I am moving around on the grid of items, I may
even see what the student on a one has for a five and call that one next. Or I
may simply move on to another number quickly to limit embarrassment.

If the item is one that we may want to address as a class and I believe no
one is highly visible due to his or her choice, I may take the time to do that
while we stand at the numbers. In a regular classroom setting, you may want
to use this activity as a break over a number of days. You may also want to collect the form after you have completed the activity as a reference list that may
influence your curriculum choices.

Adapting to Your Grade Level   The areas of adaptation are the items, the
rankings, and the visual clues.

For the lower grades, teachers have substituted pictures instead of written
items or even both to help with reading. I have seen forms that had three categories for ranking and were labeled "Not yet," "So-so," "Right on;" "This is
very hard for me," "I am okay at this," "I'm very good at this;" and my favorite:
"I'm still learning" "Fine, okay," "Great, super, terrific." Some used three smiley
faces, with a frown, a straight line, and a smile for the mouth. Some used one,
two, or three stars in each row to be circled. And a music teacher used sets of
one, two, and three connected musical notes for the rankings. Music teachers
also used items that were connected to music in all the intelligences.

For upper grades, some teachers started by having the students all write on
index cards something they were good at. Then, the teachers organized them
into intelligences and made a form just for their classes, knowing every student
would get a very good or high rating on at least one item. The form shown
here should be fine for upper graders as is.

PART II

Becoming Culturally Competent in the Classroom and Community

"Not this time. This time, we want to talk about the crumbling schools that are stealing the future of Black children and White children and Asian children and Hispanic children and Native American children. This time, we want to reject the cynicism that tells us that these children of America are not those kids, they are our kids, and we will not let them fall behind. ... Not this time."

— Barack Obama

We have so far focused on two key aspects of cultural competence—understanding racism in its various forms and understanding culture and cultural differences—and have seen how each shapes the way teachers interact with culturally different students. In many ways, the first five chapters are the more difficult steps in the journey. The underlying problems—the details of the mess we are often in—have begun to be uncovered. While there are reflections and classroom activities in the earlier chapters, in this next section, we will begin to envision larger practical solutions to some of the complexities I have raised and we have considered.

As we move into the next section of this book, we will look at facts, theories, and stories that will add strongly to your knowledge base. How do race and culture in America shape the psychological and educational experiences of Students of Color? What steps can one teacher take? We begin to look closely at classroom culture and climate as well as educators' responsibilities and abilities for adapting the curriculum and working against built-in bias in textbooks.

Introduction to Chapters 6, 7, 8, and 9

After the foundations covered in the first section of this book, we now examine how those concepts and details affect students as individuals in families and in classrooms and in schools. Chapters 6 and 7 give us underlying theories and answer questions, such as the following, that enlarge our understanding: How are human development, parenting, and family structure and dynamics affected by race and culture? What societal factors place Students of Color at special risk for stress? What types of internal problems and emotional issues are they likely to bring with them into the classroom? What is it like to be the *only* Child of Color in a classroom?

Chapters 8 and 9 focus on understanding biases in the classrooms, bilingualism, classroom management, immersion experiences, and specifics for undertaking cross-cultural teaching. The following questions are addressed: How are curriculum and textbooks inherently biased? How do these biases present barriers that lead to underachievement? Is there an achievement gap, an achievement *test score* gap or an opportunity gap? How may we center the curriculum on the students in our classrooms? Which kind of bilingual system is best for students who are learning English? Do African American students respond differently to the classroom management style taught in most teacher education programs? How effective are immersion experiences for preparing to teach cross-culturally?

The following table shows how the material we have learned in the first part of this book plays out in *instructional consequences* that we will consider in the following chapters.

Student Voices: Fellow Travelers on This Journey

- Chapter 6, "Children, Parents, and Families of Color," looks at some of the psychological issues related to child development, parenting, and family dynamics in Communities of Color. A web course student shares: "A good friend of mine who identifies as Native American/Multi-racial spoke to another class I'm in about how she has to acknowledge that she is granted some of the advantages of the people who oppressed her people because of how fair she is; her sister, however, looks more like her Native American father than her Hungarian mother and has encountered significantly different treatment throughout her life. My friend grapples with that reality—of being given those advantages and watching her sister be denied them even though they share the same heritage."

Conceptual Repertoires of Diversity

Concepts	Explanations	Teacher's Assertions	Instructional Consequences
Color-blindness (conceptions of race matter!)	Teachers avoid and reject their own and their student's racialized experiences in their decision making. Teachers see race as a taboo topic that is irrelevant and inconsequential to the success of their students. Teachers do not recognize the multiple layers of privilege associated with their race and how race can manifest in teaching, learning, and curricula experiences.	If I acknowledge the racial or ethnic background of my students or myself, then I may be considered racist. If I admit that people experience the world differently and that race is an important dimension of people's experiences, I may be seen as "politically incorrect". I may offend others in the teacher education classroom discourse if I express my beliefs and reservations about race. I should treat all my students the same regardless of who they are, what their home situations are, or what their experiences happen to be.	Teachers teach their students in a myopic manner; they do not consider how racially diverse students experience the world inside the classroom, inside the school, and in society. Curriculum and instructional decisions are grounded in a White norm that students of color just have to deal with.
Cultural conflicts (conceptions of culture matter!)	Inconsistency emerges in the teaching and learning context based on (among other factors) race, gender, geography, and socioeconomic disconnections between teachers and students. Conflicts may be historically or currently grounded and shaped.	I must teach students based on how I teach my own children, not based on their own cultural ways of knowing. I'm not going to tolerate students joking around with me or with each other during class. If they misbehave, I'm going to send them to the office—period! "Those" students need to adapt and assimilate into the culture of my classroom and accept the consequences if they do not.	Teachers refer students to the office when students of color "misbehave." Teachers refer students to special education when students are not grasping curriculum material rather than attempting to adjust their instructional practices to better meet the learning styles of the culturally diverse students. Disproportionate number of African American students are suspended and expelled.

continued

Conceptual Repertoires of Diversity *continued*

Concepts	Explanations	Teacher's Assertions	Instructional Consequences
Myth of meritocracy (conceptions of socioeconomic status matter!)	The idea that people are rewarded based (solely or mostly) on their ability, performance, effort, and talents. Systemic and institutional structures and barriers are not considered. Individual achievement is seen as an independent variable.	All groups of people were born with the same opportunities and if students or people just work hard, put forth effort, and follow the law, then (like a formula) they will be successful. My grandparents and/or great-grandparents immigrated to the United States, and they made something of their lives. There is no excuse for other groups not to succeed. If students do not succeed, it is because they are not working hard enough, not because of other factors that may be outside of their control. Some students just do not have the aptitude, ability, or skill for success; the "system" has nothing to do with academic achievement.	Teachers do not give students multiple chances for success. Teachers do not delve (more) deeply into the reasons behind student's lack of engagement or the reasons why students do not complete their homework. The reality that students' performance may be a consequence of students' economic realities is not considered in the classroom.
Deficit conceptions (mind-sets matter!)	Teachers approach their work concentrating on what students do not have rather than focusing on what	I need to distance the students of color from the "horrors" of their present cultural conditions. The students are lacking so much.	Teachers spend their time remediating students instead of building on the knowledge students actually bring into the classroom.

	students actually bring into the learning environments (their assets). Teachers have a narrow conception of what it means to be normal or successful; these views are based on their own cultural references that may be inconsistent with others.	I am being sensitive to culturally diverse students when I feel sorry for them. If I expect too much, then I am setting students up for failure. Students need teachers who try to make up for what they are lacking and not necessarily those who build on what students have because some students bring so little. It is my job to concentrate mostly on student's test scores and to close the achievement gap.	Teachers refuse to allow students to develop their own critical and analytic thinking skills. Students are expected to regurgitate a right answer that the teacher or the textbook has provided. Very little discussion and creative learning opportunities are available. Students are given busy work in hopes that the students will not talk; the classroom is viewed as the teacher's space, and students are expected to conform and to be quiet.
(Low) Expectations (optimism and efficacy matter!)	Teachers do not believe that culturally diverse students are capable of rigorous academic curriculum so they provide unchallenging learning opportunities in the classroom.	I am actually helping to build self-esteem among my students when I give them easy work that they can complete without difficulty. Those poor students cannot meet high expectations because they do not have the resources to do so. My job is to just allow students to get by and, at best, pass their standardized tests. When they accomplish this (passing of their standardized tests), my job is done.	Teachers water down the curriculum and provide only minimal curricula expectations. Teachers focus on basic skills only and push students to get a "right" answer in all academic subject matters. Students are not allowed to think outside the box, develop critical and analytic thinking skills, or question power structures in order to improve unfair, inequitable learning environments.

- Chapter 7, "Psychological and Educational Issues," provides a clearer picture of the kinds of psychological and educational issues with which culturally different students struggle and which they ultimately bring into schools. Some preservice teachers reported that culturally focused courses and an immersion program profoundly changed them. One student said my course taught her "to view life in a different light. I have come to recognize my hidden prejudices, my unearned privileges and the latent racisms that surround our society."

- Chapter 8, "Bias in the Curriculum and in the Classroom," explores various forms of bias as they play out in the educational system for Students of Color. A Latina said that "listening to the stories of White Americans who could not comprehend why it was important to discuss certain issues" startled her. Another student noticed a trend in her school: "There is a third grade class at the school I student teach at that has 8 of the 24 Latino students in the entire school. My cooperating teacher and I were discussing recently whether or not these students were purposely placed together because of race or on the reason that the classroom teacher is amazing and strives to push all students towards excellence."

- Chapter 9, "Critical Issues in Working with Culturally Diverse Students," tackles several critical and practical issues in working cross-culturally, specifically bilingualism and maintaining respectful and caring classrooms through classroom management and a safe verbal environment. There is also a section on immersion programs and experiences. One student said after leaving her immersion experience, "I miss the diversity, energy, spirit, and overall feeling of King School." Another student, in an immersion program I initiated, gained new insight into his cultural diverse placement when he went *back* to his original placement. Listen to what he says: "My students did not seem very excited to see me. I felt kind of a stranger, a person that they will need to get to know again. The kids were so quiet and subdued... . I started to cry... . It is going to be a hard adjustment for me... . I feel like I am a *new* person. I have learned that I value, respect, and need *diversity*."

CHAPTER 6

Children, Parents, and Families of Color

"How beautiful they are (yet) everywhere they turn
They are faced with abhorrence of everything that is black."

–Margaret Burroughs
From "What Shall I Tell My Children Who Are Black?"

Parents of Color face a most difficult and frustrating task: preparing their children for entry into a society that often does not truly value them. Besides suffering from psychological wounds associated with racism, Children of Color may encounter problems navigating some of the developmental tasks of childhood because of the preponderance of negative messages from the White world. Of particular concern are potential difficulties in internalizing a positive self-concept and in developing an unconflicted racial identity. Given this situation, families and schools must serve as buffer zones between Children of Color and mainstream society, protecting and nurturing them.

The structures and dynamics of Families of Color vary widely due to ethnic and cultural differences and often bear little resemblance to mainstream White families. Of special interest to educators are the biracial children whose numbers are growing rapidly and who have unique challenges adjusting to their roles in bicultural families and the larger society. Often, teachers who assume they will work with children and families similar to themselves tend not to be sensitive to these differences or prepared to teach cross-culturally.

After setting the stage with statistics on children in the United States and three scenarios, this chapter begins with a discussion of issues related to child development that particularly impact Children of Color: cultural differences in temperament at birth, the development of racial awareness and its impact on self-concept, personal identity formation in Adolescents of Color, and differences in cognitive and learning styles. Next, we turn to working with Families of Color and biracial children. Together, we will view the perspectives and unique experiences of isolated Students of Color.

The later sections of this chapter focus on questions of parenting. What unique tasks face Parents of Color regarding society and their children? How can Children of Color be prepared cognitively and emotionally for the racism they will inevitably encounter? Given the existence of racism, what child-rearing strategies and school practices are most likely to produce emotionally healthy and academically successful children? Finally, we will look at ways to encourage dialogue across differences, especially in parent/teacher interactions.

First, let us look at the reality of the demographic and experience divide in our schools. Christine Sleeter and Carl Grant have encapsulated it well:

> There is about an 85 percent chance that you, the reader, are White female. ...
> Many of you live in middle-class conditions and have never experienced poverty.
> Most of you are privileged without realizing all the options that you take for
> granted, and many of you have rarely—if ever—been in a daily situation where
> you are the minority, the only person who represents your ethnic, racial, or sexual
> orientation group. Very few of you were ever in special education. Most of you
> were educated your entire lives in your first language.
>
> The gap between your own experiences and personal identity and those of your
> students may be small, or it may be tremendous. But there is a gap, and it will continue to grow as the student population becomes more diverse. The Children's Defense Fund (1998) reports the following about children born in the United States.
>
> - 1 in 2 will live in a single-parent family at some point in childhood.
> - 1 in 5 was born poor.
> - 1 in 3 will be poor at some point in childhood.
> - 1 in 3 is behind a year or more in school.
> - 2 in 5 will never complete a single year of college.
> - 1 in 5 has a foreign-born mother.
> - 1 in 7 has no health insurance.
> - 1 in 24 lives with neither parent.
> - 1 in 60 sees his or her parents divorce in any year.
> - 1 in 1,056 will be killed by gunfire before age 20.
>
> Also, "it is estimated that 750,000 school-age children live in shelters, cars, parks,
> abandoned building door stoops, or with other families" (West, 2001, p. 1). For
> those students, "it means growing up with a future dimmed by an 'abundance of
> nothing'" (Grant & Sleeter, 2009, pp. 1–2).

Three Scenarios

The following three scenarios, drawn from real-life situations, highlight the kinds of differences, demands, and dilemmas that characterize ethnic families. Most striking is the complexity of the dynamics that impact these children, parents, and families to which they must respond and adapt. More often than not, forces in the broader environment impact them in negative ways, requiring creative intervention or accommodation for the child or family system to follow a healthy developmental course. Frequently, this involves drawing on the strengths and unique attributes of the family's cultural norms.

Scenario 1. An interracial couple came to a counselor to talk about marital problems. The Chinese-American husband and Irish-American wife disagreed bitterly about his mother's role in their lives. He said that it was normal in his culture for the mother of the family to give advice and guidance to the daughter-in-law and that, even though the advice might at times be a little "heavy-handed," it was done out of love and caring. He further believed that his wife should be more tolerant out of respect for his culture. She, in turn, responded that she had spent the last ten years trying to recover from an abusive home situation and refused to subject herself to further abuse from the mother-in-law, no matter how pure her intentions or how normal such behavior might be in Chinese culture. "I married you, not your family, and don't feel it is fair or very loving to ask me to continue to subject myself to your mother's intrusive and abusive ways." The husband just lowered his eyes, as if embarrassed by what his wife was saying.

Scenario 2. From the book *Race in the Schoolyard: Negotiating the Color Line in Classrooms and Communities,* Lewis shares the following story from her long engagement with Students of Color in the schools:

> One day in the yard I witnessed a conversation between Rodney, an African American fourth-grader, and two of his former teachers, Ms. Sullivan and Ms. Hill. Ms. Sullivan had been explaining to me her efforts to get her students to think about their futures and what they wanted to do with their lives. She stopped Rodney, a student in her class the previous year, and asked him what he wanted to do. He said he wanted to go to college but first he had to go to prison. When Ms. Sullivan looked horrified and asked him what he was talking about, he spelled it out for her: "All black men go to prison." He thought it would be more efficient to get his prison term out of the way before he went to college rather than having to do it afterward. He was impervious to both teachers' efforts to convince him that it was not true. (2003, p. 54)

Scenario 3. This case study gives a twist on isolated Students of Color:

> Jessica, a 22-year-old Mexican American from central Illinois, left home to attend college in California. A few weeks into the semester she began to notice that the majority of the Hispanic students were able to speak both English and Spanish fluently. Although her parents spoke Spanish and at home, they did not insist that their children become bilingual, so Jessica could understand Spanish if someone spoke to her, but she was not a fluent Spanish speaker. Jessica talked to the Chicano studies professor after class, who assured her that not all Mexican Americans share the same socioeconomic experience, but that all people needed to

understand and respect the values of others. He also suggested that if this situation continues to bother Jessica, she should consider seeing a counselor. In her English class, consisting primarily of white students, Jessica felt comfortable and relaxed; however, in a Chicano studies course, she felt out of place because she did not share the experiences of other Hispanic students. (Koppelman, 2011, p. 134)

These are real-life scenarios about individuals caught in society's norms of culture, beauty, traditions, and expectations. Let us explore how these values impinge on the development of children and families with different norms and challenges.

Child Development

Temperament at Birth

The characteristics and development of children from different ethnic groups vary greatly from birth. For example, it is easy to discern dramatic differences in temperament and activity levels of newborns and infants. White babies of European background cry more easily and are harder to console than Chinese babies, who tend to adapt to any position in which they are placed. Navajo babies show even more calmness and adaptability than the Chinese babies. They accept being placed on a cradleboard, while White babies cry and struggle to get out of the strapped confinement. Japanese children, in turn, are far more irritable than either the Chinese or Navajo children. Australian aboriginal babies react strongly, like Whites, to being disturbed but are more easily calmed (Freedman, 1979).

Differences are also found in the ways mothers and infants interact (Seifer, Sameroff, Barrett & Krafchuk, 1994). There is far less verbal interaction between a Navajo mother and baby than between a White mother and baby. The Navajo mother is rather silent and gets her baby's attention via eye contact. White mothers talk to their children constantly, and their children respond with great activity. However, these mothers are equally adept at gaining their children's attention. The differences result from the continual interplay of genetic predispositions and patterns of cultural conditioning through early child/parent interaction. Children's genetic temperamental tendencies are reinforced by cultural learning about the proper way to respond emotionally, and the result is children who increasingly take on the temperamental style of their culture. These early temperamental differences continue to be evident and influential as the children enter school and begin to interact with teachers and peers.

Development of Racial Awareness

Children are aware of differences in skin color and facial and body features in the early months of their lives (*Newsweek*, 2009), and by the time a child is four, it is possible to begin to discern the rudiments of racial awareness. Majority-group children are generally slower to develop a consciousness of being White because race is not as central to their families' lives as it is to the lives of People of Color. Racial identity develops in relation to the sequential acquisition of three learning processes. The first is *racial classification* ability and involves learning to accurately apply ethnic labels to members of different groups.

For example, in the classic doll studies designed by Clark and Clark (1947) to measure racial identity in African American children, the child is asked to "Show me the Black doll" or "Show me the White doll" when presented with dolls of varying skin tones. The child who can accurately perform such labeling on a regular basis is ready to move on to the next stage of forming a *racial identification* (Aboud & Doyle, 1993). This study was recently replicated by a young student and is available for viewing (see Chapter 2 and Companion Website; Edney, 2006). Racial identification involves children's learning to apply the newly gained concept of race to themselves. This process requires a kind of inner dialogue through which children learn that because of their own skin color, they are members of a certain group (the child is black or yellow or brown) and, as such, visibly different from others (Proshansky & Newton, 1968). Racial identification results from an interaction between children's comparisons of their own skin color with those of parents, siblings, and others and what they are told or discern about who they are racially. The final stage, called *racial evaluation* (Proshansky & Newton, 1968), is the creation of an internal evaluation of the child's own ethnicity. This involves how children come to feel about being black or yellow or brown. Racial evaluation develops as children internalize the various messages regarding their own ethnicity received from significant others and society in general. By age seven, most ethnic children are aware of the negative evaluation that society places on members of their group (Thornton, Chatters, Taylor & Allen, 1990).

By the time children enter kindergarten, these processes are well under way. At this point of development, children may already show racial preferences in their choice of play and learning partners (Copenhaver-Johnson, 2006). And one does periodically see children who have already been socialized within their families to avoid children of a certain skin color.

Racial Awareness and Self-Esteem

Early studies of racial awareness found that Black children had difficulty successfully completing the last two stages (Clark & Clark, 1947; Goodman, 1952). These children would deny the fact that their skin was dark, devalue people with dark skin and Black culture in general, or do both. In addition, these same Black children often exhibited conflicted self-concepts. During those years, these researchers concluded that such outcomes were almost inevitable for Children of Color. Living in a White-dominated society, they could not help but internalize the negative attitudes and messages that bombarded them daily, and the resulting negative self-judgments often translated into a diminished self-image.

As the ethnic pride movements, such as "Black Is Beautiful," of the 1960s gained momentum, the likelihood of such conclusions was successfully challenged. Some referred to this early work as the "myth of self-hatred" (Trawick-Smith & Lisi, 1994). Earlier studies were criticized as being methodologically weak or as reflecting an earlier psychological reality that was no longer accurate. Later studies showed no differences in the self-esteem of Black and White children (Powell, 1973; Rosenberg, 1979). In fact, in racially homogeneous settings, Black children often scored higher on self-esteem than their White counterparts (Spenser & Markstrom-Adams, 1990). The more extensive their interaction with Whites and the White world, however, the lower their self-concept scores. The accuracy of these findings was often challenged in turn as too conveniently fitting the researchers' political agendas.

Doll studies with both Black and White children show that preferences for skin color vary by race over time. African American preschoolers were more likely to choose White dolls and choices, which could be interpreted as indicating some early identity confusion as suggested in the pre-1960s studies discussed. By third grade, African American children were appropriately aware of their racial identity, accepted it, and often choose playmates from their own group. However, regarding racial evaluation, there do seem to be lingering pro-White attitudes among Black youth until junior high school, when there is a dramatic reversal to predominantly pro-Black responses. From these data, it seems likely that African American children to some extent internalize the attitudes of society at large. But it is not clear whether their pro-White preferences can be interpreted as indicative of negative feelings about themselves or their group. In any case, the effects are not lasting, and there is little concurrent difficulty in racial identification. It is probably fair to say that this is a critical period in the developmental life of Children of Color and may be potentially problematic for the development of self-esteem as long as pro-White attitudes linger (Williams & Morland, 1976; Spenser & Markstrom-Adams, 1990).

The Usefulness of a Dual Perspective

Critics of the earlier studies on self-esteem argued for the usefulness of a dual perspective in resolving this question: They believed that the messages sent by the child's immediate environment (which consists of home, community, and significant others) rather than those sent by the broader society can be internalized and, therefore, become the basis for self-esteem. Earlier researchers had assumed that society's negative views and stereotypes were directly reflected onto the child and internalized into the sense of self. It is useful to differentiate the child's immediate environment from that of society in general. For Whites, there is little difference between the two kinds of messages.

The situation is very different for People of Color; the two systems send very different and conflicting messages. This is being changed by the election of an African American president, as some recent studies have indicated an impact on self-esteem (Dillon, 2009). Still, the more immediate interpersonal world of the child is most critical in the development of healthy self-esteem; the family can act as a buffer between the child and the broader society and become the primary sculptor of feelings about self. A number of questions that yet need to be answered: "What happens in the interaction between Black parents and their children in those stable nurturing families from any educational or socioeconomic level who manage to rear children with a strong sense of self? How and with what patterns do these families defy the 'mark of oppression'? How can we determine the strengths and healthy coping mechanisms in the interaction between black parents and their children?" (Norton, 1983, p. 188).

Whether or not Children of Color regularly exhibit positive self-esteem and unconflicted racial identities, racism poses a risk for the developing child. Active measures should be taken to protect them, whether through creating a buffer zone around the child (Norton, 1983) or creating ethnic pride to psychologically insulate the child from the experience of racism (McAdoo, 1985).

It should be obvious by now that issues of skin color and racial identity are very powerful forces within families. Teachers should realize that balance is needed when such dynamics come into play. Teachers need strive to neither overlook or overreact to issues. Consider the following two stories. One biracial child reported long after the fact that he was referred to by the "n-word" every single school day for many months. It became clear only in retrospect that this racial slur had become a nickname used by some of his classmates, who would call this epithet across the playground to get his attention. His parents did not know the details of this labeling and believed it was only occasional. One has to ask where teachers and administrators were during this long scenario.

On the other end of the continuum, an African American mother became quite concerned when her biracial child said she hated "Suzy," the only other Black child in the classroom. After further investigation and discussions with the teacher, however, the mother discovered that it was a personality conflict (Suzy was not popular with any of the children) rather than a matter of race.

A final perspective on the impact of racism on self-esteem can be gleaned from interviews with People of Color who came to the United States as adults after growing up in countries where they were in the racial majority (Diller,

1997). Only after they arrived in this country did they have their first personal experiences with prejudice and racism. How did they respond? Their first reported reaction was shock and disbelief. However, once they had sufficient time to process what had happened and to label it as a racial attack, they were able to put up sufficient ego defenses to protect themselves emotionally as well as physically. They quickly learned to identify such situations before or as they happened and to deal with them quickly and effectively. They uniformly believed that it was only because of their own strong sense of self and well-developed ego defenses that they were able to come out of these experiences relatively unharmed. When asked how they might have felt as children facing such experiences, they indicated that they would have been overwhelmed and likely scarred in some essential way.

Formation of Adolescent Identity

Another potential area of difficulty for Children of Color involves the formation of personal identity (that is, a stable and positive sense of who one is) in adolescence. Adolescence is a time of self-exploration during which the young person tries to find a comfortable synthesis of past experiences, sense of family, present questions and concerns, and hopes and plans for the future. In a study comparing lower-class urban African American and European American adolescent boys, Hauser and Kasendorf (1983) found very different patterns of identity formation in the two groups. The African American adolescents formed a stable integration of self-image much earlier than did their European American counterparts, who seemed to experience a lot more confusion, disequilibrium, and personal exploration. In fact, it took the European American youth all four years of high school to reach the same level of identity stability achieved by the African American youth after one or two years.

At the same time, African American adolescents showed a striking sameness in how they saw themselves compared to European Americans, who showed much greater variability and flexibility in content. According to one model of adolescent identity development, the European Americans were experiencing slow but steady movement toward a coherent definition of self with extensive confusion and time out for exploration. On the other hand, the African American adolescents were seen as stabilizing their identities very early, with a premature closing off of possibilities in terms of content (Erikson, 1968).

For the African American youth, images of themselves as future parents were equally fixed and rigid, especially if the father had been absent from the home. Fathers were sometimes disparaged figures who foreshadowed what they themselves would be as fathers, and on this basis, there was little hope for being any different. In some cases, early foreclosure seemed a natural consequence (Hauser & Kasendorf, 1983).

Similarly, their image of the future was rigid and established early, connoting little hope for what was to be. Images of the past self showed great discontinuity, reflecting some discomfort and shame over the historical past (slavery and exploitation), instability in families (not knowing one parent's background), and even a kind of racial self-hatred (although there was no desire to be White). Finally, similar negative patterns were evident in relation to the kinds of fantasies they reported: lacking hope for their futures, especially in relation to what they could accomplish and become, the work available to them, and the role models they could emulate.

Although times have changed, particularly with the role models of Obama and others, and many populations have significantly improved their financial and social situations, the study still points to the difficulties that can exist for Children of Color growing up in a racist environment that dramatically limits what they can do and become. The data also show the great capacity for coping found in these Black males, for their everyday lives showed little evidence of the negativity and hopelessness that one might have predicted. In fact, their self-images differed little from those of their White counterparts. Finally, it should be acknowledged that cultural differences may be related to these findings. Erikson's model is clearly European and reflects a view of adolescence (and what should be happening during this period) that may not be accurate or appropriate for a different cultural group. Some anthropologists have even suggested that the prolonged period of confusion and moratorium that typifies European American adolescence is a symptom of the loss of much-needed rites of passage, which in many other cultures create a clear sense of direction and identity for the young person.

Families of Color

The key to understanding and working with Families of Color is an appreciation of their diversity, especially in relation to mainstream White families. First of all, their form varies from culture to culture. Each culture has "differing ways of understanding 'appropriate' family organization, values, communication and behavior" (Gushue & Sciarra, 1995, p. 588). For example, Mexican American families tend to be hierarchical and male-dominated, religious, traditionally sex typed, and often bilingual, with deep extended family roots. But to push such generalizations too far is to enter into the realm of stereotyping.

No two families are ever culturally identical. Each internalizes in its own way aspects of the cultural norms of the group. Some aspects become very important; others are disregarded. Cultural considerations and family cultural choices are starting points for understanding a given family. There are a variety of other factors that impact the way ethnic patterns surface in families:

Included here are acculturation, class, education, ethnic identity, reason for migration to the United States, language status, geographic location, and stage in the family life cycle at the time of migration.

Cultural differences in family structure should not be interpreted as cultural deficits. The Moynihan Report (1965) on the status of the Black family, also referred to as "the myth of the Black matriarchy," is an excellent case in point. The report, which had great impact on public welfare policy in the 1960s and 1970s, implied that the strong influence of the mother in African American families was an aberration caused by racism. It further implied that in more equitable times, the African American family structure would return to a more patriarchal form. Critics argued that the existence of strong women in the African American family is instead a cultural artifact that reflects greater role equality and flexibility of men and women than is true in European American families. They further pointed to strong women as an example of the creative and adaptive strategies and strengths that emerged out of the African American family to deal with a hostile social environment. The critical conceptual difference here is seeing this phenomenon as a creative adaptation of a traditional African American cultural form and as a strength rather than as a deficit.

Bicultural Families

There are two kinds of bicultural families: families in which the parents come from two different cultures and families in which parents from the same culture have adopted a child from another culture. Bicultural families and children are definitely on the increase. In 2010, an estimated 1.6 million interracially married couples inhabit the United States, an increase of about 900 percent since 1965 when I entered an interracial marriage. Before 1967, seventeen states had miscegenation laws against interracial marriages of some type. Although still a small percentage of all couples in the United States (2.6 percent in 2000), interracial couples are becoming more common.

According to government statistics, approximately one million children— or 3 percent of the population—born between 1970 and 1990 were of mixed race. This was probably a substantial underestimate because there was no formal category for counting such individuals in the 1990 U.S. census. The 2000 U.S. census—the first to inquire about multiracial backgrounds—found that 6.8 million people, or 2.4 percent of the population, identified as multiracial. However, in spite of these increasing numbers, there are still a number of myths and distorted beliefs about bicultural children.

Here are three of the most prevalent myths: (1) bicultural children turn out to be tragic and marginal individuals; (2) each must choose an identity with only one group; and (3) they are very uncomfortable discussing their ethnic identity (Kerwin & Ponterotto, 1995). Each myth is far from the truth; in fact, some recent evidence indicates that children of mixed racial heritage may be more stable than other children (Cloud, 2009). Bicultural children are quite capable of developing healthy ethnic identities and finding a stable social place for themselves. Contrary to having to choose membership in one group over the other, healthy identity development involves integrating both cultural backgrounds into a single sense of self that is a blend of both and yet uniquely different from either. Bicultural children welcome the opportunity to discuss and explore who they are ethnically. Such myths are likely created and sustained by individuals who are uncomfortable with the idea of intercultural relationships and who project their own discomfort onto the children. As a longtime member of an interracial marriage, I remember well my own family's concerns in this area.

Bicultural Couples

Extensive interviews with African American and European American bicultural couples and their children found personal attraction rather than race as their reason for involvement with their spouses (Jacobs, 1977). None of the fourteen spouses reported feeling any guilt over their relationships. Spouses seemed well-differentiated from each other and, because of this, were able to allow their children to separate and become their own selves. The parents *did* report that it seemed easier to give their children more autonomy because the children were not exactly like either of the parents (Jacobs, 1977). Perhaps this underlies stability among biracial children (Cloud, 2009).

The couples studied had varying degrees of rejection of the marriage from their own parents. Spouses reported an interesting sequence of reactions to parental rejection, which again attests to the basic maturity and emotional health of the partners in Jacobs's sample. After initial anger lasting anywhere from several months to a number of years, they were able to develop empathy and understanding for the rejecting parent and continued to attempt to re-establish contact and attachment.

Bicultural couples reported frequent focus on issues of race and ethnicity. Intimate interaction with someone who is culturally different cannot help but elicit racial material from both partners. Discussed honestly and worked through, such issues strengthen the marriage. In effect, what exists is a microcosm of race relations, with numerous opportunities to explore cross-cultural problems. Interracial couples were often much freer to discuss topics of race and ethnicity than were either Black or White monocultural couples (Jacobs, 1977).

Bicultural couples also tend to be rather isolated as a unit, often experiencing social rejection and preferring social contact with other bicultural couples who can more easily understand what they face. In reaction, they often develop patterns of strong interdependence, which may to lead to an unwillingness to acknowledge problems or seek help. On the other hand, such couples may try harder to resolve conflict on their own. At the same time, isolation and mutual dependence may make the airing of problems a particular threat.

Bicultural couples face an added challenge that monocultural couples do not. Not only must they deal with their own individual differences and conflicts, but they also need to navigate through the often complex and difficult terrain of cultural differences. Interfaith couples—for example, Jewish and Christian—must agree on shared practices and their children's religious education. Or bicultural couples may find that they have very different styles, values, priorities, or expectations that are cultural in origin. For example, Europeans become quiet and distant during interpersonal conflicts and tend to move away from their partners, while individuals from other cultures tend to become more verbal and emotional and move toward their partners in an effort to resolve conflicts (Orbé, 2004). Learning to accommodate differences in style helps bicultural couples resolve problems.

Cross-cultural marriages demand from each partner a certain kind of cultural transition. The couple must "arrive at an adaptive and flexible view of cultural differences that makes it possible to maintain some individuated values, to negotiate conflictual areas, and even to develop a new cultural code that integrates parts of both cultural streams" (Falicov, 1986, p. 431).

There are three common patterns of cultural tension in interracial marriages (Falicov, 1986). The first pattern is conflicts in *cultural code.* This involves cultural differences in how marriages are conceived and structured. Particularly important are differences in rules related to the inclusion and exclusion of others (especially extended family members) and the relative power and authority of spouses. In the hope of mutually adapting to each other's style, partners often minimize or maximize cultural differences. In either case, limited knowledge of the other's culture leads to a necessary developmental task for the marriage: negotiating a new cultural code that implies the melding of their different ways. Sometimes, this limited knowledge of cultural differences may be "mistaken for negative personality traits" of the other (Falicov, 1986, p. 431).

The second type of problem deals with cultural differences and permission to marry. Problems related to parental disapproval of the relationship and cultural artifacts, such as trends toward *enmeshment,* make separating from the family of origin a difficult task. Two patterns of adaptation in couples who had not received emotional permission to marry emerge. In the first, partners

maximize their differences and do not blend, integrate, or negotiate their values and life styles. They lead parallel lives, each holding on to their culture and/or family of origin. Often, the counterpoint of the marital distance is an excessive involvement of one or both parties with the family of origin. There may also be unresolved longings for the past ethnic or religious affiliations, even if these were of little importance previously. (Falicov, 1986, p. 440)

These types of problems have implications for the children pulled between families and caught in the tension this produces. The second pattern involves minimizing and even denying the differences, including possibly joining a third and alternative culture or cutting ties with culture and family. Such couples may develop an attitude of "us against them" (meaning the world) or "we only have each other." The third problem area in cross-cultural marriages is "cultural stereotyping and severe stress" (Falicov, 1986, p. 440). Some impending stress (such as the death of a parent) initiates the maximizing of cultural differences as well as increased cultural stereotyping of each other. Children in families reacting to stress in this manner may need extra help negotiating the stronger pull of conflicting cultures during this time. Teachers alerted to impending stress within bicultural families may need to be prepared to offer more than the usual care and empathy for such children. These three patterns of cultural tension within marriage may exacerbate the kind of unique developmental tasks that bicultural child must navigate.

Bicultural Children

ONLOOKER: "That baby looks half and half."

BABY'S THOUGHTS: "That's me: half mommy and half daddy."

Biracial children are one of the fastest growing populations in the United States, currently about 4 percent of the children in our schools (Baxley, 2008). This number will increase as 1 in 7 newlywed couples are interracial (Marcus, 2010). Although monoethnic children may eventually face the realities of a hostile social environment, bicultural children must additionally come to grips with their parents' racial drama and the perpetually repeated question, "What are you?" The interracial child represents not only the parents' racial differences but also a unique individual who must work through very personal identity issues. In many ways, the racial-identity process parallels that of monoethnic children but with the added task of simultaneously exploring two (or more) rather than a single ethnic heritage and then integrating them into a unique identity. Perhaps the most salient point to remember in teaching biracial and multiracial children is that, psychologically, they are not merely reflections of their two or more sides but rather unique integrations of them.

On average, biracial children develop awareness of race and racial differences earlier than monoethnic children (Moule, 2010). This is because they are exposed to such differences from birth in the confines of their own family. It is also likely that their parents are more attuned to these differences because of their own interracial relationship. Upon entry into school, biracial children are immediately confronted with questions that serve as major stimuli for their internal processing of "What are you?" Concurrently, they begin to experiment with labels for themselves. Children may create descriptions based on perceptions of their skin color (such as *coffee and cream*) or adopt parental terms (such as *interracial*).

Biracial children have five possible options for biracial identity:

1. Accept the racial identity given by society;
2. Identity with one of the parents (perhaps a Parent of Color);
3. Identity as White, especially if the individual physical features allow;
4. Identity as biracial (no individual race identified);
5. Identify with more than one race. (Root, 1996)

Any of these choices can be positive if the choice is freely made and the individual does not feel marginalized by the choice. Biracial children also have the right to identify differently in different situations, differently than brothers and sisters, and most importantly, differently than strangers expect them to identify (Root, 2004).

Generally, biracial children are more successful moving through the identity formation process when race is openly discussed at home and parents are available to help them sort out the various issues of self-definition. Rate of development also depends on the amount of integration in their classrooms and the availability in school of role models from their two cultural sides. During pre-adolescence, children begin to regularly use racial or cultural as opposed to physical descriptions of themselves. They become increasingly aware of group differences other than skin color (physical appearance, language, and so on) and of the fact that their parents belong to distinct ethnic groups. Exposure to racial incidents and first-time entry into either integrated or segregated school settings also accelerate learning.

Adolescence is particularly problematic for bicultural children. It is a time of marked intolerance for differences. There are likely to be strong pressures on bicultural adolescents to identify with one parent's ethnicity over the other—usually with the Parent of Color if one of the parents is White. The pressure of racial identity for biracial children is influenced by the race of each parent. For example, racially speaking, who is Obama (see Figure 6.1)?

Peers of Color may push the adolescent to identify with them, and Whites may perceive and treat the bicultural adolescent as a Person of Color. Identification with one ethnic side and the simultaneous rejection of the other and then identification with the other ethnic side is a natural part of identity formation in bicultural youth (Jacobs, 1977; Moule, 2010). Perhaps only by internalizing one aspect of the self at a time and vacillating between the two over the duration of adolescence and young adulthood can both identities be integrated. Dating begins in adolescence, which accentuates race as a central

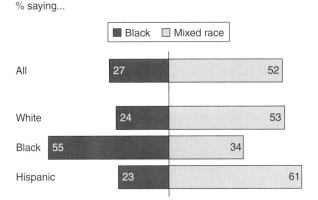

FIGURE 6.1 Do You Think of Obama as Black or Mixed Race?

Source: Pew Research Center, *A Year After Obama's Election: Blacks Upbeat about Black Progress, Prospects,* http://pewresearch.org/pubs/1459/year-after-obama-election-black-public-opinion, Copyright © 2010 Pew Research Center.

life issue. It is not unusual for biracial youth to experience rejection because of their color or ethnicity, and such experiences are likely to have a great impact on their emerging sense of identity (Tatum, 2003).

Biracial women have a particularly difficult task meshing their body images with the differences in physical appearance of their two parents. Young Black women often opt out of the mainstream society's "beauty contest." They find themselves so far from White America's standard of beauty that they sometimes do not even try to emulate that image and, as a result, may in fact pursue a healthier, more realistic self-image. Biracial women can also be torn between ideal mainstream images as portrayed in the media and identification with body image type of a Mother of Color. The heightened sexuality of adolescence also stimulates such questions as, "What will the baby look like?" if one becomes pregnant or makes someone pregnant.

Interactions between bicultural children and their parents are at times complex and conflicted. As children mature and become more aware, they are increasingly confronted with and confused by being different. They may struggle to make sense out of how the world is reacting to them. Bicultural parents often have a more difficult time understanding what their children are going through. At the root of this misunderstanding is a parent's tendency to see the child as a personal extension rather than as a blend of the couple. The parents' growing realization that the child is really not like either parent but something beyond both can rouse anxiety in both parents and child, and this very same factor may result in the earlier mentioned independence and strong self-image (Cloud, 2009).

Adopted Children

Intercultural adoption is a second source of bicultural families. Some people in Communities of Color, especially African Americans and Native Americans, have taken strong stances against adoption and foster care across racial lines. Their feeling is that European Americans are not capable of providing ethnic children with adequate exposure and connection with their cultures of birth or of training the children in how to deal with the racism they will inevitably experience. Serious efforts have been made to sensitize and train adoptive parents in cultural competence as well as to encourage them to keep their children connected to the ethnic community of origin. There are sincere questions about whether such efforts can overcome the cultural gaps—such as something as simple as styling hair—let alone a racially hostile social environment. White adoptive parents seldom understand the enormity of difficulties that their children face as People of Color. In addition, they often unconsciously deny differences between themselves and their children.

This puts children in a difficult psychological position. They may feel isolated in dealing with the very complex issues of race and ethnicity. Often, there is a sense of disconnectedness caused by the gulf between how they are treated in the world and at home. Finally, adopted Children of Color can feel confused when their adoptive parents simultaneously represent nurturance and emotional support on one side and oppression of some kind on the other.

Isolated Students of Color

Whether through individual choice, job relocation, accident of birth, or adoption, isolation of individuals from their ethnic and racial communities causes particular challenges. Isolated Children of Color experience greater pressures to assimilate, face more stereotyping, are more visible, and are more vulnerable to institutional racism. They often lack the support of the broader community and have less protection as well as more exposure to conscious and unconscious biases and racism.

An acquaintance told the following story about a simple, although often experienced, aspect of her life as an isolated Person of Color. Anecdotes like this one abound in the literature on race (Cose, 1993; Jones, 2001; Taylor & Whittaker, 2003):

> I had an encounter Wednesday morning. I was running down the main street of our town just as it was getting light. A White man approached me going the opposite direction. As he got closer, he moved far to the edge of the sidewalk. Yet, as usual, I gave him the benefit of the doubt. I spoke in a loud, cheery voice, "Good morning." His response: Silence.

At that point, my husband pulled up to pick me up. As I got in the car, I told him about the encounter. He said, "Some people are just like that." "Yes," I said. "They are just more like that if you happen to be Black."

This simple event—which highlights not a blatant, identifiable act of racism but a minor slight, a microaggression, that may indeed simply be the result of a bad day by the silent fellow—gives us a glimpse into the very different world inhabited by People of Color who find themselves surrounded primarily by White folks. The story continued:

> I find myself not as friendly as I'd like to be. I find I do not look into cars as much as other people. I do not even want to face the rejection, even if it is one in one hundred. This is a daily fact of life for me. I find my general, easy-to-please self becoming less friendly and, recently, less willing to overlook the often obvious.
>
> My husband noted a similar reluctance my African American acquaintances have in coming to my house in a predominantly European American rural setting. They want very clear directions. Their spouses call with much concern to check if "they made it OK."

Taking with us the understanding that such everyday slights and burdens occur along with more blatant racism, let us look at what happens to isolated Students of Color in the schools. The pull between the culture of the Community of Color and mainstream White culture asserts itself more powerfully on isolated Individuals of Color than on children who reside in a majority minority community. The pressure to assimilate is also greater on isolated individuals without a community to which to attach. Various authors (Delpit, 2006; Moule, 1998, Tatum, 1992a; Taylor & Whittaker, 2003) have used case studies of isolated Students of Color to highlight their particular problems. Paley (1979), in her classic book *White Teacher*, described the occasional Black students who found their way into her classroom: "One the child of the live-in maid of a prominent family, two others when the school board attempted some minor integration" (p. 7). Encounters with these children caused Paley concern. One avoided looking at her and responded to her questions with only a "Yes'm." Another, Fred, joined an aggressive group of six White children. When the teachers came into Paley's room under various pretenses to, as Paley said, "check out the two black children," they all singled out Fred. "You've got your hands full with him. Shouldn't he be in a special class?" (p. 7).

Paley's story highlights a particular burden for the isolated Child of Color—higher visibility. This higher visibility may lead to increased pressure to assimilate or to an increased tendency to exhibit or be reproofed for behavior problems (Bireda, 2002; Ogbu, 1992; Tatum, 2003). Delpit used Paley's work as a good example: "At the first faculty meeting Paley raised the issue that even though all the children in Fred's small group behaved as he did, teachers singled out Fred because of his color. After vigorous discussion, the faculty reached a consensus: 'More than ever we must take care to ignore color. We must only look at behavior, and since a black child will be more prominent in a White classroom, we must bend over backward to see no color, hear no color, speak no color'" (Delpit, 1995, p. 177).

This "color-blind" attitude probably did more harm than good. It allowed the teachers to continue to pretend that race didn't matter in the curriculum, in classroom images, and so on. Teachers in communities with only a few isolated Children of Color tend to experience their schools as monoracial. They seem unwilling to acknowledge the existence of current or increasing demographic diversity of their communities. Such reactions cannot help but make Children of Color feel invisible as well as highly visible, certainly a confusing state for young children.

In her study *Talking to Children About Race: The Importance of Inviting Difficult Conversations* (2006), Copenhaver-Johnson clearly illustrates a disconnect between what is taught—racial harmony and civil rights—with what is observed on the playground and lunchroom—racial tensions that often lead to isolating Children of Color. She finds that White teachers have a hard time talking between themselves or with their students about race. The process of silencing begins early: "White children's reluctance to discuss race and racism can be considered symptomatic of their socialization into color-blindness" (p. 16).

Isolated Children of Color also come under more intense pressure from institutionalized racism. Anderson (1988) was specific about the effects of the system on the children within it:

> In America, as White children leave the home and move on through the educational system and then into the work world, the development of cognitive and learning styles follows a linear, self-reinforcing course. Never are they asked to be bicultural, bidialectic, or bicognitive. On the other hand, for children of Color, biculturality is not a free choice, but a prerequisite for successful participation and eventual success. Non-White children generally are expected to be bicultural, bidialectic, bicognitive; to measure their performance against a Euro-American yardstick; and to maintain the psychic energy to maintain this orientation. At the same time, they are being castigated whenever they attempt to express and validate their indigenous cultural and cognitive styles. Under such conditions cognitive conflict becomes the norm rather than the exception. (p. 5)

We see these dynamics acted out in the experiences of Chris and Nicole, both biracial.

Chris

At home, the "Mom unit," as Chris affectionately calls his mother, has brought the detailed eye of her training as an engineer to matters of child-rearing and homemaking. She surrounds her biracial children with sights and sounds of their African heritage and promotes citywide events for families with children similar in color to her children. The family's frequent vacations are varied and reflect the family's high income. Chris is a typical isolated Child of Color within a community in which individuals from underrepresented groups have been heavily recruited by private companies and the university. While his socioeconomic status, home life, and parental expectations will be advantageous in his education, only time will tell how Chris's experience as an isolated Student of Color will affect his life.

The public school Chris attends is one percent African American. An African American intern teacher there observed several race-related problems, although the teachers he interviewed said that there were none. Perhaps the European American teachers had not noticed when one boy asked another to pick up a dropped ball. "What color do you think I am?" was the disdainful response. Or perhaps only the African American intern or a student whose color had been the oblique object of the reference would even have caught the racial slur in the offensive response.

What does Chris experience? Does the lens of his racial heritage reveal incidents that his European-American teachers miss—perhaps quite innocently? Is race ignored or, worse, is he asked to be a token who guides the teacher through events such as Martin Luther King Jr. Day? Does he encounter the teacher who planned to avoid racial offenses by sidestepping any mention of racial differences? Does his presence embarrass a well-meaning teacher who pretends not to hear direct student questions about racial or cultural issues? Whatever his experience, he almost certainly is learning to see the world through a double lens. He is learning to view events and interactions through the eyes of the dominant culture he is a part of, and he is also learning to view the world through the eyes of an African American, partially because others see him as different. With support from his parents, he is coming to see his multiple perspective as the positive benefit that it is. Without this support and understanding, he would be unlikely to reach his full potential as an individual and a citizen (Moule, 1998, pp. 4–6).

Nicole

Next, we meet Nicole, an isolated Student of Color in a school district that is 89 percent White, as seen by a student teacher.

> "A girl in my class … is the only Person of Color in our entire class and … she has a challenge other students don't. [She] looks for books with Black protagonists and she reads those … not as many as [with] White protagonists. One of the things we talked about [was] rules for the class. [We] brainstormed … she threw out 'Don't call Black people Indians.' People at her table group laughed at the time. So I approached them and asked her to repeat it. We decided that 'Treat

other people with respect' incorporates it. She is swimming up stream. A question I've had, what am I going to do as a teacher in school ... potentially mostly White students with a few Students of Color? What am I going to do to prepare kids to live in [this state] and be a positive influence ... with numbers becoming more diverse?

Nicole is a proud and capable artist and writer, and it is in these areas that she usually shines in the classroom—when she reads aloud or when she shows her artwork. Generally she is shy. She does not bring up racial issues in her writing, and I haven't seen her color the people she has drawn to indicate any skin color. Her mother is Black and her father is White, and she doesn't mention that in any discussions about her parents. Because of her own hesitancy to talk about race or racial issues, I have always talked generally about multicultural issues or topics, taking care not to spotlight her. I think it would make her extremely uncomfortable. ... I believe that we haven't done any damage this year to Nicole or the other students by just talking in generalities."

In this same classroom the children were rehearsing an African dance for the school awards ceremony. The mentor teacher directed a question to Nicole, asking her if she knew the tribe or culture in Africa that the dance came from. Nicole did not answer. There was no apparent reason why Nicole would know the culture in Africa the dance came from, except for the teacher's assumption that her brown skin gave her this specialized knowledge. Shortly after her silence and the unanswered question, the mentor teacher suggested that they practice the song and dance. Nicole did not join in. In the busy life of the classroom, only an observer watching one particular child was aware of a very subtle, yet seemingly disturbing event for an isolated Child of Color.

(Adapted from *My Journey with Preservice Teachers: Reflecting on Teacher Characteristics That Bridge Multicultural Education Theory and Classroom Practice* by Jean Moule, 1998, pp. 148–149. Reprinted by permission.)

The White student teacher learned some very important lessons from being in the classroom with Nicole. First, he learned how little he knew about the lives and experiences of Children of Color, especially those who are isolated in predominantly White communities. Second, he learned the value of active observation, especially when it comes to matters of race. For example, he recognized the student's hesitancy to discuss race. In time, he came to see the importance of making time for the discussion of race relations in the classroom and how such discussion works against the unstated taboo that exists in most school environments. Third, he learned the importance of self-reflection and the need to look at his own feelings and experiences in relation to what was happening to Nicole.

Finally—and perhaps most importantly—this student teacher allowed himself to remain open to the humanity of one small Child of Color. We see this particularly in relation to the teacher's question about African dances. bell hooks (1994) refers to what happened to Nicole as becoming a native informant, writing that "one lone person of color in the classroom ... is objectified by others and forced to assume the role of 'native informant'" (p. 43). The student teacher learned that instead of forcing Nicole to be a native informant, the teacher may have more appropriately asked, "Does anyone know which people in Africa created this dance?" If Nicole or anyone else knew the answer, he or she could then have volunteered it. When teachers take the time to observe individuals and apply simple strategies, the classroom becomes a more supportive and caring learning environment for all children. As strange as it may seem, simple etiquette may help us to work well with all students, "honesty, respect and consideration—never change, regardless of the political, social or cultural landscape" (Post, 2010, p. 62)

An isolated Person of Color may have adjustments to make as he or she moves into a more integrated or a predominately Black or other group neighborhood. An African American friend shared this reflection:

> When I first moved to Portland from Moses Lake Washington, a town of slightly under 9,000, mostly White residents, back in 1989, I remember driving through the predominantly Black neighborhood for the first time. The streets were run-down and dirty. The people were walking freely through the middle of the streets with paper bags shaped like bottles or cans. Cars that passed us moved either very fast, as if running from someone, or very slow as if looking for someone, maybe me. Music was loud and so were the people. I felt very uncomfortable and felt myself sink a bit in the passenger seat of my sister's car and lock my door. At that point, my sister noticed that something was wrong with me and said, "What are you scared of? They are Black just like you." Immediately, like a light had just gone on, I felt like an idiot. At 18 years old, I had never lived in a Black community. My only frame of reference was my church experiences and BET. Twenty years later, I still live in that neighborhood and haven't locked my car doors since.

Parenting

All parents face the task of creating a safe environment in which the child may move without harm through the developmental stages of growing up. Threats to the child's health or safety—both the expected kinds and ones that are random and unpredictable—are mediated or removed by the child's parents. On top of these needs for protection among mainstream White children, Children of Color are also systematically subjected to the harmful effects of racism. Having grown up under similar conditions, Parents of Color are often aware of what awaits their children and know that there is only so much they can do to protect them. What can Parents of Color do?

First, they can create a buffer zone in which children are protected from the negative attitudes and stereotypes that abound in the broader society. Part of this process involves instilling a sense of ethnic pride. In such a safe environment, the child is more likely to develop a more positive sense of self. Help your child build confidence by teaching them about their culture, where they come from, family stories, and to respect others beliefs and traditions even if they may directly contradict your own. Second, parents can teach their children how to deal emotionally with the negative experiences of racism. For example, start to build communication early with your kids by making their school stories a priority. Do not get angry if they tell you a story in which they made a mistake. Third, parents can prepare their children cognitively for what they will encounter in the world outside the buffer zone. It is possible to help children become an increasing part of the solution. One parent says, "I teach my kids that we are not better than, but we are just as good as anyone. I think that helps breaks the cycle of oppression."

In these endeavors, schools and teachers need to partner with parents. They must work to realize the importance of creating a safe and racism-free zone. They should embrace the necessity of preparing children both emotionally and cognitively for racism and focus on incorporating this as part of the curriculum. Above all, they must recognize the destructiveness of racism, both intentional and unintentional, to young psyches and realize that much harm may already have occurred as evidenced in the doll studies (Edney, 2006). "It often will not be enough just to listen; one might have to work to create an environment in which a silenced voice feels the confidence or security to speak" (Burbules, 1993, p. 33). More often than not, such efforts produce results only slowly over time. Previously silenced students or parents may require multiple opportunities based on mutual respect and trust before they feel safe enough to express what is on their minds and in their hearts.

Creating a Buffer Zone

The creation of a buffer zone in which a child can develop without harmful intrusions from the outside is the essence of good parenting. All young children must be protected and nurtured until they are able to venture forth with sufficient skills and abilities to protect themselves. Children of Color are often at risk, and it is especially critical for their parents to create within them a good psychological base grounded in a strong and positive sense of self. Research has repeatedly shown that a positive self-concept is correlated with effective social functioning, higher levels of cognitive development, and greater emotional health and stability (Curry & Johnson, 1990). The buffer zone against racism and negative racial messages can provide a place and time for optimal personal growth.

Children's concepts of self result directly from the messages they receive about themselves from the world. Psychological theories about the development of the self speak of mirroring and reflection and imply that children take in and make a part of themselves these reflected views of others. If they are loved, they will love themselves; if they are demeaned or devalued, that is how they will come to feel about themselves and treat others. In this regard, "children who are consistently rejected understandably begin to question and doubt whether they, their family, and their group really deserve no more respect from the larger society than they receive" (Clark, 1963, pp. 63–64). This is why the idea of a buffer zone is so critical to Parents of Color. By substituting the reflection of loving parents and significant others for that of an often hostile environment that may routinely negate the value of children because of their ethnicity, a more positive sense of self is guaranteed. "Early consistent, loving, nurturing interaction is the ideal process of interaction leading to a good sense of self. The child who is loved, accepted and supported in appropriate reality-oriented functioning in relationship to others comes to love himself and to respect himself as someone worthy of love" (Norton, 1983, p. 185).

However, the idea of a buffer zone should not be limited merely to parents and family. Communities, particularly Communities of Color, often serve this purpose. The African adage that "it takes an entire village to raise a child" is relevant here: In many African languages, the same word is used to mean *mother* and *aunt,* and child-rearing is the responsibility of all the adults in the whole village.

Likewise, the institutions of the entire local community, especially schools, can function to protect the children. For example, at an elementary school in Portland, where I directed a preservice teacher immersion program, children are taught and cared for by most of the staff members. The school functions more as an entity than as a series of discrete classrooms. An intangible spirit of community and of being together both in and against the outside world wraps the children in a protective envelope. Often, the older Black women who are teaching assistants function as "other mothers," a common role that has its cultural roots in African societies (Delpit, 2006).

Preparing the Child Emotionally for Racism

There are many ways to help children deal emotionally with negative racial experiences. First, children should not be allowed to feel alone in their struggle. They must not only feel the support of their parents, peers, and teachers but also understand that they are part of a long history of People of Color, who have similarly struggled against racism. Parents should model active intervention and mastery over the environment as well as help their children develop competence and the ability to achieve personal goals. If children can experience their parents as powerful, they gain a sense of vicarious power. Sometimes, children should be allowed to try to deal with racial situations on their own, with parents prepared to intervene if necessary. Other times, it is the parent's responsibility to work to resolve the situation quickly and satisfactorily and, above all, to protect the child's self-esteem.

There are a number of mechanisms that parents may adopt in the process of supporting and preparing their children for life. For example, some parents may tell their children that "Black is beautiful," hoping to reinforce positive identity and self. However, children may begin to wonder whether repeating the phrase over and over implies that maybe Black is not so beautiful after all. In a parallel dynamic in a school setting, rhetoric around "achievement regardless of race or previous academic performance" sets up the same sense that maybe the children cannot achieve after all.

Other parents adopt a permissive stance, being overly generous and accommodating with their children, as if to assuage their own guilt or make up for the harshness that the children will eventually encounter. This strategy does not allow children to test themselves and their abilities in the real world and, in so doing, develop feelings of competence and self-worth. Still other parents are overly authoritarian and feel that the best they can do for their children is to toughen them up so that they will be familiar with functioning in a hostile environment. But this strategy may lead to abuse, which teaches children to be abusive in some manner. It also gives them a green light to act out in the world. A final mechanism involves encouraging a child to remain passive and to avoid aggressive behavior of any kind, as if such a strategy would somehow mollify racial hatred (Poussaint, 1972).

Children must learn to manage the righteous anger that they will feel as objects of racial hatred. Suppressing anger eventually leads to self-loathing and low self-esteem. Overgeneralized anger is counterproductive, leads nowhere, and consumes a vast amount of undirected energy. A more balanced approach seems optimal: teaching children to assert themselves sufficiently, to display their anger appropriately, and to sublimate and channel much of it into constructive energy for actively dealing with the world. "Our job," Poussaint wrote, "is to help our children develop that delicate balance between appropriate control and appropriate display of anger and aggression, love and hate" (1972, p. 110). He continued: "As parents we must try to raise men and women who are emotionally healthy in a society that is basically racist. If our history is a lesson, we will continue to survive. Many Black children will grow up to be strong, productive adults. But too many others will succumb under the pressures of a racist environment. Salvaging these youngsters is our responsibility as parents" (p. 111).

One parent, also an educator, described this process in her home:

> I don't think that creating a safe and supportive classroom environment means that you have to give students the impression that there are not challenges in life that they will encounter. As I raise my own children as African American, I try to create a home environment that is safe for them to ask questions, get angry, and

express their feelings in a healthy way. I feel that this gives them a place to gain confidence in themselves as individuals and know what they believe and why they believe it. When they enter the world, they can speak with that same confidence and be able to support it.

I believe the same holds true in the classroom. My job as a teacher is to prepare students to be confident individuals and problem-solvers who listen to each other with empathetic ears. This creates students who are better prepared for real world experiences as adults. (A. Freeman, personal communication, February 9, 2010)

Preparing the Child Cognitively for Racism

Equally important to providing children with a strong emotional base is preparing them for the eventual experience of prejudice and discrimination to be encountered in the broader world. How may children be prepared?

First, never deny children's ethnicity or underestimate its possible impact on their lives. Some parents feel that it is best to put off such discussions as long as possible, thereby protecting children from the horror of racism until it can no longer be avoided. There are real problems with this approach. First of all, it models a denial of reality that not only confuses children but also sets them on the course of not actively dealing with their ethnicity. Parents who choose to avoid discussions of race also tend to underestimate the level of children's knowledge and may be avoiding issues that have already become real and problematic for the children (Copenhaver-Johnson, 2006; Tatum, 2003). Most ethnic children are aware of racial differences as early as two or three years of age and by seven are aware of the negative judgments that society holds about their group. Ethnic children might want and need to discuss their experiences but may feel that they must remain silent because of the family rule: "We do not talk about these things." By such tactics, parents unintentionally remove themselves as important resources for their children.

It is clearly best to allow children to bring up the subject of race and ethnicity and to deal with it in the context of their ongoing reality. Parents should answer questions in as simple a manner as possible and not overwhelm children with more knowledge than they need. More often than not, a small amount of information will suffice. Parents should answer questions in a manner that fits with the children's level of cognitive development. Similarly, children should not be overwhelmed emotionally with difficult information or stories. Preparing children for dealing with racism is not a single event; it is an ongoing developmental process. As they encounter racism in the real world, it should be discussed and processed; and as they mature, information and explanations should also grow in depth and comprehensiveness.

It is important to help children develop a strong and positive ethnic identity based on values inherent in group membership so as to internally counteract the negative experiences of being an object of prejudice. Children should be able to say: "I am an African American, and I come from a rich cultural tradition of which I am very proud. Sure, I experience a lot of racism, but that is just the way it is, although, at times, I get angry. But I would not trade it for being White or anything else, even if it meant life would be a lot easier." An ethnic identity based solely on negative experiences of racial hatred is a very fragile thing that disappears as soon as the adversity is gone. If children are made to feel bad because of how they are different, it is psychologically crucial that they have and can draw on positive feelings about who they are ethnically and individually. If they do not, they may in time come to hate their group membership, seeing it as the source of all their problems.

Racism should be presented as a social issue, not as an individual or personal problem. For example: "Why did Tommy call me that bad name? I didn't do anything to him." "Of course you didn't. Sometimes, when people get angry or unhappy, they take it out on others who are different from them. There is something wrong with people when they do that." Children must not come to believe—consciously or unconsciously—that something they did brought on the racist behavior. Parents should not assume that a child has not personalized a negative racial experience. They should check it out. In their egocentric mode of experiencing the world, young children tend to take responsibility for most things that happen to them. Parents should actively make sure they do not do so. An ethnic child can be transformed from a happy and carefree young person to one who is negative and sullen by a single experience with racism. Much of the damage could be alleviated by working through the incident with the child.

Children should learn two lessons about ethnic group membership. The first is that group membership is based not only on obvious physical or cultural features but also on an interdependence of societal pressures: Members of an ethnic group share the experience of being treated similarly by the world. This should serve to heighten awareness of being part of a single whole, yet it is easy for children to learn to vent their frustration on subgroups within their community, blaming them for the bad treatment that all group members experience. Such internalized racism can become a tyranny of its own and lead to destructive intergroup struggles. For example, I am thinking of caste systems based on lightness and darkness of skin color that exist in many Communities of Color. In my own culture, there was a time when a rushee for a Black sorority was accepted based partially on whether her skin tone was lighter than a standard brown paper bag.

The second lesson is that it is acceptable to have multiple allegiances and belong to different social groupings at the same time. If children are made to choose between alternatives, they sometimes grow resentful and may eventually get even with parents, usually by rejecting group membership at some level. For example, some parents are very critical of their children's attempts at being bicultural (of trying to become competent in the ways of dominant culture as well as their own). Fearing that their children may lose touch with traditional ways and values, they force them to choose, and the result is unhappiness for all concerned. The same result may come from forcing the child to acculturate into the mainstream culture, which may engender later yearning for identity.

Parents should realize that children's feelings about ethnicity, ethnic identity, and group belonging are not likely to be more positive or less conflicted than their own. Put in a slightly different manner, parents may pass on inner conflicts and issues about their own ethnicity to their children. In preparing children for a hostile world, parents should focus not only on their children but also on themselves as role models.

Interacting with Parents of Color

Whether Parents of Color are unique in their situation as isolated individuals or part of a larger Community of Color, interactions with teachers not like themselves will be a fact of life in all but a few of this nation's school districts.

Fox (1993), in *Opening Closed Doors*, carefully examined obstacles to trust and open communication between Black parents and White teachers. For the parents, contact with the teachers highlighted their own issues of internalized oppression and "the need to prove." For teachers, prejudice—conscious or unconscious; real or perceived—and their own use of personal power emerged as issues.

Issues that emerged as problems in interaction included differing views of institutional racism, differing levels of trust and mistrust, and conflict in communication styles. Fox showed how each group viewed the other in ways that made sense only from a single perspective and how such ethnocentrism kept them from "open communication, constructive conflict, a genuine expression of feelings, learning to act with each other in meaningful ways, and reexamining a learned fear of difference" (p. iv). Above all, she emphasized the need to develop trust.

Interaction styles is often the main cause of miscommunication: Blacks are more likely to be passionate and raise their voices verbally when fully engaged in a conversation and this is often experienced as aggression instead of engagement. "Whites invariably interpret black anger and verbal aggressions as more provocative and threatening than do blacks" (Kochman, 1981, p. 11).

Once this intereaction style is more fully anticipated and understood, deep communication increases. "The problems occur most when White people and African American people assume that the meaning they are assigning to these behaviors are the same, and therefore the motives ascribed are also justified" (Fox, 1993, p. 158). Consider the role this plays in increasing the gap between parents and teachers, particularly when this "interpretation of behaviors between White people and African Americans and the covert role that it plays in the communication process is a discussion that rarely takes place" (Fox, 1993, p. 158).

A Parent/Teacher Scenario

As an example of these differences in perspective, I end this chapter with a somewhat humorous hypothetical look at a parent/teacher interaction. In this scenario, we not only read what each individual says to the other but also get a glimpse into their thoughts. The dialogue was created by students in a multicultural issues course (Diaz-Ramos, Null, Pentland & Roush, 1996). In it, the parent of an isolated Student of Color talks with his teacher.

The scene: Mrs. Pentland, a third-grade teacher in a public elementary school, is about to have a conference with the parent of a Korean student, Jisoo. This dramatization invites the audience to be "flies on the wall," where they can hear not only the spoken words but also the thoughts of Mrs. Kim and Mrs. Pentland.

P'S MIND: Okay, now I've done my homework, I know the general Korean etiquette and this will go very smoothly. Oh, please don't let me treat Mrs. Kim as a stereotype—remember that Jisoo is a unique boy. I'm so glad I memorized how to say hello. Hope I say this right!

MRS. P: Anyung Ha So Yo!

K'S MIND: Did she say "porcupine?"

MRS. K: (smiles and nods)

MRS. P: Well, it is certainly a pleasure to have Jisoo in class! Do you have any questions I can answer?

MRS K: (after a pause) Yes. How old are you?

P'S MIND: Why is she asking this?

MRS. P: Um … 45.

K'S MIND: Ah—she is older than me. She deserves even more respect than just for being Jisoo's teacher. (silence)

MRS. P: Oh, I see you've brought Jisoo's performance report! As you can see from the marks, Jisoo is doing very well. His developmental abilities are quite adequate in most areas, reflecting his stage of growth. He's still a concrete thinker, so he needs manipulatives.

K'S MIND: I have no clue what she's talking about!

MRS. K: (smiles and nods)

P'S MIND: Oh rats—quick, Beth, drop the jargon!

MRS. P: What I mean is that Jisoo is doing very well for his age. He has excellent attention, strong cooperative abilities, and his academics are improving rapidly.

K'S MIND: Jisoo brings honor to our whole family. I must write a letter to the grandparents; they will be so proud.

MRS. K: (smiles and nods, but more genuinely)

MRS. P: I'd like to review some of Jisoo's work with you. I'm so impressed by the improvement of his writing. I do wish he'd put more detail into his stories—they're such fun to read, I'd like to see him expand on his ideas.

MRS. K: (no nod—apprehensive face)

K'S MIND: No, the honor of our family and community depends on Jisoo's performance. If he is not working hard now how can he be successful later?

MRS. P: Please, Mrs. Kim, don't worry. I shouldn't have mentioned it. The detail of his writing will come naturally as his English continues to improve. It's really not important now. It will come.

K'S MIND: What does this mean, "It will come"? It will not come unless he works hard. He must work harder. Maybe it's because we speak Korean at home. If we spoke more English he'd be more fluent by now. Maybe it's because my English is not so good. We must make sure Jisoo learns better English.
   (silence)

P'S MIND: This isn't going well. And there's way too much silence. Let's switch topics. How about ... (think, think) ... social, yes, he gets along well with other kids!

MRS. P: You know, Jisoo gets along so well with the other kids! In fact, just the other day they were playing a game of soccer when an older student took the ball, and Jisoo was very upset. At first he was yelling at the boy, but then he calmed down and gained control and spoke up for himself and his friend. He was the hero who got the ball back. The children all look at Jisoo as a leader.

MRS. K: (shocked face)

K'S MIND: AAAaacccckkk! What is he learning here? No more TV, no more video games! Jisoo knows not to let his emotions show. He should not have yelled. How could he let this happen? He needs to blend in—not stand out. He shouldn't be drawing attention to himself.

MRS. K: I apologize for Jisoo causing a disturbance.

MRS. P: No, Jisoo didn't cause a disturbance. He is a natural leader, his handling of the situation was a great model for others. ...

P'S MIND: Don't forget to ask her to come into the class!

MRS. P: I just had a thought—I'd love for you to come in and help with the class. Could you give us a presentation on Korean cooking?

K'S MIND: What?? Talk to the whole class? My English is not good enough. Jisoo would be so embarrassed—he is even embarrassed when I talk just to his friends.

MRS. K: (hesitantly—no smile) Yes.

P'S MIND: Uh oh. She doesn't really want to do that—what else?

MRS. P: Or, better yet, how about helping with our spelling lessons?

K'S MIND: What?? English spelling? That's even worse than speaking. Doesn't she realize I'm still struggling with this crazy language?

MRS. K: (still hesitantly) Yes.

P'S MIND: Uh oh …—Try painting!

MRS. P: No, wait, I have a better idea. How about painting? Jisoo mentioned that you like to paint. Perhaps you'd like to help me with the class next week?

K'S MIND: Finally, that sounds like something I will enjoy.

MRS. K: (relieved) Yes!

P'S MIND: Whew!

MRS. P: That will be great! Thank you so much for coming in, Mrs. Kim. I really am enjoying Jisoo this year.

BOTH MINDS TOGETHER: I wish we'd had an interpreter!

(From *Parent–Teacher Scenario* by S. Diaz-Ramos, K. Null, B. Pentland, and M.L. Roush, 1996. This scenario, completed as a class project, is used with permission.)

Connections and Reflections: Emerging Views

Consider the stories from the beginning of the chapter and of the isolated Students of Color as well as the thoughts that came up for you as you read the parent/teacher scenario. Choose one that particularly engaged you. Share with others why you found it compelling/interesting. Then, begin to discuss what sort of advice you would give to the student and the teacher.

This exercise involves writing a detailed autobiography focusing on issues of race and ethnicity. You might find it helpful to do this chronologically. With your reflections, *Becoming Aware of Race,* from the end of Chapter 4 as a beginning, write a personal history of your experiences with prejudice and racism and how your own ethnic background has impacted your contact and connections with those who are culturally different from you. Here is a partial example from a student in my web class:

> I recall my cousins going through a similar process of negotiating their identity as "Indians," "Natives," "Aboriginals," or "mixed-race" individuals. This was a complicated process that they began at around ten years old. They were learning the complicated history behind different labels, they recognized that they were different than other people in their family and in their world and that it was important to them to try to determine where they fit in and what their world view was in relation to others.

You can increase the power of this exercise by getting together with another person or in a small group and taking turns reading your autobiographies. Have the other person or people respond to various aspects of your writing, and follow this up with a discussion of their reactions. The classroom activity for upper grades may also be used for your own reflection.

Classroom: Adventures in Learning

- For lower grades, talk to children about the toys and games they play with and have at home. Are there pictures of both boys and girls on the packages? Are the children of different colors? Children may go to toy stores to look at packages and advertisements and begin to see who is illustrated. Also, could children who are blind play this game? What are some toys and games that would work with children of different abilities or disabilities? (Chartock, 2010).

- For upper grades, consider writing "Where I Am From" poems. The description of the activity and this reflection comes from one of my multi-ethnic preservice teachers:

  The idea behind this activity is to use two themes: *Our Foundations* and *The Journey*. With Foundations, you consider things like beginnings, family and friends, birth-place, community, values, schools, identity, significant experiences growing up, etc. In *The Journey*, you are prompted by the words personal and professional, identity development, pain and healing, joy, dilemmas, discoveries, learning, rec-ognition of help received, internalizations, transformation, etc. Using this infor-mation, you write a poem in the fashion of Linda Christensen's "Where I Am From" writing activity. Christiansen's article, "Where I'm From: Inviting Students' Lives into the Classroom" is in *Rethinking Our Classrooms* (2001), Volume 2, pub-lished by Rethinking Schools. You can also find it at http://youthvoices.net/node/2737.

  Using a brainstorm worksheet, you list as many words as you like under each topic. When you are done, go back through your words and "color them up" with adjectives or descriptive phrases. ... Then, you begin to create your poem. ... You can use whatever form or structure you like, just keeping in mind the theme. You will find an example from one of my students on the companion website. This poem may help people see their own diversity, as my student shared.

  "My oldest son has done this activity in his English class. I thought that this was amazing. He told me that he actually discovered how diverse he was in culture and heritage. He had not realized that before." (M. Bukovsky-Reyes, per-sonal communication, March 2010).

CHAPTER 7

Psychological and Educational Issues

"You may not be able to change the world, but at least you can embarrass the guilty."

—Jessica Miltford

Young people are often alienated from schools and isolated from full participation in both school culture and American society at large through no fault of their own:

> Mr. Cur ... was the teacher who sent "Jamar" out of his room because he was being "insubordinate and defiant." He perceived Jamar as rebellious because Jamar was wearing his hair in a traditional African American way. Mr. Cur interpreted this as a statement of "black power." He was immediately frightened by it ... and lashed out at Jamar.
>
> Meanwhile ... Jamar had done nothing but show up to class!
>
> Mr. Cur acted in accordance with his own limited viewpoint. Driven by both his fears and his lack of understanding about African American students, he "saw" Jamar "wearing a cloak of defiance," when, actually, Jamar was "naked" of any such emotion (Ely, 2001, pp. 91–92).

Ely suggests that such disconnects are routinely experienced by African American, Latino/a, and lower-socioeconomic children because teachers lack basic sensitivity to the cultural styles of their students. Rather than reacting unconsciously to their own prejudices and stereotypes, teachers should learn to see and understand students' behavior from within the students' cultural perspectives.

Such encounters take their toll on the innocent victims. In a most extraordinary book entitled *The Rage of a Privileged Class,* writer Ellis Cose (1993) explored the anger lurking below the surface of the African Americans. Negative perceptions of self were deeply intertwined with their experiences as African Americans in the United States. Because of having to live in, adapt to, and survive in a hostile and racist world, African Americans and other People of Color are often at perpetual risk for developing serious physical and emotional problems. These are individuals living reasonably functional lives until the microaggressions mounted up. Most do adapt, survive, and may grow even stronger. But People of Color often pay an emotional price that may, with sufficient stress and personal difficulty, result in some type of psychological struggle based primarily on race.

This chapter focuses on issues that plague People of Color, particularly in educational settings. It explores a number of factors, such as the racism described in Chapters 2, 3 and 4, that put individuals at risk for psychological and educational difficulties. Throughout the chapter, particular attention is paid to models of racial identity development that have proven particularly useful in making sense out of cross-cultural interactions. Ethnic identification and group belonging as affected by acculturation and assimilation also help us understand identity crises for Individuals and Groups of Color.

A fuller discussion of student stress from different factors and ways to provide psychological support in the classroom is included adjacent to material on academic performance and learning styles. The last sections of this chapter focus on who are the teachers and teacher characteristics that make for sound cross-cultural teaching.

Racial Identity and Group Belonging

The controversy over whether Children of Color regularly experience problems in group identification and low self-concept as a result of racism was discussed in some detail in Chapter 6. Based on several sources of evidence, the conclusion was that they did not necessarily but that without sufficient and appropriate family and community support, Children of Color were certainly at risk for such problems. Researchers have been hesitant in estimating the deleterious effects of racism and society's negative views of ethnic-group members. In this section, we expand this picture of identity difficulties.

The Inner Dynamics of Ethnic Identity

The term "identity" refers to the stable inner sense of who a person is, which is formed by the successful integration of various experiences of the self into a coherent self-image. *Ethnic identity* refers to that part of personal identity that contributes to the person's self-image as an ethnic-group member. When one speaks of African American identity or Native American identity or European American identity, what is being referred to is the individual's subjective experience of ethnicity. What does the person feel, consciously and unconsciously, about being a member of his or her ethnic group? What meanings do individuals attach to their ethnicity? What does people's behavior reflect about the nature of their attachment to the group? Answers to these questions are subsumed under the notion of ethnic identity.

Ethnic-identity formation, such as personal-identity formation, results from the integration of personal experiences each individual has as an African American or Native American or European American as well as the messages that have been communicated and internalized about ethnicity by family members, significant others, and the community. In general, ethnic identity can be positive, negative, or ambivalent (Baxley, 2008; Ngo, 2008; Torres & Rollock, 2009). The latter two situations have also been referred to in the literature as "internalized racism" and "internalized oppression." The internalized images for both oppression and domination become "deep, internal psychological qualities, characteristics, or 'marks' that are extremely difficult (if not impossible) to resist, interrupt, or abandon once they are in place" (Tappan, 2006, p. 2122).

As emphasized in Chapter 6, ethnic children raised in a hostile racist environment are likely to have unpleasant experiences associated with their ethnicity. As these negative experiences accumulate, it becomes increasingly difficult for the child—and, later, the adult—to integrate them into a coherent and positive sense of ethnic self. Inner conflicts in ethnic identity ultimately find expression in overt behavior. In the case of negative identification (where aspects of the ethnic self are actively rejected or disowned), the individual tends to deny, avoid, or escape group membership in whatever ways possible. In Communities of Color, this is often referred to as *passing*. It may include trying to change one's appearance so as not to look so typically ethnic, changing one's name, moving to a White neighborhood, dating and marrying outside the group, and taking on majority-group habits, language, and affectations. Such behaviors are usually experienced as offensive within ethnic communities. Specific derogatory terms have, in fact, been created in each of the Communities of Color to describe such individuals: "Oreos" among African Americans, "coconuts" among Latinos/as, "apples" among Native Americans, and "bananas" among Asian Americans. All refer to individuals as being of Color on the outside but White on the inside. As part of this rejection of ethnicity, the individual also takes on majority attitudes and habits, including the dominant culture's prejudices and stereotypes.

In relation to ambivalent identification, where rejecting tendencies exist concurrently with positive feelings about group membership, there is either vacillation between love and hate (where individuals move back and forth, pulling away from feeling too identified if they get too close and moving back toward the group if they grow too distant) or the simultaneous expression of contradictory positive and negative attitudes and behaviors. One form of accommodation is to compartmentalize ethnic identity (retain certain aspects and reject others).

For example, a Latino/a might refuse to speak Spanish, identify as a Catholic, or marry within the group but at the same time may have strong preferences for native foods, prefer to live in a barrio, and become involved in civil rights activities. It is perhaps most accurate to conceive of ethnic-identity formation as an ongoing and lifelong process. It involves a series of internal psychological adaptations (that may eventually translate into changes in behavior) to an ever-changing complex of unfolding ethnic experiences.

A good example of such dynamics is offered by Tatum in *Why Are All the Black Kids Sitting Together in the Cafeteria?* Tatum points out that race and racial-identity issues become particularly salient when Children of Color enter adolescence. Changes in school groupings, dating, and broader participation in the social environment increasingly highlight the existence of racism and the need to understand what it means to be Black. In adolescence, there is a greater likelihood of encountering experiences that may cause an individual to examine his or her racial identity. Boy/girl events and interactions become less racially diverse, and White peers seem less likely to understand or be able to provide support for the emerging identities of Children of Color. As a result, adolescents gravitate to like-race peers and often adopt an oppositional stance or identity, absorbing stereotyped images of being of Color and rejecting characteristics and behaviors that they see as White. "The anger and resentment that adolescents feel in response to their growing awareness of the systematic exclusion of Black people from full participation in U.S. society leads to the development of an oppositional social identity. This … both protects one's identity from the psychological assault of racism and keeps the dominant group at a distance" (2003, p. 60).

Tatum sees this attachment to the peer group as a "positive coping strategy" in the face of stress. However, it is not without difficulties. Images of blackness tend to be highly stereotyped, and academic success is often discounted as White, although this appears to be changing with the election of a highly educated biracial president (Dillon, 2009). As we shall see next, this stage of racial identity development—which Cross (1995) calls the "encounter" and which entails turning toward one's own group and rejecting the majority and its values—is followed by the emergence of greater individualization and diversification of racial identity. Models of racial identity development are helpful for exploring both student and teacher interactions across cultures.

Models of Racial Identity Development

An important but somewhat different approach to understanding the evolution of racial or cultural consciousness is offered by various researchers (Cross, 1995; Helms, 1990; McDermott & Samson, 2005; Porow, 2006; Tatum, 2003) who began in the 1970s to develop what have come to be called models of racial identity development. These models, which were first developed in relation to the experience of African Americans, assume that there are strong similarities in the ways individuals respond to oppression and racism. It is believed that People of Color go through a series of predictable stages as they struggle to make sense out of their relationship to their own cultural group as well as to the oppression of mainstream culture. Cross (1995), whose work is exemplary, hypothesizes five such stages of development. It is assumed that each Person of Color can be located in one of the five stages, depending on the level of racial awareness and identity.

In Stage 1, called *pre-encounter,* individuals are not consciously aware of the impact of race and ethnicity on their life experiences. They tend to assimilate, seek acceptance by Whites, exhibit strong preferences for dominant cultural values, and even internalize negative stereotypes of their own group. By de-emphasizing race and distancing themselves from other group members, they are able to deny their vulnerability to racism and sustain the myth of meritocracy and the hope of achievement unencumbered by racial hatred.

In Stage 2, *encounter,* some event or experience shatters individuals' denial and sends them deep into confusion about their own ethnicity. For the first time, they must consciously deal with the fact of being different and what this difference means. People of Color at this stage often speak of "waking up" to reality, realizing that ethnicity is an aspect of self that must be dealt with and becoming aware of the enormity of what must be confronted out in the world.

Stage 3, *immersion/emersion,* is characterized by two powerful feelings: first, a desire to immerse oneself in all things ethnic—for example, to celebrate all symbols of blackness—and second, to simultaneously avoid contact with Whites, the White world, and symbols of that world. The result may be an uncritical belief that everything Black is beautiful and everything White is abhorrent. During this more separatist period, people may seek out information about ethnic history and culture and surround themselves exclusively with people like themselves. The anger that is generated during Stage 2 slowly dissipates as the person grows focused on self-exploration and attachment within the ethnic world and less in need of moving away from the White world.

Stage 4, *internalization,* begins as individuals become increasingly secure and positive in their sense of racial identity and less rigid in their attachment to the group at the expense of personal autonomy. Pro-ethnic attitudes become "more open, expansive, and sophisticated" (Cross, 1995, p. 114). While they feel securely connected to their ethnic community, they also become more willing to relate to Whites and members of other ethnic groups who are able to acknowledge and accept their ethnicity.

Stage 5, *internalization/commitment,* represents a growing and maturing of the tendencies initiated in Stage 4. People at Stage 5 have found ways to translate their personal ethnic identities into active commitment to social justice and change. According to Tatum, the Stage 5 person is "anchored in a positive sense of racial identity" and can "proactively perceive and transcend race" (1992b, p. 12). Race has become an instrument for reaching out into the world rather than an end in itself, as in Stage 3, or a social reality to be denied or avoided, as in Stage 1. (Further light on Cross's model comes through in the interview with him in Chapter 12).

Racial Identity Development and the Teaching Process

The value of these models for teachers is twofold. First, they educate and sensitize teachers to the importance of cultural identity in the lives of Children of Color. Second, they suggest that individuals at different stages of development may have very different needs and values and may feel differently about what is supportive in the learning situation.

Students of Color at Stage 1 may do very well in learning from White teachers. According to Sue and Sue (2003), Stage 1 individuals may react differently to White and same-race teachers.

Those at Stage 2 tend to be preoccupied with personal issues of race and identity but at the same time are torn between fading Stage 1 beliefs and an emerging awareness of race consciousness. They may do particularly well with teachers who are knowledgeable about their own cultural group and with teaching methods that allow maximum choice and self-direction. A child may be quite comfortable with a White teacher, as long as the teacher is culturally aware.

Students in Stage 3 are absorbed in re-exploring and engaging in ethnic ways, and they may see personal problems as exclusively the result of racism (Atkinson, Morten, & Sue, 1993). In classrooms, Teachers of Color are by far preferred. Teachers, whether White or of Color, may be seen as a symbol of the oppressive society and thus challenged. The least helpful response is to become defensive and take attacks personally. White guilt and defensiveness will especially exacerbate student anger. Teachers should realize that they may be continually tested, and they often find that honest self-disclosure about race is necessary to establish credibility. Lastly, consider adopting strategies that are more "action oriented" and "aimed at external change" as well as group approaches when working with Stage 3 students (Sue & Sue, 2003). Students of Color functioning at this stage may be particularly ready for the social action level of curriculum reform, which we visit in depth in Chapter 8.

Students in Stage 4 are struggling to balance group and personal perspectives and may need help sorting out these issues. They may still tend to prefer teachers from their own group, but they can begin to conceive of learning from culturally sensitive outsiders. Those in Stage 4 appear in many ways to be similar to those in Stage 1. They tend to experience conflict between identification with their group and the need to "exercise greater personal freedom" (Sue & Sue, 2003).

Approaches that emphasize self-exploration are particularly helpful in integrating group identity and personal concerns of the self.

Those who have reached Stage 5 have developed their skills at balancing personal needs and group obligations, have an openness to all cultures, and are able to deal well with racism when it is encountered (Atkinson et al., 1993). Their preference for a teacher is most likely to be dictated by the personal qualities and attitudes of the teacher rather than by group membership.

In Chapter 4, Helms' model of White identity development was introduced. That model, which parallels and evolved from the work just described, enumerates stages of racial consciousness development in Whites and the eventual abandonment of entitlement. Just as it is useful to be able to identify the stage of identity development of individual Students of Color, so too is it valuable to be able to assess White teachers using Helms' model in order to better prepare and match them with Communities of Color. White teachers will be most effective in cross-cultural teaching when they have successfully worked through feelings about whiteness and privilege. Such individuals, located in the highest stages of Helms' model, are able to experience their own ethnicity in a nondefensive and nonracist manner. Sue and Sue also warn against mismatches, especially when the White teacher is at Stage 1 of Helms' model.

An Example of Racial Identity and Interaction

In Chapter 4, I introduced a four-stage model that uses colloquial terms and is easy to remember in everyday school situations (Moule, 2004). Here is a summary of racial interaction development:

> Stage 1, the pre-encounter stage, "I'm OK; you're OK," includes the "colorblind" perspective.
> Stage 2, the encounter stage, is "Something is not OK."
> Stage 3, "I'm OK; I'm not so sure about you," includes anger, denial, pseudo-independence, immersion, and emersion.
> Stage 4, "I'm OK, you're OK, we're OK," signals that people are ready to work together.

The following story—my own—illustrates how racial-identity stages may play out for Children of Color. It was originally written in third person, and I will share it in that form.

Jean was six years old. Her family had quietly moved into an all-White, mostly Jewish neighborhood. Despite an act of overt racism—one morning her father had seen "N_____ go back where you came from" scrawled on the outside of the house and, without telling anyone, washed it off—Jean's parents had hoped that the school personnel would treat Jean like any other child. Perhaps pretending there was no difference would allow her to "fit in." Jean's parents hoped that an "I'm OK, you're OK" attitude—a preencounter stage—would be enough to ensure Jean's safety and success.

The preencounter strategy failed, for race and culture did matter. Jean experienced being different even as she worked to assimilate, and the resulting dissonance separated her even farther from her peers. During a Jewish holiday, only two students attended school, and Jean was the sole student in her class. She wondered, "Why isn't the teacher teaching me today? I am here!" Both in school and socially, she was often alone. Something was not OK.

Jean's encounter phase, "Something is not OK," slowly progressed to anger and the "I'm OK, I'm not sure about you" stage. One day, when Jean's mother came to pick her up from second grade, the teacher said that Jean waited at the door of the classroom and stomped on the toes of her classmates as they exited.

The next year Jean and her family moved from their East Coast urban area to a West Coast suburb, from a two-parent to a one-parent family. Jean's new school was as culturally diverse as any Los Angeles could offer. Miss Thomas' room was a secure and healthy place for her own emotions and her classmates' toes. Jean was learning about her own culture and became, in ways, immersed.

Miss Thomas used strategies that seemed to validate every child in her room. Each day, she wrote a Spanish phrase in the corner of the blackboard. She read it to the class, then had the children repeat it. In less than a minute of classroom time, she acknowledged her Mexican American students and opened the door to another language for all her students. Miss Thomas' classroom was safe from disrespect toward her or among students. In this situation, as a result of a caring and skillful teacher, Jean entered, for a time, into the autonomy stage, "I'm OK, you're OK, we're OK."

(Adapted from pp. 1, 2, 16 of *My Journey with Preservice Teachers: Reflecting on Teacher Characteristics That Bridge Multicultural Education Theory and Classroom Practice* by Jean Moule, 1998. Reprinted by permission.)

Assimilation and Acculturation

"They won't learn the language. They're not assimilating. They don't look like us. I say—put them back on the Mayflower" (Keefe, 2006). This cartoon caption, as with *Body Rituals Among the Nacirema* (see online), helps us to take a very different perspective. *Assimilation* means the coming together of two distinct cultures to create a new and unique third cultural form. Ethnic group members can differ widely in the extent of their assimilation and acculturation. Many people envisioned the United States becoming a great melting pot in which different races and ethnicities would merge into a new American cultural form. In time, it became known as the myth of the great melting pot because Americans never totally assimilated into a single culture.

There are several forms of assimilation, including acculturation, structural assimilation, marital assimilation, and identificational assimilation (Gordon, 1964). *Acculturation* involves taking on the cultural ways of another group, usually of the mainstream culture. *Structural assimilation* means gaining entry into the institutions of society. It is also called "integration" by Gordon. *Marital assimilation* implies large-scale intermarriage, and *identificational assimilation* involves developing a sense of belonging and peoplehood with the host society. It is probably most accurate to say that White ethnics—of Irish, Italian, Jewish, Armenian, and other backgrounds—have assimilated into European American society on all of these dimensions but only to the extent that they have been willing to give up most of their traditional ways and values.

On the other hand, People of Color are rarely considered part of the great melting pot and have remained structurally separate. However, they have acculturated in varying degrees to the dominant European culture. In America, assimilation has always been a one-way process that is perhaps better referred to as *Americanization* or *Anglo-conformity*:

> This kind of assimilation was designed to maintain the predominance of the British-type institutional patterns created during the early years of American society. Under Anglo-conformity there is relatively little sharing of cultural traits, and immigrants and minority groups are expected to adapt to Anglo-American culture as fast as possible. Historically, Americanization has been a precondition for access to better jobs, higher education, and other opportunities. (Healey, 1995, p. 40)

Acculturation—the taking on of cultural patterns of another group—is important in two different ways. First, it is critical to be able to assess the amount of acculturation that has taken place within any individual or family and, simultaneously, to discover to what extent and in what specific areas traditional attitudes, values, and behavior still remain. Just knowing that a student is Latino/a says little about who the person is or how he or she lives. To know where the individual falls on a continuum from traditional identification to complete acculturation offers more information. However, it is important to not confuse group membership with the degree of acculturation that has occurred. The cultural values of the student may or may not be the cultural values of the student's ethnic group.

Acculturation can also create serious emotional strain and difficulties for ethnic students. A special term—*acculturative stress*—has been coined to refer to such situations. For example, take a newly arrived Vietnamese family. The children have learned English relatively quickly in comparison to their parents. As a result, they may end up translating for and becoming the spokespeople for the family. This is not a traditional role for Vietnamese children, who are trained to be very deferential to elders. Nor is it natural within the tradition for children to wield so much power. As the children Americanize, they feel increasingly less bound by traditional ways. The result is stress on the family unit, as is usually the case when traditional cultural ways are compromised or lost as a result of immigration and acculturation.

Views of Acculturation

Researchers have long argued over how best to conceptualize the process of acculturation. Is it one-dimensional or multidimensional? That is, does acculturation exist on a single continuum ranging from identification with the indigenous culture at one end to identification with the dominant culture at the other? Or does it make more sense to conceive of an individual's attachment to the two groups as independent of each other, with the possibility of simultaneously retaining an allegiance to the traditional culture and the dominant American culture? The one-dimensional view implies that a person who moves toward dominant cultural patterns must simultaneously give up traditional ways. This approach has generated the notion of the marginal person, an ethnic-group member who tries to acculturate into the majority but ends up in perpetual limbo, caught between the two cultures (Cose, 1993; Stonequist, 1961). Such an individual has transformed too much to return to traditional ways but, at the same time, cannot gain any real acceptance in majority culture because of skin color.

Others see acculturation as two-dimensional or multidimensional. Proponents of biculturalism believe that it is possible to live and function effectively in two or more cultures (Baxley, 2008; Ngo, 2008; Thompson, 2004; Torres & Rollock, 2009). Unlike the marginal person, who is suspended between cultures with little real connection to either, the bicultural individual feels connected to both and picks and chooses aspects of each to internalize. In this view, it is possible for an Asian American to remain deeply steeped in a traditional lifestyle while at the same time interacting comfortably in the White world, perhaps in relation to school, work, some socializing, and recreational activity.

Problems arise when aspects of the two cultures are in clear conflict. For example, an immigrant Latina must work outside the home yet tries to remain true to traditional gender roles. Even if she were able to integrate the two, it will be very difficult for her children, not having been fully enculturated in traditional ways, to do the same (Casas & Pytluk, 1995; Waldschmidt, 2002). Also, biculturalism is not seen as a virtue in all ethnic communities. Some view people who have become proficient in majority ways with contempt, as turncoats who have rejected their own kind.

A third perspective suggests that the impact of acculturation can best be assessed by discovering the kinds of materials that have been gained or lost through acculturation. Three proposed levels of acculturation include (Marin, 1992):

1. The superficial level involves learning and forgetting facts that are part of a culture's history or tradition.
2. The intermediate level has to do with gaining or losing more central aspects and behaviors of a person's social world (such as language preference and use; ethnicity of spouse, friends, and neighbors; names given to children; and choice of media).
3. The significant level involves core values, beliefs, and norms that are essential to the very cultural paradigm or worldview of the person. For example, Latino/a culture values "encouraging positive interpersonal relationships and discouraging negative, competitive and assertive interactions," "familialism," and "collectivism" (Marin, 1992, p. 239). When cultural values of this magnitude are lost or become less central, acculturation has reached a significant point, and one might wonder what remains of an individual's cultural attachment. For many Europeans in America traditional cultural ties progressively slipped away, generation by generation. The immigrant generation tended to trade more superficial cultural material. Their children, in turn, exchanged more immediate cultural material as they increasingly acculturated—and so forth.

Acculturation and Community Breakdown

Another dynamic is the psychological consequence of the breakdown of the broader community as a result of assimilation. As acculturation proceeds and group members feel less attached to traditional ways, they often choose to leave the community (or ghetto) in the hope of avoiding some of the animosity routinely directed toward the group. At this point, the ability of the community to protect the individual is weakened, and the use of distancing to avoid racial hatred is likely to prove counterproductive. Chapter 6 had some examples of isolation.

Immigration and Acculturation

Acculturative stress is most pronounced during periods of transition, especially during and after significant migrations (to the United States) and the exposure and necessary adjustment to a new culture. A number of factors either ease the transition or make it more difficult:

1. The reasons for the migration and whether the original expectations and hopes were met;
2. The availability of community and extended family support systems;

3. The structure of the family and whether it was forced to assume a different form after migration (for example, an extended family becoming exclusively nuclear);
4. The degree to which the new culture is similar to the old (the greater the difference, the more substantial the stress);
5. The family's general ability to be flexible and adaptive. (Landau, 1982)

When the stresses are severe, the support insufficient, and the family basically unhealthy, family members are likely to try to compensate in one of three ways, each leading to even more stresses and a compounding of existing problems (Landau, 1982). The family may isolate itself and remain separate from its new environment. It may become enmeshed and close its boundaries to the outside world, rigidify its traditional ways, and become overly dependent on its members. Or it may become disengaged, with individual members becoming isolated from each other as they reject previous family values and lifestyle. Especially problematic is a situation in which family members acculturate at very different rates.

Perhaps the most common and problematic consequence of acculturation is the breakdown of traditional cultural and family norms. For example, among Latino/a immigrants, this may take the form of challenges to traditional beliefs about male authority and supremacy, role expectations for men, standards of conduct for females, and fluency in language. Such changes may not be limited to newer immigrants, as these same changing patterns are evident within the Latino/a community as a whole.

There are differences in levels of acculturation and assimilation based on whether immigration is voluntary or involuntary. Voluntary immigrants "are people who have moved more or less voluntarily to the United States ... for economic well-being, better overall opportunities, and/or greater political freedom. Their expectations continue to influence the way they perceive and respond to events, including schooling." On the other hand, involuntary immigrants "are people who were originally brought into the United States ... against their will. For example, through slavery, conquest, colonization, or forced labor.... It is involuntary minorities that usually experience greater and more persistent difficulties with school learning" (Ogbu, 1992, p. 8).

Implications for School Achievement

Ogbu's (1992, 2003) research on immigrant populations, drawing on data from the United States and other countries, has done much to identify underlying factors in the poor achievement scores of Children of Color. These studies find that minority children do not fail in school merely because of cultural and language differences or succeed because they have internalized the culture and language of the dominant group. Ogbu gives specific examples from many places around the globe where students do much better after immigrating because they see themselves as immigrants in the new settings rather than as the lower-status oppressed group they were in their homelands.

This body of literature is key to understanding the effect of attitude on achievement. Whether a family or an individual acculturates or assimilates is partially based on how its members view themselves in the culture:

> Voluntary minorities seem to bring to the United States a sense of who they are from their homeland and seem to retain this different but non-oppositional social identity at least during the first generation. Involuntary minorities, in contrast, develop a new sense of social or collective identity that is in opposition to the social identity of the dominant group after they have become subordinated. They do so in response to their treatment by White America in economic, political, social, psychological, cultural, and language domains. (Ogbu, 1992, p. 9)

Assimilation and Acculturation in the Classroom

How do these underlying factors play out in the classroom? What differences arise from assimilation, acculturation, or schooling in a majority minority culture in contrast to schooling as a minority Individual of Color? Several factors come into play in these cross-cultural educational challenges. Poor achievement scores seemed to be most prevalent where:

- Children begin school with different cultural assumptions;
- Certain concepts in the core curriculum are foreign to the home culture;
- Students are non-English-speaking;
- Children's learning styles differ from the predominant teaching style in the classroom. (Ogbu, 1992)

Voluntary immigrants are likely to view learning English as a necessity and the playing of the school game as useful because they see a payoff later. With this accommodation without assimilation attitude, they are able to cross cultural boundaries and do well in school. On the other hand, involuntary minorities may view education as learning the culture and language of White Americans—that is, the learning of the cultural and language frames of reference of their oppressors. They may feel that such learning is "detrimental to their social identity, sense of security, and self-worth" (Ogbu, 1992, p. 10).

The acculturated Child of Color—as exemplified by a voluntary immigrant—may be strongly influenced by a collective orientation toward making good grades as well as peer pressure to do so. However, in some involuntary minority groups, there is less pressure to achieve. Less stigma is attached to being a poor student, and there are fewer community pressures toward academic achievement. The peer group may also work against academic striving, especially if academic success is seen as acting White.

Research with Black students indicates that the following strategies are used by students who have consciously overcome the pressures against achievement:

- Emulation of White academic behavior or cultural passing (i.e., adopting "White" academic attitudes and behaviors or trying to behave like middle-class, White students). Some students say, "If it takes acting like White people to do well in school, I'll do that." Such students get good grades. The problem is, however, that they may experience isolation from other Black students, resulting in high psychological costs.
- Accommodation without assimilation. Students behave ... according to school norms while at school, but at home ... behave according to Black norms.... Black students who adopt this strategy do not pay the psychological costs that attend the White emulators.
- Camouflage (i.e., disguising true academic attitudes and behaviors). Students use a variety of techniques: become a jester or class clown ... claim to lack interest in school ... study in secret, to obscure their academic efforts.
- Involvement in church activities. Students find an alternative peer group.
- Attending private school where there are fewer anti-academic norms.
- Mentors. Students find adult support for achievement.
- Protection. Students secure the help of bullies from peer pressure in return for helping bullies with their homework....
- Remedial and intervention programs. Students seek out help in areas of academic need.
- Encapsulation. Students become encapsulated in peer group logic and activities ... don't want to do the White man's thing ... don't do their school work. (Ogbu, 1992, p. 11)

While Ogbu's work gives us some understanding of the underlying reasons that many children do poorly in schools, there are larger issues than an individual child's abilities and outlook. One factor is the difference in cultural learning styles that are directly in opposition to those expected by the teacher. Another is the impact of negative cultural and personal expectations on educational achievement, which is explained and expanded by a discussion of learning styles and *stereotype threat*.

Academic Performance and Learning Styles

Why do Children of Color often perform at a lower academic level than their White counterparts in the public school system? One explanation is the differences in ethnic cultures. John Ogbu began by distinguishing between three-types of ethnic minorities and their relative success in academic performance:

autonomous, immigrant, and caste-like (1978). The first group—which includes relatively small populations, such as Jews, Amish, and Mormons—tends to experience prejudice but not widespread oppression. They possess distinctive cultural traits related to academic success as well as cultural models of success and do not suffer from disproportionate degrees of school failure. The second group includes recent immigrants to the United States, such as Koreans and Chinese. They came here voluntarily to improve their life conditions and are ready to assimilate and/or accommodate. Although mainstream individuals may view them negatively, they do not hold similar views of themselves. Their living conditions in this country are often a marked improvement over what they experienced in their countries of origin, and if they were to grow dissatisfied here, they *can* return to their home countries. In spite of cultural differences, their children perform well in school and on academic tests. The third group, what Ogbu called *caste-like minorities*, includes African Americans, Latinos/as, and Native Americans and tends to experience disproportionate amounts of school failure. They are the objects of systematic racism and disadvantage both within and outside of the schools and, according to Ogbu, often view school success not as a path to advancement but rather as acting White or "Uncle Tom" behavior.

Closely related to poor school performance among these populations is the issue of cultural differences in learning styles. As children grow, they internalize and become progressively more comfortable and proficient with learning styles congruent with their own culture. Evidence indicates that poor school performance among ethnic children is related to conflicts in learning style—that is, the U.S. school system as an institution is based on and rewards a mode of learning that is characteristic of European culture (Loewen, 2010). Those who do not adapt or do not become comfortable interacting educationally in this mode are clearly at a disadvantage and are, over time, likely to fail. When educational efforts have been made to adjust classroom interaction to the cultural needs of different individuals, the results have been dramatic increases in performance and school success (Gay, 2010).

Cultural learning styles develop pragmatically. For example, Native Americans developed their keen sense of visual observation out of necessity and in relation to their home environment. Their survival depended on "learning the signs of nature." Thus, observation became a central mode of learning: "watching and listening, trial and error" (Fleming, 1992). Storytelling was the primary mode of teaching values and traditional attitudes, and it was often stylized through the use of symbols, anthropomorphizing, and metaphor, a particularly powerful way of teaching extremely complex concepts (Boma, 2009). Today, "modern Indian children still demonstrate strengths in their ability to memorize visual patterns, visualize spatial concepts, and produce descriptions that are rich in visual detail and the use of graphic metaphor" (Fleming, 1992, pp. 161–162).

Contrast this with the very different learning paradigm emphasized in mainstream schools: auditory learning, conceptualization of the abstract out of context, and heavy emphasis on language skills. Similarly, African Americans (Hale-Benson, 1986), Hawaiians (Gallimore, Boggs & Jordan, 1974), and Mexican Americans (Kagan & Madsen, 1972) exhibit learning styles that have a heavy relational component in contrast with the European style, which emphasizes individualism and competition. For example, Mexican American children are less willing than White students to enter into rivalries or competition or to internalize a drive to perform well to meet the expectations of teachers. Neither do Hawaiian children feel any need to forsake their strong need to affiliate with peers for a more individualistic modality that reinforces goal-oriented behavior.

Although children from these cultures can learn to process information in the European manner, it is counter to their preferred mode of interacting. Put simply, it feels foreign and unnatural, and rather than adapting, many Students of Color choose to shut down and thereby exit the formal U.S. education system. A major task of education in a multicultural society is to broaden the dimensions of the classroom to make room for the learning styles of all students (Collett & Serrano, 1992; Pang, 2005). Similarly, teachers should be aware of optimal learning styles for students in order to maximize their potential during the learning process.

Children of Color learn better and show higher achievement levels when learning activities are culturally relevant and directly related to their larger lives and context. Learning to walk, talk, and internalize simple rituals and concepts occurs naturally in the family home and other familiar environments. Mainstream schools tend to introduce a basic disconnect between what is familiar in the child's life and the activities and content of the classroom. Its tendency is toward abstraction and out-of-context learning. Children of Color—indeed all children—learn best when their classrooms and activities mirror and build upon what is familiar to them and where this occurs in as many ways and at as many different levels as possible. Such an approach to teaching and learning grows most authentically out of the lives and stories of the children and their natural relationships to each other, their families, and their neighborhoods.

Examples include authentic service learning projects that address real needs in the community, focus the child on the collaborative good, and concurrently provide opportunity to develop skills and concepts that will ultimately form a foundation for achievement of mainstream learning goals. An urban child's already strong sense of buildings, cars, and movement can be used as the basis for teaching the physical sciences. Rather than start with the child, the environment, and the cultural learning style and then find creative ways to transform these learning foundations to meet school and statewide standards and goals, most mainstream teachers tend to start with a canned curriculum and then add on connections.

Stereotype Threat

> Black Americans' generations-long passage through a sea of noxious stereotypes ensured that some of those stereotypes would be absorbed, that many blacks would come to believe, as the society insisted, that black brains were somehow deficient. The result is something of a psychological Catch-22. The belief that one is not intellectually inclined can, itself, be enough to prevent one from becoming academically proficient, which can make it impossible ... to offer proof that one is not mentally inferior. (Cose, 1997, p. 65)

As reported in a personal communication to Cose (1997), Spencer found clear evidence that when Black students were told they were taking a "culture free" test, their performance paralleled that of White students. When they were told nothing about cultural considerations, they did worse. Blood-pressure readings of Black students were significantly lower when they were told a test was culture-free. Cose attributes this to "not carrying the burden of negative racial expectations" (p. 42). This pattern is substantiated by recent research that identifies concerns about race as the variable in the Black/White test-score gap (Helms, 2003). Steele (1997) refers to this phenomenon as *stereotype threat*, reporting that the threat is even more acute among individuals already performing at a high level in their respective fields (see Figure 7.1).

Similar patterns of achievement have been found in relation to gender (Schmader, 2002). Women performed at the same level as equally qualified men when the stereotype of male advantage in math was artificially removed. When women were told that particular tests showed no gender differences, none were found. When gender differences were emphasized as reasons for differences in test scores, such differences emerged in test scores (Spencer, Steele & Quinn, 1998). What incredible implications for teachers and educators!

Key factors in stereotype threat from recent research and conceptualization give us some profound understandings of how this threat operates in students and how it is a clear factor in the achievement gap we are all well-aware of. Stereotype threat explains the process "by which many bright Black students underperform on intellectual tests not because of biology, lack of preparation, or poor motivation, but due to the chance that they will confirm a stereotype" (Sue, 2010, p. 102).

The consequences of stereotype threat explain many of the problems we encounter among Students of Color:

- Negative cognition and dejection
- Lowered performance expectations
- Physiological arousal
- Reduced self-control
- Reduced working memory capacity

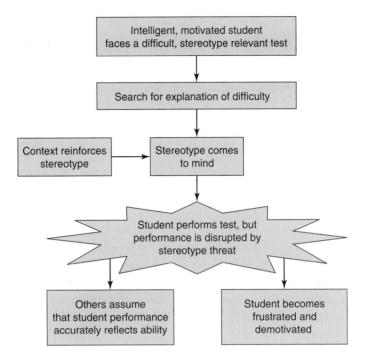

FIGURE 7.1 Stereotype Threat Flow Chart

Source: Block, C., Roberson, L., & Merriweather, T. (2008). *Responding to stereotype threat: What we know and what remains unanswered.* Paper presented at the Winter Roundtable on Cultural Psychology and Education at Teachers College, Columbia University.

- Reduced creativity, flexibility, and speed
- Anxiety
- Excess effort or attention
- Lowered performance expectations (Stroesser & Good, 2010)

Stress

How exactly do broad social factors, such as racism, acculturation, poverty, and so forth, get translated into the everyday physical and emotional distresses that disproportionately affect People of Color? The mechanism is stress. Put most simply, lacking resources and being the perpetual object of discrimination make life more stressful and increase the risks of instability and difficulty in school. Myers suggested that "for many blacks, particularly those who are poor, the critical antecedents appear to be the higher basal stress level and the state of high stress vigilance at which normative functioning often occurs"

(Myers, 1982, p. 128). In other words, poor African Americans tend to be in a stress-primed state of existence.

Certain internal and external factors either increase or decrease (mediate) the subjective experience of stress and, as a result, the risk of stress-related dysfunction (Myers, 1982). Externally, economic conditions set the stage for whether racial and social-class-related experiences will be sources of greater or lesser stress. Internally, individual temperament, problem-solving skills, sense of internal control, and self-esteem reduce the likelihood that an event or situation is experienced as stressful. With these factors as a baseline, two additional conditions that seem to mediate the individual's response when a stressful situation is actually presented: the actual episodic stressful event that occurs and the coping and adaptation of which the individual is capable. In relation to the former, episodic crises are more frequent among poor African Americans, and such crises are more likely to be damaging and disruptive because of their higher basal stress levels. "For example, the death of a relative, the loss of a job due to economic downturns is likely to be more psychologically and economically devastating to the person who is struggling to find enough money to eat, to pay the rent, and to support three or four children than it would to someone without those basic day to day concerns" (Myers, 1982, pp. 133–134). There are substantial differences among group members in their ability to cope and in the type of coping strategies used. For example, street youth resort to "cappin, rappin, conning, and fighting" as coping mechanisms for survival in the streets. For others, the "ability to remain calm, cool, and collected in the face of a crisis" is primary (Myers, 1982). Still others may turn negatively to alcohol and drugs or positively to religion and increased personal and social interactions to gain some distance from general stress or crisis events.

The stress-related risks are higher for African Americans as a group than for the general population. However, there are very real ways to reduce the risk:

> To the extent that ethnic cultural identity can be developed and stably integrated into the personality structure, to the extent that skills and competencies necessary to meet the varied demands can be obtained, to the extent that flexible, contingent response strategies can be developed, and to the extent that support systems can be maintained and strengthened, then resistances can be developed that will enhance stress tolerance and reduce individual and collective risk. (Myers, 1982, p. 138)

Microaggressive Stress

Recent research by Sue and others have conceptualized many of these stresses as related to microaggressions. The biological health effects include increased heart rate, high blood pressure, hypertension, and other physiological reactivity to chronic stressors:

- Emotional effects: Lower self-esteem, subjective well-being, and mental health (depression and anxiety). Pressures that humiliate tend to correlate to depression; stressors that produce fear are associated with anxiety.
- Cognitive effects:
  - Cognitive disruption: A study indicated that "constant, vague, just-below-the surface acts of covert racism impair performance by draining psychological energy or distracting from the task at hand" (Sue, 2010, p. 101).
  - Stereotype threat: The fear that one will be evaluated by a stereotype and confirm it, even if one does not believe the stereotype.

- Behavioral effects:
  - Hypervigilance and skepticism: Also called "healthy paranoia" or "cultural mistrust."
  - Forced compliance: One either accepts the situation or suffers the consequences (surviving or being co-opted); may mean concealing true feelings or conforming to the norm.
  - Rage and anger may be acted out or internalized; may lead to bitterness.
  - Fatigue and hopelessness: Exhaustion from constant petty humiliations and demeaning situations.
  - Strength through adversity: Thriving in a less than accepting society (Sue, 2010, pp. 96–105).

Stereotype Threat Stress

Stereotype threat produces anxiety in individuals, particularly prior to a test or another performance (Marx & Stapel, 2006). Individuals under stereotype threat may attempt to regulate their emotions in order to reduce anxiety. Unfortunately, while these efforts may work, energy is taken away from the individuals' ability to perform well on cognitive tasks (Johns, Inzlicht & Schmader, 2008). At one point, I taught a course to teachers from several schools in Portland. I called it "Addressing the Achievement *Test-Score* Gap," as I am not able to discern, as most teachers are not, which performances are based on lack of knowledge and which are due to lower performance on tests due to stereotype threat or other factors (we will discuss test bias itself in Chapter 8).

Providing Psychological Support in the Classroom

Previous sections of this chapter have focused on areas of psychological concern that may relate to some Students of Color. These included problems of racial identity development, conflicts around acculturation, and stress-related reactions. For a given student, personal issues, concerns, and stresses may be brought into the classroom by the child or by concerned parents.

Generally, such reactions interfere with student learning, may lead to behavioral problems, and should be addressed in some way. Three general strategies are suggested. The first is the creation of a classroom environment in which a sense of personal safety abounds and in which specific coping strategies can be taught as part of the curriculum. The second—seeking of counseling services—depends on the availability of resources. In an ideal situation, teachers can seek ongoing consultation from counseling professionals on how to work optimally with a student in the classroom and/or refer the student for external assessment or counseling. The third is to address stereotype threat when possible. There are opportunities to directly prevent stereotype threat when it leads to stress and lowered achievement. Most of these are "fairly simple, straightforward and importantly, cost free" (Wise, 2010, p. 179):

- Combine constructive criticism on the work done by Students of Color with regular and consistent reiteration of the teacher's belief in their potential.
- Encourage group work, team projects, group studying and a collaborative approach to learning, rather than individual work and a competitive approach.
- Challenge students with high standards, rather than demean them with remediation. In keeping with this maxim, all middle school should strive to enroll Black students in eighth grade algebra.
- Teachers should reject the notion of "aptitude" and stress the malleability of intelligence and ability.
- Provide "centering" exercises in class that allow Students of Color to reflect favorably on their identities and values.
- Get students to see academic success as part of a larger project to undo institutionalized inequality and White supremacy. (adapted from Wise, 2010, pp. 179–182)

Awareness that students may bring specific psychological problems with them is a first step in creating caring and supportive environments that can lead to successful learning situations for all children. Such a focus increases the desire of teachers to provide a safe place for students. By *safe*, we mean an environment in which the feelings of each individual are considered from an attitude of caring and willingness to dialogue across differences (Moule, 1998). Sensible and fair rules of participation are not enough to make a classroom feel safe to many students (Burbules, 1993; Ellsworth, 1990). "It often will not be enough just to listen; one might have to work to create an environment in which a silenced voice feels the confidence or security to speak" (Burbules, 1993, p. 33).

A number of other learning goals can be introduced into the classroom to help students who are at psychological risk. Promoting resiliency through classroom activities can become an increasingly important meta-goal for students for whom risk and vulnerability are everyday experiences. Promoting resiliency involves strengthening personal characteristics that permit better coping in stressful situations.

The following factors are critical to resiliency: an ability to not overreact to stress, specific coping and problem-solving skills, a history of success in coping with race-related situations, a perception of being capable of manipulating the world and controlling one's destiny, and a healthy and well-integrated sense of self (Myers & King, 1985). To the extent any of these personal characteristics can be addressed, students will benefit by the development of better coping skills. Obviously, such factors do not work in isolation but rather reinforce each other. For example, success in coping leads to personal empowerment and feelings of competency, which in turn increase the probability of future successes in adapting and coping.

In looking at specific populations, Puerto Rican children—defined as "invulnerable to risk"—tended to exhibit more sociability, dominance, endurance, energy, demonstrativeness, reflectiveness, and impulse control than those who were more at risk (Canino & Zayas, 1997). This research also pointed to the importance of ethnic identification, family values, and adaptation to biculturality as hedges against vulnerability to stress.

> For instilling resiliency in African American youth, rather than using methods that encourage African Americans to accept their negative environmental circumstances and adapt to such an environment, provide information that promotes the effective use of underutilized resources and helps them to seek strategies and greater social mobility that will enable them to survive in their environment. (Dupree, Spencer & Bell, 1997)

Another meta-goal is greater comfort and success in dealing with culture conflict and biculturality, both frequent sources of stress for Children of Color. Helping children tolerate competing cultural values and practices by learning to reduce the conflict and confusion inherent in bicultural settings is key when such conflicts find their way into the classroom. "A mother explained when I was questioning her values about allowing him to fight. 'I'll take care of his behavior; you take care of his education. Where we live he has to be tough and be able to fight. I'm not going to stop that. You set your standards here and I'll see that he understands he has to abide by them'" (Pinderhughes, 1989, p. 182). Teaching the child to negotiate this duality—inconsistencies between home and school are likely to be ongoing realities the bicultural child must learn to negotiate. Rather than unintentionally creating a conflict, educators may regularly monitor their own value judgments and teaching goals so as not to "undermine the children's ability to tolerate the inconsistency between home and school. What the children needed was a sense that while the values at school were different, those of their parents were not being undermined. The teachers ... must be able to function as a bridge, respecting the children's cultural values while simultaneously upholding the values of the school" (Pinderhughes, 1989, p. 182).

Offering Students of Color skill development in overcoming pressures against achievement helps. There is real value in teaching students how to cope with the anti-achievement attitudes sometimes found in their friends by increasing "students' adoption of the strategy of 'accommodation without assimilation' ... or 'playing the classroom game.' The essence of this strategy is that students should recognize and accept the fact that they can participate in two cultural or language frames of reference for different purposes without losing their own cultural and language identity or undermining their loyalty to the minority community" (Ogbu, 1992, p. 12).

Ogbu (1992) also emphasized the value of introducing such learning more broadly within the school curriculum, as part of counseling and related programs intended to teach students how to separate attitudes and behaviors that enhance school success from those that lead to acculturation or "acting White." Such interventions may help students avoid interpreting achievement as "acting White" and thereby as a threat to their identity and sense of security.

Who Are the Teachers?

According to Liston and Zeichner (1996), the majority of prospective teachers are White females, come from middle-class homes, and have had very little contact with other cultures or with Children of Color. Although attempts have been made to bring a more diverse population into elementary education, the vast majority of preservice teachers remain monocultural and middle to upper-middle class. In 1996, student enrollment across ethnic groups in public elementary and secondary schools was 64 percent White, 17 percent Black, 14 percent Hispanic, 4 percent Asian/Pacific Islander, and 1 percent American Indian/Alaskan Native (National Center for Education Statistics, 1999). In contrast, the 1994 teaching force was 87 percent non-Hispanic White, 7 percent Black, 4 percent Hispanic, 1 percent Asian/Pacific Islander, and 1 percent American Indian/Alaskan Native (U.S. Department of Education, 1997). In my home state, Oregon, one in every four students is a Child of Color while only one in every 20 teachers is a Person of Color (Moule, 2008).

Many Teachers of Color have been retiring, and expanded occupational options for People of Color has meant few replacements. Meanwhile, the continual increase in the percentage of Children of Color has caused an increasing cultural mismatch. One helpful solution is recruiting preservice teachers who are more likely already culturally competent by virtue of membership in a Community of Color or who have "experiences, knowledge, and dispositions that will enable them to teach well in culturally diverse settings" (Sleeter, 2001, p. 96).

While much lip service is paid to recruiting more Students and Faculty of Color, the numbers have remained consistently low. Overall, college "student enrollments become increasingly racially diverse, the teaching force is actually becoming increasingly White due mainly to the striking decline in Black, Hispanic, and Asian enrollments in teacher education programs since 1990, with a proportionate increase in minority business majors" (Hodgkinson, 2002, p. 104). In addition, both cost and the European cultural climate that predominates keep many non-White students out of the university (or contribute to their dropout rate). It is not only difficult for Students of Color, especially those who are not highly acculturated, to navigate the complex application and entry procedures that teaching programs typically require, but it is also a challenge to feel comfortable, safe, and welcome in a monocultural environment that is not their own.

An equally critical factor is the number of Instructors of Color within teaching programs. These statistics continue to remain quite low. Teachers at the university level are overwhelming White. Whether because of the lack of input from Students and Faculty of Color or cultural incompetence, teacher educators and preservice teachers continue to replicate themselves and remain prisoners of their own experiences (Liston & Zeichner, 1996). This situation will not easily right itself, for "when predominately White teacher education classes focus on race in the curriculum, without the presence of racially diverse standpoints there is the danger that the dialogue will privilege White viewpoints and add little to an understanding of how concepts of race and racism are experienced from different racial standpoints" (Johnson, 2002, p. 163).

Without a more balanced perspective, cultural learning cannot help but remain superficial, residing somewhere outside the heart of preservice teachers, accessed only when time permits and the presence of culturally diverse students compels. Promising practices for deepening the preparation for teaching diverse students are placements in diverse settings as well as work with mentor Teachers of Color (Meltzoff, 2010; Moule & Higgins, 2007).

What is it like being an Instructor or Researcher of Color? I have come to anticipate my multicultural education class with both dread and pleasure: a knotty journey we all take each quarter. When in conversations with a new graduate teaching assistant, I was reminded of the difficulty of this work and how much I have grown in order to withstand this regular onslaught. After our first day, Adrian, a Chicano comfortable in diverse environments but not yet in his role as a Teacher of Color at the college level, asks me, "Do you find the students ... resistant?" He had begun to understand the complexities of bringing others to an open understanding of cultural perspectives. I shared with him research that shows that courses in multicultural education can actually reinforce bias (Barry & Lechner, 1995). I tell him that most preservice teachers in the class struggle both with the subject matter and their reactions to having their first African American professor. Added to this is my commitment to teach in a constructivist and student-centered manner—a far different atmosphere from the usual university courses. One can begin to appreciate the kinds of barriers to growth and openness that can get erected.

As an isolated Researcher of Color, I am routinely interested in identifying the race of the researchers in the articles I review. I find that this information is very central to my eventual understanding and evaluation of the material. When I share this kind of information with colleagues, I am met with blank stares, as if I have crossed some invisible line. They just do not see it as relevant. This conflict highlights one aspect of institutional racism a Person of Color routinely faces: insistence on an exclusively Eurocentric perspective. I like what Kochman (1981) says about this: "White[s] … consider an idea authoritative when it has been published.… Blacks consider it essential for individuals to have personal positions on issues and assume full responsibility for arguing their validity" (pp. 24–25). Others assert that claiming objectivity is itself the biased stance of privileged White males (Reinharz & Davidman, 1992, p. 157). In any case, I am determined to include my personal position and the context of my current life in my work, even when my faculty colleagues want only hard objective facts (Moule, 2003).

Isolated Teachers of Color

Recruiting Teachers of Color helps faculty of schools reflect racial diversity, yet the first such teachers are often isolated individuals in their school culture and demographic. Levon (pseudonym), an African American preservice teacher, provides a perspective on the struggles of such an isolated individual during his time in a teacher education program. Levon's interaction with other members of his preservice teacher cohort showed him open to others' views, well-versed in several cultures, and acutely aware of the interactional problems that could arise during his journey toward licensure (Moule, 1998).

On the first day of the multicultural issues in education course, Levon wondered how honest and authentic the interaction would be and whether his own racial experiences and issues would "be lost in the quest for diversity among other religions, genders, groups. Hopefully, people will say what's on their minds.… Politically correct language allows Americans to hide their racist beliefs.… We can never solve any racial problems because people are always denying that racism exists in today's society.… Sometimes people's reluctance to change makes me want to holler." He spoke of his potential value as a Black man entering the teaching profession. "Considering the social, economic, and political situation of black men in America, I can bring a perspective to education that could prove quite beneficial in classroom practices.... Studies have shown that ... black males in particular ... psychologically drop out as early as third grade.... The idea and reality of black men in the classroom can serve as a catalyst for students who are otherwise 'checking out' of school" (Moule, 1998, p. 113).

While Levon sees the value of his presence and role-modeling for the Students of Color he will teach, he is acutely aware of the more difficult journey he travels to become a teacher:

> Being the only African American in the ... Cohort is a particular experience.... Sometimes I wonder how I managed to slip through the barriers (institutionalized racism) that impede the progress of my people. Being the only "one" means that I'm carrying all 22 million [African Americans] on my back.... I find it very strange that my graduate program takes pride in their diversity achievements. They need to realize that having one person of color in the program doesn't equate to true cultural diversity. (Moule, 1998, p. 114)

Along with his reflections on his future value to students and his own struggles, Levon clearly sees his value in the education of his White classmates through their interaction with him. "Some of the students found it very difficult to compromise their Eurocentric values.... As future educators, if we cannot honor another cultural perspective then we must reevaluate our decision to become educators.... Once you comprehend another person's life experiences, then you can have a meaningful conversation with them" (Moule, 1998, p. 115).

Through his experiences, Levon developed a new appreciation for the power of multicultural education, and through his observations, we are able to get a first-person sense of the experience of an isolated Person of Color struggling with the mistrust and the racial attitudes of Whites. Fortunately, the outcome was positive and motivating for Levon and his White classmates—all preservice teachers (Levon is now a middle school principal).

Teacher Characteristics That Make a Difference

Preservice teachers and teacher educators bring to their teaching a complex of personal and group identities that can serve as obstacles or as stepping-stones to successful multicultural classroom practice. Are certain traits likely to predict success in teaching, or more specifically, success in teaching a diverse K–12 student population? For example, Haberman (1996) extrapolated the following research-based list of teacher characteristics likely to enhance cross-cultural teaching:

- Teachers need to understand that it is their responsibility to engage *all* students in meaningful learning activities.

- Caring orientation: The expectation of the need for rapport with children and youth.
- Fallibility: The expectation and orientation of teachers to their own errors through reflectivity.
- Persistence: The predisposition to pursue activities at which children or youth will succeed and to solve problems that intrude on learning.
- Organizational ability: The predisposition to engage in planning and gathering of materials.
- Physical and emotional stamina: The ability to persist in situations characterized by poor home lives and other crises facing some students.
- Response to authority: The predisposition to protect children or youth against bureaucratic constraints.
- Explanation of success: The predisposition to emphasize effort rather than ability.
- Teaching style: The predisposition to engage in coaching rather than directive teaching. (p. 755)

In my research, I identified four key teacher characteristics likely to promote successful interaction of teachers and culturally diverse students: care, dialogue, passionate pursuit, and openness to learn (Moule, 1998). Two traits appear on both my list and Haberman's list. *Care* may be defined as giving *permanent value*—considering each child as of value regardless of behavior or differentiated circumstances. This permanent value is also known as "unconditional positive regard" (some would simply use the words "unconditional love"). How a teacher develops and expresses care and concern for students may depend on personal value system, character, and personal philosophy. However, if the teacher lacks care for each student as a unique and valuable human being, no step-by-step techniques will transform the classroom into a safe environment for students. Similarly, my *openness to learn* parallels Haberman's *fallibility* or *reflectivity*. They involve developing skills for lifelong growth, being open to new perspectives and ideas, and encouraging the flexibility to progress in new and different directions. In multicultural education, these characteristics allow teachers to model greater openness to a broader range of learning strategies, skills, and perspectives.

Connections and Reflections: Emerging Views

This exercise is called "Save the Last Word for Me" (Rector, 2010). Find a heading in this chapter and a paragraph within it that raises an emotional response for you. In a group of three or four, the first person shares the selection without comment. Each other person in the group takes one minute to give a response and reactions to the selection. At the end, the first person to speak spends two minutes sharing why he or she made the selection and adds comments, having the last word. Each other person shares a comment, and the group proceeds as before for each selection.

Consider a time when your abilities as a student were undervalued by a teacher. Consider a time when you came to school with a heavy psychological issue. Think: What did you do in the situation? How will you be able to not make the same assumptions or mistakes with your students?

Classroom: Adventures in Learning

Copenhaver-Johnson (2006) suggests the following classroom curriculum and material decisions to help open conversations and considerations about race in the classroom:

- Read books that deal directly and indirectly with issues of race and racism. We often underestimate what children can handle at young ages (Knapp, 2001) and simply do not think to include such books at older ages. Choose read-aloud books from some of the many multicultural book lists available. Here are two excellent sites: http://www.ipl.org/div/pf/entry/ 48493 and http://bullpup.lib.unca.edu/multconf/multcultlit.html

- Modify the expectations and participant structures of read-aloud. By making the read-aloud times more interactive, the children's thoughts and questions lead naturally to difficult conversations both in the classroom and in the children's lives: "They transformed the text—projecting racism into other settings and taking new perspectives on it" (Copenhaver-Johnson, 2006, p. 19).

- Take children's interests, curiosities, and questions seriously and provide appropriate resources. An example from Copenhaver-Johnson's study involved first-grade students asking their teacher why a picture book "about Martin Luther King, Jr. did not depict Dr. King's assassin—or any other white people, for that matter" (p. 19). While that showed a negative racial interaction, in that case, the teacher brought in material on the role of White people in the civil rights movement.

- Include Characters of Color in a range of literature (not just for Black History Month). Books showing families and children in contemporary times having experiences common to the children provided White children a subtle and important way to relate to characters who were Black and provided Black children with Black protagonists beyond the Black History Month materials. "The resulting conversations about these types of books (in which the themes were not about race, yet the characters were black) provided a chance for children to realize the similarities of their positive *and* challenging experiences. Although the children didn't speak directly to racism issues, the books deepened their sense of community and built the trust critical to open conversations about race" (p. 20).

CHAPTER 8

Bias in the Curriculum and in the Classroom

"There is not one Indian in the whole of this country who does not cringe in anguish and frustration because of these textbooks. There is not one Indian child who has not come home in shame and tears."

–Rupert Costo

"A teacher cannot build a community of learners unless the voices and lives of the students are an integral part of the curriculum."

–Bob Peterson

The following happens far too often in today's classrooms:

The Counselor was visiting a pre-Kindergarten class in another district. She entered the classroom to find five tables of three or four children each, busily working with crayons and markers.

Four-year olds are so cute! She couldn't resist stopping to watch for a moment. What she saw ... when she really watched ... was upsetting to her.

There was one table whose behavior was different....

There was nothing outstanding about what was happening.

The teacher was not ignoring these children.

The other children weren't teasing or tormenting them in any way.

But ... they were different.

Somewhere between the molecules of air ... these children had "gotten the message" already. In a world where the other groups were "bluebirds" and "cardinals" and "robins;" they were the "crows."

The young students, at four years of age, had already experienced "Animal Farm" mentality ... where they were the animals not quite as equal as the rest.

Among these children, some were "Children of Color" and all were not as well dressed ... not as clean ... not as accepted as the others. These children could see the invisible wall that separated them from the others as clearly as the children from the old fable could see that the "Emperor wasn't wearing any clothes!"

The Counselor knew that the students at the "fifth table" had already begun their educational experience lacking the "connections" necessary for success in school. (Ely, 2001, pp. 138–139)

Can such destructive practices be broken? Or, we could ask, "What will happen if the increasing numbers of teachers have no idea about what they are doing culturally, who they are working with, and what the students' circumstances are? Will we continue this cycle? Does the cycle of culturally incompetent teachers continue?" (Murtadha-Watts, 1998, p. 620).

This chapter delves into the sources of bias in cross-cultural teaching. It begins by looking at ways attitudes can shape expectations. It will become clear how certain teacher attitudes and expectations are the natural outgrowth of who teachers are and what skills and preparations they bring to the cross-cultural classroom. We see how these attitudes are inadvertently supported through bias in testing and textbooks. Next, we discover that many efforts at curriculum reform have remained superficial and may in fact do more harm than good. Finally, we focus on how to more effectively reform curriculum in regard to culture and ethnicity.

What does a culturally competent classroom look like? What are the images on the walls, the books on the shelf, the materials prepared for use? How much input has come from the students? Has racism or stereotyping played a role in how teachers relate to students? Have teachers simply added materials for cultural relevancy or have they examined deep cultural roots and adjusted the curriculum accordingly?

The Impact of Social and Racial Attitudes

Most teachers begin with their own cultural perspectives and their own unexamined classroom experiences. They often fondly remember their years as students and seek to consciously or unconsciously reproduce those classrooms. Unfortunately, such models are more often than not culturally White and middle class (Kunjufu, 2002; Sleeter, 2001). Christine Sleeter analyzed eighty empirically based research studies on preservice teacher preparation. Included were studies on the recruitment and selection of preservice teachers as well as the effects of coursework, field practicum, and program restructuring. Although these studies clearly demonstrated the existence of ethnocentric attitudes and a general lack of cultural knowledge on the part of White preservice teachers and highlighted a few promising practices, very few actually followed preservice teachers into the classroom or tried to determine optimal strategies for creating culturally competent teachers. The bottom line is that we still do not know how to populate the teaching profession with excellent, culturally responsive educators, for "racial, ethnic, and cultural attitudes and beliefs are always present, often problematic, and profoundly significant in shaping teaching conceptions and actions" (Gay, 2010a, p. 143).

Classrooms based on unexamined experiences will inevitably miss the needs of many culturally diverse students. Several websites, such as the IAT described in Chapter 3, have been developed to help people examine their racial and cultural attitudes. They offer a quick, hands-on opportunity to assess the attitudes and beliefs one might bring into the classroom. I encourage you to take the full range of tests and read the various interpretations of your scores. Together, they should provide useful information about your own built-in biases.

Teacher Expectations Affect Student Learning

As we explored in Chapter 3, a vast body of research in social psychology shows how attitudes can unconsciously affect behavior. Rosenthal and Jacobson (1968) looked at the relationship between teacher expectations and student performance. Teachers were told at the beginning of the school year that half the students in their class were high performers and the other half were low performers. In actuality, there were *no* differences between the students. However, by the end of the year, there were significant differences in how the two groups performed. Those who were expected to do well did so—and vice versa.

In another experiment, rats were assigned to beginning psychology students (Rosenthal, 1976). Some were told that their rats came from very bright strains; others were told that their rats were genetically low in intelligence. The rats were all from the same litter. By the end of the training period, each group of rats was performing as expected. In these two experiments, what the teachers and the psychology students believed and expected was translated into differential behavior, which in turn became what Rosenthal called a *self-fulfilling prophecy*. In other words, what we believe (our attitudes about people) shapes the way we treat students. Although Rosenthal and Jacobson's studies were controversial and led to a thousand studies, their findings resonate with the classroom experiences of other educational researchers and teachers (Loewen, 2010; Milner, 2010). Below and beyond teacher expectations is a fundamental and often unconscious bias: "Teachers lower their expectations of students because they do not recognize the brilliance students possess, especially when students express themselves, evaluate a problem, or address a situation in a way unlike the teacher.... Teachers' decisions to lower their expectations are made visible through all forms of explicit, implicit, and null curriculum" (Milner, 2010, p. 125).

In the classic Iowa eye-color experiment by Jane Elliott, we have a wonderful example of the power of classroom teachers. Elliott divided her class into two groups based on eye color and then manipulated the environment and her way of speaking with each group. She told the children that one group was better than the other. Within a very short time, the preferred group (blue-eyed) was learning well and the denigrated group (brown-eyed) was failing. The next day, she told the children she had gotten it wrong and that the brown-eyed children were better. Again, the children believed her. One key example: On the second day, the children who were preferred accomplished a flashcard activity in half the time of the first day.

This next story, hopefully apocryphal, underlies the insidious nature of how standardized test scores affect teacher expectations:

> A substitute teacher replaces an ill regular teacher in October and remains until the end of the school year: "He managed the class well and caused his principal no problems. In June, as he is cleaning out his desk, the principal came to his room to commend his performance. 'I'm so sorry we never really had time to chat until now,' she said. 'I was so busy last fall that I never even had time to give you a proper orientation.' 'That's OK,' the teacher responded. 'Mrs. Tyler had left me a sheet with the children's IQ scores, and I found that most helpful. As I looked back over the year, the children really behaved according to their potential.' 'IQ scores?' the principal asked. 'We don't *have* IQ scores! Let me see that sheet.' He handed it to her. 'My God, those are your children's locker numbers!'" (Loewen, 2010, p. 49)

Loewen taught in Black college, and his experiences uncover deeper issues most of us have never considered: "Before school desegregation, many teachers in black high schools expected more from light-skinned African Americans than from dark-skinned students" (2010, p. 45). He goes on to share a personal story. I share it because of his willingness to take action once he noticed the problem. How willing are we to step up, step out, and, by our behavior and words, confront the biases we see?

> Young undergraduates-to-be and their teachers milled around in a "mixer" in a large hall, trying to make small talk. So did I. Twenty minutes into this awkward affair, I looked around the hall and had my "aha moment." Ever single graduate student and faculty member—white or black, myself included—was talking with light-skinned students. Darker-skinned African Americans stood in small groups talking with each other. I spent the rest of the hour talking with the darkest students I could find. Of course, my little gesture—one person, in one setting, for 40 minutes—meant nothing. I could only hope that the darker-skinned African Americans were as oblivious to the pattern as I had been. This is hardly likely. Dark-skinned singer Big Bill Broonzy, born in the Mississippi Delta in 1893, incorporated three famous lines about the pattern in a blues song he wrote....

> If you're white, you're all right.

> If you're brown, stick around.

> But if you're black, get back! Get back! Get back!

Lighter-skinned African Americans were sometimes even admitted to parties, fraternities and sororities, and even certain colleges only if their skin color was lighter than a brown paper bag. (2010, pp. 45–46)

Loewen considers that in later years, the Black Is Beautiful movement alleviated some of the problems he had witnessed.

Teachers can create their own expectations for students. Loewen quotes Agee, "In every child who is born, under no matter what circumstances, and in no matter what parents, the potentiality of the human race is born again," (2010, p. 65). Teachers who embrace this concept will always find a way to access this potential:

> We must conclude from the research ... that teachers must not let pupils'
> appearance, their own self-expectations, or low "standardized" test scores influence
> what teachers expect from them. If a teacher cannot convince herself that a student
> has *any* ability, s/he [the teacher] can fake it. Besides, every student is good at *some-thing*, or at least less bad at it. Build on students' strengths. (Loewen, 2010, p. 64)

Whether it be unconscious, unrecognized bias, or longer wait time because you expect certain students are more likely to respond, vigilance and awareness will help you consider how your expectations affect student achievement.

Cultural Aspects of Curriculum Delivery

Some aspects of the teaching process limit its relevance to Students of Color. Many of these relate to the fact that current pedagogies and practices are often defined in terms of dominant European cultural values and norms and limit the ability of teachers to address and serve the needs of non-White populations adequately. Let us explore additional sources of this cultural mismatch as well as describe ways in which current pedagogy often portrays Students of Color in a negative light: highlighting their perceived weaknesses and assuming a lack of ability. In the next chapter, when discussing classroom management styles, I describe an incident of a supposedly out-of-control African American four-year-old. From the perspective of mainstream norms, his lack of response to a veiled request appeared to be willful disobedience. We must consider the underlying culture before making assumptions about children.

Parents socialize children into different cultures. In a Black working-class neighborhood, children were taught to tell rich, creative, embellished stories with many gestures; in a White working-class community, the emphasis was on stories that were as accurate as possible, with easy-to-discern "correct" answers. In a sense, each group was trapped by its own norms. Teachers tend to value students who tell stories the same way they do, and they negatively judge students whose styles are different as "not up to my standard" because of, for example, creativity over accuracy or succinctness over many gestures (Heath, 1983). Because the styles do not match, the teachers may begin to form conscious or unconscious opinions about the academic ability of the young storytellers (Asante, 1991; Kochman, 1981; Milner, 2010).

Teacher/student interaction styles can severely hamper the learning process for a child whose cultural discourse style differs greatly from that of the teacher. Poor Deena as she eagerly anticipated her "sharing time": the one time during the school day when children have an opportunity "to talk about their personal experiences and to bring their lives at home into the classroom" (Blair & Jones, 1998, p. 53). The teacher did not respond in an empowering or supportive manner. The teacher expected a *topic-centered* style of discourse, while Deena had a much larger, conceptually and contextually, complex story to tell. Mrs. Jones "did not have the cultural knowledge to understand the *topic-associated* style of this child" (Blair & Jones, 1998, p. 55). In her efforts to keep Deena on topic, she interrupts her twice and questions her three times. "Deena's train of thought may well have been disrupted by Mrs. Jones attempts to help her move toward a different style (topic-centered) of sharing" (Blair & Jones, 1998, p. 55).

In my classes, I am often aware that I use the topic-associated style of teaching and sharing. I bring this to the attention of my students and explain that it is a cultural difference. This metacognition of how I speak in this style may be helpful to them in their future classrooms.

Many struggle with voices from the past that echo an embedded way of communicating: "As an Anglo teacher, I struggle to quiet voices from my own farm family, echoing as always from some unstated standard." This teacher asked, "How can we untangle our own deeply entrenched assumptions?" (Finders, 1992, p. 60). She saw the need to untangle her taken-for-granted assumptions from her teaching. The deeply held beliefs did not need to change; they simply needed to be recognized for what they were: taken-for-granted assumptions about the world that may not apply to everyone.

One way to overcome our own assumptions on style is to take the time to study the communities and the students we teach. The reflection at the end of this chapter gives specifics you might consider in order to gain conscious knowledge of those you teach. If you do not think through how you interact, then you will probably assume your prior embedded style of communication. Assuming a taken-for-granted exchange is like being in a play that has memorized and recognized roles. A *script* is a set of expectations about what will happen next in a well-understood situation. In many life situations, participants seem to be reading their roles. Scripts lay out what is supposed to happen and how others' actions are to be interpreted and responded to. Seeking out additional cultural experiences and becoming familiar with various interaction styles enable people to "feel comfortable and capable of playing [any] role effectively" (Schank, 1990, p. 8).

Recognizing the boxes that keep us in our own worlds so we can understand and sometimes transcend them is the root of cultural competence. If a norm is never questioned—and many are not—then that standard is inadvertently applied, with great harm, to children with different cultural norms.

Bias in Conceptualizing Ethnic Populations

Western science has a long history of portraying ethnic populations as biologically inferior. Beginning with the work of such luminaries as Charles Darwin, Sir Francis Galton, and G. Stanley Hall, one can trace what Sue and Sue (1990) called the *genetic deficiency model* of racial minorities into the present, carried on by research psychologists such as Jensen (1972). As biological theories of genetic inferiority lost intellectual credibility, they were quickly replaced within social science circles by notions of cultural inferiority or *deficit.* While political correctness would not allow educators with negative racial attitudes to continue to embrace the idea of genetic inferiority, they could easily support theories "that a community subject to poverty and oppression is a disorganized community, and this disorganization expresses itself in various forms of psychological deficit ranging from intellectual performance ... to personality functioning" (Jones & Korchin, 1982, p. 19).

These models took two forms: *cultural deprivation* and *cultural disadvantage.* In relation to the former, non-Whites were seen as deprived (lacking substantive culture). On other hand, *disadvantaged*—a supposed improvement over the term *deprived*—implies that although ethnic-group members do possess culture, that culture had become deficient and distorted from the ravages of racism. While the critiques of the terms are well-founded, it is important that we realize and remember one key fact: Due to the overlap of socioeconomic status and race, some groups are, on average, deprived in many ways beyond the efforts of the group to improve. However, such a recognition should have little to do with our expectations of the children in our care. More recent and acceptable terms are *culturally different* and *culturally distinct.* But even these can "carry negative connotations when they are used to imply that a person's culture is at variance (out-of-step) with the dominant (accepted) culture" (Atkinson, Morten & Sue, 1993, p. 9).

Research on ethnic populations tends to find and focus on deficits and shortcomings. This body of research has been widely criticized for faulty methodology: "Studies typically involved the comparison of ethnic and white groups on measures standardized on white, middle-class samples, administered by examiners of like background, intended to assess variables conceptualized on the basic U.S. population" (Jones & Korchin, 1982, p. 19).

Two additional tendencies have been even more insidious. First, researchers have chosen to study and compare Whites and People of Color on characteristics that culturally favor dominant-group members. For example, if intelligence is assessed by measuring verbal reasoning and schoolchildren are compared on their ability to compete or take personal initiative, these variables will portray White subjects in a more favorable light and simultaneously create a negative impression of the abilities and resources of ethnic subjects, who may excel in collaborative efforts and spatial variables. There is even some evidence of test items being discarded when they favored African American populations (Loewen, 2010, p. 53).

Second, where differences have been found between Whites and People of Color, they tend to be interpreted as reflecting weaknesses in ethnic culture or character. Looking at such studies, various researchers have asked why alternative interpretations stressing the creative adaptiveness or strengths inherent in ethnic personality or culture might not just as easily have been sought. The Moynihan Report attributes various African American social problems to deterioration of the Black family and has been soundly criticized both for blaming the victim and for pathologizing to the exclusion of other possible explanations. One critic wrote: "If we regard the social oppression of blacks by whites as a total dynamic, why is the black end of this dynamic more pathological than the white end? ... And how does one distinguish a 'pathology' from an 'heroic adaptation to overwhelming pressures'?" (Hampden-Turner, 1974, p. 83). Inherent in this critique is a most important point: Negative portrayals and stereotypes of People of Color serve to justify the status quo of oppression and unfair treatment and therefore serve political as well as psychological purposes.

An interesting and provocative example about the representation of Chinese Americans as the model minority "passive, ingratiating, reticent, non–complaining and self-denying" (Tong, 1981, p. 3), follows. Were these characteristics more a survival reaction to American racism than a true reflection of traditional Chinese traits? Traditional Chinese culture includes a heroic tradition that portrays the Chinese in a very different manner: "Coexistent with the Conventional Tradition was the 'heroic,' which exalted a time-honored Cantonese sense of self: the fierce, arrogant, independent individual beholden to no one and loyal only to those deemed worthy of undying respect, on that individual's terms" (Tong, 1981, p. 15). Perpetuating the myth of the model minority has led to the confusion of necessary adaptation and culture.

The traits that allowed Asian students to conform to and assimilate into White culture—however superficially—have led to classroom success to the extent that college admissions for Asian students exceed their representation in the overall population. In this case, bias in conceptualizing People of Color seems to work in favor of a group—but at what cost?

Bias in Assessment

In no other area of education has there been more concern about cultural bias than in testing. This is because People of Color have for many years watched their children being placed in remedial classrooms or tracked as having special needs on the basis of IQ tests (remember how test scores may affect expectations?). Serious life decisions are regularly made on the basis of these tests, and it is reasonable to expect them to be culture-free; that is, scored based on what is being measured and not differentially affected by the cultural background of the test taker. In reality, there probably is no such thing as a culture-free test, and ethnic group members' abilities tend to be underestimated by intelligence tests (Loewen, 2010; Snowden & Todman, 1982; Steele, 1997; Suzuki & Kugler, 1995).

A number of factors can contribute to cultural bias in testing. Test items and procedures may reflect dominant cultural values. A test may simply be more attuned to those with more mobility or more money.

> Journalist Susan Eaton showed that many black and Puerto Rican 3rd graders in Hartford, the capital of America's richest state, live so constricted by poverty and race that they had never seen the Connecticut River, which forms the eastern boundary of the city. On a field trip, seeing it for the first time from the windows of their school bus, the children gave it a standing ovation! Although they live in New England these children have never been sledding or even seen a sled up close. What chance do such children have to pick up, semiautomatically, useful facts about historical sites, the president, or anything else in mainstream culture? (Loewen, 2010, p. 59).

I had a similar experience as a director of a migrant day care center. Many of the children had been up and down Interstate 5 in the central valley of California and Oregon for years, accompanying their parents on harvesting routes. When I arranged for a field trip to the ocean, it was the first time most of them had ever seen it. Lack of experience is often reflected in test score items. Based on location and teacher/advisor expectations, different students are often taught different things and may be tracked into less rigorous courses based on race. Due to socioeconomic factors, the quality of instruction is not the same for all students (Sciarra, 2009).

The test construction, the test preparation, and the testing situations may all be problematic. As we noted, a test may not have been standardized on populations of Color—only on middle-class Whites. Language differences and unfamiliarity or discomfort with students' culture can cause a tester to misjudge them or be unable to establish rapport in group and individual testing situations (Reynolds & Kaiser, 1990). When considering bias in assessment, remember the psychological component included in Chapter 7: stereotype threat:

> The recent No Child Left Behind Act imposed high-stakes standardized testing in elementary grades. As a result, young children are made highly aware of standardized test significance at an earlier age and have a heightened investment in their test performance. Low performance may result in retention.... The standardized test performance of early children is influenced by the situational pressures outlined in stereotype threat theory. This is of particular importance because ... stereotype threat research has demonstrated that racial performance gaps are influenced by cognitive processes that may be amenable to intervention. (Wasserberg, 2007, p. 123)

The achievement gap is known among students, and this knowledge may lead to test results compromised by physical and cognitive factors brought about by the threat of reinforcing the stereotype. In many situations, simple unconscious associations may drastically change outcomes. For example, the performance of African American students in a testing situation was cut in half by asking them to identify their race at the start of the test (Steele, 1997). This simple act unconsciously reminded students of the stereotypes connected with their race. In this particular test of verbal ability on part of the SAT, Black students outperformed White students when race was not primed (Figure 8.1).

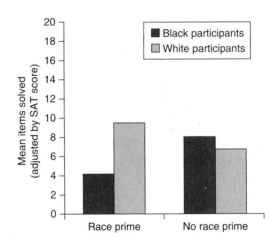

Note: SAT = Scholastic Assessment Test.

FIGURE 8.1 Mean Performance on a Difficult Verbal Test as a Function of Whether Race Was Primed

Source: Claude M. Steele, "A Threat in the Air: How Stereotypes Shape Intellectual Identity and Performance," American Psychologist, 1997; Vol. 52, No. 6, 613–629.

Moreover, when asked at the end of the test, the students who were primed to remember their race were unable to identify the reminder as a factor in their poorer test score (Steele, 1997). There is evidence that students may be mentored before testing in ways that improve exam performance (Good, Aronson & Inzlicht, 2003; see stereotype threat link in the focused bibliography for Chapter 7 in the companion website). When we consider the significant implications of stereotype threat on testing, the use of tests to measure achievement is certainly compromised.

For whatever the reason for the test score gap, another factor is almost always overlooked in regards to the size and significance of the gap. "Most people assume that the statistical gap in scores between persons of color and whites is enormous. It is not. Depending on the test the difference varies but hovers in the range of 10 percent. This difference in average scores has persisted over time, regardless of the type of test, whether it is an IQ test, norm-referenced, or proficiency test, regardless of a test's publisher, or educational level of the test taker, be it kindergarten or graduate school" (Berlak, 2009, p. 68).

Figure 8.2 illustrates the gap well. Note how much of the group overlaps and how little we may tell about any one individual. "In practical terms, the difference gap amounts to a mere handful of test items.... From an educational point of view, such differences have little if any significance. Because of the way the texts are normed and cut scores are set, however, minor differences in the number of correct answers on a multiple-choice test create grossly inflated failure rates for persons of color" (Berlak, 2009, p. 69). Regardless of the significance, test scores produce adverse impacts on Students of Color.

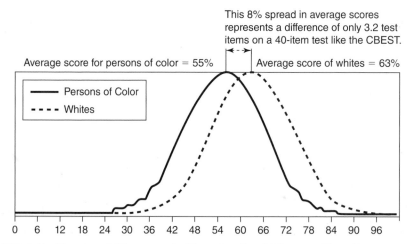

FIGURE 8.2 Percent Difference in Standardized Literacy Test Between Persons of Color and Whites

Source: Berlak, H. (2009). Race and the achievement gap. In W. Au (Ed.), Rethinking multicultural education (pp. 63–72). Milwaukee, WI: Rethinking Schools.

Furthermore, research does not show a significant correlation between the achievement test scores and actual performance: "There is no demonstratable connection between observed academic performance and standardized test scores. Test scores do not predict future success in school, the university, or in the workplace," (Berlak, 2009, p. 69).

As we have seen, assessment across ethnic groups has suffered from many problems. Racism and oppression may lead to group-wide deficits in performance on tests that have nothing to do with native ability. A test may measure different characteristics when administered to members of different cultural groups. Culturally unfair criteria, such as level of education or grade point average, may be used to validate tests expected to predict differences between Whites and People of Color. Differences in experience in taking tests may put non-White students at a disadvantage in testing situations. In short, it is difficult to ensure fairness in testing across cultures, and educators should exert great care in drawing conclusions based exclusively on test scores. They should, as a matter of validation, collect as much non-test collaborative data as possible, especially when the outcome of the assessment may have real-life consequences for the student. So, why are test scores considered so important in so many situations? For one thing, hard numbers from rigorous testing—no matter how biased—are easier to obtain and compare than are more important measures of a sound education, such as creativity, critical thinking skills, or problem solving ability, and they appear to be "reliable statistics," no matter how faulty their basis. Yet, standardized tests "fail to assess the skills and dispositions that matter most. Such tests are generally contrived exercises that measure how much students have managed to cram into short-term memory" (Kohn, 2000, p. 316). Studies of students at all levels have found significant correlations between scores on standardized tests and relatively superficial thinking. High-stakes testing should be reformed. Such tests foster a host of ills, including cheating, turning teachers against teachers, increasing overspecialization, creating defensiveness and competitiveness, driving good educators out of the profession, and narrowing the conversation about education (Kohn, 2000).

Many states, such as Oregon, have attempted to add substantial portfolio reviews to student assessment. However, as much as educators might wish to use collaborative data, such measurements are the first to fall by the wayside when budgets are tight. Policymakers often cite cost savings as a reason to rely solely on unreliable tests (Haynes, 2003).

Much culturally questionable testing still takes place. Educators tend to be over-attached to tests as a means of gaining student information. When they do try to account for cultural differences, instead of creating new instruments, they modify existing ones: adjusting scores, rewriting items, or translating them into a second language. In general, this creates new problems in the place of old ones. The end result of culturally biased assessment is a gap in achievement not only as measured by test scores but also in the placement and eventual educational attainment of students. Many are beginning to recognize the underlying problems as an *opportunity gap* and look not at test scores but at opportunities available for students. We will look at these factors later in this chapter when we consider centering the curriculum on the children.

Bias in Literature

As a basis for curriculum reform, teachers can bring a discerning eye to children's literature and textbooks. Do readers add a brown-skinned, White-at-the-core character or do they transform the curriculum to enable students to view concepts, issues, events, and themes from the perspectives of diverse racial and cultural groups? At first glance, a book that simply has a Character of Color may appear to offer a model for Children of Color as well as a sense of diversity. However, as well-intentioned as the effort may be, a high degree of superficiality can be found in books that we unquestioningly give children (Monroe, 1997).

As an example, the book *My Heart Is on the Ground* (Rinaldi, 1999) was aggressively marketed to nine- to twelve-year-old girls as an authentic fictionalized experience of a young girl in an Indian boarding school. Wide distortion from known facts as well as a disservice to specific individuals and to a culture are included in this book (Atleo et al., 1999). For example, the names of actual dead children were taken off of gravestones and used in stories that do not accurately mirror how these children probably did die. Where the author perhaps saw honor to their memories, those who know the tragedy of the boarding school see a continuation of denial and glossing over of the actual pain of individuals. Likewise, the well-intentioned efforts to share the cultural perspectives of the Sioux tribe are superficial because the author did not reflect authentic cultural roots. Educators who miss this level of understanding mis-educate their students, often relying on stereotypes, as found in this book. The culture was trivialized by resorting to a stereotypical nobility and included derogatory references to girls and women in ways that do not reflect how Native American females are actually thought of and treated.

Even harder to discern as problematic are inappropriate language choices. Overemphasis on compound words ("Friend-to-go-between-us"), romantic-sounding metaphors ("his spring is poisoned with anger"), and the stilted speech pattern that they call "early jawbreaker" ("Teacher tells it that I know some English, that she is much proud of me, but wants be more proud") were rampant (Atleo et al., 1999). Instead of bringing a young reader to a sense of shared humanity in a truly sad chapter of our nation's history, such assaults on a group's language allow the reader to remain distant and to see the group as "other" and "exoticized." Such treatment allows People of Color to be seen as appropriately excluded and oppressed by the dominant culture. Unfortunately, such details in literature meant to make a cultural connection do little to change this status.

One way to begin is to check the credentials of the writer. Has the author lived in the culture? Is she a member of the culture? Has he checked the material with members of the culture? While we cannot expect every writer to be an expert in the cultural roots of a group, we can expect a sense of humility and some indication that the author respects the culture. Does the language continually reflect respect or is it limiting? Become your own critical consumer of information and perspective before serving it to your students.

Bias in Textbooks

James Loewen's critique of eighteen history textbooks helps us to discover what is and what is not found in the textbooks we use in our classrooms. His *Lies My Teacher Told Me: Everything Your American History Textbook Got Wrong* is provocative and thoughtful. Loewen knows it is impossible to uncover the lies and distortions that are found in all the books we use. What we can do is become ourselves and teach our students of almost any grade level to become "independent learners who can sift through arguments and evidence and make reasonable judgments. Then we will have learned how to learn … and neither a one-sided textbook or a one-sided critique of textbooks will be able to confuse us" (Loewen, 2007, p. 313). I conclude that the textbook you are now reading certainly contains errors I have not caught or research results that may be challenged in the future. I hope you sift through the arguments and evidence here to make reasonable judgments.

The following seven criteria developed by a classroom teacher provide a check on multicultural sensitivity in both literature and textbooks:

- Are the authors members of different cultures? Check pictures if available.
- Does the preface make reference to multiculturalism or diversity?
- Do the illustrations, photographs, and drawings show more than one cultural group?
- Do written examples, problems, and/or samples draw from more than one culture?
- Is any reference made to help include speakers of other languages currently learning English?
- Are historical references to other cultures accurate?
- Do multicultural references emphasize individuals rather than stereotypes? (Butler, 2001)

The following list, from 10 Quick Ways to Analyze a Book for Racism and Sexism, is also useful:

- When you check the illustrations, do you see stereotypes, tokenism, or who is doing what? (Remember the child serving in the ad described in Chapter 7?)
- When looking at the storyline, what is considered the standard for success? Is "making it" in the dominant White society the only ideal? And how are problems presented, conceived, and resolved in the story?
- How are lifestyles presented? *Different* or with negative judgments?
- Weigh the relationships between people and see if cultural ways of interacting are included, who has power, who makes decisions, etc.
- Who are the heroes, and whose interests is the hero serving?
- Consider the effects on a child's self-image and if the norms established in the book will support the aspirations of the children in your classroom.
- Watch for loaded words that imply a judgment or are offensive. Examples are "primitive," "treacherous," "docile," and "backward." (Derman-Sparks & ABC Task Force, 1989)

A web search on "racial bias in textbooks" will lead you to many other checklists.

You may also want to search for relevancy for all children regarding gender, disabilities, and other marginalized groups. For example, an article on analyzing books for inclusion on disabilities suggests checking that children in wheelchairs are included in illustrations and what such children are doing in the story (Myers & Bersani, 2008/9). Items on such checklists are useful for broadening the inclusion for all children, and items for analysis may be transferred to use for racial and ethnic sensitivity.

Curriculum Reform

Head knowledge without heart empathy will lead to superficial curriculum adjustments. Although we may individually and collectively turn from overt to covert discrimination, there is little lessening of racism's powerful influence and pain unless changes are rooted in attitude and perspective shifts rather than political correctness. Once we address underlying attitudes and assumptions, we can begin to address curriculum reform that will lead to good teaching for all children. A key to developing heart empathy is to reprogram our comprehension—our head knowledge at deeper levels. Loewen unveils a global and historically entrenched perspective that reveals why the European-centric United States is the most ethnocentric country in the world:

> Eurocentrism is a special case of ethnocentrism. Indeed, imagining Europe as a continent itself exemplifies Eurocentrism. A continent is a "large land mass,

mostly surrounded by water." By any consistent definition, Asia is a continent, of which Europe is only a peninsula, or perhaps a series of peninsulas (Scandinavia, Iberia, Italy, the Balkans). Europe has no justifiable eastern boundary; the Urals are a modest mountain range that does not come within 2,000 miles of the southern edge of Asia. Yet Europe not only is "a continent," to many Americans, it is "*the* continent." As in "continental cuisine." ... Europe ... might better be known as "Far West Asia." "New World" is another Eurocentric term, of course—new to Europe, not to American Indians. Other Eurocentric terms include "discover," "savages," and "settlers." (2010, p. 137)

My own story illustrates how grounding in Eurocentrism both caused my teacher to doubt my work and also affected my relationship to history. As an eighth-grader, I had to attend a summer session to raise my low history grade. I was one of very few Students of Color in the class. We were studying pioneers and the western migration, which actually interested me. However, I was devastated when my teacher, a European American female, accused me of plagiarism. I had written what I thought was a stirring and creative beginning to my term paper. But she would not believe me when I said I wrote it myself. What was her reason for not believing the work was my own? I did not connect it with the color of my skin at the time. Nevertheless, it unconsciously took its toll on me both personally and professionally. I never bothered finishing the term paper and received another low grade. I had a strong aversion toward history for the next 30 years, avoiding it as much as possible during my education and even having some misgivings about marrying my husband more because he was a historian than that he was White. The teacher's racism as well as a history that did not embrace multiple perspectives had its impact on me for years. But finally, at the age of 38, I was encouraged by my students to do a history unit on the small Oregon town where I was teaching. As my students and I explored, learned, and researched the rich history of the town, I realized our efforts at learning had become a delight for both me and them. They won an award and much community praise, and I healed an old wound and reclaimed an excitement about learning history that had been nearly extinguished by the racist attitude of one teacher (adapted from Moule, 1998, p. 18).

Banks and Banks (2010) identify four approaches or levels of curriculum reform, each representing more extensive transformation. Their model can help educators understand the range of possibility in multicultural education as well as critically assess their own efforts at change.

- The *contributions approach* involves merely adding discrete items of culture to the existing curriculum. Examples include heroes, holidays, food, and other discrete cultural facts without any basic conceptual change in the material, sometimes called, "Tacos" and "Teepees."
- The *additive approach* involves adding content, concepts, themes, and perspectives to the curriculum, again without changing its basic structure.

- The *transformational approach* occurs when the structure of the curriculum is changed to enable students to view concepts, issues, events, and themes from the perspectives of diverse racial and cultural groups.
- The *social action approach* encourages students to make decisions on important social issues and take action to help solve them.

Most educators are content to work on the first two levels. While such efforts may *appear* to meet a multicultural mandate, they are not sufficient to ensure a culturally competent curriculum. For example, take the requirement in most educational plans for the teaching of state history. Even today, most begin with the myth of an almost empty land waiting to be discovered, overlooking the existence and contribution of Native Peoples (Loewen, 2010).

Culturally *insensitive* teachers typically begin with discrete historical units, such as those that focus on the Oregon trail or Lewis and Clark, and teach them from the perspective of "the invaders," as one Native American student put it. Waking up to the possibility that this perspective may be missing a totally different viewpoint, a teacher may decide to add a day of Native American culture or even raise controversial issues such as immigration and land ownership but is still centering the curriculum on European history. A step in a more inclusive direction might entail asking *who really discovered America?*, providing students with materials that explore the issues from various cultural viewpoints, and encouraging them to critically examine all materials.

A more comprehensive example is in the curriculum guide *Rethinking Columbus: Teaching about the 500th Anniversary of Columbus' Arrival in America*:

> The Columbus myth teaches children which voices to listen for as they go out into the world—and whose to ignore. Pick up a children's book on Columbus: See Chris; see Chris talk; see Chris grow up, have ideas, have feelings. In these volumes, the native peoples of the Caribbean, the "discovered," don't think or feel. And thus children begin a scholastic journey that encourages them to disregard the perspectives, the very humanity, of people of color. (1991, p. 3)

Rethinking Columbus includes poems and articles by Native children and writers; materials on Native rights, school mascots, and Columbus Day; historical documents; and extensive resources and references. By deconstructing Columbus and placing his historical contributions in a truly multicultural context, it is an excellent example of Banks's final two approaches to curriculum reform. Students are being sensitized to a Native American perspective on the issues and challenged to think about and take concrete action on social issues facing Native Peoples today.

Ford (1996) suggested that Banks and Banks' levels not only speak to curriculum reform but also reflect the level of cultural competence of the teachers who adopt them. For example, the *contributions* approach reflects a generally superficial understanding of racially and culturally diverse groups.

The *additive* approach tends to be adopted by individuals who fail to understand how the predominant culture interacts with and is related to racially and culturally diverse groups. The *transformational* approach tends to reflect educators who are active in seeking training and experience with racially and culturally diverse groups. Teachers who adopt a *social action* approach have become empowered to make meaningful contributions to the resolution of social issues and problems.

A culturally competent teacher devises a curriculum that enables students to view concepts, issues, events, and themes from the perspectives of diverse racial and cultural groups and/or leads students to make meaningful contributions to the resolution of social issues and problems. Teachers who add "multicultural fluff" do not meet the standard of multicultural education at a transformative level and may well *decrease* the ability of diverse students to interact effectively with the material. "Minor modifications will not suffice because Eurocentric orientations and emphases are more inappropriate now than ever before for students from culturally, racially, and ethnically diverse backgrounds" (Gay, 2010a, p. 143).

Aspects of Curriculum Transformation

We are only now beginning to discover some of the pedagogical techniques most likely to lead to successful curriculum transformation; that is, movement into Banks' final two levels of curriculum change. Consider the importance of helping students enter the reality of an historical figure. Trace the evolution of Sacagawea, the Native woman who guided the Lewis and Clark expedition, as she has been portrayed in history textbooks. For example, there has been a slow evolution away from treating Sacagawea as an actor in the White drama of exploring the West toward an image of a living, breathing Hidatsa woman with whom students can identify and into whose cultural world they can enter (Talbot, 2003). Sacajawea's story may be told through European American eyes with an emphasis on her contribution, as in Banks's contributions approach, or her story can be told from her own perspective. Taking the latter approach, it is possible to sense who she was and understand her relationships and her role in a community that was focused on the whole and in harmony with nature rather than trying to control nature. Then, her part in the journey takes on a personal perspective, and we learn more about the deep culture that surrounded her. Too often, teachers bring their students to only a limited knowing and superficial understanding of many things without letting them fully experience and know viscerally the heart of what they are learning.

Such an approach can be useful in highlighting an era as well as a historical figure. An example from a teacher in training: Sarah, who wanted her kindergarten students to more fully and directly experience Rosa Parks's defining moment as she refused to give up her seat on the bus. Sarah had already begun to investigate the use of a school bus so that children could feel what it was like to lose their freedom of movement but decided—in consultation with me, her advisor—that the students would probably think it was *fun* to sit in the back. Her solution not only connected the students to the lived experience of Rosa Parks but also through the emotions and reality of the learning experience stimulated compassion and understanding for the civil rights era.

Sarah put "no kindergartners allowed" signs on the playground equipment. She roped off part of the playground, putting one ball in the enclosed space. The children endured this limitation on their recess for several days. She also gave them two parallel art sessions: one with choice and one without. By this time, the children had internalized the message of the unit so well that one spontaneously said to another, "She's taking away our freedom." As a culminating activity, the children removed the rope around their limited space on the playground and gleefully destroyed the "no kindergartners allowed" sign. Photos showing the emotions of the children during and after the playground incident reflect the deep effectiveness of the unit (Knapp, 2001).

Such teachers in training will become risk takers as classroom teachers and will assume that they themselves have much to learn about any topic. They have *learned how to learn* and share that ability to critique and see multiple perspectives with their own students. They believe that shared lived experience is one of the few ways to change young lives. They not only engage their students in meaningful learning experiences but also illustrate the best in constructivist teaching and set the stage for self-directed lifelong learning.

Students fortunate enough to find themselves in such learning environments continue to learn and grow beyond the classroom. They are beginning to know that they can make a difference as citizens in a democratic society. Such early training may result in a later generation of teachers who are aware of and moving beyond the taken-for-granted cultural norms many current teachers struggle to even recognize.

However, such felt experiences—if not carried out with great sensitivity and caring—can become trivialized and hurtful. For example, a preservice teacher team made elaborate preparations to expose their peers to a unit on the Jewish Holocaust. At one point, they herded most of the class into a small dark section of the room draped with black plastic. On the surface, the simulation seemed to have the potential of giving the participants a taste of the horrors of darkness, confinement, and crowding. But the simulation turned to giggles, and one student turned away with tears in his eyes. His family's experience of such terror was trivialized by the activity. Another preservice teacher, hoping to generate a lived experience in relation to civil rights and the African American experience, assigned the students roles from the U.S. Civil War era.

One group decided to re-enact a slave beating. One student laughingly writhed in mock pain, and the physical horror was reduced to a game. Such experiences can be powerful learning tools, but they should be undertaken only after much thought and consultation.

Talking about race and race-related history is a challenge, yet "communities of silence cannot be moral communities. And the most pernicious and pervasive silence in primary school classrooms is the silence surrounding the subject of race. Where there is not silence, there is often a complacent orthodoxy purporting that, since Rosa Parks and Dr. Marin Luther King, Jr., changed the world, everything is just fine.... When teachers avoid the subject, pretending that is doesn't exist as an issue, or when they portray its existence as merely a fringe issue, they are sending a very strong message. Although this message may be unintentional, the result can be stifling" (Polite & Saenger, 2003, p. 275). Positioning ourselves as educators to openly discuss race and other forms of oppression is a difficult journey not for the faint of heart, especially when coupled with learning the practical skills needed to teach well. Such discussions on race may help to bridge the continued mismatch in race of students, teachers, and teacher educators (Frazier, 2009; Milner, 2006; Tatum, 2007).

Child-Centeredness of the Curriculum

Child-centeredness, especially with difficult-to-reach students, is surprisingly effective for engaging students:

> When I was an Assistant Principal, there were the "regular skippers," whom I was always chasing. When I finally caught up with the students, I asked them what it would take to get them to come to school. Many had been skipping for so long, that they really had no idea.
>
> But, I noticed a strange pattern with a few of the "skippers." There was one who would skip Periods 1, 2, 4, 5, 6, 7, 8, 9. I asked ... "So what about Period 3? Did that teacher forget to mark you absent?"
>
> "No," the Skipper replied. "That is Ms. Zachary's class. I don't miss her class."
>
> "You mean you skip Periods 1 and 2 and COME IN for Period 3?"
>
> "Yup. Every day."
>
> "You're kidding. WHY?"
>
> "Mrs. Ely, you've got to understand ... Ms. Zachary would KILL me if I didn't show."
>
> "Aw come on," I said incredulous. "ALL of your teachers would tell you that! So what makes that class special enough to get you out of bed?"
>
> Through shrugs and "ticks" and wiggles, the Skipper finally said, "Well, ya see, Mrs. Ely, I'm IMPORTANT in that class. Ya see, we do these group things. We all contribute. Sometimes, it is just an opinion. But it is MY opinion. I'm the only one who can give it! I matter. It is my PERSPECTIVE."

"And you don't feel this in other classes?"

"You kiddin'? They all just talk at me. They don't care what I think. They don't even KNOW what I think. Who cares about goin' there?"

"So, you come into Ms. Zachary's class to give your opinion?"

"That's not all of it. We do these cooperative things, too. I mean, we all have to work together on projects. We all have our parts, ya know? If I don't show with my part, I let down the whole team. Can't do that. So, I come in. Besides. It is fun." (Ely, 2001, pp. 85–86)

(From *Quo No More* by Arline Ely. Copyright 2001 by Arline Ely. Reprinted by permission.)

Ms. Zachary was able to accomplish this with the most difficult students. The traditional skippers felt a responsibility to both their teacher and their classmates. They were invested in the learning process and belonged to a learning culture. "It all relates to developing a personal connection with the students" (Ely, 2001).

Where possible begin all curriculum development, especially that related to transformation, with a thorough understanding of the students' perspective: their questions, current level of knowledge and understanding, and inner images. It is critical for teachers to be able to see the material from students' viewpoints rather than from just their own (Cooper, 2009). I suggest four factors to consider in moving toward Banks and Banks' level of transformational cultural learning:

- Focus on context-rich material that relates directly to students' life experiences;
- Allow children to engage material on their own terms, since they are usually more open to multiple perspectives than is the teacher;
- Center the investigation in student ideas; and
- Develop students' interest in how those in different times and cultures may have viewed the events and locations being studied. (Moule, 2002)

The essence of curriculum reform is that the students and their needs are central to the curriculum, not the material to be covered. It is not "Your child does not fit my curriculum" or "I teach your child through my curriculum." The child is the center, not the lesson or the curriculum. Ely distinguished the needs of today's students and compared them to the classrooms in which their teachers were educated.

Today's students ... want to know why they need to learn certain facts, have an expectation that they will be respected for who they are, are products of the "information age," who need to seek answers both alone and with peers, (and) need to have an active role in their learning process.... (They) need personal connections to both their learning and to their teachers.... But today's students are being taught by teachers who grew up in classrooms where they, as students, were listening while teachers talked, working in isolation, answering only when questioned, learning in classes of 40 students, (and) sitting in perfect rows, one "tombstone" behind the other. (Ely, p. 86)

One way to center children in your curriculum is to let them take the lead. By the second week of school, many children know the morning routines and could lead them as well as you could. One teacher in an upper-grade class pretended he was dead! He was in the room but did not respond and let the children teach that day. Ask high school students what they need, give them a reason to come to class, and they will engage (Knaus, 2009).

The last story on centering the curriculum on the students in your class comes from a high school English teacher. She had been disappointed that her tenth-grade students simply were not doing their homework and showed little enthusiasm during class discussions. After class one day, a student remained to talk:

He stood up and approached my desk. Julian was a tall, African American 16 year old ... one of my favorite students. "You ought to quit trying to make us white," he said matter-of-factly. "All these stories you're making us read are by white people, about white people." His eyes pointed to the open textbook on my desk.

"Julian, I didn't select these stories on the basis of race," I said emphatically, stunned by the implication of racism. It was the unpardonable sin in a school where 70 percent of the students were minorities. "Maybe you should have," he said, almost in a whisper, and left the classroom to silence....

I had always prided myself on conducting "colorblind" classes.... I suddenly realized the awful truth. I hadn't deliberately eliminated writers of other ethnicities, but I hadn't deliberately included them either. Clearly, the assignments reflected my own unconscious cultural biases, and one student had the courage to say so. (Blais, 2008, p. 21)

The Opportunity Gap

Even in well-integrated schools, many Students of Color are tracked into courses that do not prepare them well for either testing or college. This tracking takes various forms and all of them may be addressed in some manner. Tracking may be by choice—wanting to be with friends who are also not in these classes. Sometimes, well-meaning counselors may not be conscious of their limiting advice. And sometimes, those around them in home, community, and schools may not fully recognize the need for rigorous classes for preparing for college admission and success. Again, we see the opportunity gap, not the achievement gap, in play.

Opportunities for some children may be limited by the lack of resources available in working-class homes. And time for homework and school activity support may be difficult to find from their hard-working families who have other demands on their time. Other Students of Color simply attend schools in low-income areas that do not attract the best teachers or have funds for the best environments and supplies (Smith, 2008; Zeichner, 2010).

A few schools in the Denver area are attacking such problems in a unique and promising manner. At a presentation I attended on efforts in a northeast Denver neighborhood, one member of a panel, Teo Price Broncucia, suggested: "Ask the wearer if you want to find out if a shoe pinches" (Dray & Espinoza, 2010). Based on this idea, high school students at a very low-performing school (only 6 percent met or exceeded the math benchmark) began giving their teachers constructive and regular feedback on their teaching. As another youth leader from Project Voyce, Esmeralda Aquilar, said, "When the teachers challenged us on the whole idea, we said, 'We may not be teachers, but we ARE learners.'" Student engagement in academics at this high school has significantly increased because of the empowerment of the students and their interaction with their teachers (Dray & Espinoza, 2010). Project Voyce's main goal, according to the website, is to make youth voices real in school renewal in order to improve student achievement through action research, leadership development, and community partnerships.

Social Action at Work

Let us turn again to Banks and Banks' fourth approach—that of stimulating social action. Teachers may choose to look beyond the obvious—to address real needs in a relevant and timely manner. They may teach students to look outside the narrow confines of the given for a larger view that includes more factors, more perspectives, and alternate solutions. Teachers may begin the transformation process by helping students look for items that need action. They may then lead students to see the issue from multiple perspectives. From there, ties to curriculum items in multiple subject areas may be made.

For example, one of my young students became concerned about conflicts on the playground over the limited number of balls available during recess. Another noticed newly planted grass being trampled by students. In both cases, the problem became a classroom focus in order to enable students to see issues from alternative perspectives and then take action to solve the problems. One student found an inexpensive source of playground balls and sold the balls to classmates. Other students approached the school maintenance staff, and a small fence was soon erected to protect the grass. Even math benchmarks were addressed by action items such as fence building and ball purchases. And my students were deeply engaged in their school work.

> Loewen suggests specific social action in regard to Native Americans:
> Much of what we teach and learn in elementary schools social studies every

October (around Columbus Day) and November (Thanksgiving) amounts to a continuing canard against Native Americans. Stopping that deceit is an important first step toward redress. At the very least, students will want to let their younger siblings in on the new information they're learning about Native Americans, Columbus, and so forth. They may want to challenge their elementary school teachers or a textbook that they now find inadequate.

Other acts students can take include questioning nearby high schools or professional sports teams for their use of Indian names and symbols as mascots and logos.... If a nearby historical marker presents bad history about Native people, perhaps because of its ethnocentric us of terms like "discover," "settler," "massacre," or "half-breed," students can agitate for a corrective. (Loewen, 2010, p. 154)

Imagine the engagement of your students in such an endeavor and their increase in critical thinking skills.

There are many appropriate forums for your children's social action work or their culturally related writing and artwork. *Skipping Stones*, an award-winning multicultural magazine, is a strong example, as much of the material comes from the children themselves, including the artwork on the cover. It is also noteworthy as it recognizes books for children that are authentic and selected by input from reviewers from many backgrounds and life experiences, from age 8 to 80: "The honored books promote an understanding of cultures, cultivate cooperation and encourage a deeper understanding of the world's diversity, ecological richness, respect for differing viewpoints and close relationships in human societies" (Toké, 2010, p. 29).

Connections and Reflections: Emerging Views

Before talking with each other, imagine that you are preparing your room for the first days of school. Carefully consider each poster, list, and visual you might put on the walls. Discuss among yourselves some of your considerations and how material in this chapter may influence your choices. What cultural ways of knowing are revealed in your choices? What cultures are represented by the designs or even the colors you choose? Would you consider an approach by some teachers to leave the walls *completely* empty until your students have arrived and the choices are made by mutual agreement? Why or why not?

As you consider the questions above, either with others and on your own, would you have to give up some of what you have considered fundamental to a classroom setup? Are you willing to do that? Think of how one must be willing to give up some taken-for-granted perspectives and choices to make room for those of diverse students.

How might you improve your understanding of cultural interactional patterns? Consider watching members of a cultural group talking naturally. If possible, unobtrusively write descriptions of the following:

- What distance do they maintain between each other?
- What kinds of gestures are used?
- In what contexts do people touch each other: How do they touch and where? (Some cultural groups touch a lot; others very little.)
- What do they do to indicate they are listening?
- How does a person "get the floor" when she or he wants to speak (e.g., does the person simply start talking, wait for an opening, or use a hand gesture)?
- What level of loudness or softness of speech do people maintain?
- If you are able to watch an adult giving directions to or reprimanding a child who is a member of the adult's same sociocultural group: What does the adult say? What nonverbal behavior does the adult use? How does the child respond?
- To what extent do people "code-switch" from one set of interaction patterns to another if they move to different settings? (Grant & Sleeter, 2007, p. 146)

Classroom: Adventures in Learning

For lower grades, the following activity helps expand the world for your students. The "World in a Chocolate Bar" game may be adapted for different grade levels. You begin the lesson by holding up a chocolate bar and asking the class, "Where did this chocolate bar come from?" (Chartock, 2010, p. 188). Together, you both guess and read the ingredients to generate a list. A world map or, even better, a globe may be used to help the students get a global perspective. A typical list might include cocoa, peanuts, corn syrup, coconuts, sugar, paper wrapper, tin foil. Some may suggest how the ingredients came together or to the store and think where the truck, train, or boat was made. Corresponding possible answers to the list are Ghana, Sudan, Iowa, Philippines, Ecuador, Canada, Thailand, and Japan (Chartock, 2010). A similar activity may be done with the materials in a pencil.

For upper grades, this lesson plan from the Anti-Defamation League moves into the social action level (http://www.adl.org/education/hate_internet.asp). Students make active plans to confront hate on the Internet in one of the levels displayed on the pyramid displayed on this site.

CHAPTER 9

Critical Issues in Working with Culturally Different Students

"The world changes according to the way people see it, and if you can alter, even by a millimeter, the way people look at reality, then you can change the world."

—James Baldwin

As the proportion and number of Children of Color in the nation's schools increase, the need for teachers who know how to function in multicultural classrooms and sensitively relate to culturally diverse students heightens dramatically. Yet, we are only now beginning to learn how to prepare teachers to work with children with differences (Sleeter, 2001). The challenges are substantial. Teacher education in a pluralistic society depends on a complex set of factors. Teachers must be willing to challenge their racial attitudes and sense of privilege as well as master a body of cultural material. Educational systems must be willing to adapt their structure and style to a changing student population. There is sure to be resistance from a variety of sources, including parents and students themselves, and as you have read, gaining cultural competence is a personally demanding and at times arduous venture. Those that undertake the task will need moral courage, especially in the face of the opposition that will come from somewhere (Gay, 2010a). And, ironically, teaching about different cultural groups may actually increase or affirm preservice teachers' stereotypes (Barry & Lechner, 1995).

We have so far focused on a variety of conceptual issues related to working with culturally different students. Earlier chapters defined cultural competence—explored the meaning of racism—especially as it impacts students and teachers, and defined culture and worldview as well as the cultural limits of mainstream assumptions that have shaped most teachers' thinking. In addition, we looked at a number of factors unique to the experience of ethnically diverse students.

These included child development and parenting, differences in family structure, biracial/bicultural families, potential areas of psychological difficulty (conflicts in identity development, assimilation and acculturation, negative stereotyping, stress), and sources of bias in cross-cultural teaching.

This chapter focuses more directly on the process of working with culturally different students and also looks at some important issues unique to educating Children of Color. What is the best way to prepare for cross-cultural work? How is it different from other teaching situations? How can a teacher begin to establish rapport and maximize success with diverse student populations? What should teachers know about classroom management as well as bilingualism in the classroom? How important are times in diverse placements? We will look in depth at what is a particularly promising strategy for preparing preservice teachers for cultural competence: cultural immersion experiences.

Classroom Management and Interactional Style

Consider the following two stories. A four-year-old African American child ran past me in a brightly muraled hall of an inner-city elementary school. "Should you be running like that?" I asked in my usual teacher voice and style. He kept going, paying no attention to my question. Having taught this age group before, I was familiar with such disregard, which conjured up past visions of small crossed arms and stubborn attitudes. His seven-year-old brother appeared on the scene. "Stop running," he said, and the boy immediately did.

Then, there is "The Felon and the Fidget" (Ely, 2001):

> The school was a tiny, little K–12 building to which a judge assigned the 19-year-old boy who had been convicted of armed robbery. The class was one that I had created to assist students who had never passed a math course before. He qualified. With respect to my class, the felon came and went as inconspicuously as possible.
>
> Determined to help all of the students succeed for the first time, I buried myself in creating lessons which would interest the students. Each week, the class pretended to "be" a different type of worker and performed math from that worker's job. The math had application.
>
> One day the activity required a bit of a longer explanation than usual. The "fidgets" commenced around the fifth minute. I addressed one boisterous "fidget" and asked him to "sit still" and to "settle down." Keeping with his past behavior, the "fidget" continued to disrupt the instruction.
>
> Now, the felon had been sitting quietly, as he always did. He was becoming more and more annoyed. A single electric fright bolted through me as he turned toward the "fidget." You could see the same single electric bolt strike the "fidget" as

he became conscious of the reversed orientation of the humongous classmate in front of him. The felon and the "fidget" made eye contact.

In a quiet, deliberate, slow, firm tone, the felon leaned toward him and said, "The lady said, 'Sit down, and settle down.'"

The "fidget" was a cartoon caricature with larger-than-life "bugged-out" eyes and "strobe-light" skin that flashed comic strip colors. The "fidget" sat upright— possibly for the first time in his academic career! He folded his hands and fixed his eyes on me. The rest of the class breathed for the first time since the felon had turned around. I exhaled, too, and continued with the lesson.

The felon never said another word, outside of answering my questions. The "fidget" remained in that position, hands folded, feet flat on the floor, for the remainder of the school year!

Both the "fidget" and the felon passed the course. (Ely, 2001, pp. 83–84)

What happened in these two situations? In a study entitled *No More Mister Nice Guy*, Higgins and Moule (2009) offer advice to preservice teachers about classroom management with African American elementary students. They describe a dynamic common to inner-city schools and the interaction between White teachers and Black students that they call the "pseudo-questioning strategy of discipline" or "command versus caring." In the first example, the four-year-old processed my question not as a command or expectation but as a question, leaving him free to continue his behavior. In this case, his actions said, "Yes, I should be running." I assumed that the student's locus of internal control would say, "No, I shouldn't be running," somehow understanding the subtlety of the question. The youngster's brother, a caregiver, was aware of the need for a direct command and used the authoritative voice for safe and appropriate school behavior to simply tell him to stop. Consider a classroom teacher's statement, "Is this a good time to read your book?" This is not really a question but a statement to put the book away. Yet, from the student's viewpoint, it does not have the qualities of caring and command and is easily misinterpreted as a question to be answered freely rather than as a behavioral directive.

With prior instruction, preservice teachers are able to master a more direct disciplinary style. According to one preservice teacher: "It worked. I was having trouble keeping a young student on task. I remembered what you said and told her quite sternly to 'put away those other materials and get to work.' She did and seemed, if anything, more friendly towards me. It was as if she did see my strictness as caring" (Moule, 2003a).

The point is that conflicting cultural norms, such as questioning versus *telling with care,* often underlie the overt tension that can be found in multicultural classrooms. The storytelling and classroom language of a Student of Color may seem oppositional to a teacher who has unquestioned assumptions, adding to the cultural divide. Deeper understanding of cultural differences is the key to developing competence in working cross-culturally. How do we develop this deeper understanding? How many cultural norms are so embedded that we do not even see them? As we read in Chapter 4, in McIntosh's classic work on White privilege, the norms are, indeed, often invisible.

The experience in the hall and Ely's felon and fidget are not atypical. In a variety of ways, educators repeatedly introduce culturally insensitive understanding and curriculum choices into their teaching. By not examining their assumptions about teaching and classroom management, they do not work effectively with culturally different students. Many ethnic children, even by middle school, have already chosen to avoid school culture and teachers' misguided expectations altogether. The result has been a systematic lowering of achievement and educational attainment for many Students of Color (Garcia, 2001; Haycock, 2001; Tatum, 2003).

Many Children of Color value social aspects of the environment more than mainstream children do and tend to be especially attuned to feelings, acceptance, and emotional closeness (Delpit, 2006). African American children from lower socioeconomic groups are more influenced by the need to affiliate than by the need to achieve. In Chapter 7, we explored the possibility that such a factor might play a role in suppressing school achievement. It may also have serious implications for classroom management.

Optimal culturally sensitive classroom environments and teaching styles for some Children of Color may need to emphasize collaboration and opportunities for interaction. The teacher of such students may find it useful to view social interactions and side conversations during class in a light that recognizes the cultural value and importance of sharing and emotional closeness between students.

Due to different interactional styles, Black students may:

> Grant teachers wide latitude of emotions in which to make their expectations and dissatisfactions known. Assertive, aggressive and even angry behavior are all rated as acceptable means of communicating one's intentions as long as these emotions are perceived as genuine. If expressions of emotion are too subtle, however, students are likely to misread a teacher's intentions and become disoriented. Responses lacking a sufficient emotional quality are likely to be read as non-caring. Totally unacceptable, however, is non-responsiveness. Students expect a response, and failing to see one will generally interpret this behavior as non-concern. From students' perspective the non-responsive teacher demonstrates not only lack of control, but a non-caring attitude as well. (Foster, 1987, pp. 67–68)

In the African American community, teachers demonstrate their caring for students by "controlling the class; exhibiting personal power; establishing meaningful interpersonal relationships; displaying emotion to garner student respect; demonstrating that all students can learn; establishing a standard of achievement and 'pushing' students to achieve the standard" (Delpit, 2006, p. 142). Teachers hold student attention by "incorporating African American interactional styles in their teaching" (p. 142). The community may view a teacher as ineffectual, boring, or uncaring if he or she does not exhibit these behaviors and firmly control the class.

Consider the interactional styles of Asian students. There is a disparity between the traditional American classroom style and that expected by a recently arrived Vietnamese immigrant student. "Such a child might feel extremely off-balance and uncomfortable in a classroom environment in which teachers are informal and friendly, students are expected to ask questions and speak in front of the class, and group work is the order of the day" (Nieto, 1996, p. 144). Compare such preferred interactions with that of the child's native land, where "teachers are revered and have a formal relationship with their students, and students are expected to learn individually and by listening and memorizing" (p. 144). Asian American students perceive greater emotional and social distance between themselves and their teachers. "Without repeated urging from teachers, some may be disinclined to initiate interactions with teachers that include asking questions or participating in class discussions" (Marshall, 2002, p. 269). What to do? Marshall quoted Uba (1994), who suggested becoming attuned to "subtle body language" and noticing that students wishing to participate may sit straighter or make a bit more eye contact. Direct eye contact—viewed by most mainstream teachers as a sign of respect—is often avoided by Asian American students, who have been taught to avert their eyes in the presence of authority. Furthermore, there is some evidence that direct eye contact increases perceived threat (Sue, 2010), and some students may have come to avoid direct eye contact to ease teachers' perceptions of them as threats.

Latino/a students also bring their own unique cultural styles to the classroom:

> Indirect, implicit, or covert communication is consonant with Mexicans' emphasis on family harmony, on "getting along" and not making others uncomfortable. Conversely, assertiveness, open differences in opinion, and demands for clarification are seen as rude or insensitive of others' feelings. The use of third-person ("One could be proud of ...”), rather than first-person ("I am proud of ...") pronouns is a common pattern of indirectness, and is viewed as a way of being selfless as opposed to self-serving. Thus, Mexican Americans sometimes are left guessing rather than asking about the other's intentions; they often make use of allusions, proverbs, and parables to convey their viewpoints, which may leave an impression of guardedness, vagueness, obscurity, or excessive embellishment, obsequiousness, and politeness. (Falicov, 1996, p. 176)

Classroom interaction that calls for competition between individuals, emphasizes individual accomplishment, or promotes excessive directness or assertiveness may well make many Latino/a and Asian students uncomfortable and silent.

Regardless of cultural specifics, sound and safe classrooms depend on a few basic principles. In sound multicultural and empowering classrooms, teachers give permanent value to each student. *Permanent value* means considering each child to be of value regardless of behavior or differentiated circumstances. It could be called *unconditional positive regard* or some would simply use the words *unconditional love*. How teachers develop and express this valuing of students may depend on their own value systems, characters, and personal philosophies. "The child's realization that he has permanent value and that his value is recognized by his teacher regardless of what he is doing at the moment or where he may fail opens the way for an unselfish desire [for the child] to do his best" (Dreikurs, 1968, p. 66). Clearly, conscious solutions for narrowing the discipline gap also positively affect the achievement gap (Gregory & Mosely, 2004).

Immersion Experiences

"Most culturally diverse students and their teachers live in different worlds, and they do not fully understand or appreciate one another's experiential realities. Daily interactions with one another are sporadic and superficial," (Gay, 2010a). Immersion experiences involve placing teachers in culturally different school settings unfamiliar to them so they can learn firsthand about culturally different student populations. According to Sleeter in her work *Preparing Teachers for Culturally Diverse Schools: Research and the Overwhelming Presence of Whiteness* (2001), some weaknesses of immersion-based learning are that the immersion experience is too short in duration and intensity, that it is too superficial and lacks sufficient depth, that it does not include living within the community in which the immersion school is located, and that authentic immersion settings may be located at a distance from the teacher education program, requiring time and money to travel and relocate for the period of the experience. If these factors can be addressed, as we shall see, such a learning strategy can have powerful effects in promoting cultural competence.

Such experiences challenge the contradictory realities between theory and practice. Personal meanings are contingent upon context and the perspective of others. They are always shifting. "Consequently the meanings one makes from practice are in a state of continual and contradictory reinterpretation as other contexts and other voices are taken into account or are ignored" (Britzman, 1991, p. 15). Clearly, efforts must be made to provide ways to think through and debrief diverse field placements, a focus in most of the programs described in this section.

Immersions programs can vary widely from a four-hour cultural plunge to a community immersion practicum to a few weeks living in a foreign or intranational setting. Researchers have found that all immersion experiences have proven powerful, particularly those which include sufficient preparation, background study of the host culture, avoidance of tourist areas, sufficient duration and intensity of the actual immersion, and continual, critical reflection and feedback (Meltzoff, 2010). There is general agreement that such immersions move preservice teachers toward cultural competence in ways that course readings, discussions, and other class activities simply cannot (Lockhart, 2009; Sleeter, 2001). Considering the deep learning and self-discovery from immersion programs, whether short term or long, "preservice teachers should be required to be exposed to diversity throughout their teacher training" (Nuby, 2010, p. 42).

No matter how long or how short, the first task of an immersion experience is to establish trust and the awareness that the student teacher is an integral part of the community, even if only for a day. An often-reported outcome of immersion experience is that the participants feel less scared and uncomfortable in any new multicultural settings—a plus for life as well as teaching. Most realize that their initial discomfort came not only from previously imagined stereotypical fears but also simply from a lack of experience.

Is One Day Beneficial?

As part of my multicultural education class, I assign a visit to a culturally diverse school. The choices of schools are a bilingual one a half hour away or an inner city one two hours away. These trips are often difficult for students to arrange, especially those who must find a ride. However, it is clear during the trip, the reflections, and the end-of-quarter evaluations that these hands-on experiences are well worth the effort. I hesitate to call our one-day trips immersion experiences; however, many of the essentials are the same as for longer experiences. I will describe our visits to a school in the city of Portland, hours from Oregon State University where I teach.

When I begin a one-day experience, as the visitors arrive they list some of their expectations for the day, including their thoughts as they entered the neighborhood and building. This moment of reflection allows them to express their fears and/or note their first impressions. The completed forms also identify those who may need special attention during the day. In this one-day experience, we begin with a complete tour of the school, during which we locate their assigned rooms and see the children and staff who happen to be in the halls, gym, cafeteria, or playground. These group tours give university visitors a sense of safety and an opportunity to ask questions of their familiar and trusted teacher educator/leader. A pep talk explains their roles in the classroom as volunteers rather than as observers. I explain differences in teaching styles, classroom management techniques, and what they might be asked to do. A long-standing and positive relationship between the teacher education program, the onsite teachers, and staff is quite helpful, as is the onsite teachers' familiarity with the goals of the visiting preservice teachers and their familiarity with the university setting from which the preservice teachers come.

At the end of the day the visitors now list some of their experiences and compare them with their expectations. We debrief the time at the school. On the long drive home with their carpool partners they continue to share and reflect on their time in the school. Finally, when we next meet on campus I ask for volunteers to share their one-day experience with those who were not able to go. This reporting is usually full of emotion, passion, and changed perspectives. It also expands the learning to the whole class.

One Week in an Inner City

This example is from a college in the rural south and consists of placements in grades 9–12. As usual, student teacher preparation was a key point and prepared the students for their placements. In this placement, both students (99 percent) and most teachers (66 percent) were African American (Nuby, 2010). Beyond the more obvious increase in the student teachers' comfort levels was a willingness to consider such an in-service placement: "Before this … I wouldn't have dreamed of teaching in a place like this" (p. 45). There were a number of findings about the specific themes that arose in the student teacher papers and observations:

- School atmosphere and environment exceeded—in a good way—the student teacher expectations.
- Influence of home and community indicated that the student teachers again had lower expectations than the strong communities and stable families and students they encountered.
- Parental and extended family involvement in schooling indicated that the preservice teachers were not expecting the depth and breadth of family involvement that they encountered.
- Importance of religion was a surprise to the students as they began to understand that "public and private religious behaviors are positively associated with self-esteem among Blacks and that religious involvements cushions the harmful effects of certain types of adversities that Blacks' face," (Nuby, 2010, p. 46).
- Influence of the principal as an active, change-oriented leader and a role model was key to the experience and understanding of the participants.
- Teacher dynamics and interactional style echoed what we know from earlier studies (see the classroom management section in this chapter; Delpit, 2006) that directness and mutual respect are key to successful cross cultural teaching in predominantly African American schools.
- Vocational education was important as a means to encourage academic and future career choices for the high school students. However, focused college prep was minimal and left up to the students.
- Afterschool activities helped the preservice students more fully understand the community lives of the high school students.

These examples from a one-week program show how deeply a short time in a culturally diverse school may affect a participant.

Three Weeks in an Inner City

The material that follows is a description of a three-week immersion program I created for preservice teachers in a predominantly African American elementary school in Portland, Oregon.

In immersion programs of longer duration, preservice teachers typically develop deep rapport with cooperating teachers and quickly discover that getting to know students on a personal level is appealing and educationally sound. New relationships and experiences quickly emerge. Student teachers are usually paired onsite so perceptions and experiences can be checked out with a peer. They are required to write about their experiences, which provides an opportunity to reflect on and consolidate learning. These reflective pieces give the participants time to self-reflect before sharing in a smaller or larger group. "Dialogue with their peers is crucial because it gives teachers the opportunity to clarify their beliefs and to better understand what they felt and saw" (Pang, 1994, p. 292).

At the beginning, most preservice teachers are guarded and uncomfortable, and they offer predictable and safe expectations for the forthcoming experience. For example, one student hoped to "gain deeper insight into the African American culture and to be a better teacher for African American kids." By the end of the first week, however, they are more comfortable and begin to focus on the emotional lives of the children in their classroom, seeking them out on a human and personal level. A typical comment:

> One of the things I most want to gain from this experience is to start to form a bond with the students in the class. Now they know that I am a constant in the class and I feel with that stability some of the learners will begin to let their guard down.... On Friday one of the students wrote me a letter that said, "Thank you for believing in me." Maybe this child is my chance to form a bond and possibly make a difference. I was amazed at the compliment ... the fact that the child noticed and was thankful for someone believing in him. (Moule, 2003a, pp. 1–2)

At this point, the preservice teachers began to appreciate the important connection between emotional bonding and cultural expression. For example, as discussed earlier, discipline styles in predominantly African American schools are connected to increased emotional interactions, and that deep caring is evidenced in teacher/student and student/student relationships, even when the style seems particularly strict and authoritative.

Next, they begin to recognize the difficulties in many of the children's home lives in poor neighborhoods, where poverty influences parents' ability to provide for children and their education. They come to understand that single mothers and parents with two jobs are less likely to be able to participate in their children's schooling. They begin to realize the need to adjust their lesson plans to match the learning styles of the children and to incorporate more hands-on kinesthetic lessons and socially interactive components. The preservice teachers eventually become part of the instructional team, teaching a work sample to their assigned class. This working together appears largely responsible for a growing sense of belonging, community, and effectiveness.

Openness to discuss and understand the discipline style and the emotional interactional styles at the school were key. In difficult situations, student teachers received quick and contextual feedback on their actions that helped them gain confidence in their ability to work with culturally different populations. Significant learning also results from living in the community surrounding the school, although it took time for some to consciously relate the community to the classroom. "I have felt relatively comfortable and safe ... a lot of similarities ... inside the school. When I drive around the neighborhood I get a little nervous.... The area is like nothing I have ever experienced. It is definitely a unique experience outside the classroom" (Moule, 2003a, p. 3).

My research showed that after three weeks of the immersion experience, about half the students reported significant improvement in classroom management skills, and an equal number felt that their experience would transfer to working with other diverse populations. None showed increased bias. At worst, preservice teachers left with the same "kids are kids" attitude they came with, an attitude that may or may not cover unchanged assumptions, colorblindness, and taken-for-granted cultural norms.

The following exchange underscores the conflict around classroom management that many of the preservice teachers felt.

> I have conflicting tendencies as a teacher. One is to be the Queen of the Classroom. To be in control of the structure. The other is to be the facilitator—to shepherd students along their educational journey, letting them construct meaning as they go. I can't be both. [My cooperating teacher] is Queen, and I'm not her. I couldn't teach like her even if it were my classroom. Kids can't be chief architects of their own learning when there is a Queen or King. (Moule, 2003a, p. 3)

Most teachers struggle with the question of control—or, rather, the lack of control. Yet, it is often the ambiguity that makes things happen in the classroom. Too much control limits the educational spontaneity of students. Too little control, and the results are amorphous—which is why a "fail safe outer boundary," either physical or psychological, is necessary. In the cross-cultural classroom, the ideal situation is freedom within limits, with both the freedom and the limits carefully constructed and mindful of cultural norms and needs. Such immersion placements often take advantage of the wisdom and mentoring of African American teachers (Moule & Higgins, 2007).

A final question I asked my preservice teachers was, "What have you learned about yourself that you did not realize before this experience?" Some participants saw themselves—for the first time—through the eyes of another culture. One wrote, "I realize I am perceived as being very reserved, quiet and serious." Many expressed delight at their new adaptability: "I realized how adaptable I am to situations … in terms of grade level, academically, culturally." One reported on learning "things not to do." Others simply said, "One of the best experiences I've ever had." The following comment summed up the experience for one student teacher:

> I have also learned that I really enjoyed working in a more diverse setting here at King. I have learned that change is good. Sometimes I am very opposed to change and I was very nervous, scared and not looking forward to this experience. However, I have found that having this huge 180 degree turn in my life has been very positive, very mind altering and a very incredible learning experience. The main thing I have learned about myself from this experience is that I *really* can do whatever I put my mind to. I *can* learn from things I'm not looking forward to. (Moule, 2003a, pp. 3–4)

Two Weeks in a Foreign Country

This two-week cultural immersion experience in Trinidad and Tobago—or Jamaica depending on the year—was designed for students from a mid-sized, predominantly White Midwestern university. Students for this program were drawn by the recruitment material and were volunteers. Usually, about twelve college students and four teacher educators participated in the program. Here is a full description of the program:

> The goals of the Jamaican cultural immersion experience were to assist teacher education candidates in the development of cultural competence and to provide an opportunity for them to practice cultural competence in a diverse setting outside their "cultural comfort zones." Cultural immersion was chosen as a way to help candidates move forward with the development of cultural competence personally as well as professionally; it would allow them to become knowledgeable about people in a culture very different from their own.
>
> In this experience, students learned about Jamaica and Jamaicans through pre-trip assignments as well as through their firsthand experiences living in the country and teaching in the Jamaican schools. The teacher education candidates and an education faculty member spent ten days living at a Jamaican church-affiliated facility, which provided close contact with local people. The teacher education group had a variety of different experiences that contributed to their learning. Their major tasks were to observe and teach in Jamaican schools and to learn from and collaborate with Jamaican teachers. They taught a variety of lessons in Jamaican preschool and elementary level classrooms and presented a workshop to the Jamaican faculty. Candidates conducted individual research

projects on topics such as teaching strategies, special education, and parent involvement. Outside of the schools, the group participated in a number of experiences designed to increase the candidate's knowledge of the Jamaican people and culture. They attended church services, hosted a social gathering for community members, assisted in a Jamaican hospital, and visited the homes of Jamaicans.

The Jamaican cultural immersion experience was offered as a credit course. Students met prior to departure and were given their classroom assignments. They prepared lesson plans and materials to use in their teaching. The class met several times during the Jamaica experience to discuss challenges, joys, and learnings. Students kept journals and completed a pre- and post-trip personal/professional reflection paper. At the beginning of the fall semester, the class completed the course with a final meeting, at which time each student presented a project completed as a part of the course (L. Penland, personal communication, April, 27, 2010).

During the cultural immersion experience in Trinidad and Tobago, May 2007, participants were expected to respond to the following prompts:

1. What was the start of my "journey" (i.e., this trip)?
2. What prompted me to be involved in a cultural immersion program?
3. What were my expectations?
4. What were my concerns prior to the immersion experience?
5. What were key moments on this trip? What events impacted me?
6. Was there anything that made me feel uncomfortable?
7. What were the critical incidents, and what were their impacts on my growth?
8. What surprised me most?
9. How did I surprise myself?
10. How did this experience affect my life post-trip? What has had a lasting effect, personally and professionally?

This particular program also led to growth among the teacher educators, and their self-study underscored how much even well-educated, culturally competently trained people may benefit from continued work. After my participation as a supporter and observer, I asked Diane, a trip organizer to Jamaica, about the immersion experience. She helps me to see several benefits from such an excursion that I had overlooked:

For one thing, these soft middle class kids learn to walk a distance. They see teacher teach well with no supplies and noise coming in over the low partitions. They learn to eat or not eat what they are served. The sleep in a large room together and they bond with people they would not have gotten to know due to our communal living situation.

Once back home they think: if I could do x then I can do y. If those teachers could teach and those students learn in those conditions, what more can I do with so many resources? (D. Triplet, personal communication, May, 2007).

Targeted Immersion Program of Three Weeks

This type of immersion is designed to be specifically relevant for the participants by "focusing on the cultural or ethnic group(s) the teachers are likely to encounter in their future professional lives…. It might be more appropriate for a future teacher to complete an immersion program in a particular urban or rural area, or in a particular tribal nation or region" (Meltzoff, 2010, p. 24)

Meltzoff's data came from students who traveled with her "to the small town in the hills of Tapalpa, Jalisco, Mexico, in May-June, 2008. In this three-week program, which was established in 2001, our students typically teach English and math in local schools, volunteer after school at a community center that serves people with disabilities, host local children in a daily informal play/learning time before dark, participate in cultural events in the community, learn in workshops led by local cultural leaders, as well as engage in coursework such as book talks, journaling, reflection, on-site seminars, debriefing a formal observation in the classroom, group discussions, and paper-writing" (Meltzoff, 2010, p. 9). As with other successful programs, there was close and personal attention to the participants in preparation, onsite work, and debriefing after the experience.

Full-Year Immersion Program

As I saw the growth from preservice teachers from a one-day experience and a three-week experience, I began to wonder what would happen if preservice teachers taught in a community for a longer time. First of all, our OSU Professional Teacher Education Program (PTEP) has more contact hours than many: Students begin in August and continue in the same placement except for holidays and one 3-week alternate placement until June. I thought, what would happen if the preservice teachers lived and worked in a diverse community for the full year?

Beginning with the academic year, 2003–2004, the immersion program became a stand-alone version of our PTEP. I coordinated this program that places students in high poverty and culturally and linguistically diverse schools. Our long-term presence in the schools and communities aided our program's ability to provide supervisors and instructors who come from the host communities. The brochure for the program states:

> The Immersion Program is an intensive one-year preparation for licensure based in culturally and linguistically diverse schools. Students, who enter the program with a bachelor's degree, are placed in either a bilingual school in Salem or an inner city school in Portland. Most of the classes are held on-site in either Portland or Salem and students are encouraged to live near their host school. Experiences and classes in both communities are built into the program, as are most of the requirements for an ESL/bilingual endorsement and a master's degree.

The immersion program often attracted preservice Teachers of Color:

- Because placements and courses were held in Schools and Communities of Color, the students were able to remain in their home (or similar) communities rather than live in or travel to a predominately White town/campus. There was also a built-in connection with the K–8 student bodies of the schools.
- The goals and vision of the program were clearly aligned with teaching for a culturally or linguistically diverse program, including a built-in ESL or bilingual endorsement.

I conducted research to gather information on the effectiveness of the program for preparing preservice teachers. All the surveyed students agreed or strongly agreed that the immersion program prepared them to teach their current grade level and to teach diverse students. The following six categories of responses emerged (keywords in parenthesis). Students indicated that the placements touched them deeply and led to transformations and better curriculum choices. The following themes, in order of the number of responses in each, emerged as the agents of their growth:

- Stories (simulations/guests/films/readings)
- Empowerment (understanding/personal attention/encourage/respect/empathy)
- Transformative perspectives (reflection/experience/transform)
- Inner conflict (frustrated/discomfort)
- Dialogue across differences (conflict resolution/relationships [good/bad]/dialogue)
- Equity pedagogy (curriculum choices/race and racism discussions)

Preservice teachers seem to gain a global perspective through this program, which strongly depends on their relationships with others, particularly the cohort as a whole. Yet, as the concepts were collapsed into categories, stories—in one form or another—came into view as a major component of changed perspectives. Under the heading of stories I included: lived experiences, dialogue, guests, films—all areas that provoked reflection of both an inner and outer nature. In prior work, I have noted the ability of stories to permeate resistance and to be remembered long after specifics have passed (Moule, 2004).

As a part of the study, I followed four members of the cohort into their first year of teaching. I enjoyed connecting to these students that I had come to know well. I visited their classrooms, appreciated the environments they had created, and enjoyed watching them interact with their students. Once I began to reflect on my time with them, I tried to tease out what was different. For the students I observed, I was amazed at how completely they had mastered classroom management. I followed up my visits with calls and came to understand a few things. First of all, most of the new teachers I visited had had one student who was of special concern for them. Each teacher had decided to connect with and support this one student. What followed was a transformed classroom. As I pondered the work and success of these cohort members, I named the outcome from the program: Growing Activist Educators (Moule, 2007). Each teacher I studied was simply determined to make a difference, and several decided that meeting the needs of their most challenging student was the key. As they worked to accomplish this, their entire class and curriculum came into focus and alignment. Furthermore, these new teachers were beginning to be seen as reformers by their colleagues.

Teacher educators often lose track of the fact that what we teach our students in the rarified air of the campus classroom often does not mesh with what they experience in the field. This study of a full-year immersion program is a reminder that we need to place both knowledge and the preservice teachers themselves within historical, cultural, and social frameworks that better prepare them for a wider range of educational experiences and placements. If we do not, we set them up for failure and guilt as they try to bridge the cultural divide on their own as they begin their teaching careers.

Keys to Immersion Experiences

Once preservice teachers have had such an experience in a culturally different school—especially where staff is highly multicultural and integrated and the student population a minority majority—their previous learning about multicultural education begins to make real-life sense, and they begin to realize that practical details are easily dealt with and implemented. Without a deeper understanding of the lives of Children of Color and the cultural dimensions of their classroom, efforts at change will almost always be superficial and have little real effectiveness. The following outcomes appear at some levels across programs of every type (Meltzoff, 2010):

- Gained insight into their own attitudes, beliefs, and identities
- Felt transformed in regards to cultural and societal issues
- Increased disposition to work toward social justice
- Increased disposition toward teaching responsively
- Increased skills for teaching responsively (classroom practices)
- Increased disposition toward working with families of diverse students
- Increased knowledge of host cultures and their schools

Monocultural preservice teachers often hold pervasive stereotypes and expectations. "Once inside the school, however, students experienced the shock that accompanies a contradiction between expectations and reality"

(Aaronsohn, Carter, & Howell, 1995, p. 8). Preservice teachers placed in situations about which they have held such distorted convictions and fears need professors to be there with them to help them process the new perspectives through dialogues in class and reflective writings. These placements with support may empower preservice teachers to bridge the distance they experience between ideals and the realities of the schools and communities.

Olalde states: "It almost has to be voluntary to be effective, because it's a type of learning that relies on the individual to seek a deep connection with the culture, and a commitment to that kind of learning is personal. It is almost hard to express the depth of the learning: you get a systems overview of the culture through its institutions and services. You have the academic subculture consistent with higher education but still distinctly in a larger cultural context. On [the] streets, you are participating at the experiential level, and it changes you personally in a heart place that, sitting in the classroom, you don't often access. And finally, with all this new experience, you look at your own values and reassess, test their validity. It's quite an undertaking," (2010, p. 4).

My interpretation is that immersion opportunities work at a deep emotional level in many of the preservice teachers. These perspective changes through stories and experiences seem more valuable in moving students toward cultural competence than any specific information gained in the program.

Please see the companion website for detailed reports on these immersion experiences as well as contact information for their facilitators.

Many immersion experiences are in schools where more than one language is spoken by most students. In Oregon we have an increasing Latino/a population, currently one out of every four births. Many of these children grow up naturally bilingual. I am often surprised how few teachers appreciate this specific gift such children bring to the intellectual community in their classrooms, not to mention the cultural richness they may bring as well (Moule, 2008). This next section will expand on the details and needs of our bilingual students.

Bilingualism

(This section was written by Kathryn Ciechanowski, Oregon State University)

Today, children go to school in the United States in many languages other than English, such as Russian, Spanish, or Mandarin Chinese. Yet, there is considerable debate about whether non-English languages should be used in public settings, such as school, and if we should explicitly maintain and promote bilingualism in schools. This debate rages on given the demographic and achievement data on linguistically and culturally diverse student populations.

Thomas and Collier (2001) report that by the 2030s, the school-age population will be composed of 40 percent who speak a language other than English at home. And schools are not meeting their educational needs (Garcia, 2005).

Many think it is a new idea to provide education in a language other than English; however, bilingualism has been a part of American schooling since its early years. In the 1700–1800s, European immigrants ran non-English-speaking schools in their own neighborhoods. In 1839, at parents' request, Ohio allowed German-English instruction through its bilingual education law, and in 1847, Louisiana passed a similar law allowing French-English instruction. At the time, educational leaders, such as the superintendant of St. Louis schools, argued that suddenly eliminating one's family traditions, links to home countries, and cultural customs and habits could invoke harm and disastrous consequences on the individual; therefore, they promoted the use of multiple languages and cultures in schools. Yet, despite early acceptance and use of European languages in schools, in 1864, Congress banned Native Americans from being taught in their own languages—to the detriment of native identity, languages, and cultures.

Today, the number of speakers of other languages in the United States has grown, with over 47 million reporting that they speak a language other than English at home (Shin & Bruno, 2003). In the 2000 U.S. Census, 20 percent (approximately ten million) of the school-age population reported speaking a language other than English at home (Garcia, 2005). The 2000 Census revealed that approximately 380 non-English languages were represented in the U.S. population, with Spanish and Chinese as the most common (Shin & Bruno, 2003). The states with the highest percentage of speakers of other languages were California, New Mexico, Texas, New York, Hawaii, Arizona, and New Jersey; most of these states were in the West and Southwest. The number of speakers of other languages doubled over the decade 1990–2000 in the following states: Nevada, Georgia, North Carolina, Utah, Arkansas, and Oregon. Bilingualism is a significant and ever-present phenomenon in many locales across the United States.

The places most densely populated with speakers of other languages—in which three-quarters or more of the population spoke a language other than English at home (primarily Spanish)—are all located in California, Texas, and Florida. These states border Spanish-speaking countries or bodies of water that directly lead to these countries. More than half the speakers of other languages declared Spanish as their primary language but also reported knowing English very well. Historically, there have been hundreds of years of tense and oppressive relations between Mexico, Latin America, and the United States. In 1948, the United States and Mexico signed the Treaty of Hidalgo, allowing Mexicans the right to speak Spanish in the United States. Yet, there have been many battles brewing over the decades about the use of Spanish and

English in schools and other public settings. In 1998, the majority of Californians voted to outlaw bilingual education in Proposition 227, with English immersion required for all speakers of other languages and waivers from parents to continue any bilingual programs. In 2000, Arizona followed suit and passed its own English-only legislation: Proposition 203. Clearly, there is widespread belief that U.S. society is being threatened by the rapidly increasing population of speakers of other languages and the belief that students are not learning English (or "good" English) even after attending many years of school (Tse, 2001). These beliefs stem from fear rather than accurate information or research on English learning and bilingual education.

A renewed focus on intensive and expedient acquisition of the dominant language, English, by speakers of other languages has often led to exclusionary practices in which students are marginalized and made to feel different from their mainstream peers (Ciechanowski, 2010). Students are often pulled from their content classroom or restricted from electives such as art, music, computers, or library so they can work exclusively on their English skills. In these cases, the child's own language and culture are not considered to be resources that could benefit their own or peer learning (Ciechanowski, 2009). They are required to fit the dominant culture in order to participate and be valued in the school setting.

Here is a case in which a child is made to feel devalued and deficient because he was not proficient in the dominant language (English):

> It was reading time. The first grade teacher was asking her students to think of words that began with the letter "c." She added that she would be calling on each one to give her a different word. After calling on most of the children, she turned to Hermán, a Spanish-speaking child in her class.

> "Chancla," Hermán offered proudly.

> "What?" the teacher inquired.

> "Chancla," he answered more softly.

> "How do you spell it? ... Do you know how to spell it?"

> Being a first grader Hermán didn't know how to spell it.

> The class giggled.

> "Chank-la," the teacher repeated. "Do you have one, Hermán?"

> "No ma'am, but my mother has two."

> "What are they?" she probed impatiently.

> "Chanclas," he responded again.

> "Well, what do they do?"

> "Nothing." The class snickered.

> "You said your mother has two?"

> "Yes, ma'am."

"What does she do with them?" she pushed on....

"She wears them on her feet in the morning."

"You mean 'slippers'?"

"No ma'am, 'chanclas'." He had never heard of slippers.

Frustrated, the teacher proclaimed, "There is no such word, Hermán. Give me another word?" (Franquiz & Reyes, 1998, p. 211).

In this exemplar, the teacher made proficiency in English a prerequisite for learning and did not draw from the child's linguistic and cultural toolkit to assist in his learning. The teacher limited his opportunities for participation by limiting the use of his linguistic and cultural knowledge. This teacher worked from a *deficit model* in which a child like Hermán was problematic because his native language was viewed as inappropriate (or even inferior), intrusive, and interfering with his learning. In contrast, an *inclusive model* actively promotes the use of both dominant and non-dominant linguistic and cultural knowledge in lessons, and the students and teachers are committed learners who embrace and explore a wide variety of language and cultures. Through acts of inclusion, teachers utilize *bilingualism* as a resource in the course of literacy and content learning.

Most bilingual education models focus on the acquisition of the English; therefore, the difference between them is how the native language is included or excluded and how the child's English learning is supported. Although not considered an effective model, submersion or "sink or swim" models place bilingual students in an English-only educational setting with no support or services (Ovando, Collier & Combs, 2006). However, newcomer centers provide services and instruction in separate facilities to recent immigrants for one or two years before the learner can move to a sheltered or traditional program (Faltis & Coulter, 2008). The following two common models provide services and modified instruction primarily in English:

1. English language development pullout classes separate non-English proficient students based on proficiency level, typically for a half hour or one class period a day, to learn explicit English skills until they are tested as proficient in English.
2. Structured or sheltered English immersion programs provide content classes that use research-based strategies to promote comprehension and learning of grade-level content (Short & Echevarria, 2005). However, the following two models are considered *bilingual education* because they provide instruction in the native language:
   a. Early-exit or short-term bilingual programs instruct children in their native language until approximately second grade, often with a decreasing percentage of time in the native language as children advance through the grades.

b. Late-exit or long-term bilingual programs provide native-language instruction until approximately fifth or sixth grade, with either decreasing percentage of time in the native language or with 50 percent in each language (Ovando, Combs & Collier, 2006).

All the programs mentioned above may be considered *subtractive* when the primary goal is to learn English and the end result is that the learner loses the native language. Both languages are not maintained equally, and there is not an explicit goal to achieve bilingual proficiency.

However, an *additive* approach works from the premise that a second (or additional) language should be learned without detriment or loss of the first language. In this approach, multiple languages are promoted and used for instruction. Two-way immersion or dual-language programs instruct both native and non-native English speakers in two languages, such as English and Spanish (or Mandarin Chinese, Russian, or another language). Bilingualism is valued, promoted, and viewed as an asset for personal, functional, and psychological reasons. Research has shown that this is the most effective approach for long-term academic achievement of linguistically and culturally diverse students (Thomas & Collier, 2001).

In general, research supports the use of bilingual education as the most effective approach to promote academic achievement in children who speak a language other than English at home (Hermanns, 2010; Thomas & Collier, 2001). There are multiple reasons to explain why bilingual education is so effective:

- **Social-cultural identity:** Bilingual education promotes a feeling of student self-worth because teachers and administrators embrace non-dominant languages in their curriculum, instruction, and educational practices to demonstrate that they value the students' language and culture. Members of minority groups (regardless of their proficiency in English) often show less-than-ideal achievement in school, indicating that schools may be uncomfortable or unfamiliar institutions for many of these kids. Different cultural groups may have very different ways of communicating, teaching, and learning. So, children who have teachers or instructional aides from their own language and cultural groups often show greater academic achievement because these professionals can help children mediate between cultures and languages (Snow, 1990).
- **Cognitive consequences:** Bilingual children enjoy cognitive advantages. Meta-linguistic awareness, which is the ability to think more abstractly and broadly about language in general, typically emerges several years earlier in bilinguals than non-bilinguals (Snow, 1990).
- **Linguistic skills:** There are direct linguistic advantages to bilingual instruction. Some language skills are not limited to the language in which they

were acquired (for example, how to organize a paragraph, how to make an argument, how to hold a book) because they are *transferable* from one language to another. Studies show that children who write and read better in their native language also write and read better in English. The *interdependence* of languages suggests that academic skills, literacy, concept formation, content knowledge, and learning strategies can transfer back and forth between first and second (and additional) languages (Ovando, Combs & Collier, 2006).

- **Academic Achievement:** Native language instruction improves academic achievement. Learning content and literacy is hard work but is more easily done in the first language. Also, parents can be more involved with homework and connect to school when they can communicate with teachers and understand the schoolwork. There are long-term negative consequences for learning to read in a language that one does not speak well (Snow, 1990).

Students' academic achievement can be enhanced when academic programs use their full repertoire of languages during teaching and when lessons are contextualized in the experiences and skills of the home and community. Along these lines, the International Reading Association (2001) published a set of principles for educators about second language literacy instruction:

- Build on children's strengths by including home languages and cultures in instruction.
- Connect unfamiliar material to the familiar by linking academic content to home language and culture.
- Provide initial literacy instruction in the child's home language when possible.
- Support transfer of literacy skills from the home language to the new language (English).
- Promote literacy and proficiency in two (or additional) languages where feasible.
- Respect parents' preferences, rights, and choices regarding the child's language learning.
- Understand local, state, or provincial and national policies and their impact on language programs.

Above all, students and their families ought to be respected as contributing members of the school community who have much linguistic and cultural knowledge to be valued and harnessed to promote school success. Teachers should develop humanizing learning environments in which students are treated with respect as human beings with their own linguistic and cultural knowledge and are viewed as capable and active individuals in their own learning. It has too often been the case that those students who are learned from and valued in classrooms are the ones who come from linguistic and cultural backgrounds that more closely match those of the mainstream. "Creating learning environments that incorporate student language and life experiences in no way negates teachers' responsibility for providing students with particular academic content knowledge and skills" (Bartolomé, 2003, p. 417). Students' language and culture can be highlighted and esteemed while maintaining the highest academic expectations. "It is equally necessary not to confuse academic rigor with rigidity that stifles and silences students" (p. 417). Indeed, the strength of our teaching methods comes from the degree to which they value students' language, culture, and life experiences and construct learning contexts in which power is shared by students and teachers.

Overcoming Anxiety by Focusing on Caring

The previous chapters highlighted the kinds of life experiences that impact culturally different students as well as teaching strategies that may require modification in order to work most effectively cross-culturally. However, no amount of preparation can allay the anxiety typical of teachers who first contemplate working with culturally diverse students. Student teachers regularly ask, "But what do I do when I find myself standing in front of a room of children who are culturally different?" The usual answer is, "Just do the same thing you do with any group—begin to teach." The anxiety and hesitancy reflect a basic discomfort with cultural differences and the fact that most teachers have grown up in a racist society separated from those who are different from them. They are afraid because of their ignorance about students' cultures because they don't want to make a cultural faux pas or miss something very obvious. In addition, they are anxious and uncomfortable due to feelings of guilt over the existence of racism or feelings of embarrassment because of past indifference, the racist behavior of family and friends, or feelings of personal privilege or entitlement. It feels like dangerous territory. After reading chapter after chapter and having extended reflections and discussion about the complexity of working with diversity and how easily cross-cultural communication can break down, the prospect of facing students from a different culture and providing them with a sound education may seem daunting.

At such moments of doubt, remember several things: First, as a teacher and a student of learning, one is already—or is in the process of becoming—a skilled educator. Becoming culturally competent does not mean starting from scratch or learning everything anew. Rather, it means honing existing skills, broadening teaching concepts that are too narrow, and gaining new cultural knowledge about students. In general, culturally competent teachers are better educators because they must remain more conscious about the cultural appropriateness of tasks, methods, and perspectives that others may routinely overlook. In a certain sense, every student carries his or her own unique culture, and the teacher's task is to respectfully gain entry into that culture and offer learning that is sensitive to its rules and inner dynamics.

Second, above all, students are human beings, and this is the ultimate basis for connection. They may also be anxious about schooling, especially if they are culturally different. More than likely, they have had experiences that make them mistrust the kind of system in which the teacher works. The initial task, then, is to set them at ease in a manner that has meaning for them. Teaching and learning are human processes that start as a baby learns to walk and talk. Teaching is bound to fail (with all students, not just culturally different ones) when awareness of common humanity and caring is lost. Unfortunately, in the process of teaching people about cultural differences, there is a tendency (that should be guarded against) to objectify and stereotype students by seeing them only in terms of their differences. By attending to these too fully, the teacher can lose sight of the individuals in the classroom. Focusing too heavily on differences and thereby overlooking basic human similarities can turn cross-cultural work into a mechanical process. Cross-cultural interaction must be based on the shared humanity of student and teacher.

There are three kinds of human characteristics: those that the person shares with all other human beings, those shared with some other human beings, and those that are unique to each individual (Kroeber, 1948). Cross-cultural communication and teaching are most possible in relation to the first. A sensitivity to the second and third allows for human differences and uniqueness once a basic connection has formed. It is through the very human capacities of caring, having sympathy and empathy for others, and identifying with the basic joys and predicaments of being human that differences can be best bridged.

Preparing for Cross-Cultural Teaching

A number of concrete preparations can create support or allay some of the natural anxiety that may be felt when contemplating or actually beginning cross-cultural teaching. The development of cultural competence is a lifelong pursuit. This book is only a first step. The more you learn about racism, culture, diversity, cultural competence, and cross-cultural teaching as well as about individual groups and their cultures, the more comfortable and conversant you become. Since the late 1980s, there has been an explosion of good material in this area and a dramatic increase in the availability of excellent professional development opportunities. You should take advantage of these whenever possible.

Prepare for working with students from a particular ethnic group by doing personal research on that group's culture, history, and educational issues. This can include not only academic and professional reading and Internet searches but also novels, biographies, social histories, travel accounts, movies, videos, theater, art exhibits, lectures, and so forth.

As discussed earlier, a most valuable supplement is actual immersion in the culture. This can range from small choices—such as attending celebrations, cultural events, and political rallies; eating regularly at ethnic restaurants; and patronizing community businesses—to more sustained contact—such as volunteering in the community—to larger ones—such as learning the language and traveling to countries of origin.

Finding Support for Cross-Cultural Teaching

It is also useful to consult on a regular basis with a professional teacher who is indigenous to the community and/or the culture of the children in your class. As a beginner in cross-cultural teaching, it is particularly useful to discuss problems, especially early in their development, with someone who is knowledgeable about the workings of the students' culture. With more experience and comfort, one might need consultation only in more difficult or problematic areas.

A teacher might also consider establishing a study group or peer support group with other educators who are involved in cross-cultural teaching. Regular meetings can involve discussing shared readings, presenting problems, having guest experts, and the like. Such a group can provide opportunities to share resources and knowledge, receive observation support when helpful, and remain focused on the cultural dimensions of cross-cultural teaching (Williams, 2008).

A final suggestion is to join local ethnic teacher groups and networks. Often, teachers who work extensively with a specific population join together to share information and resources, to advocate for the needs of students and their families, and to keep knowledgeable on current research and trends in education for the population of interest. Active participation in such a group is an excellent way to learn more about a student population, connect with other teachers who might be valuable resources, and demonstrate interest and commitment to cross-cultural teaching.

How Is Cross-Cultural Teaching Different?

There is general agreement among educators and counselors that cross-cultural work is more demanding, challenging, and energy-draining than work with same-culture students. Cross-cultural work tends to be more *experiential, freewheeling,* and *bilateral* (Draguns, 1981). Experiential means that the work is more likely to directly and emotionally impact the individual. It is like culture shock: The person is immersed in a foreign culture where familiar patterns of behavior are no longer useful and new means of acting and relating must be discovered. It is more labor-intensive and more likely to result in fatigue (Draguns, 1981).

> Spilled paint on the floor, children fighting over limited crayons, the nearly completed child-sized body shapes with painted clothing lay spread all over the floor and the final bell for school was rapidly nearing. The faces and hands of the figures needed to be colored. "Ok," the teacher said, "we're all going to be White." Vickie, an experienced teacher whose classes had been slowly increasing in social class and racial diversity, thought to save time by not coloring the faces at all. As soon as the words left her mouth she realized the possible negative effects on her few Children of Color. "Children," Vickie says, "all of the shapes being White won't work, we all have different skin tones. So what can we do?" Quickly, she brought the children to their practiced KWL problem solving mode "What do we know, what do we want to know ..." Facts: There are too few crayons near flesh tones, kids are fighting, time is running out. Moving into the brainstorming solution step, Kathy, the lone African American child, said, I'll use the brown one, that matches my skin. Anavrin (Nirvana spelled backwards), envisioning his a punk-rock future, volunteered to color his figure purple. And so it went, the children openly discussing and comparing the crayons and themselves, selecting colors they felt comfortable with (V. Grantland, personal communication, June, 2005).

Another willing, resourceful teacher—in this case, giving herself the tedious, labor-intensive, clean up phase of the art project in order to have the time to work through the problem with the children. She had taken the time to turn a problem into a learning situation. This example, of a teacher making a mistake, sensing the possible emotional impact and moving on, is the kind of humanity and humility that will serve you well.

This example also illustrates *freewheeling:* the fact that the learning process must be continually adapted to the specific needs of differing students. As suggested earlier, the only constant is the shared humanity. Standard approaches are overwhelmingly culture-bound and European in nature, and even efforts to catalog cultural similarities among racially related ethnic groups are tentative and ever mindful of enormous intragroup diversity. In reference to counseling, a suggestion that will also help teachers: "Be prepared to adapt your techniques (e.g., general activity level, mode of verbal intervention, content of remarks, tone of voice) to the cultural background of the client; communicate acceptance of and respect for the client in terms that make sense within his or her cultural frame of reference; and be open to the possibility of more direct intervention in the life of the client than the traditional ethos of the counseling profession would dictate or permit" (Draguns, 1981, p. 16).

Finally, bilateral implies collaboration. By the very nature of cross-cultural work, the teacher depends more on the student for help in defining the teaching process. For example, although it is common practice for teachers to get input from students on their prior knowledge and lesson direction

(KWL: What do we *know*, what do we *want* to know, what have we *learned*), it is even more imperative in cross-cultural work. Teachers need direct and continuing student input on what is culturally valued so that what is created is culturally appropriate and useful and minimizes ethnocentric standards. Because teacher and student may begin at very different cultural places, it is reasonable to expect some mutual movement in the direction of the other. Culturally competent educators adapt and adjust their efforts to the culture of the student. At the same time, by entering into the learning process, culturally different students cannot help but gain some knowledge and insight into the workings of mainstream culture.

What Does Successful Cross-Cultural Teaching Look Like?

A number of strategies have proven successful at the college level in facilitating learning among Students of Color. From published reports and personal communication, Cose (1997) found that professors at Xavier University were able to combine attitude change and focused remediation work with a small student body of predominately African American students in order to increase academic success. Over a period of years, the university went from four or five graduates entering medical school to seventy-five. Although there were problems in the program, its overall "success in fostering an atmosphere of achievement" was clear (Cose, p. 57). The difficulties resided primarily with the educational system at Xavier, not its racially different students. Six principles of successful cross-cultural teaching:

- Find a group of young people motivated to learn or find a way to motivate them.
- Convince them you believe in them.
- Teach them good study skills, including the art of studying in groups.
- Challenge them with difficult and practical material.
- Give them adequate support.
- Demand that they perform. (Cose, 1997)

First is motivation. Without motivation that already exists or that has been stimulated by the teacher, significant learning will not occur. Implied is an expectation of student-centeredness (in other words, student needs—and not those of the teacher's—are the beginning of the learning process, see Chapter 8) as well as an acknowledgment that students from different cultural groups may be motivated in different ways and that the teacher should become cognizant of such differences.

The second principle involves the communication of caring and empathy for students. Empathy is defined as the "ability to acknowledge the feelings behind another person's lived experience" (Moule & Ingram, 2002, pp. 4–5). This "second step may be the hardest, for convincing young people you believe in them is not an easy task … unless you really do" (Cose, 1997, p. 65). In this regard, teachers can expect to have their sense of caring and concern tested by many Students of Color.

The third principle highlights the necessity of developing good study skills upon which to build further learning, acknowledging that Students of Color often find themselves left behind because of differential treatment or stereotyping early in their education. The result has often been underperformance and underachievement. Group learning reflects an understanding of the role peer pressure can play in devaluing classroom performance as well as the value placed on cooperative learning in Cultures of Color.

Principle four speaks to the use of difficult and practical learning materials— difficult so accomplishment will feel significant and challenge feelings of inadequacy in the learning realm and practical so the relevance and value of what is being learned is obvious to the student.

The fifth principle implies the necessity of close, continual contact and support in overcoming feelings of self-doubt and inadequacy. For many students, a history of learning failures saps motivation and subsequent attempts in the classroom. A culturally sensitive teacher monitors student frustration, self-criticism, and self-fulfilling prophesies and is ready to intervene and short-circuit such reactions.

The last principle—the demand that students perform—highlights the importance of ongoing caring and support—that is, communicating that "I care about you enough that I will not accept less than you are capable of." It also implies the modeling of resilience and sustained effort in educational success. As Cose implied, if a teacher demands that students perform and is really sincere, "lo and behold, they do" (Cose, 1997, p. 65).

The need for a culture that empowers students and allows for learning in open and open-minded ways is known to be crucial for all children, not just those for whom the existing school culture comes naturally. Another program was successful in training and retaining Students of Color at the college level by "creating an aura of family in which cooperation is highly valued, bonding between the students and faculty is encouraged, and a maintenance of positive ethnic identity is fostered" (Anderson, 1988, p. 8). Even with the importance of a sense of community in learning settings, "no formulas exist as yet to explain how to put together the right combination of people, things, and ideas to create a particular setting that succeeds with at-risk students" (Cuban, 1989, p. 799). In *The Power of Their Ideas: Lessons for America from a Small School in Harlem*, Meier (1995) described a New York City elementary school that came close.

Connections and Reflections: Emerging Views

This is the last regular chapter of the text with reflections and classroom activities at the end. While you will want to complete the reading on the different groups and the interviews with Educators of Color, this is a good junction in the road to take a longer look at your journey so far and compare your responses with others.

Questions About Your Journey The following questions come from those asked during one of the immersion programs. Think about your journey so far in cultural competence.

- What was the start of my "journey"?
- What were my expectations?
- What were key moments on this trip?
- Was there anything that made me feel uncomfortable?
- What surprised me most?

Cultural Competence Survey Revisited Now might be a good time to revisit the survey you took at the end of Chapter 1. Have you moved toward your self-selected goal?

Creative Problem Solving (CPS)

This practical tool of creative problem-solving (Parnes, 1967) will help you incorporate the concepts and specifics in this chapter and this book and perhaps help you solve some problems in your life. The six main steps in the process are more formally known as *objective finding, fact finding, problem finding, idea finding, solution finding,* and *acceptance finding*. I will explain the steps and then walk through my process by using a classroom problem.

The first step in the process is to recognize that there is a problem that needs solving. So, before going farther, jot down any conflict, controversy, or question that comes to mind on the material in this chapter or another. This step is sometimes called "the mess."

Next, list three to five facts that have been established about the material covered. Either think of things that particularly moved or surprised you or scan the pages again for a few details.

Based on the facts and your original concern, complete this statement: "In what ways might we _____?" We will refer to this sentence with the initials IWWMW. This restating of the problem helps us get beyond complaint into an active and collective consideration of a specific problem. You may need to generate two or three IWWMW sentences before you have one that you would like to take through the remaining steps of the process.

Use an open-ended brainstorming technique that includes the following specifics to generate ten to twelve ideas to answer your IWWMW statement:

- Do not make judgments. At this point, all ideas have value. This strategy allows you to generate rather than defend or critique your ideas.
- Come up with multiple ideas—for example, as many as you can generate in two minutes. The more creative ideas you have to choose from, the better. Having many ideas increases the likelihood of coming to a great idea.
- Build on ideas you or others have. Piggybacking and looking over each others' shoulders are allowed at this point. Perhaps ask others to help you think of or modify an idea.
- The wilder an idea, the better, for a wild idea often leads to an unexpected and viable solution. Encouraging far-out ideas expands the imagination.

Your list could contain ideas that were included in or suggested by the material in the chapter.

Now that you have generated a free-flowing and perhaps wild-eyed list, apply criteria to see which ideas are worth pursuing. Choose three to five criteria that you believe are appropriate for evaluating your ideas:

acceptance by others? adaptable to situation? advantageous? agreement of those concerned? appealing; attractive? assistance available? attitudes (positive) about idea? behavior (positive) toward idea? beneficial? challenging; holds interest? commitment: long term? commitment: short term? consistent? cooperation available? cost-effective? cost-efficient? cost for startup reasonable? creative solution? creative enhancement? (not) dangerous? deadline can be met? (not) distracting? ease in doing? effect: immediate? effect: long term? effect: short term? efficient? economical? endorsement from key people? explainable to others? financing available? fits situation? flexible to situation? functional? imaginative? improve a condition? improvement: long term? improvement: now? improvement: short term? interest will expand? lasting effect? manageable? markets available? materials and cost? materials available? measurable results? needs met? organizational acceptance? operational? performs well? performance over time? policies fit? practical? predictable? prevents _____? price? produces desired result? profitable? reasonable or logical? resources available? results immediately given? results: short term? rewarding to others? rewarding to self? rewards? risks: low? safety? socially acceptable? success likely? time? time: efficient use of? timely? transfer? transferable to other situations? useful? values intact? valuable?

Evaluate your brainstormed list by using the criteria you have chosen. You may use a simple grid with the ideas listed on the left and the criteria along the top. In each square, give zero to three points for each generated idea for each criterion you have selected. When one or two ideas have the most points, go to the next step.

Plan to implement your idea either as an actual event if you have the opportunity to do so in your current situation or in a future classroom or other community setting you may encounter. I will go through the process with a problem of my own so you may see how this process may be applied in the classroom.

Step One: The mess. I am concerned that children in a racially homogenous classroom may not have an opportunity to develop realistic perceptions of People of Color.

Step Two: The facts. I know:

- Such attitudes develop early.
- Prejudices are deeply embedded in our culture.
- Well-intentioned teachers may unknowingly perpetuate stereotypes.

Step Three: IWWMW. My statement is: *In what way might we* bring children to a more realistic view of those who are not like themselves?

Step Four: Brainstorm. I next generated a list using the brainstorming rules:

- Do not judge.
- Generate many ideas.
- Piggyback for more ideas.
- Include wild ideas.

My list of ideas includes experiences in diverse cultures, diverse books written by people from the cultures, first-person stories of children their own ages if possible, role-playing to help them move beyond their own perspectives, actively pursuing appropriate resources in the family, school, or neighborhood.

Two of these ideas did not occur to me until I was writing my list. One is to read a first-person story and then get the children involved in reflecting on it by acting parts out. The other is to gently ask the children if anyone in their family has an additional language or represents ethnic or racial diversity.

Step Five: Evaluate. The criteria I choose to evaluate all my ideas, particularly these two, include: Will it work? Is it low cost? Do I like the idea of carrying my idea out? Would the parents like it? Working with those four criteria and putting points in each box for each idea, my totals led me to I think I would start with the story-reading and role-playing idea and perhaps use it as a springboard for my other valuable idea.

Step Six: Go for it! In planning to carry out my idea, my list included:

1. Think about stories I have read. Would one work? Or ask around for good stories to read.
2. Plan a time to read the story, and think about how to present acting it out.

3. Consider how this reading would fit into my classroom curriculum and the state benchmarks. Is there anything I can do to increase the saliency of the reading and role-playing?

In this example, I have used creative problem-solving to help me glean a practical plan for improving my classroom. While we focused on ways to provide sound multicultural curricula in Chapter 8, creative problem-solving may help you apply material in each chapter to your particular educational role and beyond.

Classroom: Adventures in Learning

For both lower and upper grades, try adapting creative problem-solving for use in your classroom with your students. For lower grades you may use smiley faces instead of numbers to rate the criteria.

PART III

Working Competently with All Students

"People are what they are because of environment and heredity: Two tools over which they have absolutely no control make them what they are."

—Matthew Golson

Teachers need to be aware of the diversity that exists both across and within ethnic groups. First of all, each group has its own unique history in America. As a result, somewhat different problems have emerged for each. For example, People of Color are set apart primarily by skin color and other physical features. As a consequence, they may struggle with concerns over body image, passing for White, or peer group identity versus achieving in the mainstream White school culture. Many Latinos/as and Asians have immigrated from traditional homelands and face ongoing dilemmas concerning assimilation, bilingualism, and the destruction of traditional family roles and values. As victims of colonization in their own land, Native Americans have struggled with the representation of their histories in traditional mainstream curricula. African Americans have faced a similar psychological dislocation due to slavery and its enduring effects. In turn, European Americans from distinct ethnic backgrounds find themselves suspended between worlds; they are culturally different yet are perceived and often wish to be perceived as part of the majority. These ethnically specific circumstances shape and determine the kinds of problems diverse children bring to the classroom.

Differences among students from the same ethnic group (class, age, gender, ableness, language) can also be extensive, as suggested earlier. For example, Collins (1990) describes such differences in relation to Black women:

> All African-American women share the common experience of being Black women in a society that denigrates women of African descent. This commonality of

experience suggests that certain characteristic themes will be prominent in a Black women's standpoint. For example, one core theme is a legacy of struggle…. The existence of core themes does not mean that African-American women respond to these themes in the same way. Diversity among Black women produces different concrete experiences that in turn shape various reactions to the core themes….
A variety of factors explain the diversity of responses. For example, although all African-American women encounter racism, social class differences among African-American women influence how racism is experienced. (pp. 22–24)

The surest indicator of cultural *insensitivity* is the belief that all members of a group share similar characteristics and circumstances. A recently arrived child of a migrant worker from central Mexico—poor and barely able to speak English—faces very different life challenges than a similarly aged U.S.-born child from a wealthy Chilean family whose parents are professionals. The first task of any cross-cultural teacher is to carefully assess students' demographic and cultural situations. Some of the following information may be critical in determining the learning needs of a culturally different student: place of birth, number of generations in America, family roles and structure, language spoken at home, English fluency, economic situation and status, amount and type of preschool education, amount of acculturation, traditions still practiced in the home, familiarity and comfort with European lifestyle, religious affiliation, and community and friendship patterns.

The culturally competent teacher not only seeks such information but is also aware of its possible meaning. The child of the migrant worker may need material assistance, such as meals and clothes. The parents may be unfamiliar with the school system and fearful of authorities. The Chilean child is more likely to be concerned with cultural as opposed to economic survival: how ethnicity is impacting him or her in school, parental concern over acculturation, changing roles with the peer group, and balancing success in school with retaining traditional ways.

Each of the chapters that follow focuses on working with a different ethnic community. Each is written in conjunction with an educator from that community. Multicultural educators are divided about the value of presenting culturally specific information in this manner. Although enumerating formulas or "recipes" for understanding and dealing with groups of people is a convenient way to summarize culturally specific information, it does present certain pitfalls.

To begin with, the division of America's non-White populations into broad racial categories—although a common practice—is artificial and serves to mask enormous diversity. For example, Americans who have immigrated from Asian countries do not generally identify or call themselves Asian Americans. They may self-identify as Chinese Americans, Chinese, or of Chinese descent or even according to more regional or tribal groupings.

Some may find being called Asian American offensive. In fact, the term is bureaucratic in origin, having been developed by the U.S. Census Bureau. It is used here—as elsewhere—for convenience, but it should not be assumed to imply sameness. In actuality, as Atkinson, Morten, and Sue (1993) pointed out, the term *Asian American* refers to "some twenty-nine distinct subgroups that differ in language, religion, and values" (p. 195). The important point is that the broad categories subsume many different ethnic groups, each with its own unique culture, and lumping them together on the basis of certain common geographic, physical, or cultural features merely encourages an underestimation of their diversity and uniqueness.

Thinking about People of Color through such categories also serves to encourage stereotyping. Such thinking tends to be most common among inexperienced teachers who find the prospect of cross-cultural work anxiety-producing. Stereotyping reduces what might be experienced as unpredictability in the behavior of culturally different students. Thus, less experienced teachers often project cultural characteristics onto all individuals they identify as belonging to a specific group. It works this way: If I can be sure that all students will act similarly, I can more easily develop a general strategy of how to deal with them in class and, therefore, feel more in control. For example, if I believe that all Native American students are reticent, I can prepare myself to be more active in seeking information or if I know that all Asian Americans are taught to suppress emotions or to be hesitant to respond in class, I can be on the lookout for more subtle forms of emotionality or work to give them a safer place and manner for sharing in class. Similarly, teachers who wish to limit complexity can incorrectly assume that approaches that have been successful with a given student population are the only approaches to be adopted. In sum, then, taking the material that appears in the following chapters as gospel limits teacher creativity and adaptability and at the same time suppresses sensitivity to intragroup differences. Instead of assuming unanimity among students from the same group, a far better way to proceed is to treat all guesses about what is going on with a culturally different student as hypotheses to be verified or rejected.

As you read each chapter, use this exercise to identify your experiences with, attitudes toward, and beliefs about members of different racial and ethnic groups. Answer the following questions in relation to each of the following groups: (a) African Americans, (b) Latinos/as, (c) Asian Americans, (d) Native Americans, (e) Muslims, (f) White ethnic groups (Italians, Jews, Irish, etc.).

Consider answering the questions for each group *before* you read the corresponding chapter. Then, look at your answers *after* reading the chapter. You may discover some subtle ways your thinking is racially slanted and how this might affect your role as an educator. Your reflections and thoughts after you read each chapter will help you on your journey to cultural competence.

1. Describe in detail experiences you have had with members of this group.
2. At present, how do you feel about members of this group (describe your reactions in detail and, if possible, relate them to specific experiences), and how has that changed over time?
3. Are there any characteristics, traits, or other things about members of this group that make it difficult for you to approach them?
4. Without censoring yourself, generate a list of characteristics—one-word adjectives—that describe your beliefs and perceptions about members of this group.
5. What reactions, feelings, thoughts, or concerns come to mind when you think about teaching and working with members of this group?
6. What kinds of answers, information, learning experiences, and contacts do you need to become more comfortable with members of this group?

At the end of Chapter 9, I detailed one method of creative problem-solving—a means of working through our problems; in this case, perhaps uncomfortable feelings. You may want to revisit creative problem-solving to frame your thinking as you work through your answers to the exercise above and read Chapters 10–15. Having a means to work through our problems encourages us to solve them. Here is an example from one of my students that includes both her IWWMI statement and her answer:

> In what ways might we give all children an equal and fair amount of education based on their needs?: In order to make sure that all children will have an equal amount of education and have their needs met we have to go through several important steps. First, teachers should have special training that prepares them to be qualified to teach different students from different cultures with unbiased and fair methods. Second, teachers should make a strong connection between themselves and their students because understanding their needs will help them to find solutions for their problems. Finally, the cooperation between parents and schools will benefit the students because that connection will create a group that supports students in different ways.

Introduction to Chapters 10, 11, 12, 13, 14, and 15

What follows are five in-depth interviews focused on working with students from the five Communities of Color. The Chapter 15 focuses on students from White backgrounds. Each is written with a teacher from that community who is an educator with extensive experience working with students from his or her respective group. All were asked: What do you think is important—or even critical—for a culturally different teacher to know in relation to working with a student from your community? A number of distinct topics provide the structure for the interviews. Included are educator and ethnic autobiographical material, demographics and shared characteristics of their community, group names, family and community characteristics, cultural styles, values, worldviews, subpopulations, and learning styles. In the companion website you will find an expanded interview with each educator that adds details on the history of the various groups, ways in which socioeconomic issues affect families and individuals in the group. Each expanded interview ends with a short, often poignant and personal case study.

In the interviews included here each educator summarized his or her thinking about the general characteristics that community members share. This is not an easy task because each racial category represents diverse ethnic groups. Each interviewee tried to speak broadly enough to fairly represent the cultural and psychological characteristics shared by the majority of members of the ethnic group he or she is representing. At the same time, each tried to distinguish among subgroups where necessary. Because no single teacher can claim expert knowledge or experience working with all subgroups or divisions within any racial category, the interviewees were asked to discuss and draw examples from subpopulations with which they are most familiar. Answers to the various questions in each interview have been left close to verbatim to retain their personal and cultural flavor.

The following table gives an overview of cultural value differences for groups represented by five of the six chapters to follow. While I understand that no such chart will tell you very much about specific individuals, ponder the general insights you may gain from these cultural comparisons. As you read this section of the book, many of these cultural values—discussed in depth in Chapter 5—will come out through the introductions and the interviews.

Cultural Value Preferences

Area of Relationships	Middle Class White Americans (Eurocentric)	Asian/Pacific Americans (Sinocentric)	American Indian/ Alaskan Native	African American (Afrocentric)	Latino/a American
Man to nature/ environment	Mastery over	Harmony with	Harmony with	Harmony with	Harmony with
Time orientation	Future	Past-present	Present	Present	Past-present
Relations with people	Individual	Collateral	Collateral	Collateral	Collateral

This table is adapted from Ho (1987, p. 232) and Moore (1990). The value preference called collateral means that people are seen as individuals and also as members of many groups and subgroups; they are independent and dependent at the same time.

Student Voices: Fellow Travelers on This Journey

As you prepare to read each chapter, here are reflections from my students

- Chapter 10, "Working with Latino/a Students": "This chapter will be the most helpful to me in the future…. The area where I plan to teach has a rapidly growing Latino population. Even though I think I have an advantage simply because I am Latino, I believe that this chapter will help me."
- Chapter 11, "Working with American Indian/Alaska Native Students": "I chose to read this chapter to see if what was written would resonate as true for the community in which I work. This chapter highlights some of the tragedy of the existing reality of many Native American communities, but it also highlights some of the strengths of the Aboriginal milieu. There is a shared Native identity and a strong sense of belonging in First Nation communities, and despite the hardships experienced in these communities there is a real determination to survive and thrive. Teaching in a Native community is one of the hardest things that I have ever done, but also one of the most rewarding."
- Chapter 12, "Working with African American Students": "I believe this is the most powerful chapter in the book." (This came from an editor.)
- Chapter 13, "Working with Asian Pacific American Students": "I chose this chapter to read because of the Chinese student in my class that does not speak English. I want to learn more about what he is going through and where he is coming from, so I can approach him in an educated manner."
- Chapter 14, "Working with Arab and Muslim Americans": "I chose to read this chapter simply because I wish to reduce my ignorance. Like many Americans I have started paying more attention since 9/11. I guess sometimes it takes a crisis to get my attention. I don't want to continue to live with this part of my head in the sand. I can't if I want to be a decent teacher."
- Chapter 15, "Working with European American Students": Some of my college students were empathic: "Keep the chapter on White Ethnic Students." One said: "The idea that I've always had, that I'm just an individual, as being actually a form of 'White Privilege'—that in fact I would be shocked as being referred to racially as white, now makes perfect sense."

Other students said, "The interviews, for me, were the most powerful part of the book" and "My favorite chapters were the interviews because they taught me about different ethnic groups and labels that we give groups." Through these interviews, you will experience the words and passions of real teachers who are culturally competent experts and deeply dedicated to meeting the educational needs of students from their respective cultures.

CHAPTER 10

Working with Latino/a Students

An Interview with Aurora Cedillo

> *"The family becomes the most important element in life in this world and beyond. I have experienced the fire that melts and molds us as a community."*
>
> —Aurora Cedillo

Demographics

With the 2000 census, Latinos/as became the largest racial minority in the United States, numbering 35,204,480, or 12.5 percent of the U.S. population. These figures represent an increase of 58 percent from 1990 and are in actuality an underestimation because they do not reflect the undocumented and illegal migrants who are continually entering the U.S. Estimates of illegal immigration are approximately 500,000 per year (Passel & Cohn, 2008). Recent estimates show the number of Latinos/as in the United States at nearly 47 million, over 15 percent (U.S. Census Bureau, 2008). Projections suggest that Latinos/as will make up one-third of the U.S. population by 2060. This dramatic growth is attributed to high birthrates and fertility rates, immigration patterns, and the average young age of the population (see Figure 1.1 for a graph on this growth). As a collective, Latinos/as are quite diverse, including individuals whose roots are in Mexico, Cuba, Puerto Rico, and South and Central Americas. Those of Mexican descent, now numbering 30 million, make up 66 percent of the Hispanic population. Puerto Ricans number 4.1 million and 9 percent, Cubans number 1.6 million and 4 percent, and Central and South Americans number about 8 million, or about 18 percent.

For the purpose of the census, the government considers race and Hispanic origins as "two separate and distinct concepts." The term *Hispanic* is used to denote a Spanish-speaking background. This term, coined for the

U.S. census, is sometimes considered offensive. However, a notable exception are Latinos/as of Brazilian descent, whose native language is Portuguese. Racially, individuals of Mexican descent identify their roots as "Mestizo" (a mixture of Spanish and Indian backgrounds). Puerto Ricans consider themselves of Spanish descent, Cubans of Spanish and Black descent, and those from Latin America as varying mixtures of Spanish, Japanese, Italian, and Black. In the 2000 census, 48 percent of Hispanics identified themselves as White only and 42 percent as White and one other race.

Geographically, Latino/a populations are largely urban and are concentrated in the Southwest, Northeast, and the state of Florida. Based on country of origin, Mexican Americans are a significant proportion of the population in Texas, California, Arizona, New Mexico, and Illinois; Puerto Ricans are often found in large urban areas in the Northeast; and Cubans in the Miami area. Recently, the largest growth in Latino/a population has been in counties in the Midwest, Northeast, and South.

The vast majority of Latinos/as are Spanish-speaking and Catholic and share in varying degrees a set of cultural characteristics described below. It is very important to distinguish between traditional Latino culture and alterations in traditional cultural patterns that result from life in the United States. Three factors—generational status, language use, and adaptation to acculturative forces—play a major role in creating diversity among individuals and families within Latino communities and in the emergence of new cultural forms. The interplay between tradition and acculturation is in fact a powerful dynamic. For example, conflict within families often arises when children adapt to acculturative forces and parents struggle to maintain traditional values and beliefs. In short, one must be careful to not underemphasize the differences within and across groups, for there are as many of these as there are similarities. Compared to non-Hispanics (again, a census term rather than an identity of choice among most group members), Latinos/as tend to be younger—on average, below thirty and nine years younger than the average White American; poorer—40 percent of Hispanic children live below the poverty line; less educated—approximately 30 percent leave high school before graduation (the highest rate of all minorities); and more consistently unemployed or relegated to unskilled and semiskilled jobs. Increasingly, the younger members of this cultural group have insight into the factors that prevent their effective schooling (Orozco, in press).

A unique set of factors puts Latinos/as at high risk for physical and psychological difficulties. Included are pressures around bilingualism, immigration, and rapid acculturation, adjustment to U.S. society, intergenerational and cultural conflict, poverty, racism, the loss of cultural identity, and conscious and unconscious biases in schools. As we shall discover from our expert guest, Aurora Cedillo, central factors in understanding the educational situation of most Latino/a students are their individual experiences and the experiences of their family units in migrating to and residing in the United States.

Family and Cultural Values

As a collective, Latino/a subgroups share a language, Spanish; a religion, Catholicism; and, in varying degrees, aspects of traditional cultural values that define and structure group life. Consider the following shared values (Carrasquillo, 1991):

- Importance of the family, both nuclear and extended or *familialismo*
- Emphasis on interdependence and cooperation or *simpatico*
- Emphasis on the worth and dignity of the individual or *personalismo*
- A valuing of the spiritual side of life
- An acceptance of life as it exists

The following is an excellent description of the nature of traditional Latino/a families.

> Perhaps the most significant value they share is the importance placed on family unity, welfare and honor. The emphasis is on the group rather than on the individual. There is a deep sense of family commitment, obligation, and responsibility. The family guarantees protection and caretaking for life as long as the person stays in the system.... The expectation is that when a person is having problems, others will help, especially those in stable positions. The family is usually an extended system that encompasses not only those related by blood and marriage, but also "compadres" (godparents) and "hijos de crianza" (adopted children, whose adoption is not necessarily legal). "Compadrazco" (godparenthood) is a system of ritual kinship with binding, mutual obligations for economic assistance, encouragement, and even personal correction. "Hijos de crianza" refers to the practice of transferring children from one nuclear family to another within the extended family in times of crisis. The others assume responsibility, as if children were their own, and do not view the practice as neglectful. (Garcia-Preto, 1996, p. 151)

Family roles and duties are highly structured and traditional, as are sex roles, which are referred to as *machismo* and *marianismo*. Males, the elderly, and parents are afforded special respect, while children are expected to be obedient and deferential, contribute to family finances, care for younger siblings, and act as parental surrogates. Males are expected to exhibit strength, virility, and dominance and to provide for the family, while females are expected to be nurturing, to submit themselves to males, and to self-sacrifice (Sue & Sue, 2003). Both boys and girls are socialized into these roles early. Boys are given far more freedom than girls, are encouraged to be aggressive and act manly, and are discouraged from playing with girls and engaging in female activities. Girls are trained early in household activities and are severely sheltered and restricted as they grow older.

The authoritative structure of the family also reflects a broader characteristic of Latino/a culture. The family values conformity, obedience, deference to authority, and subservience to the autocratic attitudes of external organizations and institutions. Individuals from "high power distant" cultures are most comfortable in hierarchical structures where there is an obvious power differential and expectations are clearly defined (Marin & Marin, 1991). Professionals and helpers who do not respect this power distance—by de-emphasizing their authority, trying to make the interaction more democratic, communicating indirectly, or using subtle forms of control, such as sarcasm and causing an individual to lose face—tend to confuse and alienate Latino/a students. Respect for authority can also have a darker side by forcing individuals from high-power distant cultures to adapt to the status quo as well as restraining them from asserting their rights. Illegal migrants' cultural hesitancy is exacerbated by the fear of being caught and sent back to more oppressive and dangerous circumstances.

Personalismo—an interpersonal attitude that acknowledges the basic worth and dignity of all individuals and attributes to them a sense of self-worth—serves as a powerful social lubricant in Latino/a culture. Unlike mainstream American culture—where respect is garnered through achievement, status, and wealth—in Latino/a culture, the individual merits respect by the very fact of his or her humanity. *Simpatio,* or the placing of value on cooperation and interdependence, is a natural outgrowth of *personalismo.* Competing, undermining the efforts of another, asserting one's individuality, and trying to inflate one's ego are all viewed negatively within Latino/a culture. In cultures in which the needs of the individual are suppressed in order to better serve the interests of the group (the dimension of culture Brown and Lundrum-Brown, 1995, call "the individual versus the extended self"), the individual ego must be contained. This is done through *simpatico,* which serves to promote cooperation, noncompetition, and the avoidance of conflict between individuals.

It should again be noted that this traditional picture of the Latino/a family can be radically altered as a function of education, generational status, and income. For example, rigid sex roles are often the first cultural element to change with acculturation. Similarly, some cultural dynamics tend to go against the value patterns just described. For example, traditional culture shows a great degree of egalitarianism in decision-making and child-rearing. Latinos/as have a long history of asserting their rights in labor—for example, the mine strikes and the work of Cesar Chavez—and in education by means of litigation and community activism. And what better example is there of achievement motivation than the efforts of an individual or family to immigrate, leaving everything and everyone they know in search of a better life.

A final series of values in Latino/a culture relates to beliefs fostered by the Catholic church. These beliefs include:

- A focus on spirituality and the life of the spirit
- A fatalistic acceptance of life as it exists
- A time orientation toward the present

Latino/a culture places as much emphasis on nonrational experience as it does on the material world. Belief in visions, omens, spirits, and spiritual healers is commonplace, and such phenomena are viewed from within the culture as normative rather than as pathological. Latino/as are also willing to forgo and even sacrifice material comfort in the pursuit of spiritual goals. To a large extent, this focus on spirituality derives from the unique blend of traditional religious practices and indigenous spiritual beliefs that together have created a practice that has served as a kind of resistance to colonization that has endured for over five hundred years.

At the same time, the Latino/a church emphasizes that sacrifice in this world promotes salvation, that one must be charitable, and that wrongs against the person should be endured (Yamamoto & Acosta, 1982). Because of such beliefs, "many Hispanics have difficulty behaving assertively. They feel that problems or events are meant to be and cannot be changed" (Sue & Sue, 1999, p. 290). This relates in turn to a time orientation to the present that is shared by most Latinos/as. Focus tends to be on the here and now, not on what has happened in the past or will happen in the future. Present-oriented cultures place special value on the nature and quality of interpersonal relationships as opposed to their history or functionality (Marin & Marin, 1991). Such an orientation is psychologically related to the kind of fatalism described above and is particularly common in peoples who suffer from economic deprivation and powerlessness and find themselves at the whim and mercy of those with more power.

Latino/a Schooling Context

(Contributed by Rick Orozco, Oregon State University; see companion website for more by Dr. Orozco)

For educators to work most effectively with Latino/a students, an understanding of the context within which Latinos/as attend U.S. schools is vital. Amid mid-twentieth-century explanations of low academic achievement based on genetics to more contemporary statements of cultural deficiency, most Latinos/as have attended segregated schools that frequently have held low expectations for them (Darder, Torres & Gutíerrez, 1997). This contextualization is grounded in a long-held myth that Latinos/as do not value education (Valencia & Black, 2002). However, appreciation of the efforts of Latinos/as to improve their schooling should have two related effects: 1) a debunking of the myth and

2) higher expectations that lead to improved academic achievement. Such efforts have most notably occurred through litigation and community action.

Our Interviewee

Our interviewee, Aurora Cedillo, gives a personal voice to many of these cultural patterns and values, offering valuable insights into Latino/a students and their behavior and needs in the classroom.

Aurora is a bilingual elementary resource teacher in the Salem-Keizer School District in Oregon. She has taught grades kindergarten to adult. She graduated from Oregon College of Education with an elementary teaching major and a Spanish minor. She has a master's degree and an administrator's certificate from the University of Oregon. She is currently enrolled in a doctoral program at Oregon State University and teaches numerous in-service and teacher training workshops.

A Texas-born, Oregon-grown Chicana, Aurora migrated with her family from south Texas to the Willamette Valley in Oregon to harvest crops when she was twelve years old. Out of eighteen children born to her parents, she is the first surviving female and the fourth of ten surviving siblings. Of her personal life, she writes: "I am a single mother and grandmother who loves to dance, sing, and tell cultural and family stories. I have written books about my family, my beliefs, and my experiences. In my work, I share my culture and my perspectives on how ones' culture impacts educational experience as a learner and a teacher."

The Interview

Could you begin by talking about your own ethnic background and how it has impacted your work? I'm caught between ethnicities. As I've grown older, I realize I have a multiple identity. I describe myself as Chicana, of Mexican American heritage and experience. But as I look deeper, I realize that Mexican means mixed race. My mom is French. My dad is more indigenous, though his last name was Cedillo, a very Spanish name. Therefore, I am French and Spanish and indigenous. My father's father, or my grandfather, lived with my mom at the beginning of her marriage, so she learned a lot from him about his indigenous culture. Many of his ideas, beliefs, and practices were taught to us. Therefore, I would describe my ethnic background as Mexican American, Chicana, and all of my responses in this interview derive from my lived experience.

The political and social terms, Mexican American and Chicana, I chose to describe myself have greatly impacted all areas of my personal, social, and educational development. I am a totality of my experiences. My cultural belief on destiny, which is a very strong belief in my culture, compels me to understand that my ethnicity impacted me even before I developed any consciousness of my ethnicity. Through this belief in destiny, I have understood and accepted my place and purpose in my life, my work, and family. Through destiny and the will of God, I have been allowed to learn from others and to share with others. In my work, I have had the opportunity to experience my ethnicity directly and indirectly. I have lived, read, and shared the Chicana experience in my work, communities, and the worlds of English and Spanish speakers as well as the bilingual speakers. I have read what is written about me and others like me. I have experienced the fire that melts and molds us as a community. By that I mean the political, social, and economic oppression that limits and bars access to an appropriate education, health care, shelter, and dignity as people.

As a bilingual educator of diverse language, culture, and color, my work involves balancing the cultural, linguistic, and socioeconomic scale for students, staff, and parents. Opening means of communication and increasing awareness and acceptance between the groups are a continuous daily task. I confirm the efforts of the groups and value their input, but progress is slow in coming. Success comes one grain of sand at a time; teachers are overwhelmed with students that don't understand the language and culture of the school, parents that seem to not care about the education of their children, and administrators that can't support the teachers' efforts. Institutional, historical practices of silencing and promoting invisibility are alive and vital constantly in every element of the educational experience for Teachers, Students, and Parents of Color.

At times, the work seems to be worthless, and that is very discouraging. There is a lot of bilingual educator burnout. I've been doing this for thirty years, and nothing has changed. In fact, I think it is more difficult today. So, I embrace the little successes, the small seeds of communication, and I am hopeful for a better future for all my Mexican American community.

Who are the Chicanas/Chicanos and Latinos/Latinas? What characteristics do they share as a group? Everyone has their own definition of *Chicanismo*. To some, it is positive and proud. To others, it is negative and repulsive. My personal definition of who the Chicanos/Latinos or Hispanic are is based on personal lived experience and my readings on that topic. I used to think it meant being U.S.-born, first-generation Mexican American. Since then, I have learned that it is more than that. *Chicanismo* is a powerful inner force that energizes one to act and to self-identify as Chicano/a. It is based on a collection of similar lived experiences Mexicans—Mexican indigenous—have in common in Spanish-speaking communities throughout the United States. Experiences of oppression, invisibility, silencing, and complete rejection—yet succeeding against all odds—are the ingredients that create and define Chicanos.

Chicanos tend to be highly educated Mexican Americans or Latinos who have learned to survive in the mainstream while maintaining the barrio ways. They are advocates of the collective community. They are often excluded from top decision-making positions even if they have the required experience and education that would prepare them for that position.

A characteristic Latinos share is a belief in destiny. The belief is that we are not in complete control of everything that happens in our lives. "Si Dios quiere" (God willing) is a typical yet simple statement of such belief. A higher being, God, has a purpose and a plan destined for each of us. "Uno pone y Dios dispone" (one purposes and God disposes) states that one can plan, but if God is not willing, it will not be. To Latinos, destiny is being. No plan, no objective, no road map, no timeline. I never planned to be in this interview. I never planned to attend Oregon State University as a student participating in a doctoral program. I never planned to be a teacher—to travel nationally and internationally to share my teaching experience. Terms like *goal setting* and *objectives* and *plans* are words I learned in the mainstream world. I learned to use them; however, I can tell you that the plans I have made have very rarely been achieved. Our beliefs on destiny are based in our indigenous experience of European conquest, of genocide, of never having choice in our lives. I can't choose my place of employment; I can't choose where to live my life; I can't choose my doctor. I can't even tell you I will see you tomorrow because even that depends on someone else.

Another fundamental belief that guides Latinos is the belief that we are born into a family and that the family becomes the most important element in life in this world and beyond. The family is the centerpiece—the glue that bonds one to nature. Family is plural and multifaceted. It is elastic and fluid-like. To Latinos, family is much more than the biological members one is born into. Family is broad and deep. It is inclusive of several generations, social relationships, and local community members. Family includes mother, father, sister, and brother. It includes sister cousins, political sisters, and growth sisters. Also included are aunts, uncles, grandparents, and great-grandparents. It includes children, grandchildren, and great-grandchildren.

Latino families are united to the fifth generation. The saying "hasta la quinta pinta" (tainted to the fifth) relates the exhibition of biological traits, genes, physical similarities, language, cultural practices, and psychological beliefs being present in the lives of members through five generations: great-grandmother to great-granddaughter.

Social families are initiated and implemented by the adults in the family as family members move away or to faraway places. Through processes of religious ceremonies, the families officially unite with dear and special friends as *compadres, comadres, haijados,* and *haijadas* (co-father, co-mother, son-like, and daughter-like). This newly acquired family fills in the void of missing my family and supports new parents in rearing the young.

The community family includes members of a rural community meeting in faraway places and uniting to assist one another in surviving in the new place. Individuals share housing, food, medicine, and money. They provide guidance in survival in the community, employment, and resources. Once able to sustain themselves, they leave and set up another place to assist the newcomers. Everyone from your birth farm, community, or state is a brother and sister. The term *paisano* relates to the brotherhood.

So, we are community centered in the family, defined by destiny, and our connections extend socially, religiously, and politically. We are one. This belief, if misunderstood, creates problems on the job and in relations in mainstream culture. Something as simple as a statement in an invitation to an event can be misunderstood. For example, the statement "no children please" to some Latinos may mean that he/she wasn't really welcomed because if one is invited, all are invited.

Another characteristic of Latino culture is collaboration and cooperation. "One" does not know "it" all. However, everyone knows something. So, collectively, as a family or as a community, we Latinos are able to solve the immediate concerns. All members are responsible for something. Some are good at speaking and negotiating; others are good at thinking; others are good at math; others are more spiritually inclined; others are better caregivers. Everyone in the family is an expert in something. Depending on the task or individual funds of knowledge, different leaders arise. When we came to Oregon, my father did not speak, read, or write English. He could not read a map, a road sign, or was unable to ask for directions. My sixteen-year-old brother took the map, read it, and another brother asked directions. The rest of us participated by cleaning and feeding the crew in the cabin.

Could you talk about the various names that the group uses to describe or identify themselves and some of the names that have been used historically to identify the group by others?   Today, the most preferred term by political and social groups is *Hispanic.* Mostly used by non-Latinos describing those who speak Spanish: those coming from the Americas, Spain, Puerto Rico, Cuba, the Dominican Republic, the Caribbean islands, some from the Philippines, and anyone with Spanish surnames. Few Latinos use that term; some are offended by it. In asking about the term, I asked a peer, and he shared that *Hispanic* was a term that arose during the Reagan era. Former president Reagan was so overwhelmed with the influx and rapidly overpowering growth of Latinos in the United States that Latinos became "His Panic." I laughed and embraced that thought.

Other terms used are *Latino* or national terms such as *Mexican, Puerto Rican,* and *Guatemalan.* First-generation Latinos and a few others include *American* to their parents' nationality, as in *Mexican American.* Others use terms that identify the tribe or group. *Chicano, Cholo, Pachuco, Tarazco, Huichol,* or *Cora* are such terms.

Terms used by outsiders to describe Mexicans born in the United State are *Pochos* (those lacking or short of) Mexicans, *foreigners, los del otro lado* (those from the other side), *wetbacks, illegal aliens* and *migrant workers, braseros,* and *pandilleros.* Mexicans call us *Mexican born in the United States, Pochos. Pocho* rhymes with *mocho* (without a limb) and means diluted, incomplete, or lacking Mexicanness. To Mexicans, Mexican Americans lack proper Spanish, disrespect the Mexican culture, and have not yet acquired the English language and United State culture. As for me, I detest the term *pocho.* There is no Pochaland in this world. The French have France. The Spaniards have Spain. The Mexicans have Mexico. Pochas, what do they have? Nothing! These terms are derogatory and are used to inflict shame. It is important to realize that each individual identifies oneself according to the term that is most meaningful to them.

Could you speak more about family and community and how these shape what happens in schools with Latino students? The popular saying that "it takes a village to grow a child" is also true in the Latino community. The only difference is that in the barrio, we say, "It takes a migrant camp or a barrio to grow a child." Everyone in a community takes responsibility to assist in growing a child—parents, grandparents, co-parents, aunts, uncles, neighbors, church members, teachers, friends, and even older siblings. Authority to discipline a child if needed is given to the caregiver. My mother would say, "Spank her if she does not listen, and tell me, and I will spank her also." When you hear such words, you know you are responsible to all your elders regardless of who they are.

As a collective culture, Latinos tend to hand their child over to the teacher. They trust that the teachers and other school staff will do what is best for their child. In the subconscious mind, the teacher holds a sacred place. Next to God and Mom, the teacher is respected and honored. Parents will not invade a teacher's space unless an obvious act of violence or disregard for the child are exposed. Creating change and shaping the school culture is difficult when parents feel intrusive or rude if they question things at school. Parents will discuss issues superficially and may not confront the issues in a direct way. Added to this is the concern that parents do not speak and understand English at a level needed to address the needs. Many times, parents will bring a son or daughter to interpret for them. Schools are ill-equipped to deal with this both linguistically and culturally. They judge these actions as irresponsible, for how can parents even consider including the child in these discussions?

After many unproductive meetings with school staff, Latino families learn that coming to school alone is very ineffective. They share their experience with others. Those with typical experience share what they know. They contact support within the community, and together in a group, they call for change. Grandmothers, who are central to these activities, have been around; they experienced it with their children, and since they are elders, they carry the discussion. These grandmothers bring their whole family to come and listen. (Many different ears can understand what one set will miss.) Once again, the culture that respects the experience of elders clashes with the culture that throws elders away to retirement homes.

With time and experience, parents realize that schools will only listen when lawyers and money talk. Through the grass-roots efforts, parents can create a situation where they will be heard. They bring attention to issues and make school accountable for all students' success. What works best is to include parents as partners—informing them of school processes and getting informed of the unique cultural, linguistic, and social and academic elements of the student and his family.

Are there any subpopulations in the Latino/a community you feel deserve additional attention in the classroom? The two groups that I think deserve additional attention are the newly arrived to our communities from indigenous backgrounds and the locally born and grown Latino children. Our indigenous Indian populations intermixed racially with Latino/as as they come from Mexico, Central America, and Guatemala. We know very little about their background, how they learn, where their historical places are, or their lifestyles in their countries of origin. We are unfamiliar with their social practices and do not speak their language if it is not Spanish. Frankly, we are at a loss. Right now in our schools, we are looking for representatives from these indigenous communities who will come and share with us information on how we can reach their students and families. They tend to be even harder to reach than Chicano students, fall through the cracks, drop out, and underachieve at even higher levels.

A second group, particularly at high risk, are the first- and second-generation Latinos, both immigrant and U.S.-born. These students grow up in two worlds. They learn two languages at one time. They live between worlds and have not developed a strong foundation in either one. The minute they are born, they're listening to English as well as to the Spanish of their parents. So they must learn two languages. Educators in charge of instructing these students have little knowledge about bilingualism. In desperation, Spanish-language experts from Mexico and other Central American countries are hired to work with these students. These teachers know Spanish but do not know how to work with bilingual students. (Just because you speak two languages does not make you a teacher of bilingual students.)

Inappropriate or no assessment of these students' academic skills leads to inappropriate placement and instruction. Many of these students attend high-risk schools where the least experienced teachers tend to teach. Since they require a bilingual placement, they are taught by teachers who are just learning Spanish as their second language. They have not yet developed the depth or the breath of the language in order to provide students with rich embedded language required in academics.

Students from these two Latino subgroups tend to be the ones who drop out of school the most. They are also the fastest growing population in penal institutions. They also tend to be disconnected from the cultural practices and linguistic foundation that strengthen the first generation.

Could you talk a little more about the controversy among bilingual educators, their approaches, and what needs to be done for bilingual students?   Controversy among bilingual educators centers on pressures from the mainstream society dictating that English is the only language to be taught. Research shows that if you teach children in the language they understand, they will be successful. But there are political pressures coming from the educational establishment that allow non-English students three years in special programs and then push them out. Research, however, says that it takes five to seven years for a child to develop the academic proficiency of an English speaker. But new educators want to keep their jobs and want to make sure they are doing what the system tells them to do. Older educators who have seen the research and know from firsthand experience are more likely to challenge the political pressures and push for teaching them in their native language. But, basically, educators are caught between these forces, and what are you going to do?

Another great controversy is the misalignment in bilingual education. So-called programs are planted on hard soil. Allocated funding is misused, programs are left to the discretion of unqualified staff, and resources are either lacking or inappropriate.

Higher education institutions provide very little in bilingual education courses. Bilingual teachers have to figure it out on their own. Due to the lack of bilingual staff, multicultural education, language acquisition, and foreign language are somehow supposed to prepare bilingual educators. Bilingual education is very political. It involves learning the rights and the Constitution. It involves moving students, parents, and staff to question the system. This is very scary, and very few teachers feel strong enough to battle.

All of these misalignments take a toll on teachers who are on the front lines. She is the one who sees the failure, the student dropout rate, who attends the parent conferences, and sees the angry letters from the mainstream community against bilingualism. And, finally, she is blamed for the lack of support given to non-English speakers in such a crucial time in their development.

How do different cultural styles, values, and worldviews affect education of Latino/Latina students?   The biggest thing I see in the classroom as far as different cultural styles is that the teacher tends to come from an "I" perspective and is in charge of teaching students who are from a culture with a "we" perspective. Not being aware of this cultural difference can result in confusion and arrogance on the part of the teacher that desires to control everything. The "I" perspective is an egocentric attitude that predominates in Anglo culture. I need to plan, I need to do, or I need to fix. For the mainstream culture, the idea is that you fail because one failed to plan. This "I" perspective creates misunderstanding toward people that have a "we" perspective. In order for "I" to do something, "we" needs to happen. In order for "I" to attend, "we" need to have a car, pay the insurance, get a license, learn to read English, and learn to drive. "I" is dependent on how many resources "we" can gather.

Also, the cultural elements of destiny and family are very important. The element of time heavily impacts the class. In situations where the relationship is more important than the event, measuring time can be problematic. For mainstream culture, the clock runs the show. In Latino culture, the relationship runs the show. So, it is more important to save the relationship than it is to save time. In Latino culture, the concept of time is different; *luego, despues, al rato, al ratito, ya* all have a different time value. If a teacher does not know that, it could cause disruptions in transitioning times.

Another issue is the concept of collective ownership. In Spanish, the word[s] *la* [and] *el* [are] used instead of *my* or *mine*. In English, we say "my pencil," "my house," or "my car."

Communication style is another cultural element that needs to be considered when working with Latinos. Latinos tend to speak in colorful statements that surround the issue. This type of communication style is called "circular" and/or *peogeon* style of communication.

What are some of the common problems that Latino/a students might bring into the school setting? I guess I would not call them problems. Unless if you would consider physical challenges. Not being able to see is a problem; not hearing is a problem; not having an anus is a problem. But not speaking English is not a problem. Not being aware of the mainstream culture is not a problem. Not knowing the school system is not a problem. The problem, as I see it, is that we, the educators, want students who look like us, act like us, think like us, and see like us. We as a people, even among a common group, have problems. We have problems with teenagers, elders, obese, or thin people. Our biggest problem is "I." I need to see that I am not the center of the world. If I accept that idea, then I can move on to understand that not all people live like me. If one is late, it could be that they did not have a car. Or it could be that they had to wait on someone else and that someone else had something that they had to wait on. Or maybe they did not have a phone to call. It was raining so hard and walking to the nearest telephone would mean leaving the baby alone.

Another problem that I see could be that I accepted a job that required the use of Spanish, and my high school Spanish or my summer in Mexico did not prepare me to teach content and academics in Spanish. Another problem could be that because I was taught to make eye contact and face people to show I am attentive and sincere, I have a difficult time when students hide their eyes from me.

In Spanish, we say *el carro, la casa, el lapiz.* Even your personal parts don't belong to you. So, it's *las manos,* the hands, wash the hands. Not wash *your* hands; wash the hands, wash the face, clean the ears. But in Anglo culture, it's I washed *my* hands, I washed *my* face. So, this little boy or girl comes to school. He or she needs a pencil, so they pick one up off a desk. Not my pencil or her pencil, but the pencil. Another child yells out. "He stole my pencil. She took my pencil!" The Latino child says, "I did not take your pencil." "You have the pencil right there!" The teacher intercedes: "Is that her pencil? Give her back her pencil!" "But why?" Now, he goes home, and he takes a dinner plate. He had that plate yesterday; now his sister has it today. "That's my plate!" he says, and his mother disciplines him, feeling the need to remind him about sharing. "This is not your plate; it belongs to the family; it belongs to whoever gets it first."

Another issue is eye contact, and this is very important. In Latino culture, it is considered disrespectful to look directly at an elder when they are talking to you. However, in Anglo culture, averting one's eyes is experienced as defiant, as showing guilt, as being rude.

There is also the high respect given to food in Latino culture. It is a community where everything is shared, especially food. Nothing is thrown away, and you share your food rather than throw it away. You don't play with it. At home, one gets scolded or spanked for wasting or throwing away food. In the classroom, when food like rice or salt or macaroni or beans are used in learning activities, that is playing with it; the child is put in a difficult bind. He doesn't participate. He refuses to play with it. He may be graded down. But if the teacher is aware of these cultural things, they can use rocks or popsicle sticks—anything but food.

When teachers are unaware and cross cultural lines, they may inadvertently trample on their students and not even know it unless the child speaks up. And it is the rare classroom where Latino/a students feel free enough to speak up. There is the story of a classroom where the children obviously felt free enough to do so. The teacher gave out treats, little cakes, because it was someone's birthday. She said, "Please wait until the party person eats first and then we will all eat." But the Spanish speakers didn't understand it, because it was said only in English. So, the minute they got their cupcakes, they ate them. The teacher responded by saying, "You are eating like pigs!" One little boy responded, "Teacher, please don't call us pigs again." She began to answer "No, I said you ate like pigs" but then caught herself. "What should I have said?" The boy answered, "You could have said we ate a lot." The teacher subsequently learned that comparing a person to an animal is considered a deep insult in Latino/a culture. Again, these are not problems; they are challenges that must be discussed openly by students, parents, teachers, and other school staff.

Finally, a problem could be that because I am used to seeing groups of cowboys in Wranglers hanging out in the streets, I do not feel scared. However, because I am not used to seeing a group of Latino men dressed in khaki slacks, I feel funny and sacred. There are not problems—only challenges to overcome.

Could you discuss some of the factors important in assessing the learning style of Latino/Latina students and suggest what classroom factors could be manipulated to match these styles?   Learning styles are basically the different ways humankind learns. We learn by seeing. We learn by doing. We learn by acting out. We learn by observing others and modeling their behavior. We teach children by modeling the things we expect from them. It's a continual process in the classroom. You reach out to the kids, you model, you show, you do, you explain. You have other people explain. Look at José; he did it really well. Could you tell us how you did that? Could you show us? I do much of my teaching in the context of small cooperative learning groups. You give them tasks to practice, problems to solve, explain your expectations step by step. Put things on the wall that reinforce the lessons, always giving them references to what they need to do. Reviews for when they are absent from the classroom. All of these little efforts or bricks of support provide scaffolding for learning and succeeding. Especially where language is an issue, a spoken lecture is not enough. You have to show them many times to model behavior. In working in small groups, it is important to find a student leader who understands the lesson and is able to tell what he learned. I always tell my bilingual teachers, when you set up your cooperative groups, you want to find someone to lead who is fluent in English as well as someone fluent in Spanish. Also, a balance of gender, girls and boys. In classes for bilingual children, everyone must be a teacher to each other. English speakers are going to learn Spanish; the Spanish speakers are going to learn English. The bilingual children are going to learn every day. Also look for language ability when you're forming your groups. With different levels of ability, you're not the only teacher. You cannot teach such a classroom alone. You need your environment to help you. You need your students and their peers to help you. You need the materials to support you, and above all, you need the cultural awareness of where those kids are coming from and their home experience. Finally, learn by doing. Create the experience for and with students. Learning involves all the senses. Use them. If you do all of these things and make all of these connections, kids will be more successful.

Are there teaching strategies that are more effective in working with Latino/ Latina students? I have spoken of many strategies throughout the interview. Of all the ones I've spoken about, communicating is the most important. Be a learner and make sure to include the families; they are not there alone. "I did not get this A; we all got it." So, if you leave the parents out of the learning loop—if you leave the aunts or the grandmothers—you are only using half of your resources. You need to bring the families into the learning environment. They know their students best. They know their children the most. They know if their children are morning people or afternoon people, their abilities and capabilities, their individual histories. We have a lot of kids who bring trauma with them to the classroom: abandonment, abuse, neglect, just being poor, not having the right foods, medical care, attention. We can't expect them to read and write when their teeth are falling out or they have an ear infection that has never been corrected or when they have been abandoned by their moms in their grandmother's house without any food because mom was trying to find her husband in the United States. Having access to a counselor is very important—someone who understands these traumas and can talk to children and families about them. Even U.S.-born Latino, English-speaking students often lack resources they need to succeed. Our schools witness families who have experienced death, drownings, and fires. We tend to be quicker to help them if they are English-speaking. The school gets together, brings boxes of food and clothes, making sure that the family gets the support it needs. When Latino kids get hurt or their families have problems, there is a tendency to expect other agencies to take care of things. Somebody else will take care of it. We need the kind of system that will respond equally to all students who are hurting. And in a language and style they can understand. Who's going to counsel the immigrant child when he or she just lost their cousin in a fire? The English-speaking counselor cannot do it. And someone who can only translate is not equipped to understand the deeper concepts of counseling— what is going on in the children's minds and how to get them to discuss the issues that need attention. Such resources should be available in all of our schools.

CHAPTER 11

Working with American Indian/Alaska Native Students

An Interview with Cornel Pewewardy

> *"The most important factor impacting academic achievement today for Native students is teacher expectations."*
>
> —Cornel Pewewardy

Demographics

The estimates of the numbers of people on the continents of North and South America when people from other continents visited in the last one thousand years have varied greatly. Many times, the numbers may vary because the writer/researcher may have a theory or preconceived history to support, such as the notion that the Americas were virgin, almost empty lands before others came. Loewen (2006) estimates that there were as many people living in the "New World" (new to Europeans)—between sixty and ninety million (about twenty million in lands that became Canada and the United States)—in 1492 as there were in Europe at the same time. In those years, Hernán Cortés called the city of Tenochtitlan in Mexico "larger and more pleasant" than any in Spain (Loewen, 2006, p. 3). The population in the four corners area of the Southwest was probably higher in ancient times than it is today (Johnson, 2009). An example of the decline is graphic in this chart of changing demographics in Mexico in the sixteenth century (see Figure 11.1).

As the Americas were colonized and native populations genocided by colonizers and disease, these continents no longer looked as Columbus first saw them with innumerable people and "towns and fields without end" (Loewen, 2006, p. 2). Eventually, sheer numbers and the striving for private land caused

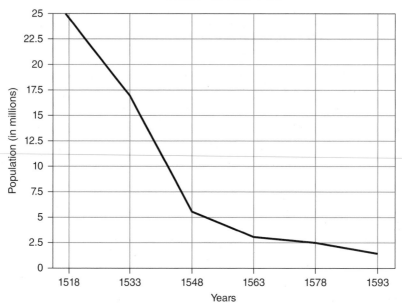

FIGURE 11.1 Estimated Native American Population of Mexico, 1518–1593

Source: James Killoran et al., *The Key to Understanding Global History,* Jarrett Publishing (adapted).

conflicts that moved American Indians and Alaska Natives (AI/AN) into reservations.

In recent years, AI/ANs have progressively moved off reservations (Machamer & Gruber, 1998). According to the U.S. Census Bureau (2000), there were 2,410,000 AI/ANs living in the United States. It is often believed that AI/ANs live in isolation on reservations (Hawkins, 2002). Actually, most AI/ANs live in urban centers; more than twice as many live in urban centers than on reservations. This portion, combined with another 1.6 million individuals from mixed racial background, equates to 4.1 million people, or 1.5 percent, of the population living in urban environments (Weaver, 2005). The urbanization of AI/ANs, through government relocation programs to cities and towns, began in the 1950s and continues to be prevalent today (Thornton, 2001).

Transitioning from rural reservations to urban environments causes some sociopolitical changes and educational adjustments in the lives of AI/AN students. This overview of AI/AN demographics sets the framework for the interplay between life issues and how they impact education.

Family and Cultural Values

AI/AN families are often accredited with the survival of AI/AN people. Despite a history of genocide, forced assimilation, unemployment, poverty, and relocation—factors that can negatively impact family function—this AI/AN sample reflects a support-oriented family profile despite the co-existence of high conflict. AI/AN families are taking more responsibility for their families by working together with the professionals that teach their children.

If another generation of AI/AN students is lost through the educational systems in this country, then at the same time, much of the hope for economic, social, and technological survival is also lost. The problem of preparing teachers to teach AI/AN students must be addressed or the consequences will be shared by members of society. Consider some of the current troubling findings regarding AI/AN students:

- Highest dropout rate of all racial/ethnic groups in the United States (Cleary & Peacock, 1998; Futures for Children, 2001; Whitener, Gruber, Lynch, Rohr, & Tingos, 1997). These educational factors are directly linked to occupational, economic, and social disadvantages (Levin, 1992; Machamer & Gruber, 1998; Sherman, 1993).
- Unemployment and poverty rates among AI/ANs negatively contribute to increased neglect and child abuse, separation and divorce rates, and single-parent families (Donelan, 1999; Harjo, 1996; Johnson & Tomren, 1999; Shanley, 2008).
- Compared to other racial groups, there is an increasing rate of alcoholism among AI/AN teenagers (American Indians/Alaskan Natives, 2004; Substance Abuse and Mental Health Services Administration, 2003).
- Suicide represents the second-leading cause of death among AI/AN school-aged youth between fifteen and twenty-four years (Shaughnessy & Doshi, 2004; Angell, Kurz, & Gottfried, 1997) and is 72 percent more common among AI/AN people compared to the general population (Indian Health Service, 2000).
- AI/AN students are the second-highest minority group referred for special education services (National Center for Educational Statistics, 1992).
- Lack of cultural awareness and understanding among educators working with AI/AN families (Pewewardy & Fritz, 2009).

These distressing statistics are impediments to academic success and are not all that describe the condition of AI/AN youth. There are some other disturbing issues that are not mentioned in this chapter and that are not easily documented, such as AI/AN push-outs, racism in schools, forced assimilation by educators, onslaught of negative advertising and stereotyping in their communities, and how gangs are becoming the major distributor of drugs.

Over half of AI/AN children who attend kindergarten today will never graduate from high school. Even with a high school diploma in hand, many AI/AN students lack the hope and motivation to achieve lifelong success. Many more finish high school without ever believing they can really make a difference in their world, and they therefore feel hopeless about life.

As mentioned in previous sections, alcoholism, family structure, and suicide have a significant impact on school completion rates for AI/AN students. Similarly, AI/AN people are experiencing an increase in the breakdown of the family unit, and the literature paints a dismal picture of the educational and social outcomes of AI/AN students. Is this enough information to sound a national alarm in education?

While we keep in mind that Native American/Alaskan Native cultures represent five hundred different tribes and more than three hundred different reservations, the following five values typify these cultures:

- Sharing and cooperation
- Noninterference
- A cyclical orientation to time
- The importance of extended families
- Building relationships with all things

Sharing and Cooperation

Sutton and Broken Nose (1996) quoted an Oglala Lakota elder on the American Indian attitude about sharing: "When I was little, I learned that what's yours is mine and what's mine is everybody's" (p. 40). Status and honor are earned not by accumulating wealth but rather by sharing it and giving it away. Gifts are profusely given, especially during life cycle events, to thank others and acknowledge their achievements. Material possessions are expected to be freely shared. Great importance is placed on hospitality and caring for the needs of strangers. Working for wages is purely instrumental. For example, a Native person may stop working once enough money has been earned to meet immediate needs. Related to sharing is cooperation. As in Latino/a culture, competition and egotism are anathema to Native ways. The family and tribe take precedence over the individual, and an individual is expected to set aside personal activities and striving in order to help others. Interpersonal harmony is always sought and discord avoided.

Of course, the selfless attitude toward material wealth and possessions may prove counterproductive in the mainstream economy. Sutton and Broken Nose (1996) described the traditional owners of a restaurant on the Navajo reservation who had financial problems because they felt obliged to serve free food to relatives, and most people on the reservation were relatives.

Noninterference

It is considered inappropriate in AI/AN culture to intrude or interfere in the affairs of others. Boundaries and the natural order of things are to be respected. Similarly, stoicism and nonreactivity are highly valued. A premium is placed on listening. "Silence may connote respect, that the person is forming thoughts or waiting for signs that it is the right time to speak, ... non-Indians may treat silence, embellished metaphors, and indirectness as signs of resistance, when actually they represent forms of communication" (Sutton & Broken Nose, 1996, p. 37).

Time Orientation

"Indian time" is cyclical, rhythmic, and imprecise. People are orientated toward the present, the here and now, not to future events and deadlines. Activities take as long as they take and have a natural logic and rhythm of their own. "Lateness" and defining time by external clocks and circumstances are Western concepts—the product of a linear timeframe. Setting long-term goals is viewed as egotism, and life events are experienced as processes that unfold in their own time and way. "The focus is placed on one's current place, knowing that the succeeding changes will inevitably come" (Sutton & Broken Nose, 1996, p. 39). This notion of time, which has a tendency to frustrate mainstream teachers who work on tight schedules, interfaces perfectly with the value of noninterference in the natural order of things.

Extended Families

Although the specifics of power distribution, roles, and kinship definitions vary from tribe to tribe, the vast majority of AI/AN peoples live under an extended family system that is conceptually different from the Western notion of family. Some tribes are matrilineal, which means that property and status are passed down through the women. For example, when a Hopi man marries, he moves in with his wife's family, and the wife's brothers, not the father, have the primary responsibility for educating the sons.

Family ties define existence, and the definition of being a Navajo or a Sioux does not reside within the individual's personality but rather in the intricacies of family and tribal responsibilities. When strangers meet, they identify themselves by who their relatives are, not by their occupations or place of residence. The individual feels a close and binding connection with a broad network of relatives (often including some who are not related by blood) that can extend as far as second cousins. The naming of relationships reflects the closeness between relatives. For example, the term *grandparent* applies not only to the parents of one's biological parents, but also to the biological grandparents' brothers and sisters. Similarly, *in-law* has no meaning within AI/AN culture; after entry into the family system, no distinctions are made between natural and inducted individuals (Sutton & Broken Nose, 1996). Thus, the woman identified as mother-in-law in mainstream culture is called mother in AI/AN culture. The responsibility for parenting is communal, shared throughout the extended family. It is not unusual for children to live in various households of the extended family while growing up.

Building Relationships with All Things

AI/AN cultures emphasize the interconnectedness and harmony of all living things and natural objects. This spiritual holism affirms the value and interdependence of all life forms. Nature is held in reverence, and Native Peoples believe that they are responsible for living in harmony and safeguarding the valuable resources human beings have been given. Sutton and Broken Nose (1996) quoted Chief Seattle: "My mother told me, every part of this earth is sacred to our people. Every pine needle. Every sandy shore. Every mist in the dark woods. Every meadow and humming insect. The Earth is our mother" (p. 40).

This message, which implies the need for noninterference in the natural order and stewardship over the environment, stands in stark opposition to the mainstream value of mastering, controlling, and taking what we want from the earth. Spiritual harmony with the natural order also underlies AI/AN beliefs about health and illness. Physical and emotional illness reflects disharmony between the person or the collective and the natural world. Only by bringing the system back into harmony can healing be achieved.

Education

(Contributed by Cornel Pewewardy, Portland State University)

Culturally responsive teaching practices cannot be approached as a recipe or series of steps that teachers can follow to be effective teachers, especially with American Indian/Alaska Native students. Instead, focus on:

- Understanding the historical context (see the focused bibliography);
- Developing certain dispositions toward AI/AN students and a holistic approach to curriculum and instruction; and
- Learning some basic principles and how these concepts tie to recent research for teaching AI/AN students.

Historically, schools in the United States have not served AI/AN students well. Not only standardized test scores reflect these disparities, but they are affirmed by the record number of dropouts for AI/AN students in school today (Gallagher, 2000; Jeffries, Hollowell, & Powell, 2004). The specific needs of AI/AN students and how their perception of schooling differs from other minorities have not been addressed (Castagno & Brayboy, 2008). A critical analysis of AI/AN education scholars (Haynes-Writer, 2001; Jeffries, Nix, & Singer, 2002; Pavel & Padilla, 1993; Pewewardy, 1998) confirms that federal government–imposed reform is specifically harmful for the children described as "disadvantaged students," the same socioeconomic groups that have historically received an inferior education. The continued underachievement and isolation of such a large and growing statistic is nothing short of a national tragedy in education. AI/AN students will continue to remain a legacy of despair in the history of this country unless more resources are placed into the resolution of this educational crisis.

Without a doubt, the education of AI/AN students should become a national priority at all levels. Educators, especially teachers, have the greatest opportunity to motivate AI/AN students to achieve success in school and in life. Despite the nature of this national tragedy in education, teachers must not lose hope. Although an ineffective teacher or school system can have a negative impact on student development, culturally responsive teachers and school districts can overcome the negative impact of prior conditioning and work well with AI/AN students.

The following sections outline some basic principles that guide culturally responsive teaching practices for AI/AN students.

Curriculum

- Textbook materials and lessons validate students' tribal culture and history.
- Teaching lessons are organized using thematic unites.
- Curriculum promotes higher-order critical-thinking skills.
- Tribal language learning is promoted.
- Sacred materials are drawn from ritual and myth.
- Maximum use is made of group collaboration work.

Instruction

- Students' tribal language and culture are valued.
- Teachers impart high expectations and provide strong motivational support.
- Teachers use students' tribal background and strengths in planning and implementing teaching episodes, matching teaching styles with student cultural learning styles, and making use of collaborative work.
- Through interactive teaching, teachers provide opportunities for students to talk and write as a way to express themselves.

- Teachers develop students' higher-order critical-thinking skills.
- A highly informal, family-like atmosphere exists in which students help each other learn.

Assessment

- Teacher and the principal monitor student progress.
- Peer-observation of classroom teaching validates teaching to the multiple intelligences of the students.
- Assessment is conducted in the Native language when appropriate.
- Testing is used for diagnostic purposes and to target help for students, not to justify inaction.
- On average, students are achieving at or very close to grade level (in multiple languages).

In summary, using the models to minimize barriers and facilitate self-efficacy in working effectively with AI/AN families is the focus of this section. Gaining trust is a necessity to work with AI/AN families before educators can implement intervention programs. Culturally responsive teaching practices can be used as a framework to work with AI/AN families.

These suggestions are for those teachers who have the inspiration and drive to facilitate the achievement and motivation of AI/AN students but who lack culturally responsive teaching practices. We hope that teachers will see AI/AN students less as "a problem" and view them from a value-added strengths perspective. May these strategies allow teachers to capture the spirit of teaching for cultural competence.

Our Interviewee

Cornel Pewewardy is the director and associate professor of Native American Studies at Portland State University. He worked primarily with AI/AN education for over thirty years as an elementary teacher, principal, and teacher educator in higher education. Dr. Pewewardy is Comanche and Kiowa and an enrolled member of the Comanche Nation. He is not only an educator, but he is also a storyteller and a musician and a founder of the National Association of Multicultural Education. Dr. Pewewardy contributed much of the material in the demographic and cultural values sections and wrote the material on education. In the following interview, we begin to understand both his background and his passion for the education of AI/AN students.

The Interview

Could you first talk about your own ethnic background and how it has led to your work in the classroom and as a teacher to AI/AN students?   My name is

Cornel Pewewardy. I am Comanche and Kiowa and enrolled member of the Comanche Nation. For me, tribal identity is a cultural base for being human. For many AI/AN students, tribal identity is built through their participation in cultural activities, such as intertribal powwows, feast days, special events at school, and cultural gatherings. AI/AN people view the tribe as the cultural foundation for their tribal identity, and the involvement of parents and grandparents is critical in the educational process. In some tribes, it is a member of the extended family who assumes responsibility for a child with disabilities. Thus, it is important for administrators and general and special educators to develop family-centered approaches while working with AI/AN parents, grandparents, and extended family members.

In urban areas, cultural identity becomes even more complex. Many times, membership in the urban community is known through informal consensus rather than validating oneself on a legal document, which usually means that they are enrolled members of federally recognized tribes. Some common descriptors associated with an urban tribal identity include ancestry, appearance, cultural knowledge, and community participation.

Teachers of AI/AN students should know that cultural identity is very important in schools, yet it is also complicated and emotionally laden with numerous descriptors and definitions about who is a tribal student and who is not. They should also know that many AI/AN students don't care about their ethnic identities because many of them are pressured to assimilate and conform to the dominant culture and school climate in the schools they attend, especially public schools. There are those individuals who self-identify, those that are identified externally from the tribe, like the Bureau of Indian Affairs, those who meet the criteria for tribal membership, those who claim their tribal identity based on ancestry and not by degree of Indian blood, those that shift their identity based on situation and geography, and there are those whose identity transforms over time by either becoming or discarding their tribal identities. Ironically, there are those that falsify their tribal identity, meaning they are conscious that they are not AI/AN yet they continue to identify themselves as such to benefit in some way from their new ethnic identity. Within the AI/AN community, this falsification of ethnic identity is referred to as ethnic fraud.

Many AI/ANs have been preoccupied with a racial identity rather than a tribal identity. This concept about identity is an abortive and externally imposed product of European colonization. Subsequently, the concept of tribal identity is an empowering element in the schooling of AI/AN students. It becomes a paradox with the inclusion of ethnic fraud cases in educational institutions because ethnic fraud infringes upon the authority of tribal sovereignty. Therefore, AI/AN must be the ones to solve the issues of identity confusion. Finally, the concept of genocide was replaced by cultural suicide simply by not claiming AI/AN ancestry.

Personally, I have never had an AI/AN teacher until I attended graduate school. I've always wondered how is it that I as a AI/AN student can attend school for twenty years and never have one AI/AN teacher in the classroom. Thirty years ago, as a Native male elementary teacher, I realized that I had a major impact upon young AI/AN children in the classroom. Young AI/AN children need positive male role models in their daily lives. Therefore, I wanted to become a principal of American Indian schools. More specifically, I've always wanted to be a Native principal of Native schools. After graduate school, I became the principal of Ojo Encino Day School on the Eastern Navajo reservation and American Indian Magnet School, a public magnet school in Saint Paul, Minnesota.

Because I attended public schools throughout my life, I confronted tremendous pressure to assimilate and emulate Western European American lifestyles and worldviews. This was my motive to design revolutionary schools for AI/AN students.

The evolution of my tribal consciousness ignited after I graduated from public high school as I went on to attend college. In retrospect, my high school experience—like many mainstream public high schools—conditioned me to see success in reductionist ways and adopt assimilationist values in school, which silently suggested to me that I should discard my tribal culture and language. But for me, this is the period in my life when I got passionate about my tribal cultures. I began to take Native American Studies classes in college. My grades improved, as did my self-esteem as a young man. The more I learned about the true history of Native Peoples, the more I began to ask myself, "Why wasn't I taught this in high school?" My thirst for tribal knowledge grew even more so in graduate school. That's when I immersed myself into critical race theory and liberation discourse ideology. Life experience and critical thinking taught me that healing will emerge once AI/ANs take a critical analysis to the processes of colonization. Liberation discourse has had a deep impact upon the development of my own cultural identity.

In my professional career, I have witnessed students move from various states of unawareness (unconsciousness) to varying degrees of self-awareness (consciousness). Working in tribal schools and mainstream university teacher education programs, I have seen how AI/AN students and White students develop their ethnic identities in teacher education programs. Therefore, for teachers of AI/AN students, I recommend that they take a deeper dialectical approach to understanding of the multiple and interconnecting relationships that speak to a more profound understanding of the politics of difference.

Those students and teachers who know themselves as cultural beings are not intimidated by those who claim cultural supremacy and hegemony.

I believe tribal people should build upon its rich past history and change approaches, as necessary, to take into account the new condition of the present. No group of people should have a monopoly on the interpretation of the human experience or on making plans for its posterity.

How would you define American Indians/Alaska Natives as a group, and what characteristics do they share?   Given the multiplicity of worldviews and perspectives on this important issue of terminological identity, I use the term American Indian and Alaska Native (AI/AN) rather than Native American to refer to the descendants of the original inhabitants of the U.S. Whenever possible, however, I attempt to refer to AI/AN people by their preferred community and tribal affiliations but understand that group members may self-identify using broader terms, such as indigenous peoples, to place their tribal identities into a wider context.

The most prevailing and common interpretation of school failure among teachers of AI/AN students is the "deficit" model. Recently, I conducted a review of the literature that revealed that AI/AN students generally learn in ways characterized by factors of social/affective emphasis, harmony, holistic perspectives, expressive creativity, and nonverbal communication. Underlying these approaches are assumptions that AI/AN students have been strongly influenced by their language, culture, and heritage and that AI/AN children's learning styles are different but not deficient. Pathologizing AI/AN student failure places the liability on a set of traits like low self-esteem, no role models, poor English speaking skills, and so on, and so forth. This attitude is alarming because school educators are unaware of their complicity and the deep detrimental effect of their interactions. Therefore, when teachers look at the research that describes characteristics of AI/AN students, they need to be cautioned that they are not pathologizing school failure.

Pathologizing AI/AN student school failure is part of a hidden curriculum that excuses teachers from their professional responsibilities to educate all students in a multicultural society. When teachers pathologize AI/AN school failure, they also protect the school from societal criticism. As a teacher educator, we need to engage preservice students in pedagogical self-scrutiny or self-appraisal of their teaching roles within the school system.

Could you describe some of the names that have been used historically to describe and identify AI/ANs and the general process of naming within the culture?   As a culturally responsive teacher, I remind myself to "start where the learner is" as it pertains to the knowledge base and life experiences of my students. I tell my classes at the university level that I have witnessed a wide range of nomenclature within my own cultural family: colored people,

Indians, American Indians, Native Americans, Aboriginals, First Nations People, Indigenous, and Indigenous Peoples. And, of course, I've heard all the racial insults and unkind words—like *pagan, savages, primitives*, and *uncivilized*—that have been carried down the generations by mainstream society. I don't want another generation to hear these obsolete words. Obviously, these name changes represented the evolution of consciousness within tribal families to take control of their own naming and self-definition process from oppressive/obsolete term like colored people or Indians. After years of critically thinking about the appropriate nomenclature, I prefer the term American Indians and Alaska Natives. The precise and primary term, of course, is writing about or naming the appropriate tribe(s), but the secondary term I use is Indigenous Peoples.

Understanding anti-oppressive practice from an AI/AN perspective involves the process of integrating tribal knowledge—implementing best teaching practices that exist within tribal cultures, traditions and languages. I still, however, use terms like Native, Native American, Aboriginal, First Nations People, and Indigenous Peoples interchangeably depending upon the context of my discussion and writings.

Are there any other things you would like to say about the nature of family, community, and culture among AI/AN that have relevance for teachers? Yes, many AI/AN teaching traditions included the education for the soul. Given this day and age of religion and public schools, how do tribal people teach when everything is connected to spiritual dimensions? Teaching to the heart is divine. Teaching from the heart is truly the heart of teaching. When a teacher touches the spirit of the student's learning, students many times develop a passion for learning and in turn the student is inspired to engage in a love for learning.

For many AI/AN families, there is the concept of the intergenerational soul wound that is commonly known as historical trauma. Individuals going through their own decolonizational process are not dismissing the orthodox Western therapeutic interventions but rather adding another approach that has stood the test of time for many AI/AN communities.

Culturally responsive teaching practices expand beyond the classroom and on to the family and community. Because many AI/AN families suffer from a soul wound, the process for healing should include the healer. In many Western therapeutic settings, the healer is supposed to be transparent, but at the same time, it dehumanizes the healer and the wounded healer spirit that is brought into the healing ceremony. Traditional healers do not pretend to be beyond the frailties of being human. Once tribal communities acknowledge their wounding and healing process, they can transition this healing into their educational processes.

You've spoken a lot about the difficult history that AI/AN peoples have faced in this country. What kinds of emotional issues are AI/AN students likely to bring with them into the classroom? And what kinds of problem behavior are they likely to exhibit in the school setting? Western European colonization is centuries old in this country and has been especially oppressive to AI/AN education. That system interrupted thousands of years of powerful AI/AN educational systems of excellence. Because of this colonization process, most AI/AN students today are uneducated about their tribal cultures and cannot speak their tribal languages.

AI/AN students are subject to misinformation and neglect in normal school curriculum. Most educators are ill-prepared to deal with hegemony related to tribal cultures. Much of mainstream curriculum offered to AI/AN students is referred to as the hidden curriculum, which is considered invalid within the field of Native Studies.

For many Native people today and especially young Native people, trying to understand and return to their traditional practices is difficult because the core of traditional Native practices is embracing the physical manifestation of spirituality through living with the land. Given that most Native populations live in urban areas today, trying to conceptualize this phenomenon is a real challenge in regaining traditional tribal knowledge. Many AI/AN students act out in school because they are not grounded in their tribal norms and cannot speak their tribal languages. Many AI/AN students are ashamed to be "Indian," particularly those that attend public schools.

Most AI/AN students are not conscious of their tribal identity and therefore struggle with the cultural norms within the schools they attend. One of the major problems of public schools is that many educators see AI/AN students as individuals and not so much as tribal families. More severely, many AI/AN students see themselves as individuals rather than tribal members. These AI/AN students are truly victims of a colonizational process.

A starting point is to focus on the antidote to colonization, which is decolonization. For those involved in leadership positions, you know that education and socialization are interrelated. There is something wrong with an education/socialization process that leaves AI/AN students uneducated of their own tribal histories—sometimes strangers to their own tribal people—and sometimes we become the oppressor and creatures of habitual shallow thought and trivial values. Many of our transformational leaders, like Vine Deloria Jr., recognized that education for AI/AN students has been, for the most part, training designed to reinforce our dehumanization and ultimately to disconnect us from the power of the AI/AN mind and spirit. Many of our tribal elders and scholars have paved the way for another generation to understand the importance of the mind and to comprehend why education is so critical to AI/AN liberation and advancement.

The lessons that I have learned are simple ones. I've learned that people that "hurt" other people are hurting within themselves and that those individuals who heal others are healed. In essence, what I'm saying is that those that hurt, hurt, and those that are healed, heal. Using that same logic, those who have been uprooted, uproot, and those that have roots do not uproot.

Can you now talk about how an understanding of AI/AN peoples cultural style and worldview can facilitate teacher interaction with indigenous students and their families?   The primary issues confronting AI/AN students today are poverty, racial discrimination, culture differences, and tribal languages. Most teachers expect students to speak standard English in school. This pressure to speak English well in school often produces negative expectations about students' personalities and academic ability.

It is critical that AI/AN students have culturally responsive teachers. Simultaneously, AI/AN students need tribal role models both within the school and community to counteract negative influences on AI/AN youth. Nothing matches the experience of having AI/AN teachers teach AI/AN students. In most cases, AI/AN teachers of AI/AN students understand the issues of culture and language more emphatically.

Additionally, there is a myth that AI/AN students have a low ability to learn in schools. This myth is rampant within many teachers and sometimes even believed by many AI/AN people. To understand the state of AI/AN education, educators must examine the intersection of power and culture. The socialization process of students is affected by a global systems of power and control. Colonization, genocide, and White supremacy are hundreds-of-years-old challenges. This global hegemonic system interrupted and destroyed indigenous knowledge and traditional educational excellence, most of which AI/AN are totally unaware of.

Hegemonic structures and ideology are the basic foundation that controls AI/AN education. This foundation formed the belief system and behaviors as well as misled AI/AN students about their own traditional teaching and learning practices. Even today, few tribes have more than minimal control over their own tribal education. Many Indian schools are templates of White educational institutions, having their school governance modeled after Bureau of Indian Affairs schools. Teachers of AI/AN students need to know that many educational reform movements are still in process to challenge these hegemonic structures.

Ultimately, teachers need to know that original hegemonic structures were designed to miseducate and colonize AI/AN people. Mission schools and BIA boarding schools were designed to eliminate an indigenous worldview and replace it with White supremacy structures. The alarming part of this process is that so many AI/AN people are unaware of their own alien socialization and miseducation (colonizational mindset).

What additional suggestions can you give regarding developing rapport with AI/AN students?   AI/AN students need social and effective motor skills that will help them confront the realities of their world. Examples of such skills include conflict resolution skills, self-esteem—building skills, and critical-thinking skills to help them understand the processes of colonization and decolonization.

Teachers can concentrate on the topics of teacher expectations, parental involvement, self-esteem, culturally responsive curriculum, focused teaching pedagogy to enhance student learning styles, test bias, and social/peer pressure.

I like what Gary Howard says about teaching: "You can't teach what you don't know." I believe that teachers can't share any cultural knowledge that they don't have or are not interested in obtaining within their own professional development plan.

Are there any learning styles that typify AI/AN students and, if so, ways to manipulate the classroom environment to match these learning styles?   AI/AN students, like all students, learn in different ways. What teachers need to do is comprise an analysis of classroom learning styles of their students and at the same time design lesson plans to match teaching styles with student learning styles. The shared variance of teaching styles and student learning styles is the shared variance where teaching and learning takes place the most.

My review of the literature on AI/AN student learning styles indicated that AI/AN students have distinct cultural values, such as conformity to authority and respect for elders, taciturnity, strong tribal social hierarchy, patrimonial/matrilineal clans, and an emphasis on experiential learning, which are deeply rooted in the teachings of the elders. These cultural traits are exhibited in family socialization patterns, which are quite different from those of other ethnic groups. Historically, these cultural values, in turn, play a dominant role in the teaching and learning process of AI/AN students.

CHAPTER 12

Working with African American Students

An Interview with William Cross

> *"Because I was so steeped in the family, the neighbors, and the good people that were around us, I didn't quite understand what they were angry about."*

> —William Cross

Demographics

The term *African American* subsumes a diverse array of peoples, including African Americans born in this country, people from Africa, and people from the West Indies and Central and South Americas. The 2000 census numbers African Americans in the United States at 35 million, or 12.3 percent of the population. Since the time of slavery, African Americans made up this county's largest minority, but the 2000 census showed that Latinos/as have become the largest minority. Recent statistics showed that as of 2007, an estimated 47,000,000 African Americans were living in the United States. This accounts for nearly 13.5 percent of the overall population—a number that is projected to start leveling off by midcentury. They are the most widely dispersed ethnic group both geographically and economically. In 2000, for example, there were eighteen states with an African American population of at least one million: 54 percent lived in the South, 36 percent in the Northeast and Midwest, and 9 percent in the West. (The statistics in the above paragraph were updated by Franklin Fisher of the Research Writing Services for the Social Sciences.)

While most African Americans are descendants of families who have been in the United States since slavery, immigration has slowly been increasing over the last two decades, leading to increasing levels of linguistic and cultural diversity. Immigrants from former British Caribbean colonies have brought a mixture of African and British customs, and those from former Spanish, French, and Dutch colonies have done the same. In 1980, only 3 percent of African Americans were foreign-born. By 2000, the figure had risen to 17 percent, with most of the increase a result of immigration from the Caribbean. Increasing immigration from sub-Saharan Africa is projected. Previous immigration from Africa has primarily come from Nigeria, Ethiopia, Ghana, Kenya, and Morocco (Pollard & O'Hare, 1999). Such diversity means we should not assume the existence of a "typical" African American family.

Family and Cultural Values

Four factors have shaped the African American experience and culture:

- "The African Legacy, rich in culture, custom, and achievement;
- "The history of slavery, a deliberate attempt to destroy the core and soul of the people, while keeping their bodies in enforced servitude;
- "Racism and discrimination, ongoing efforts to continue the psychological and economic subjugation started during slavery; and
- "The victim system, a process by which individuals and communities are denied access to the instruments of development and advancement, and then blamed for low levels of accomplishment and achievement, while their successes are treated as anomalies." (Black, 1996, p. 59)

Black slaves brought a rich amalgam of cultures from West Africa; according to Hilliard (1995), rather than eradicating African culture and consciousness, slavery actually preserved it. Aspects of an African worldview still infuse African American life: a stressed importance on religious values and spirituality, cooperation and interdependence, and a connectedness with nature. Enslavement added emphases on resistance, freedom, self-determination, and education. African culture also contributed a tradition of strong family structure in which extended families and close-knit kinship systems were the basis of larger tribal groupings (Marshall, 2002).

According to researchers who have worked to understand how the classroom can better accommodate the needs and cultural realities of African American families, three strategies are critical:

- Understanding the cultural context of the family
- Viewing differences in family dynamics as adaptive mechanisms and strengths
- Developing practices that take into account the needs, cultural dynamics, and style of African American culture

Furthermore, these researchers favor classroom strategies that educate students in the context of existing African American family structure and communities and oppose helping students adapt to a White world and its culture. Three factors are positive strengths to be built upon in the classroom: kinship bonds, role flexibility within the family, and religion (Hill, 1972). Each offers insight into the workings of African American culture, values that infuse the culture, and arenas where teachers can find additional support and encouragement for their work in the classroom.

Kinship Bonds

Many African American families are part of complex kinship networks of blood relatives and unrelated individuals. These markers of solidarity and community are based on typical patterns of "coresidence, kinship-based exchange networks linking multiple domestic units, elastic household boundaries, and a lifelong bond to three generation households" (Stack, 1975, p. 124). There exists a series of uncles, aunts, close friends, older brothers and sisters, and other relatives who operate in and out of the Black family and home. Such extended patterns should be acknowledged as legitimate by teachers and called upon as useful resources as a bridge between school and family as well as when it is necessary to involve family in educational issues that arise for individual students. An African American consultant I recently met described how frustrated she became when the teacher did not accept her mother's presence in place of her own at a parent-teacher conference. As far as the parent was concerned, her mother's presence was the same as her own presence, yet the teacher's culture was based on a more nuclear family unit. Key family members should be identified and included in educational decision-making, even if their inclusion goes beyond the teacher's personal definition of who makes up the family. It is critical that all members of the family, as defined *by the family,* be invited to participate in the process of educating their student. Such extended family networks are quite common in Latino/a families as well.

When first meeting African American students and families, teachers—especially White teachers—should exercise caution in seeking personal information about the family and its members. With good reason, African American families are often suspicious of "prying" professionals. Authors such as Hines and Boyd-Franklin (1982) and Boyd (1982) suggest delaying the seeking of personal data until adequate trust of the school situation has been developed and when information can be sought in a natural as opposed to a forced manner. Extended kinship bonds suggest that teachers consider working with subgroups of the extended family when it is necessary to involve family members in discussion about a student's classroom behavior and only those who would have direct input on a particular issue. Of course, this assumes a certain level of knowledge about a given family's members and structure. It may also be necessary to schedule home visits in order to include key figures who cannot or will not come to the school. Again, entering a home, like seeking information, should be done with sensitivity in light of past abuses of the welfare system against poor families.

Role Flexibility

Role flexibility within the African American family, like extended kinship bonds, is highly adaptive for coping with the stresses of oppression and socioeconomic ills. It is most evident in the greater role diversity found among African American men and women as well as in the existence of unique familial roles. African American males have been traditionally seen by social scientists as peripheral to family functioning (Moynihan, 1965). Hill (1972), among others, has challenged this notion. He argues that the father's frequent absence from the home does not reflect a lack of parenting skill or interest but rather the time and energy required to provide basic necessities for the family. The father's precarious economic position coupled with the need for African American females to work outside the home often lead to extensive role reversals and flexibility in child-rearing and household responsibilities. These circumstances have led White (1972) to suggest that African American children may not learn as rigid distinctions between male and female roles as their White counterparts.

Hines and Boyd-Franklin (1982) and Boyd (1982) caution against routinely excluding the father, as has frequently been done by those who subscribe to the myth of the peripheral male. Instead, they suggest doing as much as possible to include him, even if for only a cursory introduction. Teachers are encouraged, if possible, to regularly inform the father of what is happening educationally for his student if he is unable to participate more fully. The authors also caution teachers against assuming the absence of a male role model when the father has abandoned the family. Given the variety of extended family figures in the extended family and community, someone else may emerge to fill this role.

While the African American male has been viewed as peripheral, the African American female—often forced to assume responsibilities well beyond those typically taken on by White women—has frequently been mislabeled as overly dominant. In fact, African American couples are often more egalitarian than their White counterparts. More often than Whites, Black males and females grow up with the expectation that both will work. Other interesting insights into the dynamics between African American males and females: Discord tends to be dealt with indirectly, not through direct confrontation. Solutions to long-term disharmony are typically informal, and long periods of separation may occur without the thought of divorce (Minuchin, Montalvo, Guerney, Rosman, & Schumer, 1967).

African American couples tend to remain together for life, often for the sake of the children, and typically seek therapy for child-focused issues rather than for marital dissatisfaction. In spite of ill-treatment by a husband, an African American woman tends to resist the dissolution of a relationship. This may result from three factors:

- Greater empathy for the husband's frustration in a racist society
- An awareness of the extent to which Black females outnumber Black males
- A strong religious orientation that teaches tolerance for suffering (Hines & Boyd-Franklin, 1982)

In addition, economic demands and oppressive forces have created unique roles in the African American family. Included are the *parental child*—an older child who has parental responsibilities when there are many younger children to attend to or when both parents are absent from the home for considerable amounts of time—and the extended generational system of parenting, in which the parent role is shared and distributed across several generations within the home. While clearly a potential positive force, such adaptive strategies can become sources of additional problems. This occurs when their intended function becomes distorted, overutilized, or rigid. "If the mother's role is overemphasized ... it can become the pathway for all interactions within the family. This requires children to relate primarily to her moods and wishes rather than to their own needs. The result is emotional fusion of the children with the mother" (Pinderhughes, 1989, p. 113). Parental children can be forced to take on responsibilities well beyond their abilities and at the expense of necessary peer group interactions (Minuchin, 1974). Shared parenting in the multigenerational family can become chaotic or a source of open conflict and dispute. If teachers are aware of such patterns and their impact upon a student, they may better understand why a student may be chronically late, absent, or always tired or with whom to speak when they need to contact a family member about their student.

Religion

Religion is important in the African American community and provides a valuable source of social connection as well as self-esteem and succor in times of stress. Religious leaders may become part of the extended family structure and sought out by religious families for personal help and support as an alternative to White mental health or social service agencies. Such religious networks are frequently overlooked by teachers as a resource and source of support and information about the community in which a student's family lives. Educators may find it useful to seek necessary information from religious leaders, to call on church networks for help when a student's family is in crisis, or to ask a minister to intervene with a particular student or family problem. On the other hand, religiosity itself may become a source of conflict in the African American family. For example, consider the situation of a highly religious family dealing with the rejection of religion and traditional values by a pre-adolescent. An understanding of the impact of a family's religious practice on the personal development of a student (for example, strict adherence to physical punishment and discipline of children based on religious maxims such as "spare the rod and spoil the child") may help explain her or his classroom behavior or difficulties (Larsen, 1976).

The trauma of slavery and the long history of racism have shaped and defined the African American experience in the United States. It is difficult to understand the African American psyche without keeping these two events clearly in mind. "From 1619 until slavery ended officially in 1865, 10–15 million Africans were brought here, and another 30–35 million died in transport" (Kivel, 1996, p. 121). The magnitude is staggering. The effect of slavery was intensified by the systematic destruction of much of the African culture and identity by slavers and slave masters, the tearing apart of families, and the creation of myths of inferiority and subhuman status to justify what was being done. The entire nation benefited economically and socially from this cruel institution.

Racism replaced slavery as a vehicle for the continued exploitation of African Americans as well as a justification for continuing to deny them the equality guaranteed by the U.S. Constitution. As a people, they survived, grew strong, and fashioned a new culture in America, but they continue to pay an awesome price for the color of their skin—both directly due to enduring injury and continuing healing from slavery (Leary, 2005) and indirectly economically. In many ways, the United States is functionally "two nations"—Black and White—and there is an enormous disparity in the access of these two groups to the resources and benefits of this rich nation. The long list of statistical inequities—from average salaries to unemployment, from incarceration to education levels, from teenage pregnancies to poverty—is staggering. For example, poverty rates among African Americans are almost three times those of Whites. Life expectancy is six years shorter. Infant mortality rates are twice those of Whites, Asians, and Latinos/as. African American households have the lowest annual median income, while African American men experience the highest rate of unemployment among ethnic minorities (Hacker, 1995, U.S. Census Bureau, 2008).

African Americans have been the catalyst in the struggle against inequality and social injustice in this country. Through the civil rights and other social movements, they have been the voice of conscience in America, not allowing the nation to forget grave injustices that are still very much alive. African

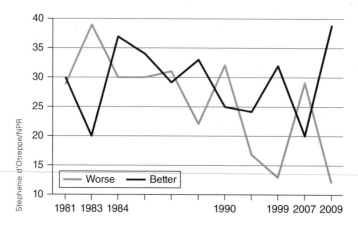

Percent of blacks who say blacks are better/worse off now than five years ago.

FIGURE 12.1 A Year After Obama's Election: Blacks Upbeat about Black Progress, Prospects

Source: Copyright 2010, Pew Research Center, http://pewresearch.org/pubs/1459/year-after-obamaelection-black-public-opinion.

Americans have been the "center of racial attention," and all other oppressed groups have learned from and modeled their fights on those of African Americans (Kivel, 1996).

With the election of Barack Obama as president, the hopes of African Americans are beginning to be raised, as this change in a "sense of progress" indicates (see Figure 12.1). Some research is also showing an increase in test scores for African American students, which has much to do with attitude and identity change (Dillon, 2009). As our guest points out, it is little wonder that the complexities around relationships and identity in America impact African American students.

Our Interviewee

William E. Cross Jr., Ph.D., is professor of counseling education in the College of Education at the University of Nevada at Las Vegas. Before taking the position at UNLV, he was professor and coordinator of the Social-Personality Doctoral Program in Psychology at City University of New York. He has taught on the faculties of Cornell University, Pennsylvania State University, and University of Massachusetts–Amherst. Dr. Cross is also a consultant to government, education, and industry on business and educational implications of America's changing demographics. As one of the leading experts on the study of African American identity, his text *Shades of Black: Diversity in African-American Identity*

(Temple University Press, 1991) is considered a classic. His model of African American identity development has significantly shaped the study of ethnic identity in the fields of psychology and African American studies and has influenced scholars theorizing and doing research on Jewish identity, Asian American identity, White ethnic-group identity, Latino/a identity, and gay and lesbian identity.

The Interview

Can you begin by talking about your own ethnic background and how it has impacted you and your work?   Because the color variation in my own family was so dramatic, when I was pretty young, I thought that being born blonde or brown was random. And so my earliest memories are not about race but that it was somehow intriguing that your mom would produce a brown child one day and a white child the next time around. As a young boy, I had mostly very rich, positive memories of youth. And there was the vaguest notion of race—it wasn't negative; it was more a sense of culture. Because I was raised on the south side of Chicago, I was growing up in the golden age of African American working class experience. I was born in 1940, so this was after World War II. The employment rate for men and women was very, very high. There were sections in the Black community that were financially stable, but they were very modest. We had baseball teams, and Jackie Robinson was in his prime. So, my primal memory, meaning when I was a young child, was being happy.

There would be these moments, however, when there were certain markers in the community; and I didn't know why we should not walk beyond that bridge or across the river. As my images of Whites evolved, this was somewhat compartmentalized because my neighborhood was a heavily integrated community. It was not uncommon for us to have White neighbors. But there was this notion of Whites—particularly White males—who were angry. And because I was so steeped in the family, the neighbors, and the good people that were around us, I didn't quite understand what they were angry about. And so I hadn't internalized their stereotypes of us. Then, we moved to Evanston, Illinois. I guess that's where I began to be more conscious of race in terms of its constructions—in terms of it being a label that somehow I was a problem to other people.

My mom, who was very fair, raised us to understand that she would use the label Negro, but then she would very quickly say, "You can be whoever you want to be." My father had more of race consciousness. But because of his alcoholism, we just didn't pay as much attention to Dad. So, in my adolescence, my mom had a greater influence on me. I probably went through adolescence knowing I was Negro but having pretty close to a racelessness notion of race.

Racelessness in the sense that I was a Negro, but so what? The school system that I attended did not teach us Negro/Black history. My father would bring me books. However, his status in the family didn't make him someone that we would listen to. I think if we had more conversations when he was sober—and he made history more, I don't want to say more fun but more engaging—it might be different. But that just didn't happen. And Mom didn't push it.

I was very much a Negro by the time I reached late adolescence. Issues across race were there. We would date White girls. I had Black and White girl-friends in high school, but I think by the time I was in high school, I probably had a distorted aesthetic in that I began to deify White beauty. Yet, all the way through college, I had mixed relationships. Sometimes, they'd be Black; sometimes, they'd be White. And I was even engaged once to a Black woman for a short time, even though before her and after her I dated White women.

In college, I was heavily affected by the Pi Lambda Phi experience. Now, anyone who knows fraternities knows that Pi Lambda Phi is a traditionally Jewish house. At the university in Denver, a radical Jewish man reorganized the chapter, and he made the point to integrate it. And so, I became the first president of what was essentially an integrated fraternity. That had a deep effect on me. It didn't cause me to become a "race-man" or "come back into a culture" man, but it meant that I could be more openly Negro, and this person could be more openly Jewish, and this person could be Catholic. So, it was a very multicultural kind of thing. So much so that in the early 1960s—I came out of high school in '59, went to Denver between '59 and '63—when the civil rights movement began picking up, I was almost unprepared for it.

When I went to grad studies in clinical psychology at Roosevelt University in Chicago in the early to mid-1960s, there was a nascent move toward nationalism and toward a more caustic discourse across racial barriers. I remember having a miserable year my first year at Roosevelt University. A lot of it was tied around the fact that I had come out of this Denver experience where we had built real bridges across—or what we thought were bridges across—race and culture. And that scaffolding had no value, for the most part, at Roosevelt. I think I began to be, also, not ashamed but wondering why I was so hesitant to just commit myself to what other Black people were saying and doing and wanting.

Then, with Martin Luther King, I got swept up in the notion of nonviolence. I certainly was not a ruffian and didn't know what value one saw in that, so there was a whole bunch of reasons I would be attracted to his philosophy. But when King was assassinated, that released a lot of my pent-up feelings, views, and so on. In my own history, my turnaround in having a Black focus would be in the sixties. The death of Martin Luther King caused me to very consciously and deliberately reconstruct what I thought was my old identity—to unload myself of the sense of shame, guilt, and anxiety about being the wrong kind of Black person and to understand to whom am I anchoring myself. Whose identity am I trying to construct? So, I just totally immersed myself in what I perceived to be Black culture—tried to go through those emotional and psychological hoops that would make me an authentic Black person. And I shyly but steadily—I should say hesitantly—began to keep notes.

Over time, this was reinforced by others, and the next thing you know, 1971, I was encouraged to publish my notes as the Black emersion experience. One other thing happened to me that was awesome is that Bill Hall, who was in counseling psychology, was mentoring me at a very key point. I was wanting to go to the clinical side of academe, but he said: "No, no, no. Go into traditional academic psychology. Become more theory-oriented because almost all clinicians use other people's theories." And he in part was right because our people needed original thinkers who are actually developing theory.

Now, as to the original question, "How do I see myself ethnically?" When I was first raised, I don't think I had a notion of race and culture. When race and culture began to evolve, it was very positive; I can still draw on that. Then, in my early adolescence, it became a stigma, and that was bad. I experienced a lot of shame because I bought into the stereotypes of the larger society. Being fair-skinned, I was sometimes able to melt into larger White society, and there'd be other times when I'd felt this sense of tension when with other Black people. Because I was so fair, my features were so sharp that even when I declared myself to be Negro, what have you, there was still in the eyes of some of the folks that I saw a sense of questioning. When I went through the Black sixties, I had an afro as long as I could get it. And wore dashikis and so on—a mirror of conformity. Like any young man, I wanted to be accepted, and loved, and have women who'd love me. I was taking blackness to another level. Being a doctoral student, I was able to fuse this sense of ethnicity and race with long-term studies.

Coming out of Princeton, I then went into Black studies, and over the next twenty years, that was a search toward solidifying my frame. I very early on went from just viewing the issue as race to viewing it also as culture. And I almost had to do that because since I racially didn't look like the very people I was identifying with, I had an existential understanding of blackness. And then once I got rid of enough shame and anxiety and guilt and rage, I became aware that actually this existential component was true for all people, whatever their ideals. So, I came to understand that existentially, identity is a choice—a choice that's often fostered by the ecological niche into which you are immersed. My boyhood flirtation with Black Nationalism in a very narrow sense was real, but it was limited. And early on, I became aware that I was an African American. An Afro American if you will. And that it was very difficult, but there were these other roots, Native American roots, White roots, because that was all there in my family. By the way, I should tell you that I received tremendous support within my family for my own identity change; they were going through changes too. But their love was so sustaining and unequivocal that even though I'd come home talking, you know, crazy ideas, they'd listen. But most importantly, my mother, who as you recall I said earlier in the interview was almost the key person for our racial ideas—and she'd work on a racelessness notion—she actually would re-engage with the children that'd been home, and she became radicalized herself in the sixties. My dad was angry because he tried to show us the power of race and culture early on, so the irony is that in becoming Black, I became even closer to my mother because she changed. And my father remained estranged, and I was close to my sisters.

I stayed with the Africana Center at Cornell for twenty-plus years; I loved it. It's the cornerstone of my being, but I shifted from a "plain" psychologist to a cultural psychologist—that's what happened to me at Africana. At Africana, I became someone who was friendly to those students who pushed the limits of a nationalist frame. Who kind of pushed us over into viewing the issue as bicultural, biracial, binational. And, of course, in some instances, even flirting with multicultural, but that would come a little bit later. Starting with the "bi-" component. We are not just Africans, we are not just Americans, we are some sort of hybrid. And where hybridity is not viewed as a negative but just simply means it's the fusion. And when Reagan took office in the eighties and his policies began to sink through—and I don't say this in any negative way toward my colleagues at the Africana Center—there was a rightful re-emergence of their nationalist frame. And I became aware I was a little bit estranged because I wanted people who were bicultural to come—I wanted people from Japan to come—to the Africana Center. I wanted the few White students who came in to succeed. And I think I was misperceived. Some people thought I spent a little too much time with these "other groups." I could see that there were actually some of our professors who were explicitly hostile to anyone who was not Black. So, I thought I was friendly to our African American students but also made the point to be the bridge to these other groups. Because my vision at Africana was that we wanted to have students graduate from our program and teach in China, Japan, Russia. Well, that meant you had to welcome someone from China, Japan, Russia. And the group as a whole, from my point of view, was not always accepting of this multicultural vision.

So, when I moved from Africana to Penn State, that was symbolic in terms of my own ethnicity—of shifting from a nationalist-focused identity to a multicultural-focused one. So, today, I see myself as very much African American but with a decided Black cultural *and* multicultural frame. My multicultural frame is limited by the fact that I don't know other languages, and I think you really do have to know other languages to pull off the multicultural frame. But I do consider myself more than a friend to movements of certain aspects of Jewish identity. I separate that out from Zionist identity—I understand Zionism, but that's not where my connection is—but to Palestinian identity, to women's identity, feminist identity, more recently gay and lesbian identity. I feel a connectivity to these other groups, which are sometimes marginalized for various reasons. I have in some cases intellectually become engaged in their concerns, and I have actually influenced the way some scholars write about them. Nonetheless, most of my writings have to do with Black people because I believe that in the short time I have on the earth, you know, I'm sixty-three, I want to do more. There's so much there you can't exhaust it, so before I spill over into a dedicated multicultural frame, I write about blackness in a way that's *friendly*—friendly to the multicultural frame.

Who are the African Americans, and what characteristics do they share as a group?   My writing since 1971 has been trying to point out to people that while in a political sense we can be called a *group*, we are really *groups*. We welcome the psychology of what I'll call human ecology—that is to say, we try to figure out in what kind of ecological niche or niches members of groups are being raised. And the material conditions, the spiritual conditions, and political conditions under which Black people are raised *vary*. Yes, we have concentrations in what we call our communities—outsiders sometimes call them ghettos—but we say ghetto in a friendly way, and there's commonality whether you're here, Cleveland, so on. But we are disbursed, and as a result, when you find someone raised in Oregon or at a distance from a large population or, in my case, where my late adolescence was in Evanston—just down the road from Chicago—there was just a different kind of frame of reference.

We are a community that is very diverse in its orientations. Now, having said that, the stigma that we have to wrestle with is real. And so, even when we achieve different class dispersion, there's a greater probability that we are a problem to other people, and as a result of being a problem to other people who have power, they do things to us that influence our lives in negative ways. And so, we are hyperconcentrated in a certain spatial sense. So, we are—we choose to live sometimes with ourselves, but oftentimes, it is more than choice; we are forced to. And as a result, we—as a group—are more likely to experience certain kinds of oppression.

But even when we have managed to escape poverty, the reach of certain types of racism—and there's not just one, there's many variations that can reach us. So, even as a bourgeoisie, middle-class academic, I have a history that I can tell of my moments of encountering racism. Moments that are going to be different across people, from the shoeshine guy, to the laborer, to the maid, and whatever. But I have not escaped that racism, although my material well-being can allow me to create some zones of comfort—some buffers. I don't equate my life with someone who has been forced to make a choice that might make them end up in prison and so on. And I certainly don't feel better, but I'm not kidding myself that my life has been the same as theirs. Now, that said, my own work has suggested that if there are a thousand ways in which African Americans come to view themselves—if there's great variation in our identity structures—some of the problems that we are almost all forced to encounter have such a repeated theme from Chicago to New York to Cleveland that I tend to focus in on these identity frames of reference to the exclusion of the others.

One cluster of identity types has to do with those people who for various reasons don't make race very important to their lives. And there could be some very positive reasons for that or some very negative. Let's just give some examples. I could be Black, but I could be so into my religion or my Pentecostal church that I see myself as being a child of God and therefore I don't place that much weight on race because I have this other positive interest. In that situation, I might be married to a Black woman, I might be going to an all-Black church, but I don't see race as a framing issue; I see it as my relationship with God. That would be a person who, from my point of view, is what I call "pre-encountered" because they have an identity, and it's a positive identity, but it's not anchored in race and culture. Whatever race and cultural dimensions they hold are under-stated, underplayed, and given secondary emphasis. Such folks do not deny being Black, but they accord "race" limited importance.

Then, there are other people who tend to have absorbed stereotypes about the group that cause them to feel some degree of estrangement from the group. They may even live in the community, but because they view the group as being about the stereotypes that are often racist, they don't often see the beauty or the strength of the community. So, therefore, they live in it, but they don't feel—they're kind of almost ambivalent about it. Such people are "miseducated"—a label taken from Carter G. Woodson's book of the same title (1933).

Then, of course, the third category that I've studied a lot is those persons that have absorbed the stereotypes—who painfully not only see the group as negative, but they see themselves as negative, and there's self-hate. Let me show you from my point of view: All three of those people end up being in the same category because if tomorrow something were to happen and there was a call to race—there was a call to culture—the first person wouldn't come forward because they don't think it's important. The second person, the mise-ducated person, wouldn't come forward because they're not so sure that Black people do anything together. And then the third person would not come for-ward because he or she is hating the group. So, therefore, all those persons end up not acting in the group's behalf. Some, again, have positive reasons—but others for real negative reasons.

And then, on the other extreme, if you will, there are a range of people who do make race and culture part of their identity. But one of the things I've done in my work is show that people who have a Black identity are not the same. Some are afrocentrically focused—that is to say, they accord black-ness importance. Others are biculturally focused. They feel very comfortable being American, and they feel very comfortable being Black. They have a real fusion. And then there are people who are emerging more recently. I guess they've been around forever, but they have more of a strong voice today. They are Black but are multiculturally focused. So, if you will, on either extreme, we have these clusters of identities. And then in the middle is something I call states of in-between-ness. There are people who you can find in the community who don't fit either of the two extremes, but they seem more volatile; they seem to be more agitated. Agitation not necessarily in a negative way. They literally are in-between. And, sometimes, they live their whole lives that way. And I call that emersion/immersion. So, from my point of view, for all the diversity of identity you find in the Black community, nonetheless, these identities are paramount. You find them in barbershops and beauty salons—in conversations you and I might have. They're the driving points of identities, though leaving off the table some other important identity frames, such as those who are Black and highly religious or spiritual.

I find more recently that I'm trying to look at how spirituality influences our identities. But I think spirituality is like gender. Gender has never been that much of a part of my discourse. And people have said, "That's because you're male, and you're leaving off women." That's the way people have said it, and I've had to walk up and look at that. I have been fortunate with the people I work with in that we have pinpointed those dimensions of Black identity that tend not to change that much across gender. So, we talk to Black women about stereotypes, and they resonate to that. And we talk to Black males about stereotypes, and they resonate to that. And we talk to Black men and women about having moments when you have doubted your identity. I mean, we have been able to hit key themes that are quite gender-neutral. Now, that said, if you go deeper into the stereotypes, we say, okay, you both agreed that you have been influenced and you know about stereotypes. Are there gender dimensions to that? Yes, there are. So, it's almost as though there's a second and third level of the discourse on identity that you can hit. And we stumbled upon those dimensions of race and cultural identity that are transcendent across gender. That doesn't make gender irrelevant. So, Black men, when they have to wrestle with the White aesthetic, they have to wrestle with the way a blonde male or a certain kind of physiology for maleness has been presented to them, and they have to work against that. And God knows we know about the stereotyping of Black men. And yet, if we ask Black women about that encounter, they're going to give you a gendered view. There's a very key component of gender that's there, but when you look at our work, and you look at our identity scales, and you look at our identity types, we find them as much in women as we do in men.

Could you talk about the various names that African Americans use to describe and identify themselves and some of the names that have been used

historically to describe and identify the group?   Now, this used to be rather easy to do when the focus was only on African Americans. We started out, of course, with our tribal or African names. Then, we had the slavery experience. We now know that who we're named after often still maintained itself during slavery. There are certain names that you can hear that have very much a Southern bent to them. In my coming up, I used to wonder who was Rufus. Rufus was always someone from Mississippi. I'm a William, but there were many Willies. And before the sixties, we used to—not that we were unique to this—but we would have fun making up names. In fact, I just met a woman whose name was Decita. And I asked her whether it was a name from the islands. And she said, "No, that was a name made up by my mom and dad based on certain letters from certain names." In the sixties and seventies, African Americans became much more friendly to African names. And now you also have a large number of African American people that were born and flew across that are now Makaza Kuminika. I don't know what percentage that would be.

But now you also have—because of immigration from the Caribbean and elsewhere—an amazing mixture in New York City, for example, of people from Panama, from Haiti, from the Dominican Republic, and so on. And now there's a cross-influence. People will hear about a Dominican name they like and they'll name their child that. So, the reality now is that you can have people with very African-sounding names—or names that would suggest ethnicity— yet when you interview them, they may be as pre-encountered as anyone else. So, names often don't tell as much about people as we might think; however, if the person was born African American and they have taken on an African name, that probably means this is someone who has a close relationship between their naming and how they think on some issues.

As a nation within a nation, we have gone through long periods of deracination. We stopped seeing ourselves as an African people. That's why the word *Negro* became so popular. In the sixties, we began to rebel against Negro, but notice how in the sixties, we didn't begin to take on African names right away. We said *Black*. It was still a struggle for us, as a people, to embrace our being African. And then, with the late movement of the sixties, there became a very self-conscious, new form of nationalism, and we now notice afrocentricity.

And then I guess it'd be in the late eighties, maybe as late as the nineties, we have this famous speech by Jesse Jackson in which he said we should stop calling ourselves simply Black because just as there are Italian Americans, just as there are Irish Americans, we are African Americans. And so today, you find that people who don't want to be called Negro—that term has almost become anachronistic. They're comfortable with Black. People from the islands, while they're in the United States, are wary of how they're going to be classified; in our research, we have found they will compromise and say "I'm Black American," and they'll feel much better if you also give them the right to say, I'm Jamaican, Panamanian, so on. So, we have a much larger spread of categories that we'll use in surveys and in general studies; people feel comfortable with the terms *White, Black, Native American,* and so on. You still find people using those categories and being OK if they were forced to make a choice.

Can you talk more about family and community and how these shape what happens in schools with African American students?   Now we get into some of the great, great distortions in African American life, the Moynihan Report (1965), and so on. From 1900 to the edges of 1960, the employment rate of Black males was usually high, and the ability of women to also work was usually high, so the existence of the two-parent household in the Black community is normative. Even when Moynihan wrote this report, 74 percent of Black families or so were two-parent households. Children were being raised in two-parent households. Recall I said that we had this transformation in the economy that takes place in the sixties, and it goes full-force in 1973 with the oil embargo. That's when we had the rapid closing down of factories and so on, and people began to lose their jobs. So, between the early 1970s and 1980s, we began to see what appeared to be a radical change in the structure of Black families. That's kind of assbackward. You can't have a family if you don't have a job.

The overall ecology of working-class life was radically affected by the pulling out of decent-paying jobs. Black people didn't stop relating to each other; they still fell in love. The irony of Black employment is that now sometimes the relationships took on more, not less, importance but also took on a distorted importance from what would happen if I was working eight hours a day, coming home to be with my wife, my children going to school, et cetera. Hope just got pulled out of that. And so, men would have relationships—and women as well—where they couldn't look forward to marriage because there was no rational reason to get married. You and I have lived through thirty years, maybe longer than that, of people still relating—still in their mind's eye wanting to be like anyone else—but not being able to afford it. That and the hyperconcentration of such people in what we know as ghettos now produces people who are estranged from larger society. They love, then divorce each other earlier and earlier. We now even see kids having kids.

The society puts almost all the pressure on the community itself and says it's the community's issue, but as you know for years and years, we continue to lose tens of thousands of good-paying blue-collar jobs in cities like New York. It's still going on, and 9/11 has exacerbated it.

How does this affect our educational institutions? Well, when I was growing up and we had the predominance of people employed, then when we went to school together, we were in segregated schools. When the really low-income kids would come along—and there were always kids who came from situations where the parents were unemployed—they were a minority. And we set the tone for conformity, and they would kind of conform to us. And they could almost discover their hope with us. They could almost discover their sense of future with us—that their life did not have to be defined by the poverty that they were experiencing.

But we had a shift in the sixties. Now at schools, the majority of kids who were in school were coming from hyperisolated, segregated, poor situations. In some cases, the percentage of single-parent moms is very, very high, and they're bringing that ethos of day-to-day *survival* with them. They're sometimes brushing up against kids who come from less risky environments, but their numbers are so big that sometimes they begin to influence the culture of the schools. So, it's almost been the reverse of earlier situations. Now add to that this interesting scenario: the Black kids who are doing OK—who want very much to communicate to their brethren who are not doing so well that "I identify with you. I am with you." And as a result, we have some middle-class kids who because they want to be viewed as part of a group will sometimes be perplexed as to how they should view school, whether or not "am I being White" in having strong performance. And we're kind of a little bit in the middle of that. I know history; we go through these cycles. And the Black communities can allow for coming out of this cycle.

Being real, being down, and so on, are driven by the underclass. But now the underclass has had a chance to play out its own agenda, and in some cases, it is no less decadent than other agendas that class has critiqued. We have our hip-hop artists who on the one hand have messages that are searing—searing, not wonderful. We can't say they're wonderful, but they're awesome because they're so truthful, and they're so raw. But we're now going through a period where people are almost celebrating pimps. Celebrating the hos, I mean—I don't see how that's any less decadent than Germany was in the 1930s. They got so hung up on sexuality and freedom that they weren't talking about political institutions. They weren't talking about rearranging society. So, we see now that some of the messages from hip-hop are very raw and very real, and we need to listen, but their political consequences are not good, and in some cases, they're as reactionary as you can find.

I think we're spinning out of that. I'm not utopian, but I think what's going to happen is the coming together of progressive Blacks and Whites and really progressively oriented folks from hip-hop culture. I don't know what that's going to look like, but it's going to be different from what we are now.

But to get to your question, the schools are often beside themselves because on one hand, they were designed for purposes of replication. The teachers were usually trained in middle-class teaching institutions. They work best when the kids come to school with attitudes like their own.

What the kids need are teachers and principals who are very competent in transformative experiences—you know, that help kids face up to and relate to their realities—but then say, "You don't have to be satisfied with that, and I can be your ally in taking you to another place." The schools want to teach about the value of American society. The kids need raw discussions on "You are a part of stigmatized groups in the United States. Here's how people have organized to get the things that they need." And that would be called radical. I mean that many people would be highly distressed if that were in the schools. But that's exactly what you need. How do you organize welfare mothers? How do you organize people who are unemployed? That's what you need for people who are trying to transform. What does it look like to have a school that actually teaches how poor people are manipulated? Not for the purposes of making them angry—and therefore wanting to go out and perform anarchy—but for the purposes of organizing.

People should understand, in the fifties and sixties, when we got angry—and we went through an angry period—we were funneled, tunneled, steered toward creating African American studies. New Black unions. New Black art. I mean, we took our energy and collectivized it. And we set the stage for individuals having a better life, but we did it through our collective action. That often was done outside of the schools.

So, when people ask me what can be done in the schools, there [are] two things. You can either change the schools in that way—and I have a very low expectation that they'll change—or you try to figure out political/economic forces that can cause the society to better distribute its resources. A better distribution will result in a higher level of employment by people that are poor, with jobs that are decent and that can sustain a family and that can sustain a community. And again, I'm not pie in the sky. We have a sanitation system that's stretched to the max, but if we were to build on a national basis for the next twenty years—it'd take us twenty years, probably more, to get the kind of sanitation system we would need—that would employ engineers, that would employ common laborers, and so on. If we had affirmative action, we'd have our fair share of such jobs. If we were to transform our bridges—we would build new ones or first start out with making sure the ones we've got are all they can be—again, we'd employ architects and engineers, and we'd also employ common laborers.

If we were to build—if not all the schools—many of the schools that we need in Washington, Chicago, Cleveland, and so on—make them up to date and so on—here we go again—that would employ engineers, architects, and so on. So, it doesn't mean we become a communist society. It means that we borrow from American history because all these things are like the Triboro Bridge again.

You know, we could identify projects that add value to all of us, but it goes against the grain in a sense. The market wants to maximize as much money as it can into those market areas that it controls. The government has an obligation to balance that somewhat. But with regard to our infrastructure—with regard to our investment in our youth—that's not something that maybe the market people want to do. That's something that we need. I'm going to make this number up: We'll make sure that 15 percent of our tax dollars—maybe 20 percent of our tax dollars—is done in these activities and ironically end up pulling out of poverty large, large numbers of common people. They don't have to have a master's, they don't have to have a B.A., they may not even have to have a high school degree, but they have to be pretty clean in their habits and so on, so they can be employed rebuilding America's infrastructure.

America thinks it's a great country. I think if we get that, we could be an awesome country. We know from studies that that would work faster than trying to change the schools. Families that have a reasonable level of good employment that allows them to remain married—some may divorce; others remain married or marry again—and where they're able to feed their children and where they're able to go to church or live out their spiritual lives, they send to school children who don't want to do battle with the school but want to learn from the school.

And it means the teachers themselves would not have to radically change; they could remain somewhat middle-class biased. Because the kids are becoming more malleable in terms of where they want to go, it'd just be easier. Things would be super better if in fact you get the teachers to be trained differently—if the schools were reorganized—in addition to the solid employment of the parents.

One thing is sure: As long as the parents of the children are devalued by the society—in the sense that you're almost treated as redundant workers or as leftovers—then there should be no surprise in us that the children of such redundant workers will reject their future and make what we call mischief. Because as they try on their own to manipulate those aspects of their environment that they can—that's what gangs are—they will produce short-run successes, but in the long run, they will likely end up in jail or in prison, and when their spirits are broken, sometimes it leads to addiction, and they commit—as we're seeing, but we don't want to see—suicide.

Right now, I don't have much hope in the short run. I think that people we have in office, such as Bush, are operating from the bell-curve agenda. I believe that they have a weird sense that the society is open, that the reason why people are on the bottom is because of their genes, that because they're on the bottom because of their genes, that nothing has to be done to assist them. And not taking action really makes a difference. That means they prolong White power. As you increase the probability of maintaining the status quo, you protect White power. They're willing to share the stage a little bit with some tokens, some Asian Americans, even some Blacks. Their image of the United States is not of a multicultural society but of a society that's multicultural in demographics only but which is still fundamentally a White man's country. And I'm sixty three (born in 1940). I don't have any expectations that there'll be any breakthrough before I die. I don't wish that on us. I just don't think change will happen that fast. I think that right now we have a president who—it's reasonable to suggest—was not elected. We have a president who distorted information on why we should send men and women off to die. We have a power system that just collapsed because of something called deregulation. In each of these instances—the question of the election, the false notions about the war, and the deregulation—there's no reason to believe that the society is going to respond.

The reason why we're at war is an impeachable offense and yet there's no movement to do that. It's ironic that we had Bill Clinton, who because of his sexual liaisons can be raked over the coals for two years, but history will show that we have a president now who committed impeachable offenses who will not be impeached and may even be re-elected. This shows you how it has little to do with justice and has more to do with might and your ability to control voters and so on. That's why I just don't have much hope.

My hope personally is working with young people. My own work is designed more recently to counter some of the vicious stereotypes about Black history and about Black people so that maybe someday later someone can say, "At least somebody was writing on these things in a way that was more truthful." But right now, I don't even know if the truth matters.

As a country we could not so much solve the problems with poverty that we have, but we could make the poverty more manageable. We can't have a zero-poverty society in a capitalist world, but we've gone through such a change—we're so imbalanced—that we're living with levels of poverty that need not be. So, I'm not utopian; I'm not a romantic; I pay a lot of attention to American history. What the society has done in the past when it steered some of its resources toward the working class has been nothing short of amazing. It is ironic that powerful Whites today who have their roots in the G.I. Bill—have their roots in forming unions and so on—could end up being so anti-poor and anti-Black in their stances when the solutions that could cause them to have a better society would, in some cases, replicate some of the things that happened to their own groups in the past. That makes for great frustration for us to see the potential of the society and to see it being wasted. It's a very painful thing to see.

Are there any subpopulations in the African American community that deserve additional attention? Yes. What's been emerging in the last ten years is that you have the Black race if you will, but there're always ethnic strands. It varies from one city to another, but in New York, it really is exploding. The Dominicans, Black Cubans, Panamanians. And now in Harlem, 123rd in Harlem is like an African street—African street in a traditional sense of the term, as it is in African American. We did research at City University of New York, and about three times we went out to collect data on African Americans, and three times we ended up with a sample that is much larger for Caribbeans and African Caribbeans than African Americans. So, these subcategories would be crucial.

The multiracial category is increasing. The last time I researched California, 17 percent of Black males are marrying out of race (22 percent by 2010). And not just White women. So, there is an explosion of biracial, multiracial children who may identify themselves as mostly Black, but they have these other connections. We are now getting more and more Black people who are successful economically. And I don't know what the spread is, but a number of them are drifting toward a conservative, right-wing orientation. So, they're becoming more of a voice. Their percentage is small, but because we're living in an era of the right, they're often better funded, and their voices often louder. There's been a diminution, in some ways, of the voices of Black progressives. But you asked for new voices.

I think that you wouldn't necessarily call this a population, but gender remains a discourse within that community—some for positive reasons; some for negative. The horrific stereotyping and stigmatization of Black males are something hard to find in Western history. But we should also look at the stigmatization that is also occurring with Black women. And the issue of sexual lifestyle is real problematic in our community. We have delayed the aggressive reaching out to our gay and lesbian brothers and sisters that are relying on us to solve the AIDS issues, although that's not the first thing one wants to think about.

Consider the incarceration of Black men and the production of a group that defines themselves as not being gay but who enjoy relationships within same-sex relationships and do so with unsafe sex. It has now spun over into heterosexual relationships, and now there's a population of Black women, often poor, relating to heterosexual men but who've been in prison and who've had same-sex relationships. So, there's a sort of category—you can't call 'em gay; you can't call them homosexual—but by their sexual activity, it's causing issues.

We have a large sector, more so than ever, of kids who are being raised in very, very poor environments, usually just with moms. Often, they're hyperconcentrated in tenement houses.

Let's not overlook, however, that we have the largest Black middle-class subpopulation that we've had in our history. And if they go through the chain that we've seen Whites go through, we will produce our bohemian group, our rebels, our people who see life differently, we'll get our entrepreneurs. There's also a certain bit of unpredictability with the very, very poor and the very, very comfortable, and it makes for wonderful history. We'll see that unfold in the years to come.

How do different cultural styles, values, and worldviews affect the education of African Americans?   Two things are going on. The kids sometimes do come with different styles, often couched in different language behaviors. But probably the biggest problem in the schools is not so much what the kids bring to the classroom—that's often varied—as much as the way our teachers have been trained and what they feel comfortable with. We had a time in the 1900s, 1920s, that people coming in were Italian, Irish, and there were Eastern European Jews from Poland or elsewhere. Over two or three generations, the schools did a pretty good job of helping them eventually achieve middle-class status.

What's kind of scary today is that the only hope that's being held out to these diverse kids, many of whom are poor, is the education system. I'll be a bit dramatic on this one. No other group—by that I mean, say, White ethnic group—has achieved social mobility from lower-class status to the middle-class status through education alone.

People are saying, well, there's the model minority: the Asian Americans. When you study the extent to which people from India, people from China, from Japan have made it very quickly—Asian Americans who have done well in our school system—you discover they didn't come in at a low point. Their parents had no money per se, but they often were middle class in the first place. So, you've got middle-class ethnic groups coming here, learning the language, taking off. That's not the same as bringing in people who are boat people. For example, when we track Vietnamese boat people who are very, very poor, they have not gone up into the system. So, it's a myth that education *alone* can make all the difference.

And this is the part that is scary with our poor kids today because society is trying to make education the *singular platform* by which social ability can be achieved. All other history shows us that it is a combination of employment of the parents in conjunction with the education of the children. If you don't have steady employment of the parents, then you don't move large masses of those kids—their progeny, if you will—into a better place. They become distracted—they get into issues of survival—and this phenomenon showed itself in the Depression when White ethnic groups became distracted, they were driven to street life, and we had a duel economy with prohibition.

So, no other group has achieved social ability in one generation through education alone. That's what education is being asked to do, and that is scary stuff. Because when the kids don't achieve, then people turn around and say,

"Ah ha! We invest in you, we have educational classes for you, and yet, you don't achieve; therefore, it must be you." They're not looking at the fact that while the children were in school, the parents were often divorced or couldn't even get married or living in tenement houses and didn't have good jobs. There has to be decent-paying jobs for the parents, and that will lead to a sense of hope. Now, do I again mean some sort of nirvana? No, but there has to be a critical mass of the parents, the adults, employed in decent jobs, not every single one. The Black community has been able to tolerate high unemployment of 15–20 percent, but the jobs had to be good-paying jobs for the other 85 or 80 percent. If not, it leads to some mischief-making by the kids.

What are some of the common problems that African Americans might bring into the school setting?   Instead of describing problems, let's call them challenges. They often bring in a different alignment system. How they codify life is different. And they work better with teachers who know the code—who can fight back for them and understand that they have to transform the kid. We should place a greater value on outside activity, as opposed to staying in a classroom. They often are more engaged if there's a way in which the curriculum can move back and forth from the classroom situation to things that happen in the street. I don't mean to bring in crime from the street. That would be ridiculous. You almost need a core of teachers and administrators who rather than view the community as enemy [instead] view the community as an anthropological wellspring. The challenge is, how do I show the students that if I'm walking down the street, there's a building and a connection, there's a building and another connection, and cognitively recognizing the connections and the differences? How to bring in that kind of everyday sense of survival and connection? Keep the kids absorbed, and bring into the classroom something that's fascinating and interesting. That's no small challenge. But if you have a school system that's busy talking about giving people tests, tracking them, and then talking about how you know that the kid can't make it, then the kid himself feels that sense of being trapped—feels that sense that you don't have much confidence in me. They fight back. They come to war. Especially by pre-adolescence and adolescence.

Could you now discuss some of the factors that you see as important in assessing the learning styles of African American students and share what environmental factors could be manipulated to match that style?   I'm impressed with the work of A. Wade Bodkins of Howard University and others. They have gone into the classroom and done anthropological studies, seeing how the classroom is arranged in terms of its activities, teacher behavior, decorations. The child comes in and sees this culture as something fully integrated into the classroom. Is the culture something new and strange or does it have enough symbols that they have from their homes? These researchers place a lot of emphasis not only on the teacher, per se, but the behavior, the language style, the competencies, and the actual physical structure of the school itself. This merging of the educational institutions and the home has value.

Is the disconnect a problem of a child or is it a problem of the teacher? Perhaps you're saying to yourself, we're going to bring in people to make a connection. It's somehow easier to understand it when they're from Hungary or Vietnam or so on. There's something about the ability of Americans to greet foreigners, strangers, in a way that it's understood that they're strangers. I'm using *stranger* not in a pejorative sense. But if the stranger is Chicano, if the stranger is Native American, or if the stranger is Black American, somehow people go brain-dead. Yet, some of the solutions that we use for bringing in a stranger who's foreign, we'd want to see them do it also with African Americans.

It's hard for people to do this because they have to face up to their racism. People have to understand that the spatial isolation of African Americans into various residencies is not an accident. Nor is it an issue of choice. And you have to own up to that.

And you have to respond to the thought that I didn't necessarily cause that, but I'm part of the solution, and I want to be part of the solution. Then, what things do I have to do structurally, pedagogically, and so on to make this not only a friendly environment—because that's a liberal solution, how to make it friendly—but more so than the issue of friendly, how do I make a child stronger? Because the issue is to push the kids—to create a sense of future—that's just as tough as it is for anyone else, and that requires people being very relaxed in taking a top to bottom look at themselves. And maybe it may mean, in a state like Oregon, going back to your schools of education and saying, "You're out to lunch." You know, you have to walk up to that and don't feel negative about it. You know, if you really, really do want to reach everyone, then tracking is not the solution. Simply cataloguing people is not the solution. As we know from history, the stories of poor White Irish kids who were done to, they were catalogued as not making it, and they have made it. We have the same scenario. How do we not make the same mistake? How do we assume from the beginning that every kid can learn? And yet take on the challenge of creating an environment where that can take place?

Considering cultural differences and learning styles, what suggestions might you have concerning establishing rapport with African American students and families? Yeah, if we did make connections earlier, that would help. But, again, I can't overstress what I said earlier. Schools can do an awful lot, and they could do more. But if the larger economic arena is not treating the parents with respect, the kids are going to come in with sand in their eye, and they're going to be distracted.

There should be a lot more participatory surveys and discussions. Ask parents, "What do you need from us?" I know I'm friendly, but we live in a world where there's racial/cultural barriers. What has to happen so that you as a parent can really feel as though you can walk in the door and feel friendly about it? How do we work together to go from low expectations for your child—you know, let's just get that on the table—to really high expectations? What kind of demands do we make of each other for that?

There should be a lot of time spent with parents and people of the community asking those kind of pointed questions, then translating those responses into programs that are doable—programs that teachers themselves can get excited about and that the various principals of the schools can be proud of. That's not an easy thing to do. You still basically use a middle-class model, and that presupposes that kids kind of look alike, sound alike, talk alike, and act alike.

CHAPTER 13

Working with Asian Pacific American Students

An Interview with Valerie Ooka Pang

"Asian Pacific American students are thoughtful, hard working, compassionate youth. Why are they often left out of equal educational opportunities?"

—Valerie Ooka Pang

Demographics

Asian Americans were the fastest growing racial group in this country from 1980 to 2000; their population nearly tripled (179 percent) during that period. The 2000 census (which divides the larger group into two subgroups) reported an Asian population of 10.2 million, or 3.6 percent of the general population, and a Native Hawaiian and other Pacific Islander population of 400,000, or 0.1 percent. Projections are for a population increase from 5 percent of the U.S. total in 2010 to 9 percent by 2050.

Like Latinos/as, Asians represent diverse ethnic groups with very different languages and cultures and, in some cases, a long history of intergroup conflict. Included are forty-three ethnic groups, twenty-eight of which are in the Asian category and fifteen in the Pacific Islander category. Included in the former are individuals who identify themselves as Asian Indian, Chinese, Filipino, Korean, Japanese, and Vietnamese; and in the latter, individuals from Hawaii, Guam, and Samoa.

With passage of the Immigration Act of 1965 and large-scale immigration from Southeast Asia and other parts of the Asian continent, the relative sizes of Asian American subgroups changed dramatically. According to the 1970 census, Japanese were the most populous, followed by Chinese and Filipinos. By 1980, however, the Japanese were in third place, Chinese first, and Filipinos second. Today, Chinese is the largest Asian subgroup with 3.5 million, followed by Filipinos at 3.1 million, Asian Indians at 2.8 million, Vietnamese at 1.6 million, Koreans also at 1.6 million, and Japanese at 1.2 million. Native Hawaiians and Pacific Islanders make up only 5 percent of the total Asian population.

Most Asian Americans come from recent immigrant families. During the 1990s, immigrants were responsible for two-thirds of the growth of the overall Asian population. For example, in 1998, 59 percent were foreign-born, with 74 percent of them arriving after 1980. However, many Chinese Americans and Japanese Americans have been here for three or more generations. Originally a source of cheap labor in the economic development of the western United States, the Chinese and Japanese experienced extensive suffering and racial discrimination:

> Legislation enacted in 1790 excluded Asians and other non-Whites gaining citizenship by limiting citizenship to "free White residents." Because most Asians were foreign-born and not citizens, they could be legally kept from owning land or businesses, attending schools with Whites, or living in White neighborhoods. Asian immigrants were not eligible for U.S. citizenship until 1952. The 1879 California constitution barred the hiring of Chinese workers, and the federal Chinese Exclusion Act of 1882 halted the entry of most Chinese until 1943. The 1907 Gentlemen's Agreement and a 1917 law restricted immigration from Japan and a "barred zone" known as the Asian-Pacific Triangle. During World War II Americans of Japanese ancestry were interned in camps by Executive Order signed by Franklin D. Roosevelt. (Pollard & O'Hare, 1999, pp. 6–7)

Recent Asian and Pacific Islander immigration has followed two different streams. The first stream came from countries such as China and Korea that already had large populations in the United States. The majority of these immigrants were college-educated and entered under special employment provisions. The second stream came from the Southeast Asian nations of Vietnam, Laos, and Cambodia after the Vietnam War to escape persecution. Most were poor and uneducated.

Forty-nine percent of Asian Americans and Pacific Islanders are concentrated in the western United States, with the largest urban populations located in Los Angeles and New York City. Sixty percent of the Chinese reside in California and New York; two-thirds of the Filipinos and Japanese live in California and Hawaii. Koreans and Asian Indians tend to be more dispersed, with the largest concentrations in California, New York, Illinois, New Jersey, and Texas. On the other hand, Southeast Asians can be found in unexpected locations due to government resettlement policies. In 1990, for example, 40 percent of the Hmong resided in Minnesota and Wisconsin (Pollard & O'Hare, 1999).

Unlike African Americans, Latinos/as, and Native Americans, Asian Americans have been educationally and economically successful, even in comparison with the White population. Asians and Whites graduate from high school at the same rate, approximately 90 percent, but Asians are more likely than Whites to complete two or more years of college and to earn graduate and professional degrees.

In 2005, the average median household income was $57,500 for Asians, compared to $49,000 for White households and $30,000 for African Americans. Although they make up only 13 percent of the non-White population, Asian Americans account for 30 percent of all minority businesses. They also score high on business ownership rates (businesses per thousand population), with Koreans and Asian Indians surpassing Whites. Asians and Pacific Islanders own about 5 percent of the businesses in the United States. The following pie chart (Figure 13.1) lists the percent of businesses owned by a number of specific cultural groups.

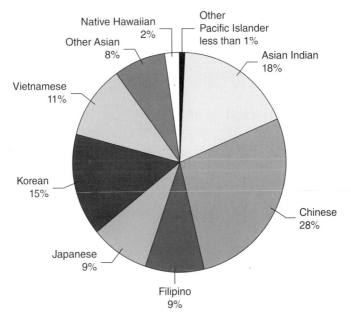

FIGURE 13.1 Distribution of Asian- and Pacific Islander-Owned Firms by Ancestral Group: 1997

Source: U.S. Census Bureau

Because of such statistics and a cultural tendency to act deferential and not compete openly with European Americans, Asian Americans have been described as a model minority and a success story. This image may be seen as a myth based on incomplete data (Sue & Sue, 2003). The myth validates the erroneous belief that any ethnic group can succeed if its members work hard enough, stimulates intergroup conflict, and shortchanges Asian communities from needed resources. A number of facts need to be understood: High median income does not take into consideration the number of wage earners, the level of poverty among certain Asian subgroups, and the discrepancy between education and income for Asian workers. Education in the Asian community is bimodal—that is, there are both highly educated and uneducated subpopulations. In large urban areas, Asians live in ghettos with high unemployment, poverty, and widespread social problems. Underutilization of services does not necessarily mean a lack of problems but may in fact have alternative explanations, such as face saving, shame, or the family's cultural tendency to keep personal information hidden from the outside world (Sue & Sue, 2003). In short, the belief in Asian success does not mean that Asian Americans experience less racism or discrimination than other groups or that there are not serious problems within crowded urban enclaves. At a psychological level, model-minority status refers to the lack of threat Whites experience in relation to Asian Americans. However, such an attitude has eroded somewhat with increased economic competition from Japan and other Pacific Rim countries and the growth in the number of Asian American students competing successfully for college and university slots.

Family and Cultural Values

The following description of traditional Asian families helps our understanding:

> In traditional Asian families, the family unit—rather than the individual—is highly valued. The individual is seen as the product of all the generations of his or her family. The concept is reinforced by rituals and customs such as ancestor worship, family celebrations, funeral rites, and genealogy records. Because of this continuum, individuals' personal action reflects not only on themselves but also on their extended family and ancestors…. Obligations and shame are mechanisms that traditionally help reinforce societal expectations and proper behavior. An individual is expected to function in his or her clearly defined roles and positions in the family hierarchy, based on age, gender, and social class. There is an emphasis on harmonious interpersonal relationships, interdependence, and mutual obligations or loyalty for achieving a state of psychological homeostasis or peaceful coexistence with family or other fellow beings. (Lee, 1996, pp. 230–231).

Depending on specific cultures and generation, family and gender roles and expectations are highly structured. Fathers are the breadwinners, protectors, and ultimate authorities. Mothers oversee the home, bear and care for children, and are under the authority of their father, husband, in-laws, and even sons. Male children are highly prized, and the strongest bond within the family is between mother and son. Children are expected to be respectful and obedient and are usually raised by an extended family system. Older daughters are often expected to be caretakers of younger siblings.

Traditional Asian values differ dramatically from those of European middle-class Americans. With immigration, there is the strong possibility of cultural conflict within the family. Lee (1996) described five Asian American family types that differ in levels of cultural conflict:

- "Traditional" families are largely untouched by assimilation and accultura-tion, retain cultural ways, limit their contact with the White world, and tend to live in ethnic enclaves.
- "Culture conflict" families are typified by traditional parents and accultur-ated, Americanized children who experience intergenerational conflict over appropriate behavior and values, exhibit major role confusion, and lack agreed-upon family structures.
- "Bicultural" families tend to include acculturated parents born either in the United States or in Asia but exposed to Western ways. They are pro-fessional, middle-class, bilingual, and bicultural. Family structures tend to blend family styles but with regular contact with traditional family members.
- "Americanized" families have taken on the ways of majority culture; their ties to traditional Asian culture are fading, and they have little interest in ethnic identity.
- "Interracial" families are formed through intermarriage with a non-Asian partner; family styles from the two cultures can be successfully integrated or there can be significant value and style conflict.

Sue and Sue (2003) similarly identified four value conflicts that may arise between Asian American students and Western-trained teachers:

- Asian students and families value a collective and group focus that empha-sizes interdependence, while Western teachers focus on individualism and independent action.
- Asians tend to be most comfortable with hierarchical relationships, in comparison with the Western emphasis on equality in relationships.
- Asian cultures see restraint of emotion as a sign of maturity, while Western culture is more likely to see emotional expressiveness as healthy.
- Traditional Asian students and families expect teachers to provide solutions, while the Western educational perspective encourages finding one's own solutions through introspection.

Our guest expert has taught school and prepared preservice teachers for many years. She has particular expertise in connecting surface and deep culture (Pang, 2004). In this interview, Dr. Pang gives us an overview of a very diverse and prominent group in the United States by drawing on her own childhood as well as Asian Pacific stereotyping, historical events, education, and communication styles.

Our Interviewee

Valerie Ooka Pang is a professor in the School of Teacher Education at San Diego State University. She was a first- and second-grade teacher in rural and urban schools. Dr. Pang was senior editor of *Struggling to Be Heard: The Unmet Needs of Asian Pacific American Children,* which is the only multidisciplinary text on Asian Pacific American children and human rights at Boston University. The second edition of her textbook, *Multicultural Education: A Caring-Centered, Reflective Approach,* more fully described a philosophical framework called caring-centered multicultural education. Her philosophy is based on the work of scholars such as Nel Noddings, John Dewey, Lev Vygotsky, Luis Moll, Jacqueline Jordan Irvine, Vanessa Siddle Walker, Geneva Gay, and Michael Cole. In addition, Pang has served as general editor with E. Wayne Ross of the series *Race, Ethnicity, and Education* published by Praeger Press. She was also volume editor of two of the texts: *Multicultural Education: Principles and Practices* and *Language and Literacy in Schools* (with Robert T. Jiménez). She is the senior editor (2010, with William Fernekes and Jack L. Nelson) of a new book entitled *Natural Disasters and Human Rights* from the National Council for the Social Studies.

Dr. Pang is a sought-after consultant for *Sesame Street,* Fox Children's Network, and Family Communications (producer of the fondly remembered *Mr. Rogers' Neighborhood*). She has published in a variety of journals, including *Harvard Educational Review, The Kappan, Educational Forum, Theory and Research in Social Education, Social Education, Equity and Excellence,* and *Multicultural Education.* She received the Outstanding Teaching Award in the Liberal Studies Program at San Diego State University.

The Interview

Could you begin by talking about your own ethnic background and how it has impacted your work? I am a third-generation Japanese American. I was born in Seattle, Washington, and grew up in eastern Washington in the town of Ellensburg. The farmers there grew corn, potatoes, Kentucky bluegrass, hay, that kind of thing. I lived in town, but I would visit my friends out in the country, and we would ride horses. I rode horses as a child, but I never rode the subway until I was thirty-nine. Many folks do not see me in this way—I mean, living in a rural town. I could milk a cow. I fed the steers. I've been to the roundup, where they brand them. I have a whole different kind of background than most Asian Americans, who tend to live in urban settings.

My interest in multicultural education began many years ago when I was a twenty-year-old, and I started teaching at the only neighborhood Black elementary school in a large urban district. It was March, and I had just received my bachelor's degree in education from a small private university. I felt I was ready to tackle the problems of the world. My first teaching assignment was in a school of three hundred children; 93 percent of the students were Black, 3 percent were Asian and Native American, and 4 percent of the youngsters were White. All my students were either on reduced or free lunch.

Of the fourteen teachers at the school, only three had more than six years of teaching experience. Most of us were new or had been teaching for less than three years. There was an underlying atmosphere of frustration and hopelessness in the school, especially in the upper grades.

Most of the staff didn't think that I—a relatively quiet, young, and short Asian American woman (barely five feet tall)—would make it at this tough neighborhood school. The week after I took the job, the principal mentioned to me, "We had a knifing in the parking lot last year, so be sure to lock your car." I was definitely a greenhorn who would learn much from the school and parents in the neighborhood in the next year and a half.

As a beginning first-grade teacher, I was unaware that young children are sensitive to ethnic differences. The first days of the school year were spent in special orientation sessions: Small groups of first-graders came with their parents to become familiar with their new surroundings before attending school for an entire day. During one such session, I noticed a child and his mother huddled in discussion outside the classroom door. Finally, this mother came inside to speak with me. She said, "My son Rodney doesn't want to come in." My tension level beginning to rise, I wondered how I would coax this anxious body into the room. Politely, I asked her, "Is he scared?" "No," she said matter-of-factly. "Rodney says he doesn't want to come in because he can't speak Chinese!" At first, I didn't understand what she meant; I don't speak Chinese either. Then, I realized that peering into the room and seeing me, a Japanese American, the youngster assumed I was Chinese. I went over and spoke to Rodney, persuading him to join the other children. This misunderstanding, though easy to correct, demonstrates that Rodney, barely six years old, had already formed certain beliefs: First, that those with Asian physical features must be Chinese and not American, and that if I were Chinese, I would not speak English.

I wish I had been a more effective teacher. I didn't know where to begin. What did I need to learn? What changes did I need to make to be a better teacher? This is how my interest in multicultural education began.

Who are the Asian Americans? What characteristics do they share as a group? You did a pretty good job answering the question in the introduction to this chapter. Rather than talk about similarities, I would like to also emphasize our differences. Asian Americans are one of the most diverse groups that you will find in the world. There are more within-group differences than are between groups. They include people who come from the islands like the

Hawaiians, and that is why we refer to the broad group as Asian and Pacific Islanders. Chamorros, they are from Guam. There's the people from the Marshall Islands, Micronesia. Then, of course, the Asians who first came to the continental United States. The first group were Filipinos, who jumped ship from Spanish galleons in 1765. I think that's the right date. They just celebrated 225 years in this country. You'll find the documentation in Fred Cordova's book: *Filipinos, Forgotten Asians.* I think that is the title. And then Chinese immigrants who came in the mid-1800s. I always think of Ah Bing, after whom the Bing cherry is named. He was here in the 1850s and 1860s, working on the Lewelling farm in Milwaukie, Oregon. Seth Lewelling, the brother of the original orchardist, Henderson Lewelling, named the cherry after Bing, his Chinese foreman. So, there are a lot of other groups—the Japanese, they also came to the United States—but most immigration from other countries stopped in 1924 with the Asian Exclusion Act and didn't really start up again until 1965 with the new immigration act. That's when you get an influx of immigrants from Asia: more Filipinos, Koreans, and Southeast Asians. So, I would say it is also diversity that is a main theme within the Asian and Pacific Island American group, each with its own unique culture.

Could you talk about the various names Asian Americans use to describe or identify themselves and some of the names that have been used historically to identify the group by others?   As you know, Asians have been called Orientals. I think that term probably came from Westerners who went to China, Japan, and Korea when those countries were just opening up. At that time, it was referred to as the Orient. But as I tell my students, I am not a rug, so that's why I'm not an Oriental. I am an Asian because that denotes where my ancestors are from in a world context. And in the sixties, Yuji Ichioka from UCLA created the term *Asian American* because it was a description that we felt more signified who we are and is devoid of the negative connotation of terms such as Oriental and Yellow Peril. Many Asians in America prefer to be referred to by their country of origin.

Derogatory names are just part of the larger problem of racial discrimination and stereotyping and how children internalize them into their identities. Consider the words of Suzanne Akemi Negoro, a Japanese American female:

> In my junior high history class, I remember sitting in the rigid single desk, resting my feet on the bookrack of the desk in front of me. I always used to sink low in my seat, and on one particular day I was sinking even lower than normal as our teacher announced that it was Pearl Harbor Day. Usually anything that is given its own day is something that's good; there's Valentine's Day, Martin Luther King, Jr., Day, President's Day, Labor Day, and Independence Day. But Pearl Harbor Day is one of the few dark-designated days, left in the same camp with D-Day. This day not only marks the day that Japan bombed the United States; it also marks that

day that my family and other Japanese Americans officially became suspected traitors. Sitting in my junior high history class, this day also marked me. I can still picture the student in the row next to me leaning toward me and whispering, "So why'd you bomb us anyway?" Four generations and forty years, and not much had changed.

The biggest problem I had in dealing with this student's comment was my own inability to reconcile my cultural identity, both Japanese and American. I remember words from my childhood: being praised, "You speak so well; Your English is so good"; being questioned, "What are you anyway?" "No, what are you *really*?" and being criticized, "You don't speak Japanese? Why not?" "How sad that you've lost your language; How sad that you've lost your culture." I remember being about three feet tall with the voice of a mouse, trying to talk as loud as possible so that people could hear how well I spoke, that is, without an accent. I remember my years of adolescent female fun that always ended up matching me with the other Asian boy in the class. And I remember always wanting to be matched with every other boy but him. I wanted to prove to people that I was American, and to me that meant proving that I was White.

I was not, however, simply just trying to prove that I was White. I was simultaneously trying to prove that I was still "Japanese enough." As a child, the most difficult part was figuring what was enough (Pang, 2001, pp. 127–128).

It is a concern of mine that Asian Pacific American students are lumped together for purpose of demonstrating that they have no academic, social, or mental health needs. Scholars and the press have used APA students against other students of color when they utilize aggregate data that reinforces a stereotype that APA youth do not need help in school. APA students, like all groups, have strengths and weaknesses. When their needs are not being met in the classroom because schools and districts have not been under enough political pressure to address them, this shows a grave lack of equity in our educational system. There are many APA students who are failing in writing, reading, chemistry, physics, and math; they drop out of school. Unfortunately, this information is not often known or listened to by policymakers, superintendents, principals, teachers, and the general public.

Could you talk more about family and community and how these shape what happens in schools with Asian American students?   I think even though you don't want to overgeneralize, for Asian Pacific American children, family is probably the most important value. Family relationships are the core of how the child develops, how the child sees the world, how the child interprets the world, and how the child behaves in relation to the world. The family. Of course, there are many differences within families and across families. We are very aware of generational differences. Like I am third-generation in this country, but my children are now fourth-generation. There are also fifth-generation Asians as well as first and second. Each generation has its own values and concerns, relationships to each other, and position in the family. Depending upon the ethnic community one comes from, even though family form varies somewhat. Like Hawaiian and Samoan families focus more on the extended family. There are some more-assimilated Asian groups—maybe the Japanese— where the family form is the nuclear family. So, even though family as a theme is important, how we interpret its meaning might be slightly different. Though from an outsider looking in, one may not be really able to understand that. Within the Asian family, I think there is still a little bit more respect for elders and education than in other communities. But even this varies across groups. There are Asian groups who have come here—like the Hmong, still a preliterate people—for whom education in a formal sense is not something they are as oriented toward. But I know they are educated in the customs and the ways of their families. Children learn culture from their families. Families are holders and transmitters of culture. Let me share a story about a friend of mine:

> When Gerry was ten years old, he went to his grandmother's eightieth birthday party in Hawaii. The family had the party at a Chinese restaurant. Everyone was smiling and talking. Gerry sat at a round table with nine other people. He sat next to his Auntie Sara. This was a big birthday celebration, and so the family wanted to honor their grandmother with a nine-course dinner.
>
> Many years ago, Gerry's grandmother traveled to Hawaii from Canton, China, by ship when she was only fifteen years old. She was betrothed to his grandfather, who at that time was about twenty-five years old. The couple eventually had eight children. His grandfather died when Gerry was four years old and left his grandmother as matriarch of the family.
>
> In honor of the grandmother, the family had golden peach pins for everyone. Peaches symbolize long life, and so every family member was given not only pins but vases with peaches painted on the front panel.
>
> As each course was brought out to the table and served, Gerry became more full. He wanted to rest his stomach, so he stuck his chopsticks into his bowl of rice. The chopsticks stuck straight up. His Auntie Sara placed her hand on his shoulder and whispered, "Gerry, don't do that because it means death."
>
> Gerry quickly took the chopsticks from his bowl of rice and placed them on his white dinner plate; his face was slightly red because he was embarrassed. He knew children were not supposed to do anything to bring disgrace to their family. Just like in school, children were supposed to act properly.
>
> One of the nine courses was a noodle dish. Noodles are served at birthday parties in many Chinese and Chinese American families because they are long and therefore represent long life. When the large blue platter of noodles was pushed before Gerry on the table's lazy susan, he took the large spoon and began to put noodles on his plate. However, some noodles were falling off the serving place so he cut them with the spoon. His Auntie Sara frowned and leaned down toward Gerry, gently whispering in his ear. This time she said, "Gerry, don't cut your noodles or you will be cutting the life of your grandmother short." The

young man quickly scooped the noodles on to his plate and pushed the lazy susan toward the next diner.

In the course of the meal, each person was also given a small packet of dried coconut and fruit that had a sugar coating. The sweetness of the dessert represented more sweetness in life for his grandmother.... Gerry, like most children, learned values and beliefs besides other cultural elements like traditions and customs through social interactions with family members (Pang, 2001, pp. 7–8).

Are there any subpopulations in the Asian American community you feel deserve additional attention?   Each is unique in its own right, but Filipino Americans are a good example. They are one of the largest groups of Asian Pacific Americans, and people know little about them. Although there are hundreds of languages in the Philippines, Tagalog is one of the main ones. It should be taught in the schools, but it's not. In California, Filipinos are the single-largest Asian group. And yet, people and teachers and other service providers have very little knowledge of their experiences. And it's hard for Filipino kids—often because their parents are immigrants. They're first-generation and trying to make it, and the children are like a bridge between old ways and new ways. I know some girls are not allowed to go out at night or go out past ten o'clock even if they're older. I had a student, a senior in college, who couldn't go out past midnight. She had to have her parents' permission. She couldn't stay overnight at anybody else's house. So, it depends on the family. It depends on how traditional. Some Asian families are very traditional and others are not as traditional. I also think Filipino Americans are often invisible within the Asian Pacific American community.

How do these various differences you have been talking about affect the education of Asian Americans?   For those Asian families who believe strongly in education and formal education and brought that to the United States, their values are more apt to mesh with mainstream America. They tend to achieve in the schools. Members of Asian groups with less formal education have a harder time. But it's not necessarily the case that Asian Americans always are assimilated. It's just that, in some cases, their values may be in line with a more mainstream view of the world. They can still remain very traditional, but their traditional culture involves beliefs and values that allow a child to function naturally within the school environment.

What are some of the common problems that Asians face or bring into the school setting?   Well, some of the problems that they see—that the children see—is prejudice. If you look at the literature and you talk to children themselves, they will tell you that the level of prejudice that they feel that they experience in public schools is absolutely phenomenal. People will be calling them Cambodian, which is kind of like using the "n-word" in the way it is used on the playground. And they're often discriminated against because of physical differences. I mean, other kids have been taught racism at home, and unfortunately, Asian American children have to deal with this. Teachers deal with them differently also. Because of the model-minority myth, teachers may expect Asian kids to do well in topics or subject areas like math and sciences. And sometimes, they do do well, but what happens to the Asian child who doesn't do well in math, like me? Then, something must be wrong with you. This is a stereotype we also internalize, which creates a problem for those students who do not fit the mold.

Another area of concern is for Asian children whose family does not encourage them to articulate verbally what they think—who are taught to be deferential and quiet. When students who have been raised with this value go to school and are asked by teachers to join in the Socratic method and other discussions, they may find it difficult to participate due to shyness or a lack of practice in verbal communication style. It is the teacher's job to mentor and help them overcome these barriers and to do it in an emotionally sensitive way. Maybe they develop activities for the child, such as a short speech of a couple minutes by way of practice. Or if the child is scared of making a mistake. Let's say they're bilingual and unsure of their language skills in English. The teacher can record a short talk of theirs on videotape, show it to them, and also provide them the opportunity to re-record if they feel they're going to make a mistake. With such an opportunity, their anxiety won't be as high. I think Asian Pacific American children have anxiety—communication anxiety.

The literature also shows that often the written work of Asian children is not as developed as it could be. I don't think enough teachers encourage Asians to be novelists, to be poets, to be actors, to be musicians, any of the fine arts or creative arts kind of careers. They are rather pushed primarily into technical areas of computer science, physics, mathematics. There are, for example, lots of children from the Black community who are great dancers. Is that because, innately, those children have genes to dance well? No, they've been practicing that ever since they were born. Similarly, Asians have been pushed into more technical fields and have had more practice at it. They have been developing those skills. I'm sure that if we had the kids dancing too, they would be great dancers. It's just a matter of, first, cultural priorities and, second, the expectations that are placed around certain types of behavior.

I want to say a bit more about the invisibility of certain Asian and Pacific American students and the need for school districts to look at disaggregate statistics. You don't hear about the dropout rates of Samoans, though in San Diego it's something like 50 percent. They have one of the highest dropout rates of any ethnic group in San Diego. But if you look at the scores of all Asian kids put together, such realities become masked over. It is critical to understand the enormous diversity that exists within the Asian American community, the needs of certain groups, and the tendency to overlook such deficits because so many of us want to believe in the myth of the model minority. Another area I want to allude to is mental health. There's a lot of alcoholism in Asian communities that people don't know about. There are also problems with self-image among our students. I did my dissertation on physical self-image in Asian American children. I looked at body image in Japanese American and Caucasian kids. Asian American kids in general may not like the way they look. They don't think they're tall enough. They don't like the shape of their eyes. The girls don't have big enough breasts. But this information gets lost with a broad analysis. If you use a general measure of self-concept where you can't separate out body image, you might not see a significant difference between White kids and Asians. Feeling good about academics or one's family may cover over the lower body image scores. Also, because of the diversity that exists across Asian American groups, it is important to not lump all Asian group members together in the analysis.

Teachers also may have little knowledge about the differences between Asian Pacific American communities. An educator shared with me that in a diverse school where the majority population consists of Students of Color—African American, Latino, and Asian—a Teacher of Color called all Asians by a derogatory Spanish term that means Chinese. However, the educator reminded his colleague that the children are from many different Asian backgrounds. The students represented families who were Northern Vietnamese, Central Vietnamese (Hue), and Southern Vietnamese, Cambodian, Lao, Hmong, Burmese, Chamorro, Cantonese-speaking Chinese, Mandarin-speaking Chinese, and Filipino. There is no one Asian Pacific American culture. There are Asians and Pacific Islanders from many states and countries in the world.

This leads to the next question. Could you discuss some of the factors you see as important in assessing the learning style of Asian American students and what environmental factors could be manipulated to match these styles? There is some research that Clara Park did on Asian American learning style. She felt that Asian students liked demonstrations but that teachers tended to use the blackboard a lot. Whenever the teacher spoke and tried to explain a concept, she would write a definition or create a graphic or a map or a model. Whatever she did, it was visual. So, in order to learn with this teacher, the kids need to be able to relate to visual representation. I think Asian American kids would benefit from hands-on methods that—unfortunately—are used least in our schools. Schools generally depend on paper and pencil–type activities, even though most kids remember more information and can process more comprehensively with a hands-on demonstration or modeling.

Say we do an experiment and then the child is given the hands-on opportunity to repeat it. What happens? My preservice students do a lot of work out in the field with kids. One of the activities they've used is making bubbles to teach the concept of surface tension. They ask the children what shapes makes the best bubbles and why is the bubble round? Talking about this is one thing, but what they did was actually go into a kitchen and try out different things as bubble makers. They tried a strainer, etc. I can't remember all the things they used. One student brought a tennis racket whose holes are square, and the teacher asked, "What do you think?" One child said, "I still think it's going to be round." But why? He wasn't sure. So, he tried the tennis racket, and it was "Ah, ha! They are round," and so that led to more discussion. Then, the issue of surface tension was introduced. When you press on the bubble, it pops because the balance of the surface tension is weak. But students don't learn as much unless they can interact directly with the materials. You can tell them all you want about surface tension, but if you don't have them actually making the bubbles and blowing them all over the playground, they don't really quite understand it. Ninety-eight percent of children, especially Asian children, like hands-on activities.

I would also like to say something about teaching students—and also teachers perhaps—about what culture is. How do we give them an appreciation for its depth, complexity, and interconnectedness. Ramon Valle provides a multidimensional model to explain culture. Culture is defined by Valle as having three layers: language, symbols, and artifacts; customs, practices, and interactional patterns; and shared values, norms, beliefs, and expectations. These three levels can also be described as means of communication, means of interaction, and values driving people [and] groups. Culture is made up of many elements, and together, they make an integrated whole. Separating culture into distinct elements—as we often do in the classroom—tends to fragment it.

There are many aspects of culture that may be invisible. In caring-centered multicultural education, teachers know that culture is an important aspect of children's lives. They try to "unpack" the layers of culture and identify what children respond to and understand in human relationships. Remember Gerry's experience at his grandmother's birthday party. Gerry was learning the meanings behind many symbols in his family culture. He gained a better understanding of what behaviors were expected of him and why. His Auntie Sara helped him to "unpack" what was going on and what was expected of him in the cultural context of his family. She explained what to do and the reasons why.

Teachers must also learn to make these connections themselves and help their students to do so. My daughter learned these lessons through origami—Japanese paper folding. Origami represents not only the tangible product of a culture but also interactional patterns and underlying values. To provide students with a more complete understanding of culture, teachers must share with them not only the how-to sequence of folding but explain how it is an art form that reinforces the importance of observational skills, working with others, and patience, and it represents simple beauty. Using a single piece of paper, a person can create a myriad of objects and artistic expressions. There are various levels of cultural significance.

Most importantly, I think it is important for educators to understand that Asian Pacific Americans perform significantly differently on standardized tests. In December of 2009, at the annual California Association of School Boards in San Diego, my team of researchers presented statistical analyses that demonstrated that in California, the achievement pattern of these groups showed their diversity. In addition, the data verified that there are many Asian Pacific American students who need educational tutoring and more effective teaching in schools. We analyzed the performance of over five million students who took the California Achievement Tests from 2003 to 2008 in third and seventh grades. A major finding is that Cambodian, Laotian, Samoa, and Hawaiian students do not do as well as Caucasian, Chinese American, and Japanese American students in reading and math. Much financial support has been devoted to the achievement of Latino and Black students, and there are also Asian Pacific American students who also would benefit from these programs.

Considering cultural differences and learning styles, what suggestions might you have regarding establishing rapport with Asian American students and families?
Since family is a core value, relationship-building is important. Even though there are many people who feel that the Asian respect for teachers has become almost stereotypical, I still believe it is true. For most children in the Asian Pacific American family—as in many other communities—the teacher is still seen as a respected and revered person. Even though a child may not necessarily always act in that way, they still know that the teacher is a person to be treated deferentially and always kept at a distance. So, I think it's absolutely critical that teachers develop relationships—trusting relationships where they actually talk to the kids—and find out about their dreams, their disappointments, and their needs. Such open dialogue is quite important because the kids are dying to get to know the teacher more closely. Because they're seen as so quiet or as the model minority, the teacher may overlook them and not spend the time that they really should have in developing a personal connection. Every child needs that relationship, and I think it's even more so with Asians because of their family background and because they're seen so often as invisible. They're the good kids. We don't have to spend so much time because they do not seem as needy or disruptive or demanding of attention.

You also have Asians students I would not consider the most upstanding citizens, but that is more rare. They may be getting straight As in school but are gang members in the evenings. So, all this is extremely complex, and merely giving a teacher a book on Asian American values is not going to do it. Because not only are Asian groups different, but each family is different and then there are individual student differences. And the context of where the child lives and all the groups that they're interacting with impact who they are and how they define themselves and how they act. There are Asian kids who know how to use the stereotype too. There's research that shows that Asian students know teachers think of them as model minority, so they'll pretend that they're behaving when they're really not. Someone else is likely to be the one that gets in trouble. Maybe the Black child, maybe the Latino child, a different child more likely to be seen stereotypically as acting out. But if you are a smart child, you know, and you use all of your abilities and cultural knowledge to get by in school.

I want to re-emphasize relationship-building because a teacher can really have so much more power in motivating and mentoring when the kid trusts you. But teachers don't realize this. Because society does not reward them, teachers often feel unimportant in the general scheme of things. But children are still coming to school every day. That says a whole lot. They're still sitting in that classroom even if it's so unbelievably boring sometimes. There is always hope; kids are always hoping for something more. Kids are also going there because of their friends. But there they are, waiting to get engaged—to get empowered. You as a teacher can send them out with knowledge and life skills so they can live and make life better when you're not there anymore. You're trying to give them the skills and the attitude and the philosophy so that they can work with anybody in all types of situations, so they can create a more compassionate, just, and happy place for all of us. We often forget about that happiness—that joy. Life is supposed to be like that! Not a burden. Not always suffering.

CHAPTER 14

Working with Arab and Muslim Americans

An Interview with Karim Hamdy

"The onus is on the educators because they are the ones who are adults, who are trained to convey knowledge, how to allow for questioning, and everything else, to make sure their worldview does not intimidate or ignore the different viewpoint, the different background that the learner brings in."

—Karim Hamdy

Demographics

Muslim and Arab Americans present many distinctive cultural, traditional, linguistic, and religious sets of features. It is important to talk "sets of features" rather than features because of the great diversity within and between these groups (El-Badry, 2001). A clear understanding of this multiple diversity—within and between—may be one of the two most critical factors that would help U.S. educators succeed in their interactions with learners from these backgrounds.

The other factor is the unenviable "group of interest" stigma imposed by the U.S. media on these groups for the past five decades—a stigma exacerbated by the events of 9/11 and their aftermath and deepened even more following the U.S. invasion of Iraq in 2003. Neither the religion of Islam nor the Arabic language unites U.S. pupils and students whose ancestry is from what is referred to as the Arab world or the Islamic world. In many instances, quite the opposite is the case. A student of Christian Lebanese descent shares very little with a classmate from an Iranian Shi'a Muslim background or with a child whose parents are Nation of Islam African Americans, except for the externally imposed stigma they all confront.

Ethnic, racial, and religious classifications are predictably fraught with inaccuracy and tentativeness. The same is true when referring to Arab Americans and Muslim Americans. We have the impression that these two designators refer to two specific groups in the United States—each distinct from the other—until we focus a bit more carefully on the ethnic characteristics of these groups. In addition to an obvious overlap between the two groups—that is, Arab Americans who happen to be Muslims (about 24 percent according to 2000 census data)—we also have the even more important fact that Muslim Americans are a much larger group, which includes such non-Arabs such as Iranians, Turks, Pakistanis, Indians, and Indonesians—just to name a few national origins of Muslims from outside the Arab region. So, even before getting into complicating geopolitical factors, we already have two important but confusing factors when we deal with Arabs and Muslims in the United States: (1) the fact that only one in five Arab Americans is Muslim and (2) the fact that all Arab Americans combined represent just a fraction of a larger Muslim American community.

While it is important to develop some reasonable shorthand classifications of students' cultural backgrounds, educators are encouraged to keep in mind the overriding diversity of each community, both to help you succeed in your instructional mission but also not to alienate some of your charges by committing avoidable blunders. The quick answers about the size of these populations can be taken from the 2000 census and from recent survey numbers:

- 1.25 to 3.5 million Arab Americans
- 1.1 to 7.0 million Muslim Americans

The wide gaps between low and high estimates are a reflection of the politically charged nature of these estimates. For the purposes of this essay, we suggest using the working estimates for 2008:

- Arab Americans: 3 million
- Muslim Americans: 5 million

We have to recognize that the U.S. Census Bureau does not provide an Arab classification option nor does it request religious affiliation in the short census form. Because the court decisions of 1913–1917 about Syrian immigrants, administratively, citizens and residents of the United States who come from the Middle East and North Africa are classified as "White." In what follows, we will discuss Muslims and Arabs in the United States under these two major classifications, provide important demographic data and other facts about them, and emphasize that one has to maintain the caution about the "within and in between" diversity of these American communities.

About one-third of Arab Americans are of Lebanese origin, and about half of all Arab Americans have ancestry in just four Arab countries (of a total of 22 Arab countries). The unaffiliated categories "Arab" or "Arabic" as well as "Other Arab" percentage from the U.S. Census Bureau from 2000 shows 29 percent of

Muslim Americans: Who Are They?	
	Total
proportion who are ...	%
Foreign-born Muslims	65
Arab region	24
Pakistan	8
Other South Asia	10
Iran	8
Europe	5
Other Africa	4
Other	6
Native-born Muslims	35
African American	20
Other	15
	100
Foreign-born Muslims	65
Year immigrated:	
2000–2007	18
1990–1999	21
1980–1989	15
Before 1980	11
Native-born Muslims	35
Percent who are ...	
Converts to Islam	21
Born Muslim	14

Source: Pew Social and Demographic Trends

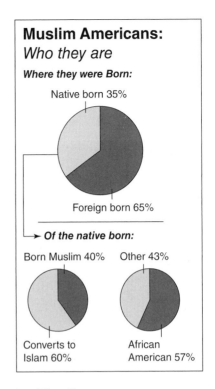

FIGURE 14.1 Muslim Americans: Who Are They?

Source: Pew Research Center, *Muslim American: Middle Class and Mostly Mainstream*, http://pewsocialtrends.org/pubs/483/muslim-americans, Copyright © 2007 Pew Research Center.

self-identified Arab Americans who did not specify which Arab country they consider to be their ancestral home. They (or their parents) may have migrated in two or more stages (to Europe and then the United States, for example).

The table and the pie charts about Muslim Americans in Figure 14.1 tell a different story. For example, a larger percentage of Muslim Americans come from the non-Arab regions of Pakistan, Iran, and Other South Asia than from Arab countries. The same applies to native-born Muslims (65 percent), of whom more than half are converts to Islam and more than half are African American (converts and descendents of Muslims).

Family and Cultural Values

Some character features and beliefs often found among Arab Americans are:

- The family is very important and everyone loves children.
- Men and women are different and complementary.

- The older you are, the wiser you are.
- Beyond a certain degree of striving, the person should accept what comes his or her way.
- Dignity, honor, and reputation are more valuable than material success.
- Honor (or shame) is collective and can affect the community, particularly one's family.
- Group solidarity is more important than individual advantage or success.
- Individuals must strive, but much depends on God's will.
- Arab cultural heritage is rich, and one can be proud of it.
- The Arab region suffered excessively from colonialism and exploitation.
- Total assimilation may be harmful to family mores.
- Arabs are wrongly stigmatized, and Western media is biased against Islam and against their culture.

Religion and Tradition

Sixty-three percent of Arab Americans are Christian. Only 24 percent are Muslim. The Christian segment includes the denomination "Orthodox," which is an Eastern Christian church older than Protestantism. Other religious communities have lived in the Arab and Muslim regions of the world. Some of them have migrated to the United States; hence, the presence of Arab Jewish Americans, Bahai Americans, Druze Americans, etc.

However, the religious factor may not be a good predictor of the main family values. In general, Arab families are tightly knit well beyond the nuclear family itself. Christian and Muslim Arabs alike may keep a family-oriented way of conducting their lives while adapting to their immigrant environment in the United states. Generationally, there is often slow but predictable erosion of certain traditional and somewhat conservative features. This conservatism would manifest itself in gender relations and the dynamic between men and women, which are affected by the mores of the host culture, and the requirements of economic struggle for survival and success. That often leads many Muslim American families to adapt, finding ways of doing things that may be quite different from what life in the former homeland taught the elders. Perhaps the most apparent change is the move to a more nuclear family, given the distance separating them from the community in their ancestral homelands and the high degree of mobility in American life. This is not to say that there would not be residual features.

Educators are well-advised to observe, listen, and inquire to discover what degree of adaptation/assimilation (or lack thereof) their students present in their behavior at school. Some male students may exhibit a typical patriarchal behavior of "protectiveness" toward female siblings and other close relatives that could be perceived as attempts to control. Just as in the case of social workers, the cultural competency of educators could make a big difference in engaging students of Muslim and Arab backgrounds. It may look like an uphill battle, struggling against multifaceted stereotyping based on media often irresponsible frenzies over terrorism incidents and the Iraq invasion, as well as over the Israeli-Palestinian long-lasting conflict.

Education

Arab Americans have a strong commitment to family and to educational and economic achievement. Ninety-four percent of Arab Americans live in metropolitan areas, and 85 percent of them completed a high school diploma. Forty percent of them have a college degree (compared to 24 percent for the overall United States), 17 percent of them have a postgraduate degree (9 percent for the overall United States). Eighty-eight percent of them work in the private sector. Their median income was $47,000 in 1999 (higher by $5,000 than the overall per capita income in the United States). Arab Americans are younger, more educated, more affluent, and more likely to own a business (El-Badry, 2001).

The involvement of parents in their children's schooling is not foreign to immigrant Arab American parents. However, as in the case of many recent immigrants, the language gap may be a deterrent. First-generation and recent immigrants in general may find it difficult to participate in an American PTA organization. Their own children would speak English more fluently—or even as a native tongue—with no accent and may be reluctant to have their parents encounter schoolmates and school officials. This situation is not unlike any other minority.

However, unlike other minorities—say, Latinos or Chinese—the traditional appearance of Arab American parents (if they maintain the use of distinctive dress in the United States) might be a particularly difficult feature for the schoolchild to share with others, given the frequently virulent vilification, bordering on racist slander, of things Arab and Muslim, by the media and by popular culture, that stigmatizes the collective groups (Shaheen, 2001).

As stated at the beginning of this section, Arab Americans have an overall higher level of education across the board. They also have a higher median income and tend be employed in the private sector close to 90 percent of the time. Both Arab and Muslim Americans are mostly middle class and mainstream. About two-thirds of self-employed Arab Americans own incorporated business—more than twice the overall U.S. average. The proportion of Arab Americans engaged in sales (33 percent) is twice the national average. Many Arab and Muslim Americans have achieved great success in business, in the arts, and in sports. Educators would be better prepared to help their students if they learned about the careers of such Arab Americans as the dean of White House correspondent Helen Thomas, boxer Muhammad Ali, ABC News anchor

Christiane Amanpour, music historian Casey Kasem, astronaut-educator Christa McAuliffe, Ford Corp CEO Jacques Nasser, football star Doug Flutie, former senator George Mitchell, former White House chief of staff John Sununu, etc.

American educators may be justified in not knowing enough about their Arab American and Muslim American students. It is the least studied ethnicity and the most stereotyped religion. The fact that the same group is at least subliminally associated with the considerable publicity their region of origin receives in the coverage of political and economic events (war and oil) makes educators even more uneasy about the presence of these "ethnic" students in their classrooms. How can they help their students go beyond the defensiveness forced upon them? Through guilt by association? The broad strokes used by the media in their coverage of violence, war, and economic turmoil as well as the lack of information are two major reasons the educators may have a tough time playing their role efficiently.

Our work as educators is to provide a safe place for our Muslim students and an informed education about Muslim and Arab individuals and families to those we influence in the schools and without. Our guest expert, Karim Hamdy, wrote the demographics and family and cultural values above in an essay that I have edited; his original essay appears on our companion website with additional graphics. In the following interview Dr. Hamdy gives us both personal and professional insights into understanding and working with these communities and children.

Our Interviewee

Karim Hamdy is the director of the Study Abroad Program in Tunis for the Oregon University System. Karim, who was originally trained as a civil and environmental engineer, has a long-term association with Oregon State University, first as a graduate student and later as a project manager and instructor. He took additional training in education and taught Arabic and French at Oregon State. Karim has published papers on "Islam and the Environment," on "Online Polemics over Islam," and on "Edward Said and Arab Intellectuals." He also published English translations of French novels (jointly with Laura Rice). His current research projects are on "Water Wars in the Middle East" and on "Globalization and ISO 14000 Certification."

The Interview

Can you begin by talking about your own ethnic background and how it has impacted you and your work?   Well, I happen to be born in a country by the name of Tunisia, which makes me an Arab and a Muslim by background. Tunisia being in North Africa, it is a place of diverse historical backgrounds, including Arabs, Berbers, and other groups, but the majority speak Arabic and consider Islam to be their religion. In terms of impact, actually it goes without saying that moving to the United States a quarter century ago, within a short time of doing that, I discovered that I needed to study my own history a bit more carefully to be able to respond to inquiries by interested friends and neighbors and classmates when I was a graduate student, but at the same time, it was even more critical because overall ... there has been already in the 80s when I arrived—the early 80s—there was an issue with misrepresentation of my culture for political reasons, with the nations that are Muslim, of who is an Arab and what features there are in terms of behavior and cultural background, and unfortunately, it only got worse after September 11th, which we will probably get to again when you to ask me other questions.

Who are the Muslim Americans, and what characteristics do they share as a group? To start off, it would be the religion that they share. Muslim Americans are a complex group because there are many—particularly African Americans— who happen to be Muslim. So, born here with a legacy of slavery or otherwise, but there are also more than four million Muslims who either are first-generation immigrants from Muslim countries around the world from Morocco all the way to Indonesia or second-, third-, fourth-generation, which means their ancestors or parents had immigrated and they themselves where born here, so that's really the diverse group of many languages and traditions in addition to their backgrounds and cultures.

Certain traditional values of Arabs and Muslims—with regard to family, community, and religion observance—are quite similar to those of some other minorities. However, two critical differences stand out and have to be seriously considered when dealing with Arab and Muslim American students. First, there is the fact that in federal statutes, no legal classification as a minority exists for either Arab or Muslim. This absence of administrative and legal recognition as a community has led to undercounting them in censuses (by a factor of three) and to their neglect in demographic and other group-centered social studies and surveys; hence, the lack of data to help us understand who the Arabs and the Muslim are. Second, there is the unwanted and traumatizing situation of being associated with terrorism and war and being perceived—irrationally—as potential threats to the United States. Those two peculiarities make it even harder for educators to equip themselves with the necessary information to understand the cultural background of Arab and Muslim students in the classroom. The confusion is made even worse by frequent publications produced by self-appointed "researchers" and pundits in ideologically loaded think tanks and media outlets. These "researchers" have a vested interest in reaching preset conclusions that justify fear of Islam and of Arabs. Educators may be at a loss trying to navigate the torrent of polemical literatures claiming to explain who

Arabs and Muslims are, how many of them live in the United States, and what makes them tick. The opposite situation is also equally problematic. Some of the pundits and "researchers" who attempt to counter the Islamophobic torrent of literature online, on TV, in the movies, and in all media may go overboard at times in their defensiveness, crossing into the territory of unjustified and unhelpful apology and bias. Even the vocabulary to describe these groups is a contested territory: Although—just like Jewish Americans—the great majority of Arab Americans are of Semitic origin, the word anti-Semitism and its derivatives do not apply to prejudice against them. The civil rights advocates of the larger group—Muslim Americans—have coined a new phrase to refer to anti-Muslim prejudice: Islamophobia—a well-justified move. However, even the latest versions of word-processing software (MS Word 2007) do not acknowledge it. The accusations, the prejudice, and the sweeping generalizations about Muslim Americans and about their religion are often borne by Muslim self-portraits.

Could you talk about the various names that Muslim Americans use to describe and identify themselves and some of the names that have been used historically to describe and identify the group? I guess maybe we need to be careful in terms of naming what is legitimate and what is pejorative (i.e., illegitimate). I'll start with by talking about legitimate ways of referring to ourselves and how others refer to us as Muslim Americans under the umbrella phrase Muslim American. As I started explaining earlier, we have Muslims from Tunisia, like I am, or Arabs like also I am, but we do have Muslim Americans from many, many regions of the world plus the natives, particularly African Americans and the smaller number of converts from White and Latinos and others. The phrase I prefer personally that people use is "Muslim Americans" to emphasize citizenship and democratic participation and having the religion be a feature, not a dominant part of who a Muslim American is. We refer to ourselves, depending on our origins, sometimes as Arab Americans, Arabs, Muslims, Asian American; these are the legitimate ways—the phrases that do not cause difficulty in terms of having racist baggage. I don't think there is a need for us to discuss the pejorative phrases.

You mentioned September 11, 2001, earlier. Could you elaborate on that because that has highlighted the Muslim American community? I think it has and in a very negative case—unfortunately. I believe one way of looking at it is comparatively: Our society in the United States has made great strides toward more justice, more acceptance of diversity, and less denigration of People of Color. I'm not saying denigration and racism have disappeared, but there are great strides toward improvement with regard to African Americans, Latinos, and some other minorities—Asian Americans and, of course, Native Americans.

When it comes to Muslim Americans, Arab Americans—whether they be natives of this land from generations ago or new arrivals—they sort of have been made to feel like they don't belong, and September 11, came to exacerbate that feeling, and I'll just share with you a few examples. On September 12—the day after the tragedy that happened in New York, Washington, and Pennsylvania—there are Whites who had the bravery to publish articles telling Americans that the United States should not go into the slippery slope of easy racism because we were angry at what happened and who did commit the tragedy. An example of something I just saw again today [an article from September 12] says "refuse and resist anti-Arab, anti-Muslim racism." Unfortunately, that was September 12, and the writer is to be commended for their bravery. Now, when you go to today, July 9, 2007, I have another article that is in the opposite way six years after the tragedy. We find, for example, an inflammatory headline that came out today that says, "Muslims declare sovereignty over U.S. and U.K." It sounds meaningless. I read the article; it is by an ultra-conservative right-wing outfit, and thanks to the Internet, anyone can publish without any control of quality and legitimacy. "Muslims declare sovereignty over U.S. and U.K." makes the reader who is uninformed extremely scared, and it is totally meaningless, but the impact is there, so six years after the tragedy, the public discourse and the media are really very mixed, and the impact on my community as a Muslim American is still felt strongly.

Can you talk more about family and community and just how these shape what happens in schools with Muslim American students? That's an issue that Muslim Americans face as a community within the larger society of the United States—and that's families. It's the occasional or frequent discrepancy between traditions brought with them based on religion or societal traditions that are related to religion and how they are trying to survive within a new society that has a total separation of church and state. But at the same time, heads of households—men or women—feel a great attachment to their culture of origin and would like to raise their children with full respect toward those traditions, and there is an occasional clash there between what the parents want for their kids and what their kids see and encounter through peers, teachers, and the educational system. The mixing of the two does not occur smoothly, and parents fear what is a potential alienation between them and their children, and actually, the alienation does happen. I know of a family in Seattle where the father is a religious leader, and the mother was a stay-at-home mom, and the children were raised with full respect of religious edicts because the father—the leader of the household—is a religious man. Well, fifteen years later, the kids are adults, and they rebel against what the father thought would be the "straight path" to goodness—to being a positive, productive member of the community. One of the children— born in Seattle and raised in Seattle— had been going to a mosque with their parents maybe since age seven or eight. Within fifteen years, they quit, and they declared sometimes that they are more than skeptics about Islam; perhaps they don't believe in the Muslim message anymore. And that is tragic for the dynamic of the family. Of course, people here are free to pursue what they come to believe in as rational individuals who learn from the education system and from society. But at the same time, educators who have Muslim American kids in their classrooms have to be really sensitive to the fact that they are struggling, and they may be confused, and the message the educator has is probably good in general but not universal in the sense that discarding what the children bring with them to school should not be a solution to adopt. Giving them a chance to voice their concerns, plus even their confusion and help them slowly and carefully to discover their new identity that has maybe a mixture of tradition and new cultural elements.

Are there any subpopulations in the Muslim American community that deserve additional attention?   Let's start by saying the Muslim population in America is probably as diverse as a big cross-section of society in general given that, as I said in the beginning, they came from various regions, and they keep links with family back in their countries of origin. So, yes, there are subgroups of Muslim populations. Arabic speakers could be considered one subpopulation— that's one way. The other way would be Asian Muslims who are American citizens or permanent residents or live here, are members of society here, and are quite different from Arab Americans. Within Arab Americans themselves, not everyone is a Muslim, which tells us already that "Muslim Americans," while it is broad enough to cover the majority, does not cover the Christians from Lebanon, or Syria, or Egypt. Other subpopulations would be different sects within the religion itself. You may have a couple of students who are Shi'a Muslims—citizens of this country—and their classmates—three or four of them—are Sunni. And those are differences that we don't expect a teacher to be conversant in. The details and nuances of the differences are difficult to discern, but awareness of the basics would be a plus to help avoid conflict and treat people equally.

How do different cultural styles, values, and worldviews affect education of Muslim Americans?   Worldview of the learner is one thing—not necessarily to be respected as is because, after all, adult educators are molding the minds and personality of the learner in combination with the efforts of the family, community, church, clubs, and everything else. The worldview of the teacher is also important, and the two worldviews are meant to contribute to the discourse between teacher and learner, not the class. And the onus is on the educators actually because they are the ones who are adults—who are trained to convey knowledge, how to allow for questioning, and everything to make sure their worldview does not intimidate or ignore the different viewpoint and the different background that the learner brings in. We are talking about Muslim American children in this case. Unfortunately, again, in the United States, I wouldn't be surprised if we conducted a survey to find out that teachers are in the rat race like everybody else and end up getting their news from mainstream media. Mainstream media, in my view, is guilty of gross misrepresentation of Muslim and Arab cultures, which leads to a backlash, which ought to be avoided between the worldviews of the learner and the teacher.

Any more on the cultural styles and values of Muslim Americans?   There is. We will have to resist stereotypes in general, and it's clear that we need to educate ourselves about the learning styles of the children we have in class. There is a stereotype that may have a small grain of truth—that people who come from Egypt, Tunisia, India, or other Muslim places ... have a tradition of rote learning—for example, particularly in grade school or preschool, sometimes referred to as madrasa in Muslim regions. Rote learning is looked down upon by many educators—the fact is it probably should be a combination of things: the idea of learning by doing, experiential learning, and other features of how to make sure that the learning happens while the children are enjoying themselves should be combined with a minimum of acquisition— not necessarily advocating rote learning but the idea of the basics of what the big features of the culture are should be included. People should be taught to be conversant in the American culture as much as learning by doing, but the diverse learning styles within the Muslim American group must be similar, I believe, to the diversity of the others other than very special cases of individual difficulties.

Any other common problems that Muslim Americans face or bring in to the school setting?   Maybe focus a bit on ... first-generation, second-generation learners—children whose knowledge of the language, for example, is not up to par with native speakers. There are literally tens of thousands of Muslim Americans who go to school—say, for example, ages 15–17 who just arrived five years ago; some arrived maybe ten years ago—still, they started learning English at age five, ten, or twelve, and it is not the same as somebody who knows English as a mother tongue and sometimes nothing else. That's when there may be other issues with food restrictions in schools, like the Muslim kid is taught at home not to eat pork, or other examples of halal food—like kosher food for Jews, there is halal food for Muslims. In some communities ... in the United States where there are good concentrations of Muslim Americans, school districts actually have started doing a good job of responding to that in a positive way. Where the problem arises is we have small numbers, like in Corvallis, Oregon—or other small little towns—who have, say, a couple dozen kids who go to three different schools, and they are always in the minority—less than 1 percent of the student body ... and that is another feature of a difficulty confronting Muslim Americans.

Considering the learning styles you have talked about and considering cultural differences, what suggestions might you have regarding establishing rapport with Muslim American students and families? I like for example the PTA system that I have read about. I haven't really experienced it myself, but I like the parent/teacher association method of having interaction between educators and the kids and their parents. I believe the association itself and the education system should make an extra effort to show that inclusion is the name of the game—that both the minority student of Muslim background and their parents to the extent that is feasible are welcome—are absolutely as welcome as others to participate, to give an opinion, to share what difficulties they have. The teachers should really have a proactive attitude about reaching out to the Muslim American community through the parents, through their own groups, going to their mosque if there is a mosque, talking to their leaders if there are leaders of the community, probably also smartly building their knowledge base to avoid reinventing the wheel repeatedly. If there is a turnover in teachers in the institution—be it a school, a school district, or other structure—someone should be developing a database of expertise and knowledge of how to deal with the group rather than leaving it to the individual initiative of the teacher, who—once they take off—take the knowledge with them.

CHAPTER 15

Working with European American Students

An Interaction with Christine Sleeter

"One can understand Euro-Americans today as an ethnic group in its own right, sharing common threads of history and experiences within the United States."

—Christine Sleeter

Background

When asked to describe themselves in ethnic or cultural terms, White Americans commonly draw a blank. An ethnographic study of White students in two high schools offers a good example. Perry (2002) found the students were puzzled when asked about their ethnic identity. Those in a school that was predominantly White were never asked to think about it and consequently had difficulty applying the concepts of race, ethnicity, and culture to themselves. Those in a school that was multiracial—where culture and ethnicity were talked about— viewed these concepts as irrelevant to themselves, seeing culture and ethnicity as attachment to a past in which they were not interested. Similarly, Frankenberg (1993) found that while White women could describe "others" as cultural, their own identity remained "amorphous and indescribable" (p. 196). To varying degrees, they could name European ancestral roots, but most saw these as relatively insignificant to their identity. In addition, while they were aware of and uncomfortable with racial inequality, they lacked knowledge with which to examine it other than "long-established modes of cultural description" (p. 196).

White people usually take ethnicity to mean that which is *not* White Anglo-Saxon Protestant and culture as something rooted in the "old country" (Sleeter, 2001). Euro-Americans that were surveyed to find out how they think about ethnic identity and culture confirmed that most regard it as fairly insignificant (Alba, 1990; Waters, 1990). Those who found ethnicity significant saw it primarily as a source of enrichment or uniqueness, expressed mainly through food, customs, family celebrations, festivals, and words or phrases from a heritage language. In fact, these kinds of expressions of culture are what Americans commonly view as the totality of culture. Ethnicity provides a language with which to talk about extended family. For many people, ethnic identity makes them feel special and links them loosely to a community without actually disrupting individualism by making demands on them (Waters, 1990).

If most White people think of themselves as not having much significant culture or ethnicity, how then might White teachers and students think about cultural competence? This question is especially difficult to consider while also grappling with White privilege. For example, White teachers "longed for a positive white identity, but lamented the fact that a negative white identity seemed to be the only kind of cultural or racial self available to them" (Marx, 2006, p. 89).

Actually, Euro-Americans do have ethnicity and culture but usually do not understand these concepts well enough to use them. Chapter 4 of this book discusses White privilege, which is a part of everyday experience that White people often do not see or want to see. Culture and ethnicity are also useful constructs to understand and may provide a sense of self from which White people can confront racism and White privilege.

According to De Vos (1995), "an ethnic group is a self-perceived inclusion of those who hold in common a set of traditions not shared by others with whom they are in contact" (p. 18). Ethnicity is a "subjective sense of belonging" to a collective that "extends beyond the self" and that has "historical continuity" (p. 25). Ethnic groups are not fixed but instead evolve over time; ethnic identity "is a continually evolving social process" (p. 17). A distinction between ancestry and ethnicity is useful because these are not necessarily the same (Lieberson, 1985). Ancestry refers to one's forebears' nations of origin, while ethnic identity refers to how individuals identify their ethnic backgrounds today. For Euro-Americans whose ancestry is dispersed and generations removed from Europe, the evolving nature of ethnicity is important to recognize. One can understand Euro-Americans today as an ethnic group in its own right, sharing common threads of history and experiences within the United States.

Euro-American ethnicity has been evolving for generations. European immigrants during the 1700s and early 1800s generally arrived identifying with towns or regions (such as Cornwall, Kerry, or Calabrese) rather than with nations; indeed, nations as we know them today, such as Germany and Italy, did not yet exist (Novak, 1996). For example, at the time of massive German immigration to the United States, Germans were in the process of shifting from seeing themselves as Prussians, Hessians, or Sachsens to seeing themselves as Germans.

"Hyphenated" White ethnics—mainly people of Eastern and Southern European descent who share a common experience of relatively recent immigration to the United States—include Italian-Americans, Polish-Americans, Greek-Americans, Jewish-Americans, and so forth. These groups had long histories of oppression and racial hatred in their native lands, were met with suspicion and rejection as newly arrived immigrants, and for a generation or two were exploited as cheap labor. Today, there are strong pockets of intact traditional culture within each of the hyphenated White ethnic communities, although many descendants have taken the path of complete and irreversible assimilation. Because of their darker physical features and appearance of many, Whites of Southern or Eastern European descent were viewed as non-White by Western Europeans and thus rejected both religiously and racially.

White ethnic groups have also formed—or are forming—entirely within the United States. Appalachian ethnicity is probably the best example. The U.S. Census Bureau does not include Appalachian as an ethnic category, but on the 2000 census, 11,945 people wrote it in. Increasingly, scholars argue that there is a distinct Appalachian culture and ethnic identity. While richly varied, Appalachian culture, is unique to the Appalachian region where it developed; one of the most prominent elements that is widely recognized today is country music (Biggers, 2006).

Euro-Americans of mixed descent (such as German-British)—who constitute the majority of White Americans—generally do not define themselves in relationship to Europe, particularly if they have multiple national origins in their family history. Knowledge of ancestry becomes blurred and distorted over time in a society that is highly individualistic and mobile and in which not only is there considerable interethnic marriage, but marriage itself is not permanent. The growing proportion of the White population that has lost knowledge of its ancestral origins entirely may be called "unhyphenated Whites" (Lieberson, 1985).

To probe into Euro-American ethnic culture, we must return to the concept of culture itself. Chapter 5 discusses deeper aspects of culture that people often take for granted as "normal" or "how things are," especially when they are members of the dominant social group. Trying to understand ethnic culture by itemizing elements like food and holidays maintains the idea of culture as something static, brought from elsewhere, to be memorized and hauled out when the occasion demands. A more useful approach is to start with the culture that one has learned in the family. Students can use Grant and Sleeter's (2007, p. 12) questions, such as: What is your family's structure? What roles do family members play? How is affection communicated? How are disagreements handled? How is time structured? What kinds of behaviors are rewarded and how; what kinds are punished and how? What do family members believe is the "good life," and how that should be achieved? How are meals handled—what is a "proper" meal, who fixes it, and when and with whom are meals eaten? These kinds of questions begin to get at the lived culture that people learn while growing up. When students compare their descriptions, they often see similarities and differences among their peers and begin to identify cultural patterns governing family life in their community.

(This background introduction was written by Christine Sleeter and used by permission.)

Our Informant

Christine E. Sleeter, Ph.D. (University of Wisconsin-Madison, 1982), is Professor Emerita in the College of Professional Studies at California State University Monterey Bay, where she was a founding faculty member. Formerly a high school learning disabilities teacher in Seattle, she had also been a faculty member at Ripon College in Wisconsin and at the University of Wisconsin-Parkside. She was recently a visiting scholar at Victoria University in New Zealand, the University of Washington–Seattle, and San Francisco State University. She served as vice president of Division K (Teaching and Teacher Education) of the American Educational Research Association. Her research focuses on anti-racist multicultural education and multicultural teacher education. She has published over 100 articles in edited books and journals, such as *Journal of Teacher Education, Teacher Education Quarterly, Teaching and Teacher Education,* and *Curriculum Inquiry.* Her recent books include *Unstandardizing Curriculum* (Teachers College Press), *Facing Accountability in Education* (Teachers College Press), and *Doing Multicultural Education for Achievement and Equity* (with Carl Grant; Routledge). She has been invited to speak in most U.S. states as well as several countries. Awards for her work include the American Educational Research Association Social Justice Award, the California State University Monterey Bay President's Medal, and the National Association for Multicultural Education Research Award.

Personal Perspective

I grew up learning an unquestioned sense of myself as White but little about myself as ethnic. My mother, when my siblings and I asked about our "nationality," would reel off a list of national origins—German, Scots-Irish, French, English, and Cherokee—usually making light of the whole question. Race, ethnicity, and nationality were conflated, then brushed off as unimportant. Only much later did I confront my identity, beginning in the context of ethnic revival movements of the 1970s, when African American friends and colleagues began to draw my attention to some of my beliefs and ways of doing things that were cultural rather than universal.

Over the last few years, I have been exploring my family history as one way to learn more about what it means to be a White American. I will first describe briefly how I am approaching this and then a little bit about what I am learning. The methodology I am using has two dimensions: genealogical research and contextual research. Genealogical research involves gathering data about the family tree and its members, using census data, birth/death records, military records, church or other religious records, marriage records, and the like; much of this is available on the Internet. I have also visited various locations in the United States where there are records (such as deeds records in courthouses) and have gathered some additional primary data, such as old records that family members have.

Contextual historical research is an important dimension that people usually do not use when researching family history, but that is crucial to helping to move from individual stories to shared experiences and to recognition of relationships among sociocultural groups. Contextual historical research involves gathering historical information about context of each family unit's life (by city, county, state, region), decade by decade. I used both primary historical material (such as books or letters written during the decade in question about the location or event in question) as well as academic research by historians and sociologists that might illuminate aspects of the family's story.

I have traced most of my family tree back to the point at which immigrants arrived in the United States (ranging between the early 1700s to the mid-1800s), and I am constructing historical portraits of the families with the data I can locate. The portraits and the entire project are at http://sites.google.com/a/christinesleeter.org/critical-family-history. Here, I would like to share two insights I have gained.

The Historical Construction of White Privilege

First, although most White Americans find White privilege very difficult to think about, when I trace how my ancestors gained land and profited from it, I can see the historical construction of White privilege and the roots of the professional class status I grew up with. For example, some of my German great-great grandparents probably arrived in the United States with money, since they purchased acreage shortly after arriving in Illinois in the first half of the 1800s. Their aim, which appears to have been common among German immigrants at that time, was to buy enough land during their lifetimes to leave good-sized farms to their offspring. But the land itself had been home to the Kickapoo Indians until they were expelled by the U.S. government in order to populate Illinois with Europeans. Further, Illinois passed a law in 1853 prohibiting Black people from staying overnight in the state. Great-great grandfather William Henry Sleeter purchased 200 acres in Illinois from the U.S. government between 1849 and 1853; his land value had tripled by the time he died in 1866. His three sons inherited the land and bought more. One of them, my great-grandfather, acquired his

TABLE 15.1 Census Data for 2002

	Home Ownership	Household Net Worth ($)	Equity of Own Home	Household Income ($)
White, non Hispanic	74.30%	87,056	121,998	54,054
Black	46.20%	5,446	58,767	33,454
Hispanic	47.50%	7,950	82,122	38,152
American Indian	54.60%			37,720

Available at: http://sites.google.com/a/christinesleeter.org/critical-family-history/Home/critical-family-history-theory/racism-and-wealth

father's original 160 acres in 1894, which he sold in 1896. By then, the land was selling for about 11 times as much as its original purchase price. My grandfather was able to complete an MD degree and become a physician, as was my father. The land—taken from the Kickapoo and unavailable to Blacks—became a springboard for class mobility. What I inherited was growing up in a second-generation professional-class family. Table 15.1 shows how this springboard for historical availability of assets reflects current economic conditions by race.

It would be inaccurate to suggest that all descendants of European immigrants who bought land around the same time became wealthy. Inheritances were subdivided, often providing a nest egg rather than a fortune to the next generation. And members of next generations used their inheritances differently; while some were able to profit, others invested poorly or had bad luck. It would also be inaccurate to suggest that European immigrants and their descendents did not work. They did, and many of them worked very hard. But it was on a playing field that had been constructed for Whites only. In this story—as well as most of the other immigration stories in my family—it is clear how the U.S. government systematically took land from the indigenous peoples, recruited Europeans or European Americans, and sold them the land cheaply, while in most states prohibiting free African Americans from buying land. Profits and other benefits Whites gained from this system were passed down through families. Knowing all of this does not make me a bad person, but it calls into question advantages I was born with and inherited. By examining the historic roots of today's racially unequal distribution of wealth and poverty and where we fit within that history, we can become more open to challenging systems that maintain racial inequalities.

Understanding How and Why Language and Culture Changed

A second insight I have gained is that many of our European or Euro-American ancestors suppressed culture and language that was not English and middle class—sometimes under forcible pressure and other times in order to advance economically and/or socially. If it feels like White culture isn't very vibrant (a feeling that can be challenged, by the way, by digging into various areas such as the arts), we really do have a history of suppressing that which is "different." For example, my mother's mother was of Appalachian descent, yet this was a term I never heard used to describe her family's origins. To the extent that Appalachian culture is associated with poverty, my mother's family wanted to pass on something "better."

In researching the German side of my family, I have become aware of the extent to which strong bilingual and bicultural German communities thrived in the Midwest for a couple of generations. Over a period of about 60 years— through the support of German churches and schools—bilingual and bicultural communities existed and were documented in newspaper articles and church records.

> Earlier, I mentioned William Henry Sleeter, or Wilhelm Heinrich Schlichter—which name he used depended on the context. He helped to establish a German Methodist Church and a German elementary school for his village. Another German great-grandfather became a German Methodist pastor. As I looked into German-American history, I learned that there had been several German religious denominations. Two seminaries trained German-American Methodists as bilingual pastors, and by the time of World War I, German Methodist congregations were serving about 60,000–70,000 members. I also learned that German-English bilingual schools became fairly common, having served about one million children by the time of World War I (Tolzmann, 2000). German books I have inherited from a great aunt who was a college German language professor attest to the bilingual nature of some of my ancestry. However, in the lead-up to World War I, followed by World War II, German-Americans were portrayed as potentially disloyal, and expressions of German culture were severely punished. Since German-American communities were bilingual and bicultural, they were able to shift into English but had to throw away a lot such as traditions, newspapers, and books. In my family, we learned virtually nothing of this history— and very little that could be identified as having German roots.

I suggest that those of us who are of European descent think of our ethnicity as created and recreated by each generation in the United States. Rather than being trapped in an inheritance we may or may not want, we have the capacity to critically examine and reshape our lives. We have the capacity, for example, to learn to help dismantle racism, to support bilingualism, to learn to curb our appetites for material acquisition. While I recognize that there is a relationship between social structure and culture and do not mean to reduce social transformation to unfettered individual will, we are not powerless to make changes. Critically analyzing our shared culture and its historic roots in our families—for the purpose of transforming our lives collectively—has exciting possibilities.

EPILOGUE

Continuing the Journey

"We can each aim a little higher, take our moral obligation a little farther, and make a difference in human relationships."

—Jean Moule

As you complete this book and some of the end-of-chapter exercises, I trust you have willingly negotiated some rugged terrain and some difficult material. Such work is essential if we are to make a difference in the classrooms and world we inhabit.

Accepting the Challenge to Make a Difference

At this juncture, I believe it is appropriate to share with you encouragement I gave to higher-degree graduates in a commencement speech at my university, Oregon State:

As a guide on the side, the first course assignment I give my students is to select a guiding quote. I often borrow from the quotes students post near my office or on the web. The one by the phone reminds me, "The first step to wisdom is silence; the second is listening." The quote on my computer gets me through writer's block: "I can do all things through Him who strengthens me." ... And the quote over my desk quiets my frustrations with: "You may not be able to change the world, but at least you can embarrass the guilty."

Our quote for today is, "A genius is someone who aims for something that no one else can see, and hits it." I would like each of us to find an application for this quote. So, let's take a moment to substitute a term for "genius" that we can live with. You could insert "innovator," or "risk-taker," "change agent," "one who makes a difference," or "tenacious going-to-get-this-done hard worker." If genius works for you, use it. Here's a little story to illustrate the quote:

> At a 4th of July picnic a few years ago at a friend's farm in the Cascade foothills, the guys held a shooting match. Although I had *never* fired a gun before, I decided to integrate the match.... They needed a woman. I was handed a rifle used by our host to protect himself from grizzly bears in Alaska—a 45.70. As I struggled to balance the heavy thing, the snickers began: "Just shoot it, Jean" and "Be careful; its loaded." There were targets at 25 and 50 yards and a 10-inch bright green saw blade in a tree 100 yards—that's a football field—away. I was about to pull the trigger when the owner of the gun leaned over and whispered in my ear *aim a little high*. I did. I nearly fell backward from the recoil.... Everyone was watching me ... except one guy looking through a pair of binoculars, who asked, "Jean, what were you aiming at?" "The saw blade," I said. He said, "It's gone."

The remnants of the saw blade hang in my office to remind me to aim a little higher *and* a little farther at those points that both myself and others can barely see.

I recall another time that I aimed high, reaching for a mark that my teacher could not see. I disliked history or, more accurately, the monocultural perspective *I* was taught, and I had to repeat a U.S. History class in summer school. I put my heart into it this time and wrote a stirring, creative beginning to my paper on the Oregon trail. My teacher did not believe me, an African American student, when I told her I wrote it myself. Discouraged by her low estimation of ethnic minorities, I did not bother finishing the research paper and received another low grade. Her skepticism and her assumptions hampered my interest in writing as well as in history.

Much later, as a classroom teacher, I found Oregon history peculiarly intriguing: Oregon hosted on its soil a moment of inclusion when a Black man, Clark's slave, York, and a Native woman, Sacajawea, voted along with the rest of the expedition for the location of its winter camp. Yet, Oregon's history is marred by racist laws, including one exclusion law that prohibited Blacks from settling in the territory altogether. Violators were to be whipped every six months, the law declared, "until he or she shall quit the state." A later version merely assessed Blacks, Chinese, and Hawaiians an annual $5 tax for the privilege of living in Oregon. This legacy of exclusion is seen today in the absence of People of Color in many Oregon communities.

In the refreshingly candid and honest work I receive from my students at OSU, I often see a willingness to consider how such matters affect us today. One student shared that when he is around people who are not from what he calls the "White Protestant norm," he sometimes feels uncomfortable. He attributes this to his lack of childhood experiences. He said, "I'm not racist, but ... I'm just not used to being around them." As he heard the subtle racism in his own statement, he realized that he had used the phrase before and had heard it said many times around him. My son says that when he hears "I'm not racist, but," it is a guarantee that the rest of the sentence is. Not willfully racist but hurtful nonetheless. Other quotes from my class: "I will never tell a racist joke, so I'm not racist, but … I have laughed at other people's racist jokes," and later in the course, "It will never again be okay to laugh at a racist joke or even to keep silent when one is being told." These students are beginning to understand their own roles in the subtle, often-hidden racism that surrounds us all. Every term, my students report to me that when they take the time to open their eyes, they notice that while shopping, while driving, while meeting, People of Color are treated differently. One said, "Race shouldn't matter, but in this country, it still does—to everybody."

Let's take my own case. I am one of very few African American faculty members at OSU. What is it like to be this brown face in a sea of whiteness?:

> It is as if we are all on a river that flows quietly and gently along. Most of my friends, students, and colleagues float on this river in a strong, sturdy boat of their majority status—a boat I cannot get into because I am not White. The river, our societal mainstream, is accepted and hardly noticed. I manage to swim or float alongside the boat as I am learning how to navigate this mainstream. Every once in a while someone in the boat notices my struggle and tosses out an inner tube or briefly holds my hand. And then sometimes, someone reaches out and pushes my head under with, "Just get over this race thing, Jean." I sputter, resurface and continue on.
>
> In the long run, I figure it makes sense to construct a raft for myself. So while I talk to those in the boat and we run difficult rapids together, at the same time I must lash together whatever supportive materials I can find. The response? "Hey, how come Jean gets a raft?" If I say, "Because I can't get in the boat with you and I'm getting tired of staying afloat without more support," some say, "What boat?" (Moule, 2003)

Many grapple with the complex issues raised by this metaphor, whether it applies to race or other areas of difference. The challenge for those in the water and for those in the boat is to reach out for each other on our common journey while aiming to make a difference in the very river that carries us all along.

A Temporary Resting Place

Exploring adds excitement, and the occasional loss of bearings makes one more acutely aware of one's surroundings. "When terrain is new … we need to be our own toughest critics.… Few people like to be lost" (Eisner, 1997, p. 9). As I continue to explore and explain, I hope to help both my students and their students along in their journeys: "There can be no doubt that issues of diversity form the crux of what may be one of the biggest challenges yet to face those of us whose business it is to educate teachers" (Delpit, 1995, p. 105).

May the insights from this book help those who choose to journey into this challenge and those whom they welcome as fellow educators and traveling companions.

> The travelers stopped to rest. They looked back the way they had come. The path seemed longer and more difficult than they had remembered: Their talk as they walked must have helped to smooth the way. Now that they had the vantage point of the ridge, they saw that what they perceived as a summit had been the beginning of the foothills. They continued on.

FOCUSED BIBLIOGRAPHY: SITES AND INSIGHTS ALONG THE WAY

"The real voyage of discovery consists not in seeking new landscapes, but in having new eyes."

—Marcel Provost

On the companion website you will find resources for every chapter in this book. You will be able to access the links electronically through the companion website or sometimes through a quick web search. While there are many collections of cultural competency weblinks, this one by a colleague, Bonnie Morihara, is particularly rich and is updated frequently: http://www.wou.edu/tri/usp/556weblinks.htm

- Also NAME, the *National Association for Multicultural Education*: Our interviewees in Chapters 11 and 15, Cornel Pewewardy and Christine Sleeter, are leaders in this organization. The national site will have links to state chapters as well as other links of interest: http://nameorg.org and http://oregonname.org
- And, The *Children's Defense Fund*: Find useful statistics and articles on the welfare of all children here: http://www.childrendefense.org

Catalogues are full of multicultural material for teachers and children. Here are ones I particularly recommend:

- *Teaching Tolerance*: Besides current articles from inservice teachers, this site includes access to free materials for educators: http://www.tolerance.org/
- *A World of Difference Institute*: Find many multicultural and anti-bias books for children and other helpful links here: http://www.adl.org/bibliography
- *Rethinking Schools*: This magazine and materials from this publisher are key to rethinking specifics for classrooms of all grade levels: http://www.rethinkingschools.org/

Cultural competency for the sound education of all children depends on our own solid foundations and basic understandings. I especially recommend the following people and materials for challenging our perspectives and gaining "new eyes." Each may be found with a search on the web. For influential individuals, check the websites of James Loewen and Tim Wise. For two classic articles look for Peggy McIntosh's 1989 *White Privilege: Unpacking the Invisible Knapsack* and the 1956 piece: *Body Rituals of the Nacirema*.

While specific resources for each cultural group is included in the focused bibliography for each chapter 10 to 15 on the companion website, *Stereotype Threat*, a key concept for working with all Students of Color, is carefully researched and shared here: http://www.reducingstereotypethreat.org.

REFERENCES

Aaronsohn, E., Carter, C. J., & Howell, M.
(1995). Preparing monocultural
teachers for a multiethnic world:
Attitudes toward inner city schools.
Equity & Excellence in Education, 28,
5–9.

Aboud, F., & Doyle, A. B. (1993). The
early development of ethnic identity
and attitudes. In M. E. Bernal, & G. P.
Knight (Eds.), *Ethnic identity*
(pp. 46–59). Albany, NY: State
University of New York Press.

Adoff, A. (1973) *Black is brown is tan.*
New York: Harper & Row.

Alba, R. D. (1990). *Ethnic identity: The
transformation of White America.*
New Haven: Yale University Press.

Al-Hazza, T., & Lucking, B. (Spring, 2007).
Celebrating diversity through
explorations of Arab children's
literature. *Childhood Education, 83*(3)
132–135.

Allport, G. W. (1954). *The nature of
prejudice.* Cambridge, MA: Addison-
Wesley.

Anderson, J. A. (1988). Cognitive styles
and multicultural populations. *Journal
of Teacher Education, 39*(1), 2–9.

Angell, G. B., Kurz, B. J., & Gottfried, G. M.
(1997). Suicide and North American
Indians: A social constructivist
perspective. *Journal of Multicultural
Social Work, 6*(3/4), 1–26.

Applebaum, B. (1997). Good, liberal
intentions are not enough: Racism,
intentions, and moral responsibility.
Journal of Moral Education, 26(4),
409–421.

Asante, M. K. (1991). The Afrocentric idea
in education. *Journal of Negro
Education, 60*(2), 170–180.

Atkinson, D. R., Morten, G., & Sue, D. W.
(1993). *Counseling American minorities: A
cross-cultural perspective, 4th edition.*
Dubuque, IA: William C. Brown.

Atkinson, D. R., Whitely, S., & Gin, R. H.
(1990). Asian-American acculturation
and preferences for help providers.
*Journal of College Student Development,
31,* 155–161.

Atleo, M., Caldwell, N., Landis, B., Mendoza,
J., Miranda, D., Reese, D., et al.
(September, 1999). My heart is on the
ground and the Indian boarding school
experience. *Multicultural Review, 8*(3),
41–46.

Banks, J. A., & Banks, C. A. (2010).
*Multicultural education: Issues and
perspectives (7th ed.).* Hoboken, NJ:
Wiley.

Banks, J. A., & Banks, C. A. M. (2004).
Handbook on multicultural education.
New York: Macmillan.

Banks, J. A., Cookson, P., Gay, G., Hawley,
W. D., Irvine, J. J., Nieto, S., et al.
(2001). *Diversity within unity: Essential
principles for teaching and learning in a
multicultural society.* Seattle, WA:
Center for Multicultural Education,
University of Washington.

Barry, N. H., & Lechner, J. V. (1995). Preservice teachers' attitudes about and awareness of multicultural teaching and learning. *Teaching and Teacher Education, 11*(2), 149–161.

Bartolome, L. (2003). Beyond the methods fetish: Toward a humanizing pedagogy. In A. Darder, M. Baltodano, & R. Torres (Eds.), *The critical pedagogy reader*. NY: Routledge.

Baxley, T. P. (June, 2008). "What are you?" Biracial children in the classroom. *Childhood Education, 84*(4), 230–234.

Bay Area Association of Black Psychologists. (1972). Position statement on use of IQ and ability tests. In R. L. Jones (Ed.), *Black psychology* (pp. 92–94). New York: Harper & Row.

Begley, S. (November 19, 2004). Racism studies find rational part of brain can override prejudice. *Wall Street Journal*, B1.

Begley, S. (March 1, 2010). West brain, East brain: What a difference culture makes. *Newsweek, 155*(9), 22.

Bennett, M. B. (1993). Towards ethnorelativism: A developmental model of intercultural sensitivity. In R. M. Paige (Ed.), *Education for the intercultural experience* (pp. 1–51). Yarmouth, ME: Intercultural Press.

Berlak, H. (2009). Race and the achievement gap. In W. Au (Ed.), *Rethinking multicultural education* (pp. 63–72). Milwaukee, WI: Rethinking Schools.

Bertrand, M., & Mullainathan, S. (2004). Are Emily and Greg more employable than Lakisha and Jamal? *American Economic Review, 94*(4), 991–1013.

Biggers, J. (2006). *The United States of Appalachia*. New York: Shoemaker & Hoard.

Bireda, M. R. (2002). *Eliminating racial profiling in school discipline: Cultures in conflict*. Lanham, MD: Scarecrow.

Black, L. (1996). Families of African origin: An overview. In M. McGoldrick, J. Giordan & J. K. Pearce (Eds.), *Ethnicity and family therapy* (pp. 57–65). New York: Guilford Press.

Blair, T. R., & Jones, D. L. (1998). *Preparing for student teaching in a pluralistic classroom*. Boston: Allyn & Bacon.

Blais, D. (2008, Summer). The perils of colorblindness. *Greater Good, 4*(1), 21.

Boal, A. (1979). *Theatre of the oppressed*. London, UK: Pluto Press.

Boal, A. (2006). *The aesthetics of the oppressed*. New York: Routledge.

Bollin, G. G., & Finkel, J. (1995). White racial identity as a barrier to understanding diversity: A study of preservice teachers. *Equity & Excellence in Education, 28*(1), 25–30.

Bowman, K. (2001). The new face of school desegregation. *Duke Law Journal, 50*(6), 1751–1808.

Boyd, N. (1982). Family therapy with Black families. In E. E. Jones & S. J. Korchin (Eds.), *Minority mental health* (pp. 227–249). New York: Praeger.

Boykins, W. (2009, May 4). *Fostering high achievement for African American students: What the research says*. Presentation at the Institute for the Study of the African American Child (ISAAC) Conference on Research Directions Program. Hilton Head Island, SC.

Britzman, D. P. (1991). *Practice makes practice: A critical study of learning to teach*. Albany, NY: State University of NY Press.

Brown, M. T., & Lundrum-Brown, J. (1995). Counselor supervision: Cross-cultural perspectives. In J. P. Ponterotto, J. M. Casas, L. A. Suzuki & C. M. Alexander (Eds.), *Handbook of multicultural counseling* (pp. 263–287). Thousand Oaks, CA: Sage.

Brown, T., & Wiessler, D. (2009, January 14). U.S. school segregation on the rise. *Reuters.*

Burbules, N. C. (1993). *Dialogue in teaching: Theory and practice.* New York: Teachers College Press.

Burke, D. (2007). *An autoethnography of Whiteness.* Unpublished doctoral dissertation, Oregon State University, Corvallis, Oregon.

Burroughs, M. (1968). *What shall I tell my children who are Black?* Chicago: M.A.A.H. Press.

Butler, K. (2001). *Evaluating textbooks for bias.* Unpublished manuscript, Oregon State University, Corvallis.

Calhoon, M. (2006, May 18). Culture of whiteness: The UO fails to recruit and retain a critical mass of black students and faculty. *Eugene Weekly.* Retrieved September 15, 2010, from http://www.eugeneweekly.com/2006/05/18/coverstory.html

Canino, C., & Zayas, L. H. (1997). Puerto Rican children. In G. Johnson-Powell, J. Yamamoto & W. Arroyo (Eds.), *Trans-cultural child development: Psychological assessment and treatment.* New York: Wiley.

Carpenter, S. (2008, May 1). Buried prejudice: The bigot in your brain. *Scientific American Mind*, April, 2008.

Carrasquillo, A. (1991). *Hispanic children and youth in the United States: A resource guide.* New York: Garland.

Casas, J. M., & Pytluk, S. D. (1995). Hispanic identity development: Implications for research and practice. In J. P. Ponterotto, J. M. Casas, L. A. Suzuki & C. M. Alexander (Eds.), *Handbook of multicultural counseling* (pp. 155–180). Thousand Oaks, CA: Sage.

Castagno, A. E., & Brayboy, B. M. J. (2008). Culturally responsive schooling for indigenous youth: A review of the literature. *Review of Educational Research*, 78(4), 941–993.

Castro, A. J. (2010). Themes in the research on preservice teachers' views of cultural diversity: Implications for researching Millennial preservice teachers. *Educational Researcher, 39*(3), 198–210.

Charles, G. (January 21, 2010). Stop calling quake victims looters. *CNN.* Retrieved September 15, 2010, from http://www.cnn.com/2010/OPINION/01/21/Charles.haiti.earthquake.looting.race/index.html

Chartock, R. K. (2010). *Strategies and lessons for culturally responsive teaching: A primer for K–12 teachers.* New York: Pearson.

Ciechanowski, K. M. (2010, February). *Integrating language development and content area instruction for ELLs.* Paper presented at the 20th West Regional Conference of the International Reading Association, Portland, Oregon.

Ciechanowski, K. M. (2009). *Sociocultural resources: Expanding conceptions of funds of knowledge.* Unpublished manuscript, Oregon State University, Corvallis, Oregon.

Clark, K., & Clark, M. (1947). Racial identification and preference in Negro children. In T. H. Newcomb & E. L. Hartley (Eds.), *Readings in social psychology* (pp. 169–178). New York: Holt.

Clark, K. B. (1963). *Prejudice and your child.* Boston: Beacon Press.

Cleary, L. C., & Peacock, T. D. (1998). *Collected wisdom: American Indian education.* Boston: Allyn & Bacon.

Cloud, J. (2009, February 21). Are mixed-race children better adjusted? *Time,* February 21, 2009.

Collett, J., & Serrano, B. (1992). Stirring it up: The inclusive classroom. In L. L. B. Borders & N. V. N. Chism (Eds.), *Teaching for diversity* (pp. 35–48). San Francisco: Jossey-Bass.

Collins, P. H. (1990). *Black feminist thought: Knowledge, consciousness, and the politics of empowerment.* Boston: Unwin Hyman.

Cooper, P. (2009). *The classrooms all young children need: Lessons from teaching from Vivian Paley.* Chicago, IL: University of Chicago.

Copenhaver-Johnson, J. (2006). Talking to children about race: The importance of inviting difficult conversations. *Childhood Education, 83*(1), 12–22.

Correll, J., Park, B., Judd, C. M., & Wittenbrink, B. (2002). The police officer's dilemma: Using ethnicity to disambiguate potentially threatening individuals. *Journal of Personality and Social Psychology, 83*(6), 1314–1329.

Cose, E. (1993). *The rage of a privileged class.* New York: HarperCollins.

Cose, E. (1997). *Color-blind: Seeing beyond race in a race-obsessed world.* New York: HarperCollins.

Cross, T. L. (Summer, 1988). Services to minority populations: What does it mean to be a culturally competent professional. *Focal Point, 2*(4). Portland, OR: Research and Training Center, Portland State University.

Cross, T. L., Bazron, B. J., Dennis, K. W., & Isaacs, M. R. (1989). *Toward a culturally competent system of care.* Washington, DC: Georgetown University Development Center.

Cross, W. (1991). *Shades of Black: Diversity in African-American identity.* Philadelphia, PA: Temple University Press.

Cross, W. E. (1971). The Negro-to-Black conversion experience: Toward a psychology of Black liberation. *Black World, 20*(9), 13–27.

Cross, W. E. (1995). The psychology of Nigrescence: Revising the Cross model. In J. G. Ponterotto, J. M. Casas, L. A. Suzuki & C. M. Alexander (Eds.), *Handbook of multicultural counseling* (pp. 93–123). Thousand Oaks, CA: Sage.

Cuban, L. (1989). The "at-risk" label and the problem of urban school reform.

Phi Delta Kappan, 70(10), 780–784, 799–801.

Curry, N. E., & Johnson, C. N. (1990). *Beyond self-esteem: Developing a genuine sense of human value.* Paper presented at the National Association for the Education of Young Children, Washington, DC.

Darder, A., Torres, R. D., & Gutíerrez, H. (1997). Introduction. In A. Darder, R. D. Torres & H. Gutíerrez (Eds.), *Latinos and education: A critical reader* (pp. xi–xix). New York: Routledge.

Davis, W. (2009) *The wayfinders: Why ancient wisdom matters in the modern world.* Toronto: Anansi Press.

De Vos, G. (1995). Ethnic pluralism: Conflict and accommodation. In L. Romanucci-Ross & G. De Vos (Eds.), *Ethnic identity: Creation, conflict and accommodation* (3rd ed., pp. 15–46). Walnut Creek, CA: Altamira Press.

Delpit, L. (1988). The silenced dialogue: Power and pedagogy in educating other people's children. *Harvard Educational Review, 58*, 280–298.

Delpit, L. (1995). *Other people's children: Cultural conflict in the classroom.* New York: The New Press.

Delpit, L. (2006). *Other people's children: Cultural conflict in the classroom* (2nd ed.). New York: The New Press.

Derman-Sparks, L., & The A. B. C. Task Force. (1989). *Anti-bias curriculum: Tools for empowering young children.* Washington DC: National Association for the Education of Young Children.

Devore, W., & Schlesinger, E. G. (1981). *Ethnic sensitive social work practice.* St. Louis, MO: Mosby.

Diamond, S. (1987). *In search of the primitive: A critique of civilization.* New Brunswick, NJ: Transaction.

Diaz-Ramos, S., Null, K., Pentland, B., & Roush, M. L. (1996). *Parent-teacher scenario.* Unpublished manuscript, Oregon State University, Corvallis.

Diller, J. V. (1997). *Informal interviews about self-esteem and racism with People of Color raised outside of the United States.* Paper presented at the Conference on Race and Ethnicity in Higher Education, Orlando, Florida.

Dillon, S. (2009, January 22). Study sees an Obama effect as lifting Black test-takers. *New York Times.* Retrieved September 15, 2010, from http://www.nytimes.com/2009/01/23/education/23gap.html

Dollard, J. (1938). Hostility and fear in social life. *Social Forces, 17,* 15–26.

Donelan, B. (1999). The unique circumstances of Native American juveniles under federal supervision [electronic version]. *Federal Probation, 63*(2), 68–71.

Dovidio, J. F., & Gaertner, S. L. (Winter, 2005). Color blind or just plain blind. *The Nonprofit Quarterly, 12*(4).

Draguns, J. G. (1981). Dilemmas and choices in cross-cultural counseling: The universal versus the culturally distinct. In P. B. Pedersen, J. G. Draguns, W. L. Lonner & J. E. Trimble (Eds.), *Counseling across cultures* (pp. 3–22). Honolulu, HI: University of Hawaii Press.

Dray, B., & Espinosa, M. (2010, April). *Making the invisible visible: Environmental Justice. Project Voyce.* Panel presentation at the annual conference of the American Education Research Association, Denver, Colorado.

Dreikurs, R. (1968). *Psychology in the classroom (2nd ed.).* New York: Harper & Row.

Dresser, N. (1996). *Multicultural manners: New rules of etiquette for a changing society.* New York: Wiley.

Dupree, D. B., Spencer, M. B., & Bell, S. (1997). African American children. In G. Johnson-Powell, J. Yamamoto &

W. Arroyo (Eds.), *Transcultural child development: Psychological assessment and treatment.* New York: Wiley.

Duran, E., & Duran, B. (1995). *Native American postcolonial psychology.* Albany, NY: State University of New York Press.

Edney, H. T. (August 18, 2006). New "doll test'" produces ugly results. *Portland Medium, 13*(32), 1, 2, 7.

Eisner, E. (1997). The promises and perils of alternative forms of data representation. *Educational Researcher, 26*(6), 4–10.

El-Badry, S. *Arab American demographics, Arab-Americans well-educated, diverse, affluent and highly entrepreneurial, over 4 million Americans trace ancestry to Arab countries.* Retrieved September 15, 2010, from http://www.allied-media.com/Arab-American/arab%20american%20demographics.htm

Ellsworth, E. (1990). Why doesn't this feel empowering? Working through the repressive myths of critical pedagogy. *Harvard Education Review, 59*(3), 297–324.

Ely, A. (2001). *Quo no more.* Unpublished manuscript.

Erikson, E. (1968). *Identity, youth and crisis.* New York: Norton.

Fair, D., Cohen, A. L., Dosenbach, N. U. F., Church, J. A., Miezin, F. M., Barch, D. M., et al. (2008, March 11). The maturing architecture of the brain's default network. *PNAS, 105*(10), 4028–4032.

Falicov, C. J. (1986). Cross-cultural marriages. In N. Jacobson & A. Gurman (Eds.), *Clinical handbook of marital therapy* (pp. 429–450). New York: Guilford Press.

Falicov, C. J. (1996). Mexican families. In M. McGoldrick, J. Giordano & J. K. Pearce (Eds.), *Ethnicity and family therapy* (pp. 169–182). New York: Guilford Press.

Faltis, C., & Coulter, C. A. (2008). *Teaching English learners and immigrant students in secondary schools.* Upper Saddle River, NJ: Pearson.

Fennimore, B. S. (1994). Addressing prejudiced statements: A four-step method that works! *Childhood Education, 70*(4), 202–204.

Finders, M. (1992). Looking at lives through ethnography. *Educational Leadership, 50*(1), 60–65.

Fleming, C. M. (1992). American Indians and Alaska Natives: Changing societies past and present. In M. A. Orlandi (Ed.), *Cultural competence for evaluators: A guide for alcohol and other drug abuse prevention practitioners working with ethnic/racial communities* (pp. 147–171). Rockville, MD: U.S. Department of Health and Human Services.

Ford, D. (1996, November). *Adaptation of Banks' curriculum model.* Paper presented at the National Association of Gifted Children, Indianapolis, Indiana.

Foster, M. (1987). *"It's cooking now": An ethnographic study of teaching style of a successful Black teacher in a White community college.* Unpublished doctoral dissertation, Harvard University, Cambridge, Massachusetts.

Foster, M. (1994). Effective black teachers: A literature review. In E. R. Hollins, J. E. King & W. C. Hayman (Eds.), *Teaching diverse populations: Formulating a knowledge base* (pp. 225–241). Albany, NY: State University of New York, NY Press.

Fox, K. C. (1993). *Opening closed doors: Perceptions of African American parents and White teachers.* Unpublished master's thesis, Lesley College Graduate School, Cambridge, MA.

Frail, T. A. (2010). Americans look to 2050. *Smithsonian, 41*(4), 70–71.

Frankenberg, R. (1993). *The social construction of whiteness: White women, race matters.* Minneapolis, MN: University of Minnesota Press.

Franquiz, M., & Reyes, M. (1998). Creating inclusive learning communities through English language arts. *Chanclas* to *Canicas. Language Arts, 75*(3), 211–220.

Frazier, K. (2009). *Diversity and teacher preparation.* Unpublished manuscript, Capella University, Minneapolis, Minnesota.

Freedman, D.G. (1979, January). Ethnic differences in babies. *Human Nature, 2,* 36–43.

Futures for Children. (2001). *Futures for children.* Retrieved September 15, 2010, www.futuresforchildren.org.

Gallagher, B. T. (2000). Teaching (Native) America. *The Nation, 270*(22), 36–38.

Gallimore, R., Boggs, J., & Jordan, C. (1974). *Culture, behaviorism and education: A study of Hawaiian-Americans.* Beverly Hills, CA: Sage.

Garcia, E. E. (2001). *Hispanic education in the United States.* Lanham, MD: Rowman & Littlefield.

Garcia, E. (2005). *Teaching and learning in two languages: Bilingualism and schooling in the United States.* New York: Teachers College Press.

Garcia-Preto, N. (1996). Latino families: An overview. In M. McGoldrick, J. Giordan & J. K. Pearce (Eds.), *Ethnicity and family therapy* (pp. 141–154). New York: Guilford Press.

Gay, G. (2000). *Culturally responsive teaching: Theory, research, and practice.* New York: Teachers College Press.

Gay, G. (2010a). Acting on beliefs in teacher education for cultural diversity. *Journal of Teacher Education, 61*(1-2), 143–152.

Gay, G. (2010b). *Culturally responsive teaching: Theory, research, and practice, (2nd ed.).* New York: Teachers College Press.

Gibson, M. A. (1976). Approaches to multicultural education in the United States: Some concepts and assumptions. *Anthropology and Education, 7,* 7–18.

Gladwell, M. (2005). *Blink: The power of thinking without thinking.* New York: Little, Brown and Co.

Gladwell, M. (2008). *Outliers: The story of success.* New York: Little, Brown and Co.

Good, C., Aronson, J., & Inzlicht, M. (2003). Improving children's standardized test performance: An intervention to reduce the effects of stereotype threat. *Applied Developmental Psychology, 24,* 645–662.

Goodman, M. E. (1952). *Race awareness in young children.* London, UK: Collier.

Gordon, M. (1964). *Assimilation in American life.* New York: Oxford University Press.

Grant, C. A., & Sleeter, C. E. (2007). *Doing multicultural education for achievement and equity.* New York: Routledge.

Grant, C. A., & Sleeter, C. E. (2009). *Turning on learning, (5th ed.).* Hoboken, NJ: Wiley.

Greenwald, A., McGhee, D. E., & Schwartz, J. L. K. (1998). Measuring individual differences in implicit cognition: The implicit association test. *Journal of Personality and Social Psychology, 74*(6), 1464–1480.

Gregory, A., & Mosely, P. (2004). The discipline gap: Teachers' views on the over-representation of African American students in the discipline system. *Equity & Excellence in Education, 37,* 18–30.

Gushue, G. V., & Sciarra, D. T. (1995). Culture and families: A multicultural approach. In J. P. Ponterotto, J. M. Casas, L. A. Suzuki & C. M. Alexander (Eds.), *Handbook of multicultural counseling* (pp. 586–606). Thousand Oaks, CA: Sage.

Haberman, M. (1996). Selecting and preparing culturally competent teachers for urban schools. In J. Sikula, T. J. Buttery & E. Guyon (Eds.), *Handbook of research on teacher education* (2nd ed., pp. 247–760). New York: Macmillan.

Hacker, A. (1995). *Two nations: Black and White, separate, hostile, unequal.* New York: Ballantine.

Haggis, P. (2004). *Crash.* Los Angeles, CA: Bob Yari.

Hale-Benson, J. (1986). *Black children: Their roots, culture and learning style.* Baltimore, MD: Johns Hopkins University Press.

Hampden-Turner, C. (1974). *From poverty to dignity: A strategy for poor Americans.* Garden City, NY: Anchor Press.

Hardy, K. V., & Laszloffy, T. A. (1995). The cultural genogram: Key to training culturally competent family therapists. *Journal of Marital and Family Therapy, 21*(3), 227–237.

Harjo, S. S. (1996). Now and then: Native peoples in the United States. *Dissent, 43,* 58–60.

Harris, G. S. (2008). *White racial identity development in transitional space: Discourse and praxis among Christian teacher educators.* Unpublished doctoral dissertation, Oregon State University, Corvallis, Oregon.

Harvard University. *Project implicit.* Retrieved September 15, 2010, from https://implicit.harvard.edu/implicit

Hauser, S. T., & Kasendorf, E. (1983). *Black and White identity formation.* Halabar, FL: Kreiger.

Hawkins, J. M. (2002). The pit boss: A new Native American stereotype? *Multicultural Education, 9*(4), 15–17.

Haycock, K. (2001). Closing the achievement gap. *Educational Leadership, 58*(6), 6–11.

Haynes, D. (2003, February 8). CIM and CAM on the block again. *Statesman Journal,* p. 1.

Haynes-Writer, J. (2001). Identifying the identified: The need for critical exploration of Native American identity within educational contexts. *Action in Teacher Education, 22*(4), 40–47.

Healey, J. F. (1995). *Race, ethnicity, gender, and class: The sociology of group conflict and change.* Thousand Oaks, CA: Pine Forge Press.

Heath, S. B. (1983). *Ways with words.* Cambridge, UK: Cambridge University Press.

Helms, J. E. (1990). An overview of Black racial identity theory. In J. E. Helms (Ed.), *Black and White racial identity: Theory, research and practice* (pp. 9–32). Westport, CT: Greenwood Press.

Helms, J. E. (1995). An update of Helms' White and People of Color racial identity models. In J. P. Ponterotto, J. M. Casas, L. A. Suzuki & C. M. Alexander (Eds.), *Handbook of multicultural counseling* (pp. 181–198). Thousand Oaks, CA: Sage.

Helms, J. E. (2003, February 21). *How to use Black racial identity theory to solve the Black–White test-score gap.* Paper presented at the Winter Roundtable, Teachers College, Columbia University, New York City, New York.

Hermanns, C. B. (2010). *Leveling the playing field: Investigating vocabulary development in Latino preschool-age English language learners.* Unpublished doctoral dissertation, Harvard University, Boston, Massachusetts.

Higgins, K., & Moule, J. (2009). "No more Mr. Nice Guy": Preservice teachers' conflict with classroom management in a predominantly African American urban elementary school. *Multicultural Perspective, 11*(3), 132–138.

Hill, R. (1972). *The strengths of Black families.* New York: National Urban League.

Hilliard, A. G. (1995). *The maroon within us.* Baltimore, MO: Black Classic Press.

Hines, P. M., & Boyd-Franklin, N. (1982). Black families. In M. McGoldrick, J. K. Pearce & J. Giordano (Eds.), *Ethnicity and family therapy* (pp. 84–107). New York: Guilford Press.

Ho, D. R. (1994). Asian American perspectives. In J. U. Gordon (Ed.), *Managing multiculturalism in substance abuse services* (pp. 72–98). Thousand Oaks, CA: Sage.

Ho, M. (1987). *Family therapy with ethnic minorities.* Newbury Park, CA: Sage.

Hodgkinson, H. (2002). Demographics and teacher education. *Journal of Teacher Education, 53*(2), 102–105.

Holbrook, C. L. (2006). Low expectations are the worst form of racism. In J. Landsman & C. W. Lewis (Eds.). *White teachers, diverse classrooms* (pp. 110–121). Sterling, VA: Stylus.

Hooks, B. (1994). *Teaching to transgress: Education as the practice of freedom.* New York: Routledge.

Hoopes, D. S. (1972). *Reader in intercultural communication, volumes 1 and 2.* Pittsburgh, PA: Regional Council for International Education.

Howard, G. (2007). As diversity grows, so must we. *Educational Leadership, 64*(4), 16–22.

Ignatiev, N. (1995). *How the Irish became White.* New York: Routledge.

Implicit association test. Retrieved September 15, 2010, from http://www.tolerance.org/activity/test-yourself-hidden-bias

Indian Health Service. (2000). *Regional differences in Indian health 1998–1999.* Rockville, MD: Dept. of Health and

Human Services, Public Health Services.

International Reading Association. (2001). *Second-language literacy instruction: A position statement of the International Reading Association.* Newark, DE.

Jacobs, J. H. (1977). *Black/White interracial families: Marital process and identity development in young children.* Unpublished doctoral dissertation, The Wright Institute, Berkeley, California.

Jeffries, R., Nix, M., & Singer, C. (2002). Urban American Indians "dropping" out of traditional high schools: Barriers & bridges to success. *The High School Journal, 85*(3), 38–46.

Jeffries, R. B., Hollowell, M., & Powell, T. (2004). Urban American Indian students in a nonpunitive alternative high school. *American Secondary Education, 32*(2), 63–78.

Jensen, A. R. (1972). *Genetics and education.* New York: Harper & Row.

Jensen, R. (2010, March 4). What White people fear. *Yes! Magazine.* Retrieved September 15, 2010, from http://www.yesmagazine.org/issues/america-the-remix/what-white-people-fear

Johns, M., Inzlicht, M., & Schmader, T. (2008). Stereotype threat and executive resource depletion: Examining the influence of emotion regulation. *Journal of Experimental Psychology: General, 137,* 691–705.

Johnson, B. (2009). *Archeology of the Southwest.* Retrieved September 15, 2010, from http:// www.angelfire.com/trek/archaeology

Johnson, L. (2002). "My eyes have been opened": White teachers and racial awareness. *Journal of Teacher Education, 53*(2), 153–167.

Johnson, T., & Tomren, H. (1999). Helplessness, hopelessness, and despair: Identifying the precursors to Indian youth suicide. *American Indian Culture and Research Journal, 23*(3), 287–301.

Jones, D. L. (2001). *Retaining African Americans in higher education.* Sterling, VA: Stylus.

Jones, E. E., & Korchin, S. J. (1982). Minority mental health: Perspectives. In E. E. Jones & S. J. Korchin (Eds.), *Minority mental health* (pp. 3–36). New York: Praeger.

Jones, W. T. (1990). Perspectives on ethnicity. In L. V. Moore (Ed.), *Evolving theoretical perspectives on students* (pp. 59–72). San Francisco, CA: Jossey-Bass.

Judy, R. A. T. (1993). *(Dis)forming the American canon: The vernacular of African Arabic American slave narrative.* Minneapolis, MN: University of Minnesota Press.

Juster, N. (2006). *The hello-goodbye window.* New York: Hyperion.

Kagan, S., & Madsen, M. (1972). Experimental analysis of cooperation and competition of Anglo-American and Mexican-American children. *Developmental Psychology, 6,* 49–59.

Kayyali, R. A. (2006). *The people perceived as a threat to security: Arab Americans since September 11. Retrieved September 15, 2010, from* http://www.migrationinformation.org/Feature/print.cfm?ID=409

Keefe, M. (2006, April 4). Editorial cartoon. *Denver Post.* Retrieved September 15, 2010, from http://www.denverpost.com/keefe

Kendall, F. E. (1997, June). *Understanding White privilege.* Paper presented at the National Conference on Race and Ethnicity in Higher Education, Orlando, Florida.

Kerwin, C., & Ponterotto, J. G. (1995). Biracial identity development: Theory and research. In J. P. Ponterotto, J. M.

Casas, L. A. Suzuki & C. M. Alexander (Eds.), *Handbook of multicultural counseling* (pp. 199–217). Thousand Oaks, CA: Sage.

Kivel, P. (1996). *Uprooting racism: How White people can work for racial justice.* Gabriola Island, BC: New Society.

Knapp, S. (2001). *Fighting for freedom: Kindergarteners allowed.* (Unpublished work sample). Oregon State University, Corvallis, Oregon.

Knaus, C. B. (2009). Shut up and listen: Applied critical race theory in the classroom. *Race, ethnicity and education, 12*(2), 133–154.

Knight-Richardson, N. (2005, November). Back from New Orleans. *Newsletter Department of Psychiatry, 1-5.* Portland, OR: OHSU.

Kochman, T. (1981). *Black and White styles in conflict.* Chicago: University of Chicago Press.

Kohn, A. (2000). Burnt at the high stakes. *Journal of Teacher Education, 51*(4), 315–327.

Koppelman, K. (2011). *Perspectives on human differences: Selected readings on diversity in America.* Boston: Pearson.

Kotkin, J. (2010). Ready set grow. *Smithsonian, 41*(4), 61–67.

Kroeber, A. L. (1948). *Anthropology: Race, language, culture, psychology, prehistory.* London, UK: Harrap.

Kuhn, T. S. (1970). *The structure of scientific revolutions.* Chicago: University of Chicago Press.

Kunjufu, J. (2002). *Black students—Middle class teachers.* Chicago: African American Images.

Ladson-Billings, G. (1994). *The dreamkeepers: Successful teachers of African American children.* San Francisco: Jossey-Bass.

Landau, J. (1982). Therapy with families in cultural transition. In M. McGoldrick, J. K. Pearce & J. Giordan (Eds.), *Ethnicity and family therapy* (pp. 552–572). New York: Guilford Press.

Landsman, J. (2004). Confronting the racism of low expectations. *Educational Leadership, 62*(3), 28–32.

Larsen, J. (1976, October). *Dysfunction in the evangelical family: Treatment considerations.* Paper presented at the American Association of Marriage and Family Therapists, Philadelphia, Pennsylvania.

Leary, J. D. (2005). *Post traumatic slave syndrone: America's legacy of enduring injury and healing.* Milwaukie, OR: Uptone.

LeCompte, M. D. (1994). Defining reality: Applying double description and chaos theory to the practice of practice. *Educational Theory, 44*(3), 277–298.

Lee, E. (1996). Asian American families: An overview. In M. McGoldrick, J. Giordan & J. K. Pearce (Eds.), *Ethnicity and family therapy* (pp. 227–248). New York: Guilford Press.

Levin, B. (1992). Dealing with dropouts in Canadian education. *Curriculum Inquiry, 22*(3), 257–270.

Lewis, A. E. (2003). *Race in the schoolyard: Negotiating the color line in classrooms and communities.* New Brunswick, NJ: Rutgers University Press.

Lewis-Charp, H. (2003). Breaking the silence: White students' perspectives on race in multiracial schools. *Phi Delta Kappan, 85*(4), 279–285.

Lieberson, S. (1985). Unhyphenated Whites in the United States. *Ethnic and Racial Studies, 8*(1), 159–179.

Lindsay, R. B., Robins, K. N., & Terrell, R. D. (2009). *Cultural proficiency: A manual for school leaders (3rd ed.).* Thousand Oaks, CA: Corwin.

Linton, R. (1945). *The cultural background of personality.* New York: Appleton-Century-Crofts.

Liston, D. P., & Zeichner, K. M. (1996). *Culture and teaching.* Mahwah, NJ: Lawrence Erlbaum.

Lockhart, J. (2009). *Critical investigations into interns' urban teaching apprenticeship experiences.* Unpublished doctoral dissertation, Michigan State University, Lansing.

Loewen, J. (1992). *Lies my teacher told me about Christopher Columbus: What your history books got wrong.* New York: New Press.

Loewen, J. (2006). *Sundown towns: A hidden dimension of American racism.* New York: New Press.

Loewen, J. (2007). *Lies my teacher told me: Everything your American history textbook got wrong (2nd ed.).* New York: New Press.

Loewen, J. (2010). *Teaching what really happened: How to avoid the tyranny of textbooks and get students excited about doing history.* New York: Teachers College Press.

Lum, D. (1986). *Social work practice and People of Color: A process-stage approach.* Monterey, CA: Brooks/Cole.

MacDonald, C. D., & Sperry, L. L. (1995, February 15–19). *Predicting changes in preservice education students' ethnocentrism.* Paper presented at the National Association for Multicultural Education, Washington, D.C.

Machamer, A. M., & Gruber, E. (1998). Secondary school, family, and educational risk: Comparing American Indian adolescents and their peers. *The Journal of Educational Research, 91*(6), 357–369.

Marcus, M. B. (2010, June 4). 1 in 7 newlywed couples are interracial. *Statesman Journal,* p. 3A.

Marin, G. (1992). Issues in the measurement of acculturation among Hispanics. In K. F. Geisinger (Ed.), *Psychological testing of Hispanics* (pp. 235–252). Washington, DC: American Psychological Association.

Marin, G., & Marin, B. V. (1991). *Research with Hispanic populations.* Newbury Park, CA: Sage.

Marshall, P. L. (2002). *Cultural diversity in our schools.* Belmont, CA: Wadsworth.

Marx, S. (2006). *Revealing the invisible: Confronting passive racism in teacher education.* New York: Routledge.

Marx, D. M., & Stapel, D. A. (2006). It's all in the timing: Measuring emotional reactions to stereotype threat before and after taking a test. *European Journal of Social Psychology, 36,* 687–698.

McAdoo, H. P. (1985). Racial attitude and self-concept of young Black children over time. In H. P. McAdoo & J. L. McAdoo (Eds.), *Black children: Social, educational, and parental environments* (pp. 213–242). Newbury Park, CA: Sage.

McDermott, M., & Samson, F. L. (2005). White racial and ethnic identity in the United States. *Annual Review of Sociology, 31,* 245–261.

McIntosh, P. (1989, July/August). White privilege: Unpacking the invisible knapsack. *Peace and Freedom,* 10–12.

McLain, T. (2005, April 18). Cultural-competency bill hits a roadblock. *Statesman Journal, C3.*

Meier, D. (1995). *The power of their ideas: Lessons for America from a small school in Harlem.* Boston: Beacon Press.

Melser, N. A. (2006). Ain't nothin' like the real thing: Preparing teaches in an urban environment. *Childhood Education, 82*(5), 279–282.

Meltzoff, N. (2010). *The influence of targeted immersion experience on preservice teachers.* Unpublished manuscript, Pacific University, Eugene, Oregon.

Milner IV, H. R. (2006). The promise of Black teachers' success with Black students. *Educational Foundations, 20*(3-4), 89–104.

Milner IV, H. R. (2009). *Diversity and education: Teachers, teaching, and teacher education.* Springfield, IL: Thomas.

Milner IV, H. R. (2010). What does teacher education have to do with teaching? Implications for diversity studies. *Journal of Teacher Education, 61*(1-2), 118–131.

Miner, H. (1956). Body rituals of the Nacirema. *American Anthropologist, 58*, 503–507.

Minuchin, S. (1974). *Families and family therapy.* Cambridge, MA: Harvard University Press.

Minuchin, S., Montalvo, B., Guerney, G., Rosman, B., & Schumer, F. (1967). *Families of the slums.* New York: Basic.

Monroe, S. (1997). Beyond Pocahontas: Authentic images of Native American female protagonists in children's literature. *The New Advocate, 10*(2), 149–159.

Morihara, B. (2010). Literacy and cultural competence weblinks: Online annotated bibliography. Western Oregon University. Retrieved September 15, 2010, from http://www.wou.edu/tri/usp/556weblinks.htm

Moule, J. (1998). *My journey with preservice teachers: Reflecting on teacher characteristics that bridge multicultural education theory and classroom practice.* Unpublished doctoral dissertation, Oregon State University, Corvallis.

Moule, J. (2002, November). *Fighting for freedom: Kindergarteners allowed.* Paper presented at the National Association for Multicultural Education, Washington, D.C.

Moule, J. (2003a). *Immersion for cultural competency and pedagogical strength in math and science.* (Final Report for Eisenhower Professional Development Grant). Oregon State University, Corvallis.

Moule, J. (2003b, June). *Aiming to make a difference.* Commencement Address at Oregon State University, Corvallis.

Moule, J. (2004). Safe and growing out of the box. In J. J. Romo, P. Bradfield, & R. Serrano (Eds.), *Reclaiming democracy: Multicultural educators' journeys toward transformative teaching* (pp. 147–171). Upper Saddle River, NJ: Merrill Prentice Hall.

Moule, J. (2005). Implementing a social justice perspective in teacher education: Invisible burden for faculty of color. *Teachers and Teacher Education Research, 32*(4), 23–42.

Moule, J. (2006). Giving all, getting half. In S. Smith & M. Taylor-Archer (Eds.), *Our stories: The experiences of Black professionals on predominantly White campuses.* Cincinnati, OH: JDOTT.

Moule, J. (2007, April). *Immersion for cultural competency: Growing activist educators.* Poster session presented at the annual meeting of the American Education Research Association, Chicago.

Moule, J. (2008). Cultural competence in a global society. *Teacher Education & Practice, 21*(4), 467–469.

Moule, J. (2009). Understanding unconscious bias and unintentional racism. *Phi Delta Kappan, 90*(5), 320–326.

Moule, J. (2010). Nana Jean: Biracial identity. *Skipping Stones, 22*(3), 6.

Moule, J., & Higgins, K. (2007). The role of African American mentors in preparing White preservice teachers for African American student populations. *Journal of Negro Education, 74*, 609–622.

Moule, J., & Ingram, M. (2002, April). *Developing the cultural competency of White preservice and inservice teachers using socio-cultural poetry or "White girl what you got in your bag?"* Paper presented at the American Educational Research Association, New Orleans.

Moule, J., & Waldschmidt, E. D. (2003). Face-to-face over race: Personal challenges from instituting a social justice perspective in our teacher education program. *Teacher Education & Practice, 16*(2), 121–142.

Moynihan, D. P. (1965). *The Negro family: The case for national action.* Washington, DC: Office of Policy Planning and Research, U.S. Department of Labor.

Mukhopadhyay, C., & Henze, R. C. (2003). How real is race?: Using anthropology to make sense of human diversity. *Phi Delta Kappan, 84*(9), 669–678.

Murtadha-Watts, K. (1998). Teacher education in urban school-based, multiagency collaboratives. *Urban Education, 32*(5), 616–631.

Myers, C., & Bersani, H. (2008–2009). 10 quick ways to analyze children's books for ableism. *Rethinking Schools, 23*(2), 52–54.

Myers, H. F. (1982). Stress, ethnicity, and social class: A model for research with Black populations. In E. E. Jones & S. J. Korchin (Eds.), *Minority mental health* (pp. 118–148). New York: Praeger.

Myers, H., & King, L. (1985). Mental health issues in the development of the Black American child. In G. Johnson-Powell, J. Yamamoto, A. Romero & A. Morales (Eds.), *The psychosocial development of minority children* (pp. 275–306). New York: Brunner/Mazel.

National Center for Educational Statistics. (1999). *Digest of Education Statistics.* Washington, DC: U.S. Department of Education, Office of Educational Research and Improvement.

Ngo, B. (2008). Beyond "culture class": Understandings of immigrant experiences. *Theory into Practice, 47*(1), 4–11.

Nieto, S., & Bode, P. (2007). *Affirming diversity: The sociopolitical context of multicultural education (5th ed.).* White Plains, NY: Longman.

Nile, L. N., & Straton, J. C. (2003, Summer). Beyond guilt: How to deal with societal racism. *Multicultural Education,* 2–6.

Norton, D. G. (1983). Black families life patterns, the development of self and cognitive development of Black children. In G. Johnson-Powell, J. Yamamoto, A. Romero & A. Morales (Eds.), *The psychosocial development of minority children* (pp. 181–193). New York: Brunner/Mazel.

Novak, M. (1996). *Unmeltable ethnics (2nd ed.).* New Brunswick, NJ: Transaction Publishers.

Nuby, J. (2010). An awakening through an inner-city immersion experience. *Multicultural Perspectives, 12*(1), 42–49.

Ogbu, J. U. (1978). *Minority education and caste: The American system in cross-cultural perspective.* New York: Academic Press.

Ogbu, J. U. (1992). Understanding cultural diversity and learning. *Educational Researcher, 21*(8), 5–14.

Ogbu, J. U. (2003). *Black American students in an affluent suburb: A study of academic disengagement.* Mahwah, NJ: Laurence Erlbaum.

Olalde, J. (2010). Immersion learning. *Education Matters 14*(2), 4–5. Eugene, OR: University of Oregon College of Education.

Orbé, L. V. (2004). *Racial identity, recognition of spouses' conflict resolution styles, and marital satisfaction in interracially married individuals.* Unpublished doctoral dissertation, Columbia University, New York City, New York.

Oregon University System. (2006). *Lift every voice.* Eugene, OR: Author.

Orozco, R. (2010). Prefunteme!: Toward a Chicana/o student paradigm of schooling. *Unpublished manuscript, Oregon State University, Corvallis.*

Ovando, C., Combs, M., & Collier, V. (2006). *Bilingual and ESL classrooms: Teaching in multicultural contexts.* Boston: McGraw-Hill.

Paley, V. G. (1979). *White teacher.* Cambridge, MA: Harvard University Press.

Pang, V. (2005). *Multicultural education: A caring-centered, reflective approach (2nd ed.).* New York: McGraw-Hill.

Pang, V. O. (1994). Why do we need this class? Multicultural education for teachers. *Phi Delta Kappan, 76*(4), 289–292.

Pang, V. O., & Park, C. D. (in press). Creating interdisciplinary multicultural teacher education: Courageous leadership is crucial. In Ball, A. & Tyson, C. (Eds.), *Studying diversity in teacher education,* Washington, DC: American Educational Research Association.

Parnes, S. (1967). *Creative behavior guidebook.* New York: Scribner.

Passel, J., & Cohn, D. (2008a). Trends in unauthorized immigration: Undocumented inflow now trails legal inflow. *Pew Research Center.* Retrieved September 15, 2010, from http://pewhispanic.org/reports/report.php?ReportID=94

Passel, J. S., & Cohn, D. (2008b). US population projections: 2005–2050. *Pew Research Center.* Retrieved September 15, 2010, from http://pewhispanic.org/files/reports/85.pdf

Passel, J. S. (2010). Race and the census: The "Negro" controversy. *Pew Research Center.* Retrieved September 15, 2010, from http://census.pewsocialtrends.org/2010/race-and-the-census-the-"negro"-controversy

Pavel, D. M., & Padilla, R. V. (1993). American Indian and Alaska Native postsecondary departure: An example of assessing a mainstream model using national longitudinal data.

Journal of American Indian Education, 32(2), 1–23.

Perry, P. (2002). *Shades of white: White kids and racist identities in high school.* Durham, NC: Duke University Press.

Petersen, P. B., Draguns, J. G., Lonner, W. J., & Trimble, J. E. (1989). *Counseling across culture.* Honolulu HI: University of Hawaii Press.

Pew Social and Demographic Trends. (2008). Retrieved March 18, 2008, from http://pewsocialtrends.org/pubs/483/muslim-americans

Pewewardy, C. D. (1998, Spring). Our children can't wait: Recapturing the essence indigenous schools in the United States. *Cultural Survival Quarterly, 22*(1), 29–34.

Pewewardy, C. D., & Fitzpatrick M. (2009). Working with American Indian families: Disabilities, issues, and interventions. *Intervention in School and Clinic: Working with Families from Diverse Backgrounds, 45*(2), 91–98.

Pinderhughes, E. (1989). *Understanding race, ethnicity, and power: The key to efficacy in clinical practice.* New York: Free Press.

Polite, L., & Saenger, E. B. (2003). A pernicious silence: Confronting race in the elementary classroom. *Phi Delta Kappan, 85*(4), 274–278.

Pollard, K. M., & O'Hare, W. P. (1999). America's racial and ethnic minorities. *Population Bulletin, 54*(3), 3–48.

Ponterotto, J. G. (1988). Racial consciousness development among White counselor trainees: A stage model. *Journal of Multicultural Counseling and Development, 16,* 146–156.

Ponterotto, J. G., Casas, J. M., Suzuki, L. A., & Alexander, C. M. (1995). *Handbook of multicultural counseling.* Thousand Oaks, CA: Sage.

Porow, M. A. (2006) *Biracial identity development in Black/White biracial individuals.* Paper presented at the annual meeting of the American Sociological Association, Montreal, Quebec, Canada. Retrieved September 15, 2010, http://www.allacademic.com/meta/p105264_index.html

Poussaint, A. F. (1972). *Why Blacks kill Blacks.* New York: Emerson Hall.

Powell, G. J. (1973). The self-concept in White and Black children. In C. V. Willie, B. Kramer & B. Brown (Eds.), *Racism and mental health* (pp. 299–318). Pittsburgh: University of Pittsburgh Press.

Proshansky, H., & Newton, P. (1968). The meaning and nature of Negro self-identity. In M. Deutsch, I. Katz & A. Jensen (Eds.), *Social class, race and psychological development.* New York: Holt, Rinehart and Winston.

Rector, E. (2010, April). *Having the last word.* Presentation at the annual conference of the Oregon Chapter of the National Association for Multicultural Education, Portland.

Reid, F. (Producer/director). (1995). *Skin deep: College students confront racism film.* Berkeley, CA: Iris Films.

Reinharz, S., & Davidman, L. (1992). *Feminist methods in social research.* New York: Oxford University Press.

Rethinking Schools (1991). *Rethinking Columbus: Teaching about the 500th anniversary of Columbus's arrival in America.* Milwaukee, WI: Author.

Reynolds, C. R., & Kaiser, S. M. (1990). Test bias in psychological assessment. In T. B. Gutkin & C. R. Reynolds (Eds.), *The handbook of school psychology* (pp. 487–525). New York: Wiley.

Rinaldi, A. (1999). *My heart is on the ground: The diary of Nannie Little Rose, a Sioux girl.* New York: Scholastic.

Rokeach, M. (1960). *Beliefs, attitudes, and values.* New York: Basic.

Romero, M. (1992). *Maid in the USA.* New York: Routledge.

Root, M. P. P. (1996). *Multiracial experience: Racial borders as the new frontier.* Thousand Oaks, CA: Sage.

Root, M. P. P. (2003). Bill of rights for racially mixed people. In M. P. P. Root & M. Kelly (Eds.), *The multiracial child resource book: Living complex identities* (p. 32). Seattle, WA: Mavin Foundation.

Rosenberg, M. (1979). *Conceiving the self.* New York: Basic.

Rosenthal, D. (1976). *Experimenter effects in behavioral research.* New York: Halsted Press.

Rosenthal, R., & Jacobson, L. (1968). *Pygmalion in the classroom: Teacher expectations and pupils' intellectual development.* New York: Holt, Rinehart and Winston.

Rowe, W., Behrens, J. T., & Leach, M. M. (1995). Racial/ethnic identity and social consciousness: Looking back and looking forward. In J. P. Ponterotto, J. M. Casas, L. A. Suzuki & C. M. Alexander (Eds.), *Handbook of multicultural counseling* (pp. 218–235). Thousand Oaks, CA: Sage.

Saeki, C., & Borow, H. (1985). Counseling and psychotherapy: East and west. In P. B. Pedersen (Ed.), *Handbook of cross-cultural counseling and therapy.* Westport, CT: Greenwood Press.

Schank, R. C. (1990). *Tell me a story: A new look at real and artificial memory.* New York: Scribner.

Schmader, T. (2002). Gender identification moderates stereotype threat effects on women's math performance. *Journal of Experimental Social Psychology, 38*(2), 194–201.

Sciarra, D. J., Dorsey, A. G., & Lynch, E. (2009). *Developing and administering a child care and education program.* Belmont, CA: Cengage.

Seifer, R., Sameroff, A., Barrett, L., & Krafchuk, E. (1994). Infant temperament measured by multiple observations and mother report. *Child Development, 65,* 1478–1490.

Shaheen, J. (2001). *Reel bad Arabs.* Boston: Interlink.

Shaheen-McConnell, Y. (2009). *Demographics of Arab-Americans.* Retrieved September 15, 2010, from http://www.aaiusa.org/arab-americans/22/demographics

Shanley, J. (2008). Educating a closed population pool. In The Harvard Project on American Indian Economic Development (Eds.), *The state of the native nations: Conditions under U.S. policies of self-determination* (pp. 213–215). New York: Oxford University Press.

Shaughnessy, L., & Doshi, S. R. (2004). Attempted suicide and associated health risk behaviors among Native American high school students. *The Journal of School Health, 74*(5), 177–182.

Shin, H., & Bruno, R. (2003). *Language use and English-Speaking ability: 2000.* Census 2000 Brief. United States Census Bureau.

Short, D., & Echevarria, J. (2005). Teacher skills to support English language learners. *Educational Leadership, 62*(4), 8–13.

Sleeter, C. E. (1994). White racism. *Multicultural Education, 1,* 5–8.

Sleeter, C. E. (2001). Preparing teachers for culturally diverse schools: Research and the overwhelming presence of Whiteness. *Journal of Teacher Education, 52*(2), 94–106.

Smith, M. J. (2008). Right directions, wrong maps: Understanding the involvement of low-SES African American parents to enlist them as partners in college choice. *Education and Urban Society, 41*(2), 171–197.

Snow, C. (1990). Rationales for native language instruction: Evidence from research. In A. Padilla, H. Fairchild & C. Valadez (Eds.). *Foreign language education: Issues and strategies.* Thousand Oaks, CA: Corwin Press.

Snowden, L., & Todman, P. A. (1982). The psychological assessment of Blacks: New and needed developments. In E. E. Jones & S. J. Korchin (Eds.), *Minority mental health* (pp. 227–249). New York: Praeger.

Solorzano, D., Ceja, M., & Yosso, T. (2000, Winter). Critical race theory, racial microaggressions, and campus racial climate: The experience of African American college students. *Journal of Negro Education, 69,* 60–73.

Spencer, S., Steele, C., & Quinn, D. (1998). Stereotype threat and woman's math performance. *Journal of Experimental Social Psychology, 35,* 4–28.

Spenser, M. B., & Markstrom-Adams, C. (1990). Identity processes among racial and ethnic minority children in America. *Child Development, 61,* 290–310.

Stack, C. (1975). *All our kin: Strategies for survival in a Black community.* New York: Harper & Row.

Steele, C. (1997). A threat in the air: How stereotypes shape intellectual identity and performance. *American Psychologist, 52,* 613–629.

Steele, C., & Aronson, J. (1995). Stereotype threat and intellectual test performance of African Americans. *Journal of Personality and Social Psychology, 69*(5), 797–811.

Stonequist, E. V. (1961). *The marginal man: A study in personality and culture conflict.* New York: Russell & Russell.

Stroessner, S., & Good, C. (2010). *Reducing stereotype threat.* Retrieved September 15, 2010, from www. ReducingStereotypeThreat.org.

Substance Abuse and Mental Health Services Administration (2003).

Substance use among American Indians or Alaska Native Adults. http://www.oas .samhsa.gov/2k10/182/ AmericanIndian.cfm

Sue, D. (2010). *Racial microaggressions in everyday life: Race, gender, and sexual orientation.* Hoboken, NJ: Wiley.

Sue, D. W., Capodilupo, C. M. Torino, G. C., Bucceri, J. M.. Holder, A. M. B., Nadal, K. L., et al. (2007). Racial microaggressions in everyday life. *American Psychologist, 62*(4), 271–286.

Sue, S. W., & Sue, D. (1990). *Counseling the culturally different: Theory and practice (2nd ed.).* New York: Wiley.

Sue, S. W., & Sue, D. (1999). *Counseling the culturally different: Theory and practice (3rd ed.).* New York: Wiley.

Sue, S. W., & Sue, D. (2003). *Counseling the culturally diverse: Theory and practice (4th ed.).* New York: Wiley.

Sutton, C. E. T., & Broken Nose, M. A. (1996). American Indian families: An overview. In M. McGoldrick, J. Giordan & J. K. Pearce (Eds.), *Ethnicity and family therapy* (pp. 31–44). New York: Guilford Press.

Suzuki, L. A., & Kugler, J. F. (1995). Intellectual and personality assessment: Multicultural perspectives. In J. P. Ponterotto, J. M. Casas, L. A. Suzuki & C. M. Alexander (Eds.), *Handbook of multicultural counseling* (pp. 493–516). Thousand Oaks, CA: Sage.

Takaki, R. (1993). *A different mirror: A history of multicultural America.* Boston: Little, Brown.

Talbot, M. (2003, February). Searching for Sacagawea. *National Geographic.* 68–85.

Tappan, M. B. (2006). Reframing internalized oppression and internalized domination: From the psychological to the sociocultural. *Teachers College Record, 108*(10), 2115–2144.

Tatum, B. D. (1992a). *Assimilation blues: Black families in a White community.* Northampton, MA: Hazel-Maxwell.

Tatum, B. D. (1992b). Talking about race, learning about racism: The application of racial identity developmental theory in the classroom. *Harvard Education Review, 62*(1), 1–24.

Tatum, B. D. (2003). *"Why are all the Black kids sitting together in the cafeteria?": And other conversations about race.* New York: Basic.

Tatum, B. D. (2007). *Can we talk about race: And other conversations in an era of school resegregation.* Boston: Beacon.

Taylor, L. S., & Whittaker, C. R. (2008). *Bridging multiple worlds: Case studies of diverse educational communities.* Boston: Allyn & Bacon.

Taylor, L. S., & Whittaker, C. R. (2009). *Bridging multiple worlds: Case studies of diverse educational communities (2nd ed).* Boston: Allyn & Bacon.

Teaching tolerance. *Hidden bias: A Primer.* Retrieved September 15, 2010, from http://www.tolerance.org/activity /test-yourself-hidden-bias

Thomas, W., & Collier, V. (2001). *A National study of school effectiveness for language minority students' long-term academic achievement.* Berkeley, CA: Center for Research on Education, Diversity & Excellence.

Thompson, A. (2003). Tiffany, friend of People of Color: White investments in anti-racism. *International Journal of Qualitative Studies in Education, 16*(1), 7–29.

Thompson, G. (2004). *Through ebony eyes: What teachers need to know but are afraid to ask about African American students.* San Francisco, CA: Jossey Bass.

Thornton, M. C., Chatters, L. M., Taylor, R. J., & Allen, W. (1990). Sociodemographic and environmental correlates of racial socialization by Black parents. *Child Development, 61,* 401–409.

Thornton, R. (2001). *Studying Native America: Problems and prospects.* Madison, WI: University of Wisconsin Press.

Toké, A. N. (2010). The 2010 skipping stones honor awards. *Skipping Stones, 22*(3), 29.

Tolzmann, D. H. (2000). *The German-American experience.* Amherst, NY: Humanity Books.

Tong, B. R. (1981). *On the confusion of psychopathology with culture: Iatrogenesis in the "treatment" of Chinese Americans.* Unpublished manuscript, The Wright Institute. Berkeley, CA.

Torres, L., & Rollock, D. (2009). Psychological impact of negotiating two cultures: Latino coping and self-esteem. *Journal of Multicultural Counseling and Development, 37*(4), 219–228.

Trawick-Smith, J. W., & Lisi, P. (1994). Infusing multicultural perspectives in an early childhood development course: Effect on the knowledge and attitudes of inservice teachers. *Journal of Early Childhood Teacher Education, 15,* 8–12.

Tse, L. (2001). *"Why don't they learn English?": Separating fact from fallacy in the U.S. language debate.* New York: Teachers College Press.

Uba, L. (1994). *Asian Americans: Personality patterns, identity, and mental health.* New York: Guilford Press.

U.S. Census Bureau. (2000). *Statistical abstract of the United States.* Washington, DC: U.S. Government Printing Office.

U.S. Census Bureau (2002). *Profile of selected social characteristics: 2000.* Washington, DC: Government Printing Office.

U.S. Census Bureau. (2003). *The Arab population: 2000.* Retrieved September 15, 2010, from http://www.census.gov/prod/2003pubs/c2kbr-23.pdf

U.S. Census Bureau. (2008a). *Historical income table: Households* Retrieved September 15, 2010, from http://www.census.gov/hhes/www/income/data/historical/household/index.html

U.S. Census Bureau. (2008b). *Population projections.* Washington, DC: U.S. Government Printing Office.

U.S. Census Bureau. (2008c). *Wealth and asset ownership detailed tables, 2002.* Retrieved September 15, 2010, from http://www.census.gov/hhes/www/wealth/2002_tables.html

U.S. Census Bureau (2010). *Population projections.* Washington, DC: U.S. Government Printing Office.

Valencia, R. R., & Black, M. S. (2002). "Mexican Americans don't value education!": On the basis of the myth, mythmaking, and debunking. *Journal of Latinos and Education, 1*(2), 81–103.

Vedantam, S. (2005, January 23). See no bias. *The Washington Post,* 3. www.vedantam.com/bias01-2005.html.

Wah, L. M. (1994). *The color of fear.* Ukiah, CA: Stirfry.

Wah, L. M. (2003). *Last chance for Eden.* Ukiah, CA: Stirfry.

Waldschmidt, E. D. (2002). Bilingual interns' barriers to becoming teachers: At what cost do we diversify the teaching force? *Bilingual Research Journal, 26*(3), 537–561.

Wasserberg, M. J. (2007). Stereotype threat and the standardized test performance of Black children: When does the threat become a relevant performance inhibitor? In S. M. Nielsen & M. S. Plakhotnik (Eds.), *Proceedings of the sixth annual college of education research conference: Urban and international education section* (pp. 120–126). Miami: Florida International University. Retrieved September 15, 2010, from http://coeweb.fiu.edu/research_conference

Waters, M. C. (1990). *Ethnic option: Choosing identities in America*. Berkeley, CA: University of California Press.

Watson, B. (1997). "The storyteller is the soybean ... the audience is the sun." *Smithsonian, 27*(12), 60–62, 64, 66–68, 70.

Weaver, H. N. (2005). *Explorations in cultural competence*. Belmont, CA: Thompson Brooks/Cole.

Weinstein, G., & Mellen, D. (1997). Anti-Semitism curriculum design. In M. Adams, L. A. Bell & P. Griffin (Eds.), *Teaching for diversity and social justice* (pp. 170–197). New York: Routledge.

White, J. (1972). Towards a Black psychology. In R. Jones (Ed.), *Black psychology* (pp. 43–50). New York: Harper & Row.

Whitener, S. D., Gruber, K. J., Lynch, H. F., Rohr, C. L., & Tingos, K. (1997). *School and staffing survey*. Student records questionnaire: School year 1993–94, with special emphasis on American Indian and Alaska Native students (Report No. NCES 97-449). Washington, DC: National Center for Education Statistics.

Wijeyesinghe, C. L., Griffin, P., & Love, B. (1997). Racism curriculum design. In M. Adams, L. A. Bell & P. Griffin (Eds.), *Teaching for diversity and social justice* (pp. 82–109). New York: Routledge.

Williams, J. (2008). *Unspoken realities: White, female teachers discuss race, students, and achievement in the context of teaching in a majority Black elementary school*. Unpublished doctoral dissertation, Oregon State University, Corvallis.

Williams, J. E., & Morland, J. K. (1976). *Race, Color and the young child*. Chapel Hill: University of North Carolina Press.

Williams, R. M. (1947). The reduction of intergroup tensions. *Social Science Council Bulletin, 59*, 119–127.

Wise, T. (2005). *White like me: Reflections on race from a privileged son*. Brooklyn, NY: Soft Skull.

Wise, T. (2009). *Between Barack and a hard place*. Brooklyn, NY: Soft Skull.

Wise, T. (2010). *Colorblind: The rise of post-racial politics and the retreat from racial equity*. San Francisco, CA: City Lights Books.

Wong, K. (2007). Building alliances among Women of Color and White women: Be an ally, not a friend. *On Campus with Women, 36*(1), 1. Association of American Colleges and Universities. Retrieved September 15, 2010, from http://www.aacu.org/ocww/volume36_1/feature.cfm?section=2

Wong, P., & Fernandez, A. E. (2008). Sustaining ourselves under stressful times: Strategies to assist multicultcultural educators. *Multicultural Education, 15*(3), 10–14.

Woodson, C. (1933). *The mis-education of the Negro*. Washington, DC: The Associated Publishers.

Yamamoto, J., & Acosta, F. X. (1982). Treatment of Asian-Americans and Hispanic-Americans: Similarities and differences. *Journal of the Academy of Psychoanalysis, 10*, 585–607.

Zeichner, K. (2010, May). *Toward a knowledge democracy: The nature and quality of social relations in social justice teacher education*. Paper presented at the annual meeting of the American Education Research Association, Denver.

INDEX